SAGE was founded in 1965 by Sara Miller McCune to support the dissemination of usable knowledge by publishing innovative and high-quality research and teaching content. Today, we publish over 900 journals, including those of more than 400 learned societies, more than 800 new books per year, and a growing range of library products including archives, data, case studies, reports, and video. SAGE remains majority-owned by our founder, and after Sara's lifetime will become owned by a charitable trust that secures our continued independence.

Los Angeles | London | New Delhi | Singapore | Washington DC | Melbourne

An Introduction to Social Psychology

An Introduction to Social Psychology

Suhas Shetgovekar

Associate Professor, Discipline of Psychology,
Indira Gandhi National Open University (IGNOU), New Delhi

SAGE | TEXTS

Los Angeles | London | New Delhi
Singapore | Washington DC | Melbourne

First published in 2018 by

SAGE | TEXTS

SAGE Publications India Pvt Ltd
B1/I-1 Mohan Cooperative Industrial Area
Mathura Road, New Delhi 110 044, India
www.sagepub.in

SAGE Publications Inc
2455 Teller Road
Thousand Oaks, California 91320, USA

SAGE Publications Ltd
1 Oliver's Yard, 55 City Road
London EC1Y 1SP, United Kingdom

SAGE Publications Asia-Pacific Pte Ltd
3 Church Street
#10-04 Samsung Hub
Singapore 049483

Published by Vivek Mehra for SAGE Publications India Pvt Ltd, typeset in 10/12 pt Berkeley by Diligent Typesetter India Pvt Ltd, Delhi and printed at Chaman Enterprises, New Delhi.

Library of Congress Cataloging-in-Publication Data

Names: Shetgovekar, Suhas, author.
Title: An introduction to social psychology / Suhas Shetgovekar.
Description: Thousand Oaks : SAGE Publications, Inc., [2018] | Includes bibliographical references and index.
Identifiers: LCCN 2017019429 | ISBN 9789386446831 (print (pb) : alk. paper)
Subjects: LCSH: Social psychology—Textbooks.
Classification: LCC HM1033 .S494 2017 | DDC 302—dc23 LC record available at https://lccn.loc.gov/2017019429

ISBN: 978-93-864-4683-1 (PB)

SAGE Team: Amit Kumar, Indrani Dutta, Sunil Koli and Rajinder Kaur

Contents

Detailed Contents

Foreword

When Dr Suhas Shetgovekar requested me to write the foreword to her textbook on social psychology, I was indeed delighted for two reasons. First, in India, we have very few books by Indian authors on social psychology and they are all not typically the textbooks that would help students understand the very rapidly growing field of social psychology. Second, there are very few books by Indian authors that make an effort to put across the complex concepts, theories and applications of social psychology to students, highlight the essential points in each chapter and make students question themselves regarding their understanding of the concepts. The chapters covering cultural psychology, aggression, social behaviour and application of social psychology in real-life situations are hallmarks of this textbook.

Social psychology is a field that is now making inroads into many areas such as health, mental health, counselling and so on. The various researches that are being carried out in the field of social psychology, and related fields such as personality psychology, organisational psychology, judgement and decision-making, are published in many journals such as the *Journal of Social Psychology*, *Journal of Personality and Social Psychology, Journal of Applied Psychology* and other journals of social research. Many papers published in the *International Journal of Social Psychiatry* and *Indian Journal of Social Psychiatry* include considerable social psychology methods and materials. In India, however, we are yet to see an Indian journal exclusively devoted to social psychology. Such a journal will promote publication of research articles based on Indian data that could be used in a textbook of this kind. Despite the current inadequate number of research-based India-centric articles on social psychology, Dr Shetgovekar has been able to give many examples to illustrate and substantiate the various difficult concepts in a manner that would be understandable to students.

My congratulations to Dr Shetgovekar for bringing out a most needed textbook with examples from her own personal experience and from the Indian scenario in one of the important and major fields of psychology. I am sure this book will be of great benefit not only to the students by helping them understand social psychology, its concepts, theories and applications, but would also help the teachers to impart knowledge in the field with considerable ease, focusing on the difficult concepts and theories of social psychology and its applications to various fields.

Vimala Veeraraghavan
Former Professor and HoD Psychology, Delhi University
Emeritus Professor, Psychology, IGNOU

Preface

Social psychology is one such subject area that we are introduced to after we have understood the basics of psychology. The fundamentals that we learn in general psychology are applied here to social dimension.

The book has been divided into four sections. Section I is titled 'Introduction' and mainly introduces the field of social psychology and describes research in social psychology. The first chapter of this section forms the foundation for the entire book. Social psychology has been defined in this chapter, and theories of social psychology have also been explained, besides highlighting the historical developments in social psychology. The second chapter in this section discusses research in social psychology. Research, in simple terms, can be described as adding to the existing fund of knowledge, and is crucial for any subject area. Though the topics discussed under this chapter could be similar to those discussed in the context of other subjects as well, there could be certain research methods that are more applicable to a certain subject area than others. Thus, with regard to social psychology as well, there are certain research methods more applicable compared to others. Besides discussing the definition and key concepts in research, the chapter also focuses on the types of research and qualitative research in social psychology. Ethical issues in research have also been discussed in the chapter. In addition, the chapter highlights the challenges and problems a researcher may face while carrying out research in social psychology.

Section II is titled 'The Individual', and the topics covered under this are mainly related to the individual, his/her self, social cognition, social perception, interpersonal attraction and attitude. The first chapter under this section is on self and encompasses certain relevant concepts like self-concept, self-esteem and self-efficacy. Two other important concepts, namely, introspection and self-perception, have also been covered in this chapter, which play a significant role in understanding one's self. Besides highlighting certain other concepts related to self, such as self-awareness, self-focusing and so on, the chapter also discusses gender identity. A relevant topic 'self in cyberspace' has been included in this chapter, keeping in mind the space occupied by Internet and social networking in one's life. The next chapter deals with social cognition that has to do with cognitive processes involved in the way we perceive the world and the people in it. Besides discussing the concept of social cognition, the chapter also describes automatic and controlled processing. Schemas, which can be termed as mental representations and cognitive heuristics, and also referred to as mental shortcuts, are elucidated in the chapter. The chapter, in the end, covers the relationship between cognition and emotion. The next chapter titled 'Social Perception' deals with social cognition, although it mainly focuses on how we perceive people around us. The chapter includes discussions on person perception besides impression and impression formation. Attribution is also highlighted in the chapter, with a focus on the dimensions of causality and attributional biases. In addition, non-verbal communication is discussed, with special reference to facial expressions, body language, eye contact and touching. Chapter 6 discusses interpersonal attraction, which is a crucial topic when we want to study about individuals in a social set-up. In the context of this chapter, affiliation and interpersonal attraction are discussed. Theories of attraction are also focused on, besides determinants of attraction, with a special emphasis on similarity and proximity. Online attraction is elucidated, keeping in mind the increase in frequency of interactions online. Friendship and close relationships are also highlighted, and a section has been devoted to homosexual couples and relationships. Lastly, troubled relationships and breakups are explained. The last chapter in this section is on attitude that denotes how one thinks or feels about a thing, person, place or event. Three main components of attitude are discussed here, namely, cognitive, affective and behavioural. How attitudes are formed is discussed at length in this chapter. The chapter also describes the influence of attitude on behaviour. A section on attitude change has been included in the chapter, with emphasis on cognitive dissonance theory and persuasion. Further, the chapter encompasses the concepts of stereotype, prejudice and discrimination and ways to overcome them.

Section III is titled 'The Individual and the Society', and this section discusses individual in the context of the society. The topics covered under this section are social influence, pro-social behaviour, aggression, group dynamics and culture. The first chapter under this section is on social influence that focuses on how others influence our behaviours, actions and attitudes. The chapter elucidates the concepts of conformity, compliance and obedience, and also deals with normative and informational social influence. Social reality in the context of social influence is also explained in the chapter. In addition, the chapter highlights social norms and social impact theory. Chapter 9 is titled 'Pro-social Behaviour', which is described as one person helping another in the absence of any obligation. The chapter is initiated with the definition of pro-social behaviour and moves on to explaining approaches to and perspectives on the same. The chapter also covers the situational factors that determine pro-social behaviour, besides providing details about who is likely to receive help, encompassing the characteristics of the person that determine whether he/she will receive help or not. Bystander's apathy is also discussed in this chapter. The chapter then culminates with a discussion on the outcome of receiving help and the concept of social support. Chapter 10 deals with aggression that, in simple terms, can be described as any behaviour that hurts someone. The term 'anti-social behaviour' has also been touched upon in the chapter besides the concept of collective aggression. Within the chapter, various theories of aggression are discussed, and the determinants of aggression—categorised as person-centred and situation-centred determinants—are explained. The concept of anger is also described. Lastly, the chapter focuses on the ways to prevent and control aggression. The next chapter is on group dynamics and includes topics like nature of group and roles and norms. The concept of group cohesiveness is discussed in detail in this chapter. In addition, the chapter highlights the performance of individuals in groups and explains the term 'deindividuation'. Decision-making in groups and leadership are also explained in this chapter. The chapter culminates with a discussion on conflict and conflict resolution. The last chapter in this section is on culture. The chapter opens with the concept of culture and moves on to explain the association between culture and individual. The term 'socialisation' has also been discussed in this chapter. Further, it highlights the psychological perspectives on the influence of culture on behaviour. The last topic discussed under this chapter is cross-cultural research, and a detailed discussion on issues and challenges faced while carrying out cross-cultural research is included.

The last section, Section IV, is titled 'Applied Social Psychology' and focuses on understanding the field of applied social psychology and application of social psychology in various fields. Chapter 13, which falls under this section, opens with a discussion on the concept of applied social psychology. The historical developments in applied social psychology are highlighted in the chapter. The chapter then moves forward to discuss the social psychology theories. A section on the role of applied social psychologist has also been included in the chapter to ascertain how the roles of a researcher, a programme designer, an evaluative researcher, a consultant and an advocate are discharged. Further, a section on social issues and problems has been included in the chapter besides a section on social change, which has been discussed in detail. Finally, the chapter highlights two significant terms in the context of applied social psychology—intervention and evaluation. The last chapter of this book is titled 'Application of Social Psychology'. The subtopics in this chapter are devoted to applications of social psychology in fields such as health psychology, organisational psychology, sports, clinical and counselling psychology and other areas.

For me, this book is like a journey towards the final destination of understanding social psychology. We go from one destination to another, understanding various aspects of this field of knowledge, and ultimately reach our final destination, having developed a fair idea about the subject matter. As it is said that the 'journey is more important than the destination', I hope the readers will enjoy the journey through this book and take significant learning lessons from it, as I did while writing it.

Acknowledgements

Writing of this book has not only been an extensive exercise but also a learning experience. Besides helping me develop more understanding about the concepts and theories in social psychology, it has also helped me become more aware of my social set-up and more appreciative of people in my life.

I would like to dedicate this book to all my teachers from my school, Sister Nivedita English Medium School, Dombivali, Maharashtra; my college, V. G. Vaze College, Mulund, Maharashtra; Carmel College for Women and St. Xavier's College, Goa; and Karnatak University, Dharwad, Karnataka. Special thanks to all my psychology teachers. A special gratitude goes to Professor Vimala Veeraraghavan, who is an epitome of a teacher, and who has been a constant guiding light in my life since I met her.

I also want to acknowledge the presence of unconditional love and support that I have in my life in the form of my husband, Kaushal Kumar. I can never thank him enough for bearing with me through the excitements and nervousness that I experienced during the process of writing this book.

Parents are the foremost persons in a child's life, who mould the child with all their care, love and encouragement. I express my deep sense of gratitude to my parents, Gauri and Bhavanishankar, for 'doing it right'. I attribute everything I have achieved so far in life, and that I will achieve in the future, to them. A special thanks also goes to my brother, Viraj.

I also need to appreciate the help provided by my colleague and friend Dr Monika Misra. I thank her for being accommodating and for her valuable suggestions regarding various social psychology books I could use as reference. I would also like to acknowledge the reviewers for their constructive feedback that helped me to improve and enrich the contents of this book.

About the Author

Dr Suhas Shetgovekar is presently an Associate Professor with Discipline of Psychology, IGNOU, New Delhi. She joined IGNOU as a Reader in December 2010. She is a Programme Coordinator for PhD programme in psychology and PhD programme in disability studies at IGNOU. She has earlier served as a Course Director at the Abbé Faria Post Graduate Department of Psychology, St. Xavier's College, Mapusa, Goa, and has been visiting faculty/resource person for institutions like Goa Institute of Management, National Institute of Construction Management and Research, Goa and Central Board for Worker's Education, Goa, and V. V Giri National Labour Institute, Noida.

She completed her MA in psychology (gold medallist) and PhD from Karnatak University, Dharwad, Karnataka. She has been actively involved in teaching psychology, management and related subjects in varied institutions. She has conducted numerous training programmes on behavioural skills in various industries and organisations in Goa. She has presented and published papers on topics pertaining to health modernity, women-related issues, couple relationship, ethics in psychological research, culture and industrial and organisational psychology. She has co-authored *Textbook of Parametric and Nonparametric Statistics* with Professor Vimala Veeraraghavan (by SAGE in 2016).

SECTION I

Introduction

CHAPTER 1

Introduction to Social Psychology

Do you look forward to social gatherings such as marriages, feasts, 'melas', get togethers and so on?

Do you think that family and friends play an important role in your life and they also have an influence on your behaviour?

Are you aware that individuals from certain cultures greet each other by rubbing their nose?

How do you feel when you hear about a brutal crime?

What kind of attitude do you have towards health, women and members of other communities?

All the aforementioned questions, in some way or other, probe about one's social dimension.

The moment an individual gets conceived, he/she in a way becomes a part of the society. Social dimension, thus, is one of the most significant dimensions of an individual's life. It is a framework in which an individual's behaviour can be interpreted and understood. The social also environment has an immense influence on an individual's life.

Psychologists study human behaviour, and its antecedents and consequences. Various fields in psychology such as developmental psychology, health psychology, forensic psychology, and clinical psychology study the application of principles of psychology to different areas. In this book, the focus will be on social psychology, which is also one of the subfields of psychology.

Going back to the aforementioned questions, most of us look forward to social gatherings not only because they are fun to attend to but also because we tend to meet people, relatives and friends, and we have need to belong. Human being is a social being and his/her interaction with others, and also how others influence him/her, is one of the main focuses of social psychology. Further, the behaviour of an individual when in a group is also different from that when he/she is not in a group. In our life, family, friends and significant persons are not only the sources of social support but they also have a significant influence on our behaviour and decisions.

If you see two persons rubbing nose with each other, you may find it absurd to some extent. However, if you come to know that this is a traditional 'Inuit' greeting called 'kunik' and a way in which some groups of Eskimos greet each other, mainly close relatives and friends, your reaction will probably differ and you may even start appreciating this unique way of greeting. This provides us an insight into how cultures differ and how important it is to understand individuals' culture to understand their behaviour.

News related to rape and violence against women in India makes us angry. We may sympathise and empathise with the victims/survivors and their families but at the same time we also wonder why the perpetrator behaved the way he/she did. Aggression is also one of the main aspects covered in social psychology. The nature of aggression and crimes prevalent in a society and measures that can be taken to prevent and avoid them can become an important part of research in social psychology.

Attitude is another significant aspect that is focused on under the umbrella of this subject. What kind of attitude you have towards health, women, members of other communities and so on can also be studied under social psychology.

This chapter is necessarily an introduction to social psychology and lays the foundation to develop a better understanding about other chapters in this book. In this chapter, an attempt will be made to understand the term social psychology with the help of its definitions. How social psychology can be termed as science will also be discussed. Further, theories of social psychology will also be explained. Historical developments in the field will be traced, and the chapter will also highlight current trends and challenges in social psychology.

Learning Objectives

After reading this chapter, you will be able to

- Describe social psychology
- Describe social psychology as science
- Discuss the historical developments in social psychology
- Discuss social psychology in India
- Elucidate the theories of social psychology
- Discuss current trends and challenges in social psychology

WHAT IS SOCIAL PSYCHOLOGY?

Social psychology is a combination of two terms 'social' and 'psychology'. 'Social' can be described in terms of the social environment as well as social behaviour (Staat, 1983). The social environment refers to the social set-up and includes groups, norms, structures and so on, whereas social behaviour includes emotions, attitudes and activities, driven with reference to the social set-up.

When we discuss about social psychology, it is also important to understand the concept of social behaviour. Social behaviour is described as our behaviour in social context or in the presence of others.

An individual's behaviour would differ when he/she is alone or with his/her family members, colleagues or strangers. This is mainly because of the significance that we attach to others in our lives. Given the fact that whether in school, college or at work or even during some kind of leisure activity, most often we interact with someone or other and during these social interactions our behaviour is influenced by others and the way they behave.

'Psychology' can be described as a scientific study of human and animal behaviour. Psychology mainly focuses on individual differences and on identifying factors that lead to those differences. Social dimension is one such factor that can help us understand why individuals are different. This and many other aspects related to social dimension are covered under social psychology.

Social psychology can be referred to as one of the branches of psychology. It can be described as the application of principles of psychology to understanding social set-ups, social issues and individual behaviour in varied social situations. It also denotes a discipline that engages empirical methods to understand human behaviour in a social set-up.

Defining social psychology in a way is a complex task because of its broad scope and the rapid changes that take place in a society and that have a strong influence on human behaviour. For example, social networking has not only become an important aspect of an individual's life but it also has a strong influence on an individual's behaviour and more importantly his/her social interactions.

Social psychology, as defined by Baron and Byrne (2006), is a scientific field that seeks to understand the nature and causes of individual behaviour and thoughts in social situations.

Some of the key points of this definition are as follows:

1. **It is a scientific field:** As is applicable to the wider area of psychology, social psychology as a branch of psychology employs a scientific and systematic procedure to study individuals in a social set-up. Various experimental and non-experimental research studies can be carried out to study social issues (these will be discussed at a greater length in Chapter 2) such as violence against women and individuals' attitude towards education.
2. **It seeks to understand individual behaviour:** Social psychology focuses on individual behaviour in social context and seeks to understand its nature and the underlying causes. For example, explaining the behaviour of a rapist or a violent behaviour of sportspersons during a game. The nature and predictors of such behaviours need to be focused in order to understand the individual behaviour in specific and society/community in general.
3. **Individual behaviour studied in social context:** An addition to the aforementioned point is that the individual behaviour is studied not only to understand the underlying causes but also to interpret it in the context of a social framework. Further, an individual's behaviour will differ in different setting, at home, in school/or at work, with friends and in public places. Also, behaviour many a time is determined by social norms prevalent in society. Any deviation from these norms is interpreted as deviation from normality.

Gordon Allport in 1968 defined social psychology as a discipline in which people attempt to understand, explain and predict how the thoughts, feelings and actions of individuals are influenced by the perceived, imagined or implied thoughts, feelings and action of others (Raven & Rubin, 1983). This definition highlights the influence of thoughts, feelings and actions of individuals on each other. Thus, to re-emphasise, an individual's behaviour in the presence of strangers may vary from that when they are with family and friends.

Gerrig and Zimbardo (2006, p. G-II) define social psychology as 'the branch of psychology that studies the effect of social variables on individual behaviour, attitudes, perceptions, and motives; also studies group and intergroup phenomena'. This definition again focuses on the social dimension of an individual and how does it impact his/her behaviour.

Yet another definition explains social psychology as the scientific study of how people think about, influence and relate to one another (Myers et al., 2012, p. 1). Barrett (2017, p. 5) defined social psychology as 'the scientific study of the social experiences and behaviours of individuals'. Barrett's definition of social psychology is in a way similar to that of Baron and Byrne which defines social psychology as a scientific field and focuses on the individual. Barrett also speaks about social experience that can be described by including thoughts and feelings that are conscious, processes that are non-conscious, such as the regulation of hormones and brain activation (Barrett, 2017). This definition encompasses the neuropsychological changes as well.

Social psychology mainly deals with understanding various causes underlying social behaviour and thoughts. These causes can be related to cognition, culture or environment; they can either be social or biological. These factors mainly determine the behaviour of an individual in a particular situation. Further, the subject also focuses on individuals' behaviour in social context; thus, the scope of psychology also includes social interactions. Social contacts, relationships and communications are three important factors of any social interaction. According to Baron, Byrne and Branscombe (2006), the following five factors have an influence on the social interaction:

1. The characteristics and actions of others
2. Cognitive processes
3. Ecological aspects
4. Cultural context of the individuals
5. Biological or genetic variables

The presence, traits, characteristics and actions of others do have an influence on an individual's behaviour. As will be discussed in Chapter 8, significant persons in one's life can have an influence on his/her behaviour and decision-making. Social psychology majorly focuses on how individuals influence each other. It also deals with how groups have an influence on an individual and the role played by social norms in determining human behaviour. Further, the influence that an individual has on a group, and interrelationship between groups, is also covered under this subject area. Yet another important area that has now been embedded in social psychology is the influence of social networking on human behaviour and relationships. The developments of technology like Internet has provided an altogether new perspective to understand 'the self', online attraction and relationships, aggressive behaviours like cyber bullying and also to understand the effect of the increased interactions and communications through cell phones and Internet.

Our social interactions are also influenced by various cognitive processes such as memory, learning, perception and so on. As will be discussed in Chapters 4 and 5, there are various automatic and controlled processes that determine how the social world is perceived by an individual. Schemas and heuristics also play a role in this context, as they are, respectively, the mental representations and mental shortcuts to the way the social world is perceived and interpreted. Various ecological factors such as temperature, pollution and crowding can also have an effect on our interactions. Studies indicate that feelings, thoughts and behaviour of an individual can be influenced by his/her physical environment (Bell et al., 1990). Thus, social psychologists need to focus on the ecological variables for their possible connections with aggressive behaviour, overall performance and various actions of the individual.

Culture is one of the major aspects that influence our behaviour and interactions. Social norms may differ based on culture, and thus the way people sit or stand in public, the way they greet, their clothing and verbal and non-verbal behaviours and interactions will, to a greater extent, depend on their culture.

Social behaviour and interactions may also be influenced by certain biological or genetic factors. Very often, certain physical characteristics are perceived as more attractive than others, and an individual's behaviour and interactions may be positive or negative based on certain physical features of the person he/she is interacting with.

The scope of social psychology is thus very broad and encompasses the whole of human behaviour in a social set-up, ranging from their behaviours, performance, attitudes, ideas, beliefs and values. In the process, it also touches upon how the individual perceives his/her own self and his/her interpersonal relationships.

Social psychology can also be understood through social neuroscience. The term social neuroscience was put forth by Cacioppo and Bernston in 1992. It denotes a field of study that is interdisciplinary and focuses on how brain determines social behaviour. Cacioppo and Bernston define social neuroscience as 'interdisciplinary field devoted to the study of neural, hormonal, cellular and genetic mechanisms, and to study the associations between social and biological levels of organisation' (Barrett, 2017, p. 47). Thus, behaviours in a social set-up can be mapped onto certain regions of the brain. For example, a study was carried out by Spunt and Liberman (2013) in which they made use of functional MRI to study automaticity in the mirror neutron system and the mentalising system. These two brain systems are considered significant in the comprehensions of the behaviour of other individuals. The participants of the study had to remember either an easy phone number that denoted a lower cognitive load or difficult phone numbers that denoted higher cognitive loads. In addition, the participants had to do this as they watched the videos. The goals assigned to the participants varied and included passive observation, active recognition, and understanding the motive behind the action and the implementation of the action. The results indicated that action understanding and social cognition were based on a dual-process model of the brain system, that automatic behaviour identification was supported by the mirror neuron system and that the controlled social causal attribution was supported by the mentalising system.

Social psychology also has an applied dimension, and its principles and theories can be applied to various fields ranging from sports and health psychology to clinical and counselling psychology, which will be discussed in the last section of this book.

There are various reasons why social psychology as a discipline or an area of knowledge is significant. Besides the fact that social psychology focuses on us, human beings, it also helps us understand how humans behave and why they behave the way they do. After understanding social psychology, you are more likely to pay more attention to certain non-verbal behaviours of persons you are interacting with or be more empathetic when your friend has had a breakup in his/her relationship. Social psychology can also be applied to deal with various issues around us (will be dealt with in the last section of this book), from violence to attitude towards women or members of other communities to promoting health behaviours and so on. Some facts about individual behaviour in a social set-up have been given in Box 1.1. These will be discussed in various chapters of this book.

BOX 1.1 ***Some Facts About Individual Behaviour in a Social Set-up***

- Individuals will obey authority figures to such an extent that it can even be dangerous for others. This was displayed in an experiment carried out by Stanley Milgram.
- Our social behaviour, to a large extent, is determined by situational variables. This was well displayed in an experiment called 'Stanford Prison Experiment' carried out by Zimbardo.
- More the number of people present while witnessing an accident, least is the possibility that one of them will help the victim/s. This is called the bystanders apathy effect.
- We predominantly attribute our success and accomplishments to internal factors and failures and negative outcomes to forces that are external to us. However, when it comes to others, we attribute their behaviours to internal factors and characteristics. This is called the actor–observer bias.

Principles of Social Psychology

Based on research carried out over the years in social psychology, the following principles could be discussed (Barrett, 2017):

1. **The purposive nature of social behaviour:** Any human behaviour, according to this principle, is directed towards achieving a goal. For example, human beings develop friendship to achieve certain goals. Thus, behaviours do not take place randomly. The fact that behaviour is purposive actually motivates the social psychologists to understand the purpose behind a certain behaviour.
2. **Dispositional and situational influences determine social behaviour:** When we hear about an incident of sexual abuse or a gruesome murder, we try to understand why the perpetrator behaved the way he/she did. Can the behaviour be attributed to some psychological problems or his/her upbringing or past negative experiences. Here, we basically want to know whether the determinants of such behaviour were dispositional or situational. Most often, any behaviour is attributed to interactionism, where both dispositional and situational factors play a role.
3. **How situations are interpreted, influencing the social behaviour:** A presentation in the office, in front of the superiors may be seen by one employee as an opportunity to express himself/herself, whereas another employee may see it as a threat. Thus, a single situation can be interpreted in different ways by different individuals and that has an influence on the social behaviour of the individuals.
4. **Social behaviour is cultural:** As was also discussed under the scope of social psychology, culture also has an influence on our behaviour in a social set-up. Cross-cultural differences are found in the way individuals behave. This will be dealt in detail in Chapter 12, where the relationship between culture and behaviour will be studied.

Based on the aforementioned four principles, the theories and concepts in social psychology can be comprehended.

■ SOCIAL PSYCHOLOGY AS SCIENCE

Even if you ask a passerby about why there is an increase in crime against women or an increase in road accidents, he/she will come up with some explanation. Such explanations fall under lay theories. Lay theories can be described as explanations regarding social behaviours that are demonstrated by lay persons who neither have any training in psychology nor they do employ any empirical methods (Barrett, 2017). Nevertheless, social psychology is termed as a science and it employs empirical methods while studying social behaviour.

Psychology is explained as a scientific study and, being a part of psychology, social psychology also renders itself to being a science. The two main elements of science are scientific understanding and core values. When we talk about scientific understanding, we mainly speak about the use of various research methods that employ empirical tests or rely on systematic observation to evaluate ideas, concepts and propositions to derive conclusions. Thus, a systematic procedure with a suitable research methodology is used and the ideas and propositions may be rejected or accepted. The conclusions of such research can also be generalised and can be used by other researchers.

Social psychology employs scientific methods to test the assumptions and ideas with regard to human behaviour in a social set-up. An empirical perspective will thus be adopted in order to study the influence that friends and family have on an individual, or to study the aggressive behaviour and its antecedents or to understand how attitudes develop. In this process, there is no reliance on folk wisdom or common sense. The process, though, can be challenging due to the complex nature of the very focus of this subject, that is, human being.

While carrying out research in social psychology, both scientific understanding and core values need to be considered to study the issues and phenomena under social psychology and to ensure valid evaluation.

As the discussion is carried out about social psychology as science, the goals of science also need to be highlighted. Science has four main goals, namely, description, prediction, determining causality and explanation. These are discussed as follows:

1. **Description.** It involves detecting and reporting the details about a particular phenomenon/issue. For example, a research could be carried out on adjustment problems among the adolescents. These adjustment problems could be related to home or school, or could be emotional or social in nature. Adjustment problems among the adolescents are thus described in detail.
2. **Prediction.** This has to do with identifying factors that may be related to or correlated with the phenomenon/issue. For example, with reference to the research on adjustment problems among the adolescents, there could exist a relationship between parenting style or peer influence and adjustment patterns and problems displayed by the adolescents. If such a relationship exists, then adjustment problems can be predicted based on the parenting style or peer influence.
3. **Determining causality.** This means establishing a cause-and-effect relationship between variables/factors and the phenomenon. That is, when changes occur in one variable, they lead to changes in the other variable, thus denoting a cause-and-effect relationship between the two variables. It is to be noted here that the existence of a mere relationship between two factors does not denote causality. For example, although there may exist a relationship between parenting style or peer influence and adjustment problems among the adolescents, peer influence may not necessarily cause adjustment problems among the adolescents. However, if there is a cause-and-effect relationship between the previously discussed variables, then, based on the results obtained, interventions can be developed (with a focus on parenting style or peer influence) to prevent adjustments problems among adolescents.
4. **Explanation.** This has to do with describing the reasons why a particular phenomenon occurs. This will include explaining why parenting style and peer influence lead to the adjustment problems among the adolescents. Thus, under explanation, the reasons why a relationship of causality exists between the factors are explored.

Further, there are also core values that need to be adhered to by scientists to ensure the validity of the study. These are as follows:

1. **Accuracy.** The collection of information has to be accurate using an error-free measurement and the information collected also has to be precise.
2. **Objectivity.** While collecting data and testing the idea or proposition, the bias should be kept at the minimum.
3. **Scepticism.** The findings should be rigorously verified before deriving conclusions.
4. **Open-mindedness.** The scientist should openly accept the evidence that may be inconsistent with his/her belief or theories.
5. **Ethics.** It is extremely important to follow ethical guidelines while carrying out any research.

THEORIES OF SOCIAL PSYCHOLOGY

Theories are important in organising varied observations about the subject area. It is important to focus on theories as they mainly assist in organising varied observations about the subject area. They also help us to predict behaviours and actions, based on the existing knowledge and information available, in certain other situations that probably have not been studied. They further help in promoting research based on the predictions of the theories.

Before we go on to discussing the current major theories in social psychology, we need to discuss three theories that form the basis for other theories. These are psychoanalytic theory, behaviourism and Gestalt psychology.

Psychoanalytic theory was developed by Sigmund Freud. According to Freud, the internal drives and impulses motivate behaviour. He also believed that the unresolved psychological conflicts during childhood could play a significant role in determining individual behaviour. The focus of this theory is on conscious and unconscious inner forces that determine behaviour. He believed that childhood experiences do have an important influence on the behaviour of an individual during adulthood. In social psychology, the theory of psychoanalysis can be of great use in understanding motivation and emotions in the context of social life (Sears, Peplau, & Taylor, 1991).

Ivan Pavlov, John B. Watson, B. F. Skinner and others contributed to the development of behaviourism perspective. The main focus of this theory is the observable behaviour and the external stimuli that can have an effect on the observable behaviour. They, thus, focused on overt behaviour and did not provide any significance to feelings and thoughts. The behaviourism perspective is of great help in social psychology to explain how behaviours are learned and to understand the role of experiences in determining individual behaviour.

Gestalt psychology was developed by Wolfgang Kohler, Kurt Kofka, Kurt Lewin and others. Gestalt is a German word that can be translated as a 'shape or form'. Gestalt psychologist believed that 'the whole is greater than sum of its parts'. They also believed that individuals perceive situations as 'dynamic wholes'. Social cognition can be well understood from a Gestalt perspective. Kurt Lewin used the principles of Gestalt psychology to understand the concepts in social psychology. According to him, both the individual characteristics and social environment have an impact on an individual's behaviour (Sears et al., 1991).

The three basic theories, discussed earlier, were developed with a goal to explain human behaviour and, thus, were also used to understand the social behaviour of individuals. They served as a basis of various social psychology research as well. However, problems and issues studied by social psychologists have in a way become complex and therefore cannot be solely dealt from the perspective of these theories (Sears et al., 1991). Thus, other theories in psychology also need to be discussed so as to understand social issues and aspects in a better manner. These are discussed as follows.

Learning Theories

The development of learning theories, in general, can be traced to behaviourism, and they can be termed as one of the dominant theories in the field of psychology. These theories mainly state that an individual's behaviour is determined by previous learning or past experiences. They also give relevance to an external environment in which the individuals exists and believe that the stimulation from this environment will determine their behaviour. Also, the focus in these theories is mainly on overt behaviour rather than on covert behaviour. Three main theories fall under learning theories. The first is classical conditioning by Ivan Pavlov that mainly focuses on association. Pavlov's experiment on his dog, where the dog would salivate on hearing a bell (as he associated the ringing of bell with the presentation of food) is quite famous. We learn many things, words and so on through association.

The second learning theory is that of operant conditioning by B. F. Skinner which deals with reinforcement. Operant conditioning states that our behaviour is determined by its consequences, whether positive or negative. If any behaviour is followed by positive consequences, it is more likely that it will be repeated, whereas if it is followed by negative consequences, it is more likely that it will be avoided. For example, if spitting behaviour, especially in public places is discouraged with strict repercussions, then that behaviour is less likely to occur again. Similarly, if a healthy behaviour of following safety regulations in organisations is rewarded, then it is more likely to continue.

The third theory of learning is the social learning theory by Albert Bandura who focused on covert learning or thinking. He also focused on observational learning, that is, learning various behaviours by observing others. For example, a child may learn to pray (as per his/her religious practices) by observing his/her parents. We also develop our social behaviours and attitudes in a similar manner. Here, we also discuss the concept of modelling or imitation, which occurs when the behaviour of another person is imitated or repeated in the same manner as displayed. For example, children may learn aggressive behaviours through imitation.

Cognitive Theories

Cognitive theories mainly focus on cognition that includes sensation, perception, thinking, memory and so on. These theories state that the behaviour of a person is based on his/her perceptions. Thus, an individual's behaviour in social set-ups can be understood by understanding his/her perceptions.

Cognitive perspective puts forth that individuals, naturally, tend to group or categorise objects and people (Sears et al., 1991). Things and individuals may be categorised on the basis of similarity, proximity and past experiences. Further, the principle of figure and background is also considered under cognitive theories. Figure is something that we pay attention to and ground is something that exists in the background. For example, when we look at a traffic police controlling traffic, he/she is the figure and all the moving vehicles are the background. Thus, the two basic principles, that is, grouping or categorising and figure and background determine the way we perceive our social environment and individuals within it (Sears et al., 1991).

In cognitive perspective, we also need to focus on the concept of causal attribution that can be described as how people utilise information in order to determine the causes of certain social behaviours. Social cognition is yet another term that is relevant in this context, which will be extensively discussed in Chapter 4. It mainly deals with how we derive conclusions based on encoding, storage, retrieval and processing of information with regard to individuals and so on.

Motivational Theories

This is the next category of theories that can help us determine individual behaviours in social context. Motivation can be described as a need or drive and, very often, our perceptions, attitudes and even behaviours are determined by our needs and drives (Sears et al., 1991). These needs and drives have a special place in social psychology as they can determine our social relationships as well, besides our social behaviour. Need to belong, for instance, can be one reason that influences youngsters to indulge in substance abuse, as they want to be accepted by a group and not to be left out and be labelled as 'not cool' or 'not having enough guts' to try out a drug or liquor. Similarly, motivation of not doing wrong along with strong moral principles would probably restrain these youngsters from indulging in such behaviour.

Decision-making Theories

These theories mainly focus on the costs and benefits of behaviours and actions. They also highlight how individuals rationally measure costs and benefits before making decisions and taking actions. Obviously, the decision that has less risk and more benefits is generally taken. For example, before leaving a job to become a freelancer, an individual will think in terms of the benefits and costs of leaving a job and becoming a freelancer. Also, in a similar manner, a person who is a witness to an accident will think about the benefits and costs before helping the person injured in the accident. Two relevant theories in this regard, which we need to discuss, are incentive theory and expectancy-value theory.

Incentive theory deals with decision-making that takes place as a result of assessing the pros and cons of each option available and then deciding upon or choosing a single option. However, the relative likelihood of each option may not be considered.

Expectancy-value theory, on the other hand, includes the likelihood of each option, besides the consideration of pros and cons. The theory is based on two factors that determine the decision: the value of each option and the probability of each option resulting from the decision (Sears et al., 1991). Thus, the decision taken here is based on both the expectancy and the value.

Social Exchange Theories

These theories focus on the behaviours of more than one individual who interact with one another. They are based on both learning theories and decision-making theories and state that individuals tend to exchange costs and benefits while interacting with each other. These theories can be applied to various familial, organisational and social set-ups where individuals may have mutual benefits or, in certain cases, some individual may benefit at the cost of others. Social issues with reference to infrastructure developments that probably benefit a larger population but at the cost of a few who probably have to relocate or are disadvantaged because of the situation can be studied with the help of social exchange theories. These theories can also be applied to bargaining situations.

Role Theories

These theories mainly focus on the social norms that most often determine the roles played by the individuals in a society. Social norms are the rules and expectations that are laid down in a particular community or a society. In this context, the social role refers to the norms that are applicable to certain individuals, based on their position in the community or the society. The social structure of the community and society will determine the social role to be played by the individual. These are, to a greater extent, influenced by the socio-economic status of the individuals. Members of a society have certain roles and norms that are to be followed by them. For example, there could be different gender-based roles that are expected to be followed by the members of a society.

Roles are also to be learned with reference to other complementary roles. Teachers need to be aware of the role of parents when it comes to the development of a child. In a similar manner, as citizens, we need to have an idea about one's own role and that of others while maintaining garbage-free surrounding.

Thus, the aforementioned theories can help us in comprehending various aspects and issues in social psychology. Also, more than one theory can be used to understand complex issues, thus employing an eclectic approach, where there is an integration of principles of more than one theory.

HISTORICAL DEVELOPMENTS IN SOCIAL PSYCHOLOGY

To start with the discussion about historical developments in social psychology, we need to acknowledge and mention viewpoints of the great thinkers, Aristotle and Plato. According to Aristotle, who adopted an individual-centred approach, humans were naturally sociable. However, Plato believed in a socio-centred approach and felt that individuals were controlled and provided with social responsibility by the state.

The concept of society was introduced by Hegel (1770–1831) who said that society has direct links with social mind, implying the significance of 'group mind' in social psychology. This in a way is responsible for focus on 'group mind' in social psychology.

Although the emergence of social psychology can be traced to ancient times, its beginning can be traced to 1897 when the first experiment in social psychology was carried out by Norman Triplett.

The experiment highlighted the co-action effect that describes how an individual's performance increases when others doing the same task are present.

In 1901, Starbucks tried to apply social psychology to study the psychology of religion and this, in a way, is considered a milestone in social psychology (Krech, Crutchfield, & Bellachey, 1962). The field of social psychology, however, emerged as an independent field during 1908–1924 (Baron & Byrne, 2006). Year 1908 marked the publication of a text with the phrase 'social psychology' in it by William McDougall. This text mainly dealt with the relationship between instincts and social behaviour. He argued that various instinctive tendencies determined human nature and the basis of human behaviour. He was influenced by the evolutionary theory of Darwin, which was much spoken in anthropology and sociology. He also spoke about evolutionary psychology. By evolutionary psychology, he meant the application of social psychology to comprehend the evolution or development of civilised human being. The year also marked the publication of a book titled *Social Psychology* by E. A. Ross who was an American sociologist.

According to Albert Pepitone (1981), a book with 'social psychology' in its title was published in Europe much before 1908 by Gabriel Tarde (1843–1904).

At this point, it is also necessary to introduce the term 'Völkerpsychologie' of Moritz Lazarus (1824–1903), Herrmann Steinthal (1823–1899) and Wilhelm Wundt (1832–1920). It was developed in Germany in the late 19th century. Völkerpsychologie, a German term, when translated in English, means the psychology of people. It can be termed as an earlier form of socio-cultural psychology dealing with cultural aspects such as language and custom that are the results of social interaction. Wundt proposed that an individual's thinking and perception of his/her social world can be affected by the grammar and vocabulary of his/her language.

During almost the same time that social psychologists spoke about Völkerpsychologie, a book on 'crowd psychology' was published by Gustave Le Bon in 1896. The book stressed on the concept of 'group mind'. Le Bon proposed that in certain situations, 'mob' is seen as being active as a single entity than individual human beings. Also, in this case, the mob functions at much lower intellectual and moral levels than its members would otherwise function. Year 1890 saw the publication of the book *The Laws of Imitation* by Tarde who worked on the influence that cities have on neighbouring areas. He also speculated the impact on a nation when it is conquered by another nation.

In 1924, Floyd Allport in his book emphasised that social behaviour was as a result of various factors such as the presence and actions of others. After the publication of Allport's work, social psychology developed with rapid strides, and experimentally oriented social psychology also emerged. During the 1930s, the scientific principles of precision and objectivity received attention, and there was a lot of interest shown in the group dynamics. During this period, social influence was researched in social psychology to a considerable degree. Further, in 1935, Muzafer Sherif conducted studies on social norms that can be described as rules that guide the individual behaviour in groups. Year 1935 saw the publication of the first *Handbook of Social Psychology* by Murchison. Theodore Newcomb in 1943 investigated the attitudes of young females, studying at Bennington College in Vermont, towards social and political aspects. The results indicated strong peer influence that led to the modification of attitudes held by the young females. Another research during this time focused on how individuals accepted opinions of certain prestigious people. These studies also led to developing an understanding about the concept of conformity. In 1939, Kurt Lewin, Ronald Lippitt and Ralph White conducted research on leadership and group processes.

Thus, numerous developments took place in the 1930s that paved the way for further expansion of social psychology as a prominent area of study.

The measurement of attitudes in a way was one of the major achievements in the 1930s and 1940s. The racial stereotypes of college students were studied by Katz and Braley in 1933. Methods for measuring attitudes were developed by Thurstone and Chave in 1929 and by Likert in 1932. Systematic polling of public opinion was started by Gallup during this period. Further, the use of questionnaires, interviews and observations in order to collect information was also explored by social psychologists. Sociometry that can be used to measure interpersonal preferences of individuals was developed by Moreno (1934). In 1936, Society for the Psychological Study of Social Issues (SPSSI) was established, which was mainly committed to the use of social science for human welfare. The society later became a division under American Psychological Association (APA).

Social psychology continued to develop through the 1940s and 1950s. Numerous research studies and speculations were carried out on groups and their membership. In 1941, Millar and Dollard published their work on imitation and leadership that highlighted how individuals follow their leaders without any thought or consideration. In 1946, Solomon Asch revealed that individuals develop a gestalt, form or shape while developing or forming impressions about others.

During the post-World War period, Carl Hovland et al. (1953) from Yale University conducted a research on attitude change. It mainly dealt with how an individual could develop attitudes as a result of practicing certain ideas. This was compared with how an individual would develop a motor skill by practising motor responses.

The year 1948 in a way led to a swift change in the field of social psychology. During this time, Research Centre for Group Dynamics was established by Kurt Lewin. Two other organisations by the name Commission on Community Interrelations and the National Training Laboratories were also established by him during this time. A text on social psychology was published by David Krech and Richard Crutchfield during the same year.

Leon Festinger developed the theory of cognitive dissonance in 1957. The theory proposed that human beings avoid inconsistency and try to reduce it. Thus, any inconsistency between attitudes or between attitude and behaviour will be eliminated. The 1960s was a period of rapid social change that contributed to the overall development of the field of social psychology.

During the 1970s, several new topics such as gender issues and behaviour, gender differences and discrimination, and environmental psychology caught the attention of social psychologists. Further, the focus was also on the cognitive aspect of social psychology that mainly dealt with attitudes, beliefs, values and so on. The role of cognitive factors in social behaviour was highlighted during this time. Further attention was paid to the application of social knowledge to the areas such as personal health, legal processes and work setting. In 1971, Tajfel and Turner introduced social identity theory, which states that people require maintaining a positive sense of personal and social identities. This positive sense can be, in a way, achieved by accentuating the desirability of one's own group and by focusing on dissimilarity with other groups.

In 1986, Weiner introduced the Attribution theory. He discussed about three main areas that can be attributed to experiences of failure and success. These three areas are the locus of control that can be either external or internal, stability or instability and controllability (Weiner, 1986).

Some of the prominent contributors to the field of social psychology have been mentioned in Box 1.2.

Thus, the aforementioned researchers and many more contributed to the establishment of social psychology as one of the most important branches of psychology. We will now discuss the development of social psychology in India. Some latest research in social psychology will be discussed in the course of this book.

SOCIAL PSYCHOLOGY IN INDIA

India has been a much different society than the Western countries. The varied cultures, religions, multiple languages, caste system, beliefs, attitudes and so on do make India a complex society. The social issues and problems in India also vary from that in the West. Thus, the issues dealt with under the field of social psychology also differ to a greater extent.

BOX 1.2 ***Some Prominent Contributors to the Field of Social Psychology***

Allport (1920) introduced the concept of social facilitation that deals with how the presence of others facilitates certain behaviours among individuals. For example, sports persons may benefit and perform better in the presence of the audience, especially belonging to their own nation.

Bandura (1963) spoke of social learning theory that mainly discusses how behaviour could be modelled by others. He carried out the 'Bobo doll experiment' that also confirmed the same. Children, for example, often model the behaviour of others.

Festinger (1950) proposed the term cognitive dissonance that denotes how we experience an imbalance when we behave in a way that may not be congruent with our attitude, values and beliefs.

Tajfel (1971) spoke about the social identity theory that stresses on how we develop an identity with our own group and thus develop an in-group and out-group attitude and preference.

Weiner (1986) discussed attribution theory that deals with how individuals seek attributions of their success and failure. He also spoke about the locus of control that can be internal or external, stability, whether stable or not and controllability, the extent to which one has control over the situation.

Although social psychology in India is influenced by the Western ideologies, we can find the roots of social psychology in the Indian context in ancient India. References to social relationship analysis and interpretations in India can be found even earlier to 1500 BC. References can also be found in the Vedic and post-Vedic literatures (Dalal & Misra, 2002). Various scriptures such as Vedas, Upanishads, Smritis, Puranas and Manusmriti provide insights into significant aspects of an individual's social life. The Mahabharata and Ramayana also provide significant insights into social aspect. *Arthashastra* by Chanakya (also known as Kautilya) provides descriptions and analyses of power and politics. Writings by Sufi saints and the *dohas* (poetic verses) of Kabir also help understand the social dimension even in the present context. The socio, political and religious movements spearheaded by leaders such as Maharishi Karve, Raja Ram Mohan Roy, Ishwar Chandra Vidyasagar and Swami Vivekanand have in a way contributed to the notion of social psychology in India. The folk tales from the likes of Panchatantra are yet another example of the prevalence or application of principles of social psychology as we see it today. Panchatantra to a greater extent discussed about moral and social behaviour.

During the British era, social psychology did not gain much of attention as compared to sociology and anthropology that had become a part and parcel of Indian academics (Dhangre, 1985).

Year 1926 saw one of the earliest experiments on the effect of group on performance by Sengupta and Singh. The experiment was based on the experiments carried out by Allport and his colleagues. This experiment in a way laid the foundation for growth of experimental social psychology in India. The first book on social psychology by an Indian was published by R. K. Mukherjee and Sengupta in 1928. The book had an interdisciplinary approach as R. K. Mukherjee was a sociologist and Sengupta was an experimental psychologist.

In 1935, Jamuna Prasad carried out a research on the reaction to the earthquake in Bihar that took place in 1934. He used the technique of serial production that was developed by Bartlett in 1932. Prasad analysed around 35,000 rumours and later published his work on earthquake rumours in 1950. In 1952, Durganand Sinha also conducted studies on rumours and on how people behave in catastrophic situations. The findings of the aforementioned studies were used by Leon Festinger (1957) while developing the theory of cognitive dissonance.

In 1941, Adinarayan conducted a research on colour prejudice that was also published in the *British Journal of Psychology*. This research work later formed the basis for further studies on prejudice and attitudes. After India became independent, the first prime minister of India, Pandit Jawaharlal Nehru, took numerous measures to promote the economic development of the country. UNESCO was invited to conduct research on communalism and social violence. One of the UNESCO team members was Gardner Murphy who also worked with other Indian psychologist in order to study communal hatred and its psychological impact. His work was later published in 1953 in his book titled *In the Minds of Men*.

The 1960s and 1970s saw major development and change in the research carried out by social psychologists in India. A number of researches were carried out on topics such as prejudice, attitude, stereotype and public awareness programmes. Year 1961 saw the release of the book *An Introduction to Social Psychology* by B. Kuppuswamy. Another area that received much attention was achievement motivation. The N-Ach theory developed by McClelland (1961) was also focused on, though experiments carried out by J. B. P. Sinha and Pandey (1970) revealed that the McClelland's theory was not applicable in Indian context (Dalal & Misra, 2002).

A National Seminar on Perspectives on Experimental Social Psychology in India was organised in 1979 at Allahabad. This seminar provided an opportunity for the discussion on experimental social psychology.

The debates and discussions that took place during the 1970s and 1980s in India with regard to research and experiments in social psychology further paved the way for the development of the subject in the country. Social change and development became a major focus during this time. The Indian Council of Social Science Research (ICSSR) was established in 1969, which was another milestone as it promoted further research in the general field of social science.

There was also an increased concern with regard to social psychology research in India that was seen as more of an imitation of research carried out in the Western countries. This concern was expressed by many; one among them was Ashis Nandy who in 1974 raised questions regarding the replicative and imitative nature of research in India. Over the years, social psychology established itself as an important subject area in India. Research carried out during the 1980s mainly reflected that findings of the Western studies cannot necessarily be applied to the Indian context and various social psychological processes needed an explanation that was embedded in the context of Indian culture. In 1987, a National Seminar on Applied Social Psychology in India was organised in Bhopal. The seminar mainly focused on social problems and the role of social psychology in dealing with these problems. The proceedings of the seminar were later published as an edited book titled *Applied Social Psychology in India* by Misra (1990). Since then, various studies have been carried out in the Indian context.

Research and studies in social psychology, especially in the Indian context, were further encouraged with the initiation of doctoral programmes with course work at the Indian Institute of Technology Kanpur and the Department of Psychology, University of Allahabad.

In 1992, research was carried out by DeRidder and Tripathi indicated that when norms are violated by a group, it results in a series of negative reactions by both the groups involved and, if continued, the situation could aggravate into behaviour that is violent. This was a significant cross-cultural research that was carried out in Netherlands and India.

Research in Indian context has also been carried out on selfhood. Studies have pointed out to the complexity of Indian self-hood and have stated that the categorisation of this Indian selfhood into individualist and collectivist is not easy. Thus, a 'coexistence of opposites', that is, where both individualist and collectivist self are present, was indicated by Sinha and Tripathi (1994).

In 1995, Sudhir Kakkar in his book titled *The Colours of Violence* discussed self-hood and intergroup relations based on the cultural–historical aspect. He emphasised the use of macro aspects in comprehension of systems that are psychosocial in nature.

The diversity in the mindsets of Indians was highlighted by Sinha and Pandey (2007), where they stated that in the context of a multicultural organisations, a materialistic mindset was displayed by Indians, whereas in more traditional, bureaucratic organisations or those owned by family, a collective mindset was displayed. In addition, an indigenous conceptualisation of intelligence was developed by Srivastava and Misra (2007). They termed it as integral intelligence that included four dimensions, cognitive competence, social competence, competence in action and emotional competence. Research in India has also seen a movement towards indigenisation. One such example is the cognitive processes, for example, described by Rao (2002, 2011) from Sāṁkhya-Yoga system perspective.

Thus, various researches in both psychology and social psychology have now been carried out in India, which have contributed to the overall development of the field of social psychology in India.

CURRENT TRENDS IN SOCIAL PSYCHOLOGY

One of the main trends in social psychology is its application to varied fields. Some of these fields have been discussed in the last chapter of this book. The principles and theories of social psychology can be applied to various other fields, for example, sports where leadership influences and group behaviour can be understood in a better manner. The behaviour of audience and the influence of their presence can also be studied. Social psychology also finds application in organisational set-ups, health care, clinical psychology, counselling and so on.

Another trend in social psychology is studying the interactions and influences of social media and Internet on human behaviour. Media has become a part and parcel of our lives so much so that we might be interacting with our best friends on Facebook and WhatsApp all the time but may not have met them in person for days. There are individuals who are so addicted to using Internet that they need to have constant connectivity or they feel alienated. Further, lot of Internet and cyber bullying also takes place that can have a severe effect on individuals. Considerable research has been conducted on these aspects.

A lot of research, in present times, also focuses on understanding the antecedents of social issues and problems and how principles of social psychology can be applied to deal with these social issues. In India, for example, we hear about growing crime rate, especially against women and even minors. Research is also underway to cement the gap between the social issues and principles of social psychology. The theories and principles of social psychology can possibly help in developing suitable strategies and intervention to deal with such social issues and many more. Research in social psychology is also being carried out using action research that can be termed as research with a purpose.

Another trend in social psychology is the application of cognition to studying social psychology concepts like attitudes, beliefs and so on. Behaviour and thinking are closely related and paying attention to cognitive process can help us understand human behaviour in different contexts in a much better way.

There is also a focus on studying culture especially by using methods of indigenous psychology. Various qualitative methods of research like ethnography can be used to understand cultural practices and rituals. The Western ways and methods of studying culture may not be applicable while carrying out research on cultural practices in India, therefore methods of indigenous psychology can be applied in this context. Cross-cultural research has also been carried out to understand the influence of culture on behaviour and to identify any universality.

Studies have been conducted to explore the genetic and biological basis of social behaviour. Thus, we have the development of the field of socio-biology that attributes the social behaviour to evolutionary processes. The field of social neuroscience is fast developing and various social behaviours can be explained from this perspective.

Social psychologists could thus constantly be on their toes in their attempts to understand numerous developments that take place in the society and how they have an impact on human behaviour.

SUMMARY

In this chapter, we initially discussed about the meaning of social psychology. Social psychology is defined as the scientific field that seeks to understand the nature and causes of individual behaviours and thoughts in social situations. We also discussed how social psychology is a scientific field with a goal to understand individual behaviour in social context and discussed how social psychology can be termed as science. The two main elements of science, that is, scientific understanding and core values were also discussed. While doing so, the four main goals of science, namely, description, prediction, determining causality and explanation were discussed. Along with the core values that scientists need to adhere to, such as accuracy, objectivity, scepticism, open mindedness and ethics.

We then dealt with the vast scope and nature of social psychology that covers numerous topics related to human behaviour in social context ranging from aggression, attitude to self and social cognition and so on that will be one by one discussed in this book. The theories like learning theories, cognitive theories, motivational theories, decision-making theories, social exchange theories and role theories were also discussed in this chapter. The milestones and key players in the field of social psychology were then dealt with in order to understand the developmental timeline of social psychology in general and specifically in Indian context. The chapter also focused on the current trends in social psychology including the influence of social media, understanding the antecedents of and possible solutions to deal with social issues and social problems, application of cognition to studying concepts in social psychology, focusing on cultural practices in India and exploring the biological basis of social behaviour.

QUESTIONS

1. Discuss the key points in definitions of social psychology.
2. 'Social psychology is a science', comment.
3. Discuss the principles of social psychology.
4. Describe the learning and cognitive theories of social psychology. Explain social exchange theories and role theories.
5. Identify the key contributors to the development of social psychology and discuss their contributions.
6. Describe the milestones in development of social psychology in India.
7. Highlight the current trends in social psychology.

REFERENCES

Bandura, A. (1963). *Social learning and personality development*. New York, NY: Holt, Rinehart and Winston.

Festinger, L. (1950). *Social pressures in informal groups* (1st ed.). New York, NY: Harper & Bros.

Festinger, L. (1957). *A theory of cognitive dissonance*. Evanston, IL: Row & Peterson.

Hovland, C. I., Janis, I. L., & Kelly, H. H. (1953). *Communication and persuasion: Psychological studies of opinion change*. New Haven, CT: Yale University Press.

McClelland, D. (1961). *Just because there's snow on the roof* (1st ed.). New York, NY: Vantage Press.

Mishra, G. (1990). *Applied psychology in India*. New Delhi: SAGE Publications.

Moreno, J. L. (1934). *Who shall survive? Foundations to sociometry group psychotherapy and sociodrama*. Beacon, NY: Beacon House.

Myers, D., & Spencer, S. (2006). *Social psychology* (1st ed.). Toronto: McGraw-Hill Ryerson.

Tajfel, H. (1971). *European monographs insocial psychology* (1st ed.).

Weiner, B. (1986). *An attributional theory of motivation and emotion*. New York, NY: Springer-Verlag.

FURTHER READINGS

For further reading on development of social psychology in India, the following can be read:

Dalal, A. K., & Misra, G. (2001). Social psychology in India: Evolution and emerging trends. In A. K. Dalal, and G. Misra (Eds.), *New directions in Indian psychology: Social psychology* (pp. 19–52). New Delhi: SAGE Publications.

For more information on social psychology, the following can be referred to:

Gilovich, T., Keltner, D., Chen, S., & Nisbett, R. E. (2013). *Social psychology*. London: Norton.

Gough, B., McFadden, M., & McDonald, M. (2013). *Critical social psychology: An introduction*. London: Palgrave Macmillan.

Jones, E. E. (1998). Major developments in five decades of social psychology. In D.T. Gilbert, S.T. Fiske and G. Lindzey (Eds), *The handbook of social psychology* (vol. 1). Boston: McGraw-Hill.

For more definitions and information on social psychology, you can follow the given link:

http://www.simplypsychology.org/social-psychology.html

CHAPTER 2

Research Methods in Social Psychology

In 2013, Mahakumbh was held from 27th January to 25th February in Allahabad, India. As per the official website of Kumbh Mela, the Kumbh Festival is held at the banks of holy rivers every 12 years. In Prayag, it is held on the banks of the rivers Ganga–Yamuna and the mythical Saraswati, in Haridwar at Ganga and in Nasik at the Godavari. The newspapers in India vehemently carried the news of our own Mahakumbh being the subject of study by Harvard students and researchers. Such researchers and many others are mainly interested in the overall phenomenon of Mahakumbh and look for reasons that draw such huge crowds. They are also, interested in studying the management of such extravagant events.

Research in social psychology is not only carried out to understand social events like Mahakumbh, but various social behaviours, social issues and social problems can also be studied with the help of research methods in social psychology.

Various experiments and researches pertaining to social psychology have been covered in different chapters of this book.

Research methods help us to scientifically understand social behaviour amongst human beings. Social psychologists, like other psychologists and scientists, use various research methods in order to understand human beings and their environment. Research methods can be described as the procedures that are carried out in order to obtain or gather information in any field. For example, if we want to know why youngsters indulge in rash driving, then research methods are going to help us obtain more information in this regard. Thus, a mere idea about this behaviour of youngsters can be translated into a research with the help of methods. Methods need to be distinguished from methodology. Methods are mainly the procedures, methodology deals with all the facets involved in the application of methods.

Most often, however, a question is asked whether research on human beings, especially in a social set-up, is adequately scientific, as a lot of research in this case is carried out in field. The answer to this is that there are many physical or pure sciences where research is not restricted to a laboratory. For example, subjects such as Botany and Geology require certain research to be carried out in a field set-up. Further, there are a number of researches in social psychology that have been carried out under controlled conditions.

Thus, in social psychology as well, to a greater extent, a research can be carried out in a scientific manner, provided the necessary conditions are fulfilled.

Research is an important aspect of any subject area as that is how the subject grows. Thus, this chapter is very relevant in understanding the nuances of how research can be carried out in the field of social psychology.

Learning Objectives

After reading this chapter, you will be able to

- Discuss research in social psychology
- Describe the key concepts in research
- Explain the components of the research process
- Describe research methods in social psychology
- Explain qualitative research
- Discuss the ethical issues in research
- Discuss deception in social psychology research
- Discuss the challenges and problems while conducting research in social psychology
- Describe trends and prospects in social psychology research

RESEARCH IN SOCIAL PSYCHOLOGY

Research can be described as adding to the existing fund of knowledge. It is a critical and complex enquiry and an intensive and cumulative process. It can be described as a systematic and objective analysis and recording of controlled observations that may lead to the development of generalisations, principles and theories, resulting in prediction and possibly ultimate control of events. It is a search for knowledge to find a solution to a problem.

Some of the definitions of research are as follows:

Research, in simple terms, can be defined as an investigation that is systematic in nature and directed to seek answers to a problem (Burns, 2000).

Best and Kahn (1999) have defined research as 'systematic and objective analysis and recording of controlled observation that may lead to the development of generalisation, principles or theories, resulting in prediction and possibly ultimate control of events'.

Kerlinger (1995, p. 10) defines scientific research as 'a systematic, controlled, empirical and critical investigation of natural phenomenon guided by theory and hypotheses about the presumed relations among such phenomena'.

The aforementioned definitions highlight the following aspects of research:

1. **It is an investigation.** Necessarily some phenomenon or other is investigated.
2. **The investigation is carried out in a systematic and objective manner.** Scientific research methods, and valid and reliable tools are used while carrying out research.
3. **Research is directed towards seeking answers to certain problems.** Research helps in obtaining answers to the problem in a systematic and objective manner.
4. **Generalisations can be carried out.** The results obtained can be applied to the larger population from which the representative sample was taken.

Thus, if a researcher wants to study the relationship between self-concept and academic achievement of adolescents, he/she will employ empirical methods and valid and reliable tools to collect data from the representative sample of adolescents. The data thus collected can be analysed and results can be interpreted and the findings can then be generalised to the population of adolescents.

Research can be categorised as basic research and applied research. Basic research is directed towards obtaining answers to questions related to why individuals behave the way they do. Thus, basic research is mainly based on the intellectual curiosity (Aronson et al., 2014). Applied research, on the other hand, is focused towards deriving solutions with regard to certain social problems.

Research in social psychology mainly helps to understand certain issues or areas that we already know about. It can also be a certain aspect of social life. For example, group 'A' has a negative attitude towards group 'B' and this information is already available, but further probing can be carried out with regard to why group 'A' has a negative attitude towards group 'B'. Similarly, a particular practice or a ritual prevalent amongst a group of people or in a particular culture can also be researched. Research in social psychology can help us understand certain social issues or problems such as child labour or violence against women.

The main goals of research in social psychology are discussed as follows:

1. One of the goals of research in social psychology is the systematic description of behaviour in a social set-up in order to make generalisations. While conducting research, a systematic and specific methodology needs to be followed to derive generalisations. The findings need to be based on systematic research rather than on what one feels.
2. Research in social psychology also deals with cause and effect relationship. For example, does education level have an effect on health-related behaviour?
3. Developing theories is yet another goal of social psychology. Theories can be derived with regard to certain behaviours of people. Goal of any science is developing theories. Theories mainly help understand the reasons behind certain processes and events. Thus, in social psychology, a theory regarding aggression will help understand the reasons behind this behaviour. Theories explain certain basic concepts and also the relationships between these basic concepts.
4. Further, the information and knowledge about social psychology and its principles can be applied to various social problems. For example, the knowledge about groups and group dynamics can be applied to effective functioning of groups and teams in an industrial set-up.

KEY CONCEPTS IN RESEARCH

Some of the key concepts of research are discussed as follows:

1. **Construct:** Construct is a theoretical concept that is necessarily abstract in nature. A concept becomes a construct when it is used in a research and thus it also needs to be operationally defined. For example, happiness as a concept when used in a research will be termed as construct and then it has to be defined based on what the researcher really means by happiness. The researcher will then have to use a tool for measurement of happiness based on its operational definition. Operationalisation thus converts the construct into a variable that is measurable.
2. **Variable:** Variable can be described as a concept or a construct that varies or that can have varied value. Variable can be categorised as independent, dependent and extraneous variable.

   i. ***Independent variable.*** This is a variable that can be manipulated by the researcher or experimenter. For example, in a research on effect of light on the performance of the individuals, the independent variable 'light' can be manipulated from dim to bright. In certain situations, it is not possible to manipulate the independent variable(s) because it/they have already occurred. For example, if a researcher wants to study the bereavement process of persons who have lost their siblings owing to unnatural death, the independent variable (i.e., the death of the sibling) has already occurred.

ii. ***Dependent variable.*** This is the variable that is studied for any changes as a result of changes in the independent variable. Thus, in the aforementioned two examples, the performance of the individuals and bereavement process are the dependent variables.

iii. ***Extraneous variables.*** These are the variables that can interfere in the relationship between the independent and dependent variables and thus negatively affect the internal validity of the research. In the experiment on light and its effect on performance, discussed earlier, it is possible that the group of individuals performing under bright light had a lot of noise in the room. Thus, the deterioration in their performance can be attributed to the noise (that can be termed as an extraneous variable) and not the variation in the light (bright). It is necessary that the extraneous variables are identified and controlled.

3. **Experimental and control group:** An experimental group is the one where the independent variable is manipulated or the group that gets the special treatment. On the other hand, a control group is the one that receives normal treatment. Here, the independent variable is not manipulated. In the example related to the effect of light on performance, the groups performing under bright or dim light are experimental groups and the group that performs under normal light is the control group.
4. **Confederates:** Most often in social psychology research, we may also have confederates. These are the individuals who in reality are accomplices of the researcher, who play a specified role. For example, in an experiment on social influence, some of the participants may in fact be confederates who may deliberately try to influence the decisions of the other participants so as to understand whether social influence takes place or not. Various prominent social psychology experiments, such as Milgram's experiment, involved confederates.
5. **Internal and external validity:** Psychologists predominantly discuss about validity in the context of psychological testing. Although while carrying out research, one needs to focus on the validity of the research. Internal validity mainly has to do with whether the change(s) in the dependent variable are due to the change(s) in independent variable and not due to any extraneous variables. If such changes in dependent variable are due to independent variable then the internal validity is high, otherwise it is low. Most often research carried out in a field set-up will have lower internal validity. External validity mainly has to do with generalisation of the results. External validity can be of two types, ecological validity and population validity. Ecological validity has to do with whether the results obtained can be generalised to wider situation or set-up or not. For example, if a study is carried out on children in a laboratory set-up, whether the results of the same can be applied to children in a realistic set-up or not. On the other hand, population validity has to do with whether the results of the study carried out on a certain group of individuals can be generalised to the individuals in general. For example, whether findings of a study that is carried out on a group of adolescents in India (sample) can be generalised to all the adolescents in India or not.

COMPONENTS OF RESEARCH PROCESS

The research process includes formulating problem and hypothesis/es, making decisions about sample and sampling technique, finalising research design, deciding tools for data collection, analysis of data, deriving conclusion and making generalisations. These are discussed as follows:

1. **Problem:** Problem provides an idea about the general objective of the study or research to be carried out. For example, if you are interested in studying emotional competence of victims of violence, the problem will be 'to study the emotional competence of victims of violence'.
   Hypothesis/es: Hypothesis is a tentative statement about the problem. Hypothesis can be alternative hypothesis or it can be null hypothesis. Alternative hypothesis can be one-tailed or two-tailed. An example of one-tailed alternative hypothesis is 'the victims of violence who receive suitable counselling/support have higher emotional competence when compared with the victims who do not receive any counselling or support'. An example of two-tailed hypothesis is 'there will exist a significant difference in the emotional competence of victims of violence who receive counselling/support and victims who do not receive counselling/support'. An example of null hypothesis is 'there will exist no significant difference in the emotional competence of victims of violence who receive counselling/support and victims who do not receive counselling/support'. Hypothesis formulation can be carried out on the basis of the review of literature or previous studies conducted on the related topics. Hypothesis could be formulated based on the existing theories and research.
2. **Sample and sampling technique:** The nature of sample included in a study will depend on what is being studied. And based on the nature of the sample, probability or non-probability the sampling technique can be used.
3. **Research design:** Research designs can be described as the structure and plan of the research. Based on the topic, a research design can be employed by the researcher. Research designs can be simply described as the structure of the research. They provide an outline to carry out the research. The research design has two main purposes, to find answers for research question and to control any variance, which includes maximising the true variance (variance in the dependent variable because of the independent variable) and minimising the error variance (variance in the dependent variable because of any random fluctuation or extraneous variable). As Kerlinger (1995) puts it, 'Research Designs are invented to enable researchers to answer research questions as validly, objectively, accurately and economically as possible'. There are various designs that can be used by a researcher based on the topic and objectives of the research.

   - ***True designs.*** These designs are most applicable for studies that are carried out in a laboratory or a controlled set-up. In these designs, the independent variable can be manipulated. There is also high control, and it is possible to use randomisation and matched randomisation. An example of such a design would be when we carry out a study on the effect of brightness of the light on the writing activity of the participants. Many experiments in social psychology have also been carried out in a controlled situation. In a simple example, if a researcher wants to study the effect of noise on performance, he/she will select, say, students in a certain college using randomisation and then randomly divide the participants into experimental and control groups. The experimental group may then be asked to perform under a noisy condition and the control group may be asked to perform under a noise-free condition. Their performance will then be studied for the effect of noise.
   - ***Faulty designs.*** These designs mainly find their application in field studies where the independent variables cannot be manipulated because they have already occurred. These designs are characterised by the inability to manipulate independent variables. Since the study has been carried out in a field set-up, the control is also poor and randomisation cannot be used. An example of a faulty design would be a study carried on coping strategies

employed by female victims of violence, where the independent variable that is being subjected to violence, has already occurred. Further, in such a research, randomisation cannot be used due to the nature of the sample.

- ***Quasi-experimental designs.*** These designs resemble true designs and can be used in the context of field experiments. These designs have good control though randomisation cannot be used. An example would be when we try to compare the mental health and social adjustment of persons who are HIV positive and persons suffering from cancer. In such a study, we cannot use randomisation as the two groups are distinct.
- ***Factorial designs.*** These can be used to study the effect of two or more independent variables on the dependent variable. The independent variables can be studied for their main effect (independent) or for interactional effect.
- ***Small n designs.*** These can be used for research with small samples or when the case study approach is used. Thus the research is carried out on a single or small sample, but the study is in-depth.

There are various such designs that can be used by the researcher.

4. **Data collection:** Data can be collected using suitable methods such as interview, questionnaire, observation, psychological tests and so on. Some of the methods of data collection have been discussed briefly in Table 2.1.
5. **Analysis of data**: The collected data can be tabulated and analysed using qualitative or quantitative techniques of analysis. The techniques used for data analysis will depend on the objectives and the hypothesis/es of the research.
6. **Deriving conclusions and making generalisations**: Conclusions can be derived on the basis of the interpretations of the results obtained after analysis of data. The conclusions can then be generalised to the larger population.

Though the main components of the research process were discussed in this section, the research process necessarily starts with the selection of a topic that can be based on the review of literature, on interaction with experts as well as on the events in the social set-up. Based on the selection of the topic, a research proposal needs to be prepared that is a blueprint or plan of how the researcher will go about the research. The main components of such a research proposal include background and theoretical information about the topic, review of literature and research methodology employed, which includes statement of the problem, objectives, hypothesis/es, sample and sampling technique, research design, tools of data collection and tools for statistical analysis. References in a suitable format also need to be included in the research proposal. Research can also include comparison of results across studies using meta-analysis (Box 2.1).

TYPES OF RESEARCH IN SOCIAL PSYCHOLOGY

As we will see in various chapters, a number of studies that employ various types of research have been carried out in social psychology. Understanding these types is significant not only to understand the existing research but also to take decisions regarding which method would be most suitable when one wants to study a certain phenomenon in social psychology. Various types of research have been discussed further in this section.

Table 2.1 *Methods of Data Collection Used in Social Psychology*

Method	Details
Observation	• Behaviour is observed in an artificial or naturalistic set-up. • Could be participant or non-participant and structured or unstructured. • Most often, a checklist or a video aid could be used with due permission of the participants. • Can also involve participant observation, where the researcher studies the group from within. • Subject to the Hawthorne effect, that is, the awareness about being observed has an impact on the performance or behaviour of the participants.
Psychological Tests	• These are standardised and systematic measures of sample of behaviour. • The tests are valid and reliable. • Need to be culture-fair or to be adapted to different cultures and social set-ups.
Projective Techniques	• In this, the participant is presented with a stimulus to which he/she is expected to respond with what he/she can see. • The respondent projects his/her motives, needs, values and so on onto the stimulus. • These could be structured (sentence completion test), unstructured (Rorschach inkblot test). • These techniques lack objectivity.
Interview	• These are one-to-one processes where the interviewer asks certain open-ended and close-ended questions to the participant. • These could be structured, unstructured or semi-structured. • Recording devises could be used after seeking permission from the participants.
Questionnaire	• Could include open-ended or close-ended questions. • Rating scales may also be used (for example Likert's five-point rating scale). • The language used needs to be simple and clear.
Sociometry	• Can be of great help to study social interaction in groups. • Mainly involves collection and analysis of data with regard to communication, interaction pattern and choices of individuals when in groups. • Based on the information obtained sociometric matrices or sociograms can be created.

Source: Author.
Note: A research could involve use of more than one method of data collection.

Experimental Method

The experimental method has been described by Aronson et al. (2014, p. 34) as 'the method in which the researcher randomly assigns participants to different conditions and ensures that these conditions are identical except for the independent variable (the one thought to have a causal effect on people's responses)'.

BOX 2.1 *Meta-analysis*

Meta-analysis can be described as 'a statistical analysis that averages the results of two or more studies to see if the effect of an independent variable is reliable' (Aronson et al., 2014, p. 41). Thus, for example, we may look at 30 studies on a particular topic to understand the impact of an independent variable on a dependent variable and if we find that out of 30 studies, only one study indicated that the independent variable does not have an impact on the dependent variable, then we can conclude that with an exception of one study, on an average, the independent variable has an impact on the dependent variable.

Source: Author.

The experiments are carried out in a controlled environment, for example, a laboratory set-up. This is done in order to minimise the problems that may occur because of variance in all or most of the independent variables. It also involves manipulation of one or more than one independent variable/s. The cause and effect relationship between variables is studied in a controlled situation that is mostly free from interference of extraneous variables. The participants are randomly assigned to the groups, whether control or experimental. This means that each participant of the study has equal chance of being in either experimental group or control group. The extraneous variables are controlled so that they do not interfere in the cause and effect relationship between independent variables and dependent variables. The experimental method follows systematic steps while conducting research. The important steps involved in this method are as follows:

1. Define the problem to be studied
2. Develop a research design or procedure
3. Collection of information
4. Interpretation of information

The experimental method has high internal validity but low external validity. High internal validity (as discussed earlier) means that the experiment will determine the strength of cause and effect relationship between independent and dependent variables. However, it may not be possible to generalise the results obtained to the population (population validity) or other situations (ecological validity) as the experiment is carried out in a laboratory set-up that is far from a realistic situation. Thus, it can be said that the experimental method has lower external validity. In the context of ecological validity, social psychologists could also focus on increasing the psychological realism (that focuses on the degree of similarity between the psychological processes that were precipitated in an experiment and psychological processes that take place in day-to-day life) of the social psychological research (Aronson et al., 2014).

Replications can also be used in order to test external validity. Replication can be described as repeating a particular study with either different population or in a different setting.

Field Research

One way in which the external validity of a research can be increased is by carrying out field research. In field research, independent variables cannot be directly controlled as these valiables have manifestations that have already occurred and it is not possible to manipulate them. It is not possible to employ randomisation in a field research. In field studies, inferences about the relationship between the independent and dependent variables are carried out on the basis of naturally occurring variations in them and not through direct intervention. This method has high external validity, as stated earlier, and thus the results can be generalised to the populations and other situations. However, it has low internal validity, as there are various extraneous variables that may not be possible to control and that may interfere with the cause and effect relationship between the variables.

Descriptive Research

Observation and recording are two main components of descriptive research. It involves description, as the name suggests, and does not provide information about cause and effect relationship. With the help of this method, the researcher can describe patterns of behaviour and also discover associations between variables, but causation cannot be implied. This type of research is mainly used when a researcher cannot manipulate the variables under study. The methods of descriptive research are naturalistic observation, case studies and surveys. In naturalistic observation, the behaviour is observed and recorded in a naturalistic situation. There is no control over the situation, for example, watching crowd behaviour. In a case study, a single person or situation is studied in depth, for example, a study of person suffering from a major psychological disorder. With regard to the survey method, information is collected from a large number of individuals.

Correlational Method

Correlational method is especially useful in certain settings where it is not possible to apply the experimental method. In the correlational method, no attempt is made to manipulate one or more variable. The variables are observed as they occur naturally so as to study if changes in one variable are related to changes in another variable. Measuring such relations or associations is called correlations. Correlation can range from –1.00 to +1.00. A value of '0' indicates lack of relationship and value of '1' indicates strong correlation. The signs – and + indicate whether the relationship is negative (inverse) or positive (direct), respectively. One of the drawbacks of this method is that it does not provide any information about the cause and effect relationship between the variables.

Survey Research

Survey research mainly involves collection of data from a representative sample of a population or whole population (in case of census) regarding some behaviour or to obtain their opinion. A very common example would be exit polls. Surveys can be carried out with the help of interviews or questionnaires. Surveys can also be carried out through telephone calls and emails. A survey can help gather a large amount of information from a large sample; however, they are not in-depth. Further, one of the main concerns in survey research is having a sample that is truly representative of its population. In this case, various techniques of probability sampling such as simple random sampling, quota sampling among others can be used. Survey research is also time-consuming and can be costly as well.

Action Research

According to Lewin, an action research is comparative in nature and studies the conditions and effects of various social actions and leads to social action (Fisher, 1982). Thus the focus here is on intervention.

The steps in action research are as follows:

1. *The panning phase.* Here, an attempt is made to understand the situation.
2. *Fact-finding phase.* This can also be called the phase of data collection that will help to understand the situation in a much better manner.
3. *Action or execution phase.* The results can now help in developing a suitable plan of action or intervention.

Various types of action research as stated by Chein, Cook and Harding in 1948 (Fisher, 1982) are as follows:

- *Diagnostic action research.* Here the problem or issue is analysed or studied in such a way that certain recommendations can then be made in the direction of some action.
- *Participant action research.* The individuals or the members of the community/organisation who will be taking action are directly involved right from the initial stage of the research. This also reduces resistance to change and motivates these individuals to take action.
- *Empirical action research.* Here an action is taken and then monitored on a day-to-day basis. An external researcher in this regard may be appointed in order to objectively evaluate the action.
- *Experimental action research.* Here, in order to study effectiveness of a particular action, experimental research is utilised.

While discussing action research, it is important to remember that this research can help deal with a particular social issue or problem, however results may be slow, and immediate and sure success cannot be ensured.

QUALITATIVE RESEARCH IN SOCIAL PSYCHOLOGY

For a considerable period of time, the research in psychology has been predominantly quantitative in nature. But recently there has been a movement towards the use of qualitative research as well.

The data involved in qualitative research is mainly non-numerical in nature and it mainly involves, interviews, written evidences, recorded evidences and even descriptions of events. Thus, it can be said that qualitative research lacks overemphasis on quantification and that is the core of qualitative research. Further, qualitative research involves inductive and exploratory research. Whereas quantitative research involves testing of certain theories and is deductive in nature. A lot of interdisciplinary research is now carried out which may require the use of qualitative approach or mixed approach, that is, having both qualitative and quantitative angles.

To some extent, the qualitative research emerged as a kind of reaction to the positivism of the research that is quantitative in nature, which mainly aims to adopt the methods of natural sciences (David & Sutton, 2011). And most often the researchers using qualitative approach highlight that in the qualitative approach, the participants are not treated as mere objects to obtain data. The methods used for data collection are also more open in nature which helps the researcher in carrying out the research in depth.

The research design employed in qualitative research are also more descriptive and exploratory in nature. The methods of data collection used could be interview method, observation, focused groups and so on. These are discussed in detail here.

Qualitative Interviewing

Qualitative interviewing necessarily involves asking questions which to a great extent are open-ended. This is mainly a one-to-one process, though it is sometimes possible that there is more than one interviewer (e.g., in a case where a student is still in the learning phase, he/she may need some help in interviewing correctly). Interview could be structured, unstructured or semi-structured in nature. A lot of work is needed in developing the interview schedules and framing the questions.

Also, the interviewer needs to develop a suitable rapport with the participants and create a conducive environment for the participants to respond to the questions and interact with the interviewer. Listening and observing are two skills that are extremely important here, as a researcher not only has to listen carefully and intuitively to what the participants have to say but also has to observe the non-verbal behaviour of the participants. The researcher also needs to be sure that the participants have understood the questions. Therefore, the questions need to be asked in the language that the participants understand. Questions asked could be of various types; some of them are mentioned here.

- **Warm-up questions:** These are used mainly to create rapport with participants.
- **Demographic questions:** These are used to obtain demographic details about the participant, for example, age, religion and so on.
- **Core questions:** These are the main questions related to the objective(s) of the research. In this regard, certain prompts and probes can also be used to get more information regarding the core questions.
- **Clarifying questions:** These will help researcher understand what the participant has to say and may also provide another dimension to the information provided by the participants.
- **Piloting:** This involves taking the opinion of the experts and have them critically analyse the questions developed, and also asking these questions to a smaller group (of the population under study) so as to know whether they are alright. Based on the results of piloting, certain questions could be dropped, added or modified.

The interviewer also needs to be cautious regarding the bias that may creep in, especially when the data gathered is interpreted. It is possible for the interviewer to use a recorder, provided the necessary permission has been obtained from the participant.

Focus Group

Focus groups can be described as a group interview where instead of asking direct questions, the questions are discussed by a group of participants. Focus groups were developed in the 1940s in social sciences but have been quite popular with market-related research (David & Sutton, 2011). Focus groups, like interview, can be structured or unstructured. Further, they may include experts discussing on some aspect or latest developments in their fields; this is referred to as Delphi groups. For examples, neuropsychologists could discuss latest developments in neuropsychology. They could also include individuals from different walks of life, for example, when groups of people belonging to different strata of society discuss about crimes against women or health-related issues. The individuals may or may not know each other. The groups thus can be either homogeneous or heterogeneous in nature based on the research objectives. Groups could also be naturalistic, that is, groups that pre-exist, for example, a group of colleagues, or it could be constructed by the researcher, which will have participants who are more likely not to know each other.

However, what is even more important here is the size of the group. This again depends on the research objective. A group can be as large as having even 12 participants. A Delphi group, on the other hand may have up to four participants.

Though focus group discussions can help gather relevant information, problems and issues can crop up while selecting the participants, directing the group discussion and during interpretation of the results obtained.

With regard to ethical issue, on one hand it gives more control to the participants, on the other, confidentiality of the participants cannot be assured.

The researcher plays an important role in coordinating and facilitating the discussion. He/she plays an important role in encouraging the members who may not contribute much or in directing the discussion which may go astray from the main topic. Social desirability can also be an issue here, and the participants may not be frank in their responses. Besides, as in the interview method, the researcher also needs to work on the questions involved and also on the location where this discussion will take place. The participants need to be given clear instructions and should also be acquainted with the rules for the focus group. Audio or video recording can be carried out with due permission of the participants. Lastly, as in interview where the interviewer needs to create a rapport with the interviewee, in a focus group, the researcher not only needs to create a rapport with the participants but the participants also need to have adequate rapport with each other for smooth discussion to take place.

Case Study

This is again an in-depth study. A case study approach, for example, can be used to study a person with peculiar medical or psychological condition. It could also be used to study an organisation, for example a university or an industry (to carry out an in-depth study on its structure, processes, etc.). Case study involves, as mentioned before, an in-depth study that requires both time and attention on the part of the researcher. Thus, the researcher can develop greater understanding of a unit, its traits and qualities. Case study also includes use of various tools of data collection such as tests, interview methods and observation. Case studies can also be longitudinal in which the units are studied over a period of time. As a case study involves in-depth study of single or few units, the results of the case study cannot be generalised to a larger population.

Ethnography

Ethnography can be described as the study of behaviour of people in a naturalistic set-up. The data is thus collected in a naturalistic set-up using the methods that are naturalistic. It is comparatively less structured and involves observation that is informal in nature and also includes conversation with the people being studied. The researcher, in fact, may directly participate in the setting or even in the activities. This method is descriptive in nature and most often uses smaller number of cases. Thus, people are studied in their natural set-up. Ethnography can be effectively used to study a particular community of people.

The researcher most often lives with the individuals that he/she is studying. Thus, ethnography also involves participant observation. Further for data collection, various methods such as interview, observation and documental sources can be used.

Ethnography has various advantages. This kind of naturalistic method may have higher validity than the research that is carried out in a laboratory set-up. A large number of information can be collected by the researcher, that is, mainly first-hand. A particular event, practice or case can be studied in depth.

Some of the disadvantages of ethnography are that the results cannot be generalised. Also, there is no information obtained regarding cause and effect. It is not simple to describe what is seen while using ethnography. Ethnography has same ethical issues, as we discussed with regard to the interview method and focus groups.

The researcher also develops a kind of intimacy with the participants or with the individuals belonging to the community that he/she is studying, which can be both an advantage and a disadvantage.

The overall process of using ethnography is also difficult right from identifying what the researcher wants to study, giving reasons for the choice of the cases and area, to actually getting an entry into that community or group of people and forming rapport with them. Further, data collection also involves being alert so as to adequately understand the behaviour of the group. Leaving the field after the research culminates can also be a challenging task because of the relationships that develops between the researcher and the group members.

All this definitely requires expertise on the part of the researcher and a new researcher may require help while using this method.

To some extent, deception can also be used in ethnography where the researcher enters the group but the members of the group are not made aware that he/she is a researcher.

Grounded Theory

Introduced by Glaser and Strauss in their book, *The Discovery of Grounded Theory*, in 1967 (David & Sutton, 2011), this method of data collection mainly focuses on the relationship between the scientific enquiry and theory in such a way that data collection is not merely for seeking answers to predetermined questions but to facilitate the emergence of theory from the data. The main focus of this method is discovering, which again brings the focus to the data collection process. The three main concepts in grounded theory are Grounded, Theory and Discovery. Besides, in this context, yet another term 'constant comparison' also needs to be focused on. In grounded theory, the analysis of data starts the moment the data collection commences, and there is a constant comparison in the process between data units or between the data and the possible explanations and so on.

Qualitative research, though, can raise an ethical issue as the researcher may not be in position to explain the research beforehand as he/she may not be aware about what findings might be revealed through the use of this inductive approach using open-ended methods of data collection. Thus, obtaining necessary ethical approvals for research can also be a challenge. Further, the participants may also be in the way of danger owing to the kind of information (i.e., in-depth) revealed by them during the research and as most of the qualitative research involves smaller samples, their anonymity may also be at stake. Thus, the researcher needs to be very cautious in this regard. Further, it may not be possible to obtain informed consent from the participants because of the very nature of the qualitative research. For example, when observation is used to study the interaction of adolescent students in a classroom set-up, the researcher will not be able to take informed consent, as if the adolescents, who will be observed, are informed about the research, they will become more cautious, which will have an impact on their behaviour and, in turn, will defeat the very purpose of the research.

ETHICAL ISSUES IN RESEARCH

As psychologists and social psychologists, it is important to take into consideration ethics in research. Some of these ethics have emerged as a result of various experiments carried out in social psychology, such as Milgram's experiment and Zimbardo's experiments. Ethics are to be followed at various stages of research such as selecting a research question, research design, data collection, analysis of data and reporting the findings. Following ethics in research in social psychology can be challenging because of its complex nature, and the researcher has to be very cautious while balancing between protecting the rights of the participants and not compromising the research process. Most often, research in social psychology requires the use of deception, which can clash to a greater extent with the ethical issues. For example, if we want to understand pro-social behaviour of students in a particular college and create a fake accident scene to study the reaction of the students, it will not be possible for us to seek informed consent from the participants. However, after the data collection is done, the participants can be debriefed about the study and can then be ensured about confidentiality and anonymity.

Further, it is also important to consider the risk and benefits of the research, to assess the vulnerability of participants and decide if any compensation needs to be given to the participants. If the benefits are high and risk is low, we can go ahead with the research. On the other hand, if benefits are low and risks are high, we will not go ahead with the research. When, risk and benefits are both low, again there is no point in continuing with the research as it will not add considerably to the field or benefit the participants. However, when risks are high, but benefits are also high, the question of ethics will become even more prominent and the researcher will have to think of ways in which the risk factors can be lowered or minimised before he/she carries on with the research.

Compensations needs to be decided as per the rules and laws of the country where the research is carried out. Some of the ethical issues to be considered are as follows:

- **Beneficence and non-malfeasance:** The research should be conducted keeping in mind the benefits of the research to the participants. Any research that is carried out should be beneficial to the participants. The researcher should ensure that the participants are not harmed in any way during the research. This issue mainly has to do with the risk and benefit ratio. As much as possible, the risk involved in the research needs to be minimised and further if any minimal risk exists, the participants need to be informed about the same.
- **Informed consent:** A proper consent is to be sought from the participants before conducting the research. According to Berg (1998, p. 47), informed consent means 'the knowing consent of individuals to participate as an exercise of their choice, free from any elements of fraud, deceit, duress, or similar unfair inducement or manipulation'. In informed consent, the participants are informed about the objectives of the study and also about the possible risks involved. Further, the benefits of the research are also informed. Various formats of informed consent are available, that can be used by the researchers as per their requirement. Further, it is also to be noted here that seeking informed consent can be difficult when deception is used in a study or when the participants are to be observed in a naturalistic situation.
- **Privacy, confidentiality and anonymity:** Privacy and confidentiality of the participants should be strictly maintained. The identity of the participants cannot be divulged and due care needs to be taken by the researcher in this regard. Most often, some kind of coding can be used, especially when the research involves large data. We also need to distinguish between

the terms confidentiality and anonymity. In confidentiality, the researcher assures that the information regarding the participants is not available to others. However, in this case, it is possible for the researcher or someone else to figure out who the participant is (based on, say, the personal details given in the data). In anonymity, even the researcher may not be able to identify the participant based on the data given as the data is coded. We can also differentiate between privacy and anonymity. Privacy is related to the content (information related to the performance/results of the participants) that needs to be kept private, whereas anonymity is related to the concealment of the participants' identity.

DECEPTION IN SOCIAL PSYCHOLOGY RESEARCH

As stated by Baron and Byrne (1995, p. 31), 'Deception involves efforts by researchers to withhold or conceal information about the purpose of a study from the persons who participate in it'. Though use of deception can be questioned, in certain cases it may not be possible to carry out research without deception (especially with regard to the phenomena studied in social psychology). Discussing about deception in social psychology is significant because if the participants know that their behaviour has been studied for a particular purpose, they are most likely to display a socially desirable behaviour. For example, if a study is being carried out on the attitude towards use of certain safety devices and the participants are informed about the purpose of the study, they may manipulate their responses based on what is perceived as socially desirable. To avoid this, the actual purpose of the study is not disclosed and the participants are informed that they will just be asked certain general questions about day-to-day life. Thus, in order to be able to achieve the objectives of the research, use of deception might be necessary. Most social psychology researchers also do believe that the use of deception, at least, on temporary basis, is necessary (Suls & Rosnow, 1988).

Use of deception can lead to certain issues and problems, discussed as follows:

1. When the participants come to know about the real purpose of the researcher they may not feel happy and may resent their participation in the research and may also react in a negative manner.
2. Further, once the participants come to know that they have been deceived during the research, they may never participate in any research in future.
3. The use of deception can actually harm the participant. They may feel anxious and stressed.
4. Deception also raises ethical and moral issues.

Any deception should be avoided. But in case it is extremely necessary, the safety of the participants should be ensured. If deception is used, then the researcher should carry out debriefing after the research. Deception in a research should be used keeping in mind 'minimal risk', that is, any possible risk to the participants should be minimum. Further, the use of deception also depends on the risk and benefit ratio. Debriefing, after the data is collected from the participant, can help reduce the negative effect of deception.

Thus, deception should be used only when it is absolutely necessary and it should be used in a condition where the risks are minimal because the well-being and safety of the participant are of utmost importance. While using deception, the researcher has to be extremely careful and cautious and should be prepared for any negative effects.

CHALLENGES AND PROBLEMS WHILE CONDUCTING RESEARCH IN SOCIAL PSYCHOLOGY

- **Issues and threats related to internal validity:** One of the major problems in conducting research in social psychology is that of issues related to internal validity. As most of the research in social psychology is carried out in a field set-up, it is not possible to control all the extraneous variables. Thus, the internal validity of such research can be low. However, on the other hand, the major advantage is that the research in social psychology when carried out in a field set-up can help study behaviour in a realistic situation, which will lead to high external validity.
- **Issue with regard to generalisation of the findings:** Besides the aforementioned issue, in certain cases when a social psychology experiment is carried out in a laboratory set-up, the external validity can get affected as the findings obtained in a laboratory set-up, which is a controlled condition, cannot be generalised. The sample size employed in such experiments is also, most often, small and thus population estimations are not possible. Although most often, experiments are conducted with the purpose to study the cause and effect relationship and not to make estimations for population (Berkowitz & Donnerstein, 1982).
- **Social desirability:** Most often, while carrying out social psychology research, despite assuring confidentiality and anonymity, the participants may give responses that are socially desirable. For example, while studying the attitude towards tobacco consumption, the participants may provide responses that are socially desirable, that is, they may display a negative attitude towards tobacco consumption, which may not be consistent with their actual attitude or behaviour.
- **Demand characteristics:** Besides social desirability, demand characteristics, can also mislead the findings of a research. Demand characteristics are certain cues or ideas about how the participants are expected to behave. The participants may get these cues during the research and may behave accordingly. The participants may get these cues even through the experimenter's behaviour, mainly non-verbal. Demand characteristics can be dealt with by having in-depth introspective report at the end of the experiment, ensuring that the participants are not aware about the main objective of the research or by having a different cover story regarding the research or by using deception.
- **Experimenter's expectancy effect:** Rosenthal (1966) stated that experimenter's expectancy effect can frequently occur while carrying out experiments in social psychology. In this, the experimenter who is involved in the experiment may unknowingly influence the participants. This mainly happens because the experimenter knows the study or research well and is aware about the hypothesis/es and may have an impact on the behaviour/performance of the participants. This obviously is not done consciously by the experimenter, but he/she may display certain cues that may then encourage the participant to behave in a particular manner. One way this can be dealt with is by using double blind, where neither participant nor the experimenter/ researcher is aware about the objective of the research.
- **Making a choice between maintaining discipline identity and interdisciplinary approach:** A large number of researches have now become interdisciplinary and, in fact, it is also suggested that more and more interdisciplinary research could be carried out. However, in this case, the researcher may face a challenge whether to uphold the discipline identity or go with interdisciplinary research.

TRENDS AND PROSPECTS IN SOCIAL PSYCHOLOGY RESEARCH

The field of social psychology is fast developing and that has led to broadening of the research area in social psychology. Social psychology researchers are now treading in newer areas to develop better comprehension about human behaviour. In this section of the chapter, we will discuss about both trends and future prospects in social psychology research.

- **Testing of evolutionary hypothesis:** Charles Darwin proposed the evolutionary theory that focuses on the adaptation of animals to their environment. In this context, it is inevitable to discuss about natural selection that can be described as 'the process by which heritable traits that promote survival in a particular environment are passed along to future generations; organisms with these traits are more likely to produce offsprings' (Aronson et al., 2014, p. 43). This mainly has to do with survival of the fittest. You may have watched on the discovery channel how a stronger lion would win a fight between two lions, thus, ensuring its survival, and also produce offspring and ensure that its genes are passed on to the next generation. Evolutionary theory can be used not only to explain biological aspects but also social behaviour. And this is what is focused on by evolutionary psychology, where an attempt is made to understand the role played by genetic factors (that have developed over a period of time based on natural selection) in social behaviour. Research can thus focus on testing these evolutionary hypotheses with reference to social behaviour. To test such hypothesis/es, the experimental method cannot be used and thus the researchers will have to rely on other methods.
- **Cross-cultural research:** Cross-cultural research will be discussed in detail in Chapter 12. More and more cross-cultural researches have been carried out mainly to establish universality with regard to human behaviours and also to find out variations in individual behaviour that are a result of cultural influence. As will be discussed in Chapter 12, there are a number of challenges that researcher may face while carrying out cross-cultural research.
- **Social neuroscience:** We briefly touched on social neuroscience in Chapter 1. Many social psychology researchers are now interested in understanding the role played by biological processes in social behaviour. Studies, thus, are carried out on hormones, neurological processes and so on to study their influence on social behaviour. Most of such researches also involve the use of advanced technologies such as electroencephalography (EEG), functional Magnetic Resonance Imaging (fMRI) and so on. Such researches also contribute significantly in understanding the brain and behaviour relationships.
- **Multiple perspectives:** Research in social psychology can also be carried out from multiple perspectives. Thus, social behaviours can be understood using more than one perspective so as to broaden theoretical relevance and application of the research.
- **Expansion of database:** As it may be noticed, most of the researches in social psychology have been carried out on a very specific group, mostly students or persons belonging to middle class. The database needs to be expanded and research needs to be carried out on other sections of the society as well.
- **Indigenisation:** Yet another trend in social psychology research is indigenisation, which focuses on carrying out more and more research by employing symbolic resources and practices related to a particular culture (Dalal & Misra, 2002). Indigenous psychology will be further touched in Chapter 12.

SUMMARY

In this chapter, we discussed about what is research and also focused on what are the goals of research in social psychology. Research can be described as adding to the existing fund of knowledge. We also discussed certain key concepts in research, such as constructs, variables (that could be independent, dependent and extraneous variables), experimental and control groups, confederates, and internal and external validity. Further, the research process was also described. The chapter also discussed various research methods in social psychology such as experimental method, non-experimental method, descriptive research, correlational method, survey research and action research. Based on the topic and objective of the research, the methods can accordingly be used. Qualitative research was also described in detail with a focus on its methods of data collection like qualitative interview, focus group, case study, ethnography and grounded theory.

Further, the chapter also discussed about ethical issues and use of deception in research. The challenges and problems while conducting research and trends and prospects in social psychology research were also highlighted.

To conclude this discussion on research methods in social psychology, Ronald J. Fisher (1982) in his book *Social Psychology: An Applied Approach*, very beautifully explains how some of us try 'doing science the easy way'. He writes about a story of a fellow, clearly looking drunk, frantically searching for something below a lamp post. A minister who is passing by sees him and stops to ask whether he requires any help. The fellow says that he is searching for the key of his house that he lost by the bushes in dark shadow that were little further than the lamp post. The minister was surprised and explained to the fellow that he should be looking for the keys near the bushes and not under the lamp post. But the fellow replied that 'this is where the light is'. Well, at the end of this chapter, we need to decide not to 'look under the lamp post' but explore the darker areas that probably will contribute to the existing fund of knowledge of social psychology.

QUESTIONS

1. Define research and discuss the goals of research in social psychology.
2. Explain the key concepts in social psychology research.
3. Compare between the experimental and correlational methods of research.
4. Explain in detail qualitative research with a focus on its methods of data collection.
5. Describe ethical issues in research. Which is the most significant ethical issue according to you? Give reason.
6. What is deception?
7. Describe the challenges and problems while conducting research in social psychology.

REFERENCES

Aronson, E., Wilson, T. D., & Akert, R. M. (2014). *Social psychology*. Pearson.

Berg, B. L. (1998). *Qualitative research methods for the social sciences*. Needham Heights, MA: Allen and Bacon.

FURTHER READINGS

For more information on research, the following books can be referred to:

Bauer, M. W., & Gaskell, G. (2000). *Qualitative researching with text, image and sound: A practical handbook for social research*. London: SAGE Publications.

Best, J. W., & Kahn, J. V. (1999). *Research in education*. New Delhi: Prentice Hall of India.

David, M., & Sutton, C. D. (2011). *Social research: An introduction*. New Delhi: SAGE Publications.

Kerlinger, F. N. (1995). *Foundations of behavioural research*. Bangalore: Prism Books.

Maynard, P., & Grayson, A. (2000). *Introducing psychological research*. Newark: Palsgrave.

Following are some prominent journals in social psychology:

- *American Psychologist*
- *Annual Review of Psychology*
- *Asian Journal of Social Psychology*
- *Basic and Applied Social Psychology*
- *Journal of Personality and Social Psychology*
- *Journal of Experimental Social Psychology*
- *Journal of Applied Social Psychology*

For more information on journals in social psychology, you can follow the link given:

http://www.socialpsychology.org/journals.htm

SECTION II

The Individual

CHAPTER 3

The Self

Take a few minutes here to describe yourself, write the description down and then notice how you described yourself.

Did you focus on the physical appearance or traits?

Did you describe yourself in terms of your gender or your religion?

Did you mention your hobbies and interests?

Did you mention what you are doing presently (studying or working)?

What were the other aspects on the basis of which you described yourself?

These are some questions that are relevant for understanding how individuals describes themselves. And these also, in a way, determine how we see ourselves.

Self in a social set-up determines an individual's identity and can have an influence on his/her behaviour, thus making it inevitable to escape the purview of social psychologists.

In this chapter that focuses on 'the self', the subtopics that will be covered are self-concept, besides self-esteem and self-efficacy. The terms introspection and self-presentation will also be discussed in detail. Other concepts related to self such as self-awareness, self-motive and so on will also be discussed. The chapter in the end will cover self in cyberspace and gender identity.

Learning Objectives

After reading this chapter, you will be able to

- ❒ Discuss the concept of 'self'
- ❒ Describe the terms self-concept
- ❒ Explain self-esteem and self-efficacy

- Discuss the concept of introspection and self-perception
- Describe other concepts related to self such as self-awareness, self-motive and so on
- Discuss self in cyberspace
- Explain gender identity

THE CONCEPT OF 'SELF'

Self can be described in terms of three main features (Baumeister & Bushman, 2009). The first is to do with how aware is an individual about his/her own self. Second feature is related to how self is understood in the context of social situation when we relate with others. Third is the behaviour and decisions that are largely determined by self.

Willian James, 1890, was one of the first proponents of 'self' (Gerrig & Zimbardo, 2006). He stated that anything and everything with which an individual associates himself/herself becomes part of his/her self. He proposed three elements of self experience: the material me, which deals with self related to one's body as well as physical objects present in his/her environment; the social me, which has to do with the awareness of an individual about how others view him/her; and the spiritual me, which deals with personal thoughts and feelings of an individual.

Freud also considered the concept of self as significant, as insight in one's self is an important aspect of psychoanalysis. Jung was yet another proponent who focused on the relevance of acceptance and integration of conscious and unconscious aspects of an individual in order to promote complete development of self.

Individual differences can be explained to a greater extent by 'self'. Self influences the behaviour of an individual, especially in a social set-up. It also has a strong influence on cognitive processes such as perception, thinking and learning, and it also plays a role in decision-making, setting of goal and performance. Self can be seen as responsible for regulating various psychological processes including motives.

Studies also indicate that not only human beings but other species as well have a sense of self, though rudimentary (Gallup, 1997). A study was carried out by Suddendorf and Collier-Baker (2009) on the evolution of primate visual self-recognition. In this study, a mirror was kept in the animal's cage until it became a familiar object. The animal was then anaesthetised and its brows or ears were marked with a red dye that was odourless. The chimpanzees and orangutans touched the spots marked with the dye as they saw themselves in the mirror; however, the same was not displayed by monkeys. Studies have also indicated that mirror self-recognition has been displayed by dolphins (Reiss & Marino, 2001). With regard to human beings, self-recognition develops by around two years of age and the rudimentary self-concept becomes more and more complex as they grow older (Aronson, Wilson, & Akert, 2014).

There are two main views of self, especially when cultural difference with regard to self are discussed. These are independent view of self and interdependent view of self. In self, as independent view, individual's identity is seen as not dependent on the interaction with others. In fact, self is determined by attributes that are internal to an individual. These attributes are relatively consistent across situations and periods of time. Individual differences exist with regard to these attributes. This view was referred to as the self-contained model by Markus and Kitayama (1991).

The other view indicates self as interdependent. This view proposes that an individual's identity is to a greater extent influenced by their relationship with others. The self also depends on the roles played by the individual with reference to others.

Gender differences have also been observed with regard to self. Women display more of relational interdependence where the focus is on close relationships and men display more of collective interdependence where the focus is on a larger group membership (Aranson et al., 2014).

SELF-CONCEPT

During a workshop on self, the trainer carried out a simple exercise with the participants. She asked participants to provide their answer to the question 'Who are you?' Each participant thus had to write down who they felt they were or, in simple terms, how they perceived themselves. Most of the participants described themselves in terms of their physical appearance (in terms of their height, weight and so on) or in terms of their traits (being extrovert or introvert, calm, honest and so on). Many participants also informed about their goals in life (such as they want to pursue medicine, want to become a singer and so on). Such descriptions can help understand the concept that the individuals have about themselves. Self-concept is thus 'a complex collection of diverse information that somehow is held together as you' (Baron & Byrne, 1995, p. 175).

Self-concept, in simple terms, can be described as a mental picture that an individual has about his/her own self. It can also be described as the perception that an individual has about his/her own self, for example, 'I am a good employee', 'I am honest', 'I am smart and have potentiality to do well', 'I am lazy' and so on.

Self-concept can be described as a multifaceted entity and is nothing but how you see yourself. It can be described as the collection of beliefs that an individual has about his/her own self. These beliefs are organised and are also referred to as self-schemas. These self-schemas are separately characterised by unique thoughts and feelings. Thus, various self-schemas constitute a self-concept of a person. Schemas are described as mental representations (will be covered in detail in the next chapter). Self-concept is also one such schema that an individual will have about his/her own self. Self-schemas, or schema about one's self, can be described as the beliefs, feelings and knowledge we have about ourselves. These beliefs, feelings and knowledge are organised and they determine the way in which the information about ourselves is processed by us. Like other schemas, self-schemas are also influenced by past experiences and expectations and social situations and people in the social set-up, especially the significant people in our lives.

Further, the information that is significant with reference to ourselves is also rapidly processed as compared to other information. Such information is easily detected, remembered and recalled as well. This can be termed as self-reference effect, which occurs as a result of elaborative and categorical processing. In elaborative processing, meanings of words and situations are thought about, whereas in categorical processing, various stimuli are specifically categorised. Both these processes are enhanced and facilitated by the self-referencing effect and, thus, the information related to one's self is better remembered and recalled (Klein & Loftus, 1988; Klein, Loftus, & Burton, 1989).

Self-concept are largely determined by one's past experiences, goals in life, roles played in social settings, traits and abilities and even physical characteristics. A boy who is obese and, thus, has to face taunts from his classmates may possibly have lower self-concept. A girl who wins gold medal in a swimming championship will have higher self-concept.

Relationships (both past and present) and significant others in our lives greatly influence our self-concept. Parents, friends, siblings, spouse and other significant people in one's life will determine one's self-concept.

R. F. Baumeister (1995) defined self-concept as 'the total organised body of information that any given person has about himself/herself'.

As suggested by William James (1980), there are following two main aspects of self-concept:

1. Self as a subject of experience is also denoted as 'I'. This develops early in our life and is followed by the development of self as an object of experience.
2. Self as object of experience is also denoted as 'me'. Thus, self-concept develops as we become more aware about self as an object of experience.

Self-concept can be categorised into working self-concept, a term introduced by Hazel Markus to describe the self-concept that can be retrieved at any moment or at any given time, and looking glass self-concept, a term introduced by Cooley (1902) that explains how our self-concept is determined by the evaluation of others or how others view us.

Development of Self-concept

The development of self-concept can be understood with the help of terms such as self-recognition, self-description and autobiographical memory (Eysenck, 2013).

- **Self-recognition:** Self-concept is developed very early in life, and is apparent in the self-recognition expressed by the infants. The development of sense of self amongst infants can be apparent when they start recognising themselves in a mirror. Self-recognition also indicates the presence of self-awareness among infants. Various research studies in this regard have been carried out that confirm the development of visual self-recognition that indicates the existence of self-awareness (Courage, Edison, & Howe, 2004; Lewis & Brooks, 1978).
- **Self-description:** As the name suggests, self-description denotes how an individual depicts or describes himself/herself. Research in this regard was carried out on older children, and it was found that they often distorted information in order to create a positive impression on the researcher, but at the same time they had a tendency to ignore relevant facets of self-concept (Eysenck, 2013).

  Based on the descriptions given by these children, there are four main categories of self-description as stated by Damon and Hart in 1998 (Eysenck, 2013).

  1. The first category has to do with the physical characteristics, for example, height and weight.
  2. The second category is related to various activities that are carried out by the child, for example, studying, playing and watching cartoon.
  3. The third category is that of the social aspect of the person, for example, how he/she describes self in relation to others.
  4. The last category is that of psychological features or the characteristics that are internal to an individual. For example, being honest, friendly and so on. The psychological features can also be categorised into two: one is a relatively permanent aspect that can be termed as disposition and the other is internal states that are temporary (Wellman & Gelman, 1988).

- **Autobiographical memory:** This deals with memories with regard to events in our lives. For example, we easily remember events such as weddings and get-togethers. Addis and Tipette in 2004 found that individuals with impaired autobiographical memory about childhood and early adulthood had weaker self-concept (Eyesenk, 2013). Autobiographical memory promotes social relationships, influences ones behaviour and actions in future, and also leads to the development of a sense of self continuity over a period of time. Thus, it is of relevance when we speak about self-concept. Self-concept and autobiographical memories are also interrelated as to a greater extent, self-concept will influence which autobiographical memory is relevant for us.

Theories of Self-concept Management and Maintenance

Various theories of self-concept management and maintenance are described here.

1. **Control theory of self-regulation**: This theory states that self-regulation involves four main phases, these are as follows:
   i. *Test phase*. During this phase, the individuals compare themselves with either of the two standards, private or public. The individuals who are privately self-aware will compare themselves with the private standard and the individuals who are publicly self-aware will compare themselves with the public standard. For example, an individual with private self-awareness will compare his/her own self with the values that he/she believes in and, on the other hand, the individual with public self-awareness will compare his/her own self with the values of say his/her family members (Crisp & Turner, 2010).
   ii. *Operate phase*. Individuals reach this stage when they feel that they do not meet the required standards, that is, individuals with private self-awareness not meeting the private standards and the individuals with public self-awareness not meeting the public standards. This results in the individuals changing their behaviour so as to meet the standards.
   iii. *Test phase*. During this phase, the individuals get involved in retest, that is, they again compare themselves with the standards to see where they fall. If they fall short when compared to the standard, then they further change their behaviour to match the standard and this will go on till they feel that their behaviour matches the standard.
   iv. *Exit phase*. Once the individual feels that he/she has met the standard, they exit from the vicious circle of operate and test.

Thus, if a person with private self-awareness values relationships, he/she will first compare his/her own self with this value, and if it does not match, he/she will put in more efforts in his/her relationship with others to attain the private standard. Taking another example, if a person with public self-awareness feels that respecting the elders is valued by his/her family, he/she will compare his/her self with this standard and then put in more effort towards gaining this public standard.

The theory, thus, helps in understanding how self-awareness as well as self-regulation play an important role in improvement of the self. However, as stated by Baumeister et al. (1998), when one aspect of self is self-regulated, it becomes difficult to self-regulate some other aspect, mainly because the resources for self-regulation have decreased (Crisp & Turner, 2010).

2. **Self-discrepancy theory:** This theory focuses mainly on how aware the individual is about the discrepancies that exist between his/her actual identity and ideal identity. The theory also focuses on how the individuals respond (emotional) to such discrepancies. Higgins has proposed that there are three types of self-schemas, the actual self, the ideal self and the ought self (Crisp & Turner, 2010). The actual self is mainly about how an individual is in present. The ideal self, on

the other hand, is like a reference point with regard to how an individual would like to be. The ought self, lastly, is related to what the individual feels he/she should be like.

The theory also states that individuals strive to have their actual self match the ideal self and the ought self and if these don't match, then there will be discrepancies. For example, if an individual is a student of law but wants to be an actor, but his/her parents want him to become a businessperson. In this case, the actual self (student of law) is discrepant from the ideal self (actor) and the ought self (businessperson).

In this context, the emotional responses of the individuals having these self discrepancies also need to be discussed. If the discrepancy is actual–ideal discrepancy, then the individuals will be disappointed and sad as he/she in reality is not what he/she wants to be. On the other hand, actual–ought discrepancy may lead to experiencing emotions related to anger, agitation, fear and so on as the individual is reminded of what he/she actually is and what others expect from him/her.

Although the theory states that the individuals get motivated to change as a result of self discrepancies, the experience of such emotions as anger, nervousness, fear and so on can, in fact, have a negative impact on self-regulation that may push individuals to be impulsive. Although this may give individuals immediate but temporary satisfaction, it will take them away from their goals.

3. **Social comparison theory:** The theory states that an individual will carry out the assessment of his/her abilities and opinions by comparing them with the abilities and opinions of others. Thus, one's success, for example, is determined by comparing how successful other people are. Social comparison theory not only helps us in assessing our opinions and abilities but also helps to enhance our skills and maintain self-image. Many times, such a comparison is with a group of people with peculiar characteristics, referred to as reference groups. The reference group can be your classmates, colleagues and so on, and will depend on what ability or opinion you want to compare.

   Social comparisons can be upward or downward. Upward social comparison occurs when we compare ourselves with people who are better than us. This will help us do better in life. We may compare our communication skills with that of a colleague and would make attempts to be as good as him/her. In addition, downward social comparison takes place when we compare ourselves with people weaker than us.

   In certain cases an individual may also compare with his/her own self. He/she may compare his/her current position, skills, opinions with his/her position, skills, opinions in the past. This will help an individual realise how far he/she has come along in life or what mistakes he/she has committed. This serves as feedback and helps the individual improve further.

4. **Self-evaluation maintenance model:** This model was put forth by Tesser in 1988 (Crisp & Turner, 2010). The model explains the effect of someone else's success on an individual's self-esteem. In this context, we can discuss about social reflection that has to do with the derivation of one's own self-esteem based on the achievement of others whom one is close to rather than that based on one's own accomplishments. For example, a person will feel proud when his/her younger sibling stands first in the state swimming championship, or the parents are going to be very happy when their child tops the high school examination. In these cases, the person and the parents, will experience an increase in their self-esteem. Social reflection—rather than social comparison—will take place because the skills that the other person has achieved or the field wherein he/she is successful is not important for that individual. Thus, that person's achievement is not a threat or a challenge to his/her self-concept and in a way adds to it. Furthermore, if that individual is also successful and confident about his/her abilities, the other

person's achievement is not a threat or a challenge to his/her self-concept and thus the outcome again is social reflection and not social comparison.

However, if the area in which the other person is successful is important, then the individual will engage in upward comparison and if he/she is uncertain about his/her own capabilities, then again there would be upward comparison, as in these cases his/her self-concept is under threat.

There are four main strategies to maintain self-esteem that need to be focused on while we discuss this model.

- **Exaggeration of the abilities of the person who is successful:** We might end up saying that no one can achieve as much as a certain person because he/she is a genius and there can be no comparison between him/her and normal people.
- **Changing the comparison target:** We often hear people say 'compare yourself with less fortunate than those who are more fortunate than us'. In this case, we can go for a downward comparison and compare with a person who is comparatively less successful.
- **Distancing from the successful target:** This involves emotionally distancing one's self from the target and implying how one is not similar to that target.
- **Reducing the value of the dimension of comparison:** An individual might say that the target person is successful as he/she is earning more but is not as secured in his/her relationship as this individual. Thus, the dimension of comparison has changed from earnings to relationship. And the value of the original dimension of comparison, that is, earning, is reduced.

5. **Social identity approach:** According to this approach, the self can be categorised into aspects related to personal identities (e.g., personality traits) and those related to social identities (e.g., identity related to nationality, religion and caste). Thus, a single individual holds many identities, and the identity (personal or social) that an individual is most aware of will determine the sense of self at a given time and this awareness will in turn depend on the context or the situation the individual is in. For example, when you are talking to your best friend, you will be aware of your personal identity but when you are abroad representing your nation at an international event, you will become aware of your social identity (being Indian). Furthermore, when an individual becomes aware of his/her social identity, he/she will become depersonalised and see his/her own self as having features of a particular group. As a result, he/she will start thinking and behaving as per the norms of that group. This is also known as self-categorisation theory, which can be termed as an extension of social identity theory (Crisp & Turner, 2010).

Factors that Influence Self-concept

There are various factors that determine our self-concept; they are discussed as follows:

1. **An individual's observation of his/her own self:** The main factor that affects our self-concept is how we perceive our own self. The theory of social comparison explains how we go about observing our own self and making inferences. Although our observation about ourselves is one of the relevant factors in determining our self-concept, it is not necessarily objective and subjectivity often creeps in. The self-perception (discussed later in this chapter) that we have can be biased, misleading and distorted.
2. **How others perceive the individual:** Besides how we observe ourselves, how others see us is equally important in determining our self-concept. This has mainly to do with the feedback given

by others. If we believe that we have a great sense of dressing, it will elevate our self-concept. However, when one of our classmates/colleagues ridicules us for the way we have dressed, our self-concept will, to some extent, take a dive. Thus, what others think about us does have an influence on our self-concept. In this regard, how parents perceive us is of extreme importance and can greatly affect our self-concept, especially during early childhood. However, later in life, our friends, teachers, spouse and colleagues also play an important role in determining our self-concept. The Michelangelo phenomenon can be discussed here, which occurs when a spouse/life partner or a close friend plays a relevant role in bringing together the ideal self and actual self-concept of a person. This is referred to as the Michelangelo phenomenon as it is similar to sculpting carried out by the spouse/life partner/close friend to bring about the ideal self in an individual (Weiten, Hammer, & Dunn, 2012).

3. **Social set-up:** The social setting will also have an impact on self-concept. Whether the social set-up is formal or informal will determine how the individual perceives himself/herself. For example, how an individual sees him/herself will differ when he/she is with friends, when with boss and when with teachers.
4. **Cultural aspects:** One's cultural aspects also influence self-concept. Cultural values, beliefs and practices can have an impact on our self-concept. The patriarchal system prevalent in our country may induce a lower self-concept amongst girls when compared to boys. This, in turn, affects their priorities and life goals. The feeling of not being good enough because of being a girl can be detrimental to one's functioning and self-confidence. This can also be observed in the caste system prevalent in the country. When the position in society is determined by what caste or sub-caste an individual belongs to, it may become difficult to break these barriers and achieve full potentiality in life. The information about how cultural difference exists in self-concept can help in understanding other psychological aspects that can also possibly differ across cultures.

Further, the factors that can help change self-concept include the social interactions, influences and one's identity in a social set-up.

SELF-ESTEEM AND SELF-EFFICACY

As an understanding about self-concept has been developed, the concepts of self-esteem and self-efficacy are discussed in this section.

Self-esteem

Self-esteem, in simple terms, can be described as one's attitude towards oneself. It deals with the evaluation of his/her own self-worth. It is mainly a reflection of how an individual feels about who he/she is. It can also be termed as an internal evaluation of one's self. Self-esteem can be influenced by both our assessment of ourselves and by others. Such assessment is not necessarily realistic and can be influenced by biases. To discuss an example of self-esteem, Sonam is seen by many as being comfortable with herself and has a positive outlook towards self. She often indulges in activities she enjoys and is confident in all the activities that she carries out. Sonam, here, can be termed as having a high self-esteem.

Self-esteem can have a significant influence on our behaviours in social set-ups. This is mainly because we are constantly motivated to enhance our self-esteem. Thus, an individual with high self-esteem will see himself/herself in a positive light and as confident, admirable and so on, and an individual with low self-esteem will see himself/herself as unworthy and incapable. The higher the self-esteem, the less will be the gap between one's self and ideal self. That is, with higher self-esteem, the self–ideal discrepancy is lower and with lower self-esteem, the discrepancy between the self and ideal self is higher.

Sociometer theory proposed by Leary and Downs in 1995 stated that 'self-esteem is an internal assessment of the extent to which we are accepted and liked by other people' (Eyesenk, 2013, p. 306).

Self-esteem can also be described in terms of trait self-esteem, state self-esteem and domain-specific self-esteem, these are described as follows:

1. **Trait self-esteem.** This is consistent or constant sense of worth, capability and confidence that individuals have about themselves. The trait self-esteem is comparatively constant and thus will not change over a period of time. Thus, if an individual had a lower self-esteem during childhood, it is likely that he/she will have similar self-esteem even later in life. Rosenberg Self-esteem Scale is a tool that can be used to measure this trait.
2. **State self-esteem.** As opposed to trait self-esteem, state self-esteem is not constant but can change, as it is dependent on situations or experiences. A negative situation will bring down the self-esteem and a positive experience will increase it. Achieving high marks in psychology paper will lead to higher self-esteem. An inability to win a cricket match for one's college team may lead to lower self-esteem. It is to be noted, however, that a highly fluctuating self-esteem can be detrimental to the overall well-being of the individual, even leading to depression. Depression, in fact, is greatly related to variable self-esteem that can be described as a self-esteem which fluctuates and thus sometimes is low and sometimes high, based on situational factors (Roberts & Monroe, 1992).
3. **Domain-specific self-esteem.** This has to do with a particular domain of an individual's life. An individual may feel that he/she is a good actor or a poet or writer and so on and that will determine his/her self-esteem.

Self-esteem develops mainly during early childhood. Although self-esteem is considerably high during the middle childhood, during adolescence there is a decrease in it (especially amongst girls), which later increases during adulthood, and may again decrease during old age (Weiten et al., 2012). Parenting plays an important role in the development of self-esteem and the parental styles along with involvement, attachment, support and so on can have an impact on the self-esteem of the child.

Gender difference also exists in self-esteem and women and men show differences in their experience of lowered self-esteem. Men, on the one hand, display lowered self-esteem when they are rejected on the basis of their capabilities and status, and women, on the other, display lowered self-esteem when they are rejected on the basis of their physical attractiveness (Pass, Lindernberg, & Park, 2010).

Self-esteem also differs according to whether the culture is individualistic or collectivistic. High self-esteem is most often appreciated in an individualistic culture like that in the United Stated of America, but it is not seen as desirable in collectivistic cultures like that of Japan as it may interfere with the interdependence that is valued in these cultures.

There are also certain bias that may exist with regard to self-esteem. One of them is self-serving bias. Self-serving bias is an important term in this context in which our success is seen by us as a result of efforts put in by us and the failures are attributed to external factors like luck and faith, difficulty level of the task, other individuals and so on. For example, an individual will attribute high marks achieved by him/her in an examination to the hours of in-depth study carried out by him/her. However, achievement of less mark in an assignment will be attributed to bias by the teacher. Self-serving bias is relevant as it helps in maintenance of self-esteem.

Yet another bias is false unique bias. This bias again can help enhance self-esteem. In this, individuals have a predisposition of being better than others, or unique, compared to others whether that is reality or not. Such a bias, though, can also lead to development of arrogance in individuals, and their social behaviour may also change as they see others as inferior to them. This can be because of attractive physical features, wealth and so on.

Studies have found that there is high level of bias in the Western countries that are individualistic in nature (Mezulis et al., 2004).

Individuals with high self-esteem are less likely to experience loneliness. This can also be true because individuals with high self-esteem may possess better social skills. Such individuals are less prone to depression. High self-esteem is related to happiness and it enhances academic performance and achievement. Individuals with high self-esteem are also better able to deal with failures and have positive expectations, and are optimistic. Such individuals are secured and realistic. Studies have also been carried out on relationship between self-esteem and academic achievements, which indicate that educational achievements can be influenced by high self-esteem (Marsh, Byrne, & Yeung, 1999).

However, despite the advantages mentioned here, extremely high self-esteem may lead to over confidence and arrogance that will have a negative effect on the individual, his/her social life and actions. It can also lead to narcissism, that is, a tendency of an individual to perceive himself/herself as important in an exaggerated manner. Such individuals are also extremely sensitive to criticism from others. They can develop ego problems and can also resort to aggression. Figure 3.1 displays low to extremely high self-esteem.

Self-efficacy

The term self-efficacy was proposed by Albert Bandura as he discussed about the social learning theory (Ashford & LeCroy, 2010). Self-efficacy can be described as perception and belief about whether an individual can achieve his/her goal and whether he/she has capabilities and necessary skills to deal with activities at hand. It depends on situations and, thus, a single individual will have different self-efficacy in different situations. Self-efficacy is influenced mainly by our experiences, especially our successful experiences, and social comparisons.

Self-efficacy refers to 'one's belief about one's ability to perform behaviours that should lead to expected outcomes' (Weiten et al., 2012, p. 198). As stated by Bandura (2000), variations will exist in self-efficacy with reference to the skills possessed by individuals. However, self-efficacy does not have to do with skills, it deals with the beliefs that the individual has about what he/she can do with those skills.

Figure 3.1 ***Low to Extremely High Self-esteem***

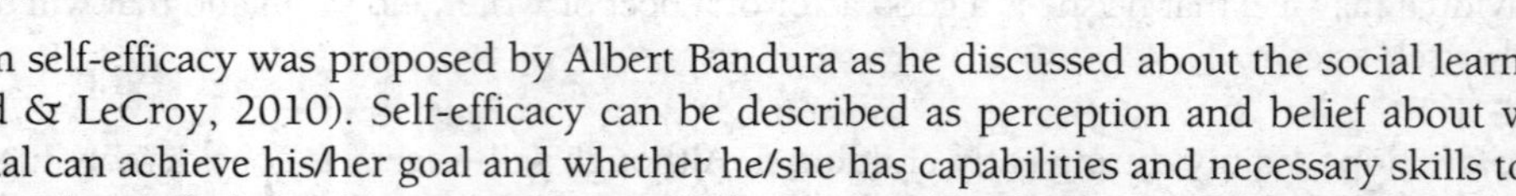

For example, Chintan had this golden opportunity to make a presentation during the annual meet of his organisation, but he felt that he will not be able to make an impressive presentation. He had no confidence and felt he did not possess adequate communication skills to make a presentation in front of all the senior officials of his organisation. Chintan, here, can be termed as having low self-efficacy.

Self-efficacy has a significant influence on the goals of the individual, performance of tasks and also the consistency with which the goals are pursued and achieved. It is related to various aspects like health, education or academics and career.

High self-efficacy can enhance overall performance and can also be related to success in academics. It is also positively correlated with job involvement. Persons with high self-efficacy also experience lower social anxiety and adjustment. High self-efficacy can help deal effectively with various psychological problems. Various healthy practices can also be promoted with the help of high self-efficacy. In a study carried out by Valle et al. (2009) amongst university students in Spain, the results indicated that students with higher self-efficacy were more likely to put in higher efforts in academic-related studies.

Sources of Self-efficacy

Four sources of self-efficacy have been suggested by Bandura (2000). These are discussed here in this section.

1. **Developing and mastering new skills:** One way in which self-efficacy can be enhanced is by developing and mastering new skills. Skills ranging from communication skills to skills related to the use of certain technology can help develop self-efficacy as the person may feel more confident in carrying out certain activity.
2. **Improving skills by observing others perform those skills:** Self-efficacy can also be increased by observing others perform those skills. This can also be termed as vicarious experiences. New employees learn a lot from their observation of certain senior employees in their organisation. Children too learn from observing their parents and significant others in their lives.
3. **Encouragement from others:** Although not a strong source, encouragement from others can enhance our self-esteem. For example, encouragement from a parent while learning to ride a bicycle can lead to better learning and enhancement of self-efficacy.
4. **One's interpretation of physiological responses and emotional arousal:** Last but not least, is how we interpret our physiological responses. Emotional arousal can also influence our self-esteem. If such responses and arousals are negatively interpreted, the self-efficacy will deteriorate and if they are interpreted positively, then self-efficacy will be enhanced.

INTROSPECTION AND SELF-PERCEPTION

Introspection and self-perception can play a role in understanding oneself and therefore they have been discussed in detail in the present subsection of this chapter. Introspection can be defined as 'looking internally at the self to examine who we are, how we feel and so forth' (Barrett, 2017, p. 116). Aronson et al. (2014, p. 131) defined introspection as 'the process whereby people look inward and examine their own thoughts, feelings and motives'. Thus with the help of introspection, an individual is able to look within himself/herself so as to examine the information available within his/her own self.

Most often, human beings lack knowledge about the internal processes and though we may know the outcome of our thought process, we may not be able to know how the outcome was arrived at. This is how our introspection could be limited.

A study carried out by Nisbett and Wilson (1977) indicated that higher order cognitive processes cannot be accessed with the help of introspection. The participants were found not to be aware about the existence of the response or the stimulus that affected the response. Thus, the study indicated that when participants attempt to confident with reference to the cognitive process, it is not done based on the true introspection but is based on certain judgements and indirect causal theories with regard to the extent to which a stimulus leads to a certain response.

Further, introspection can also be inadequate as the way one feels may change based on the process of thinking about how one feels. This was revealed by a study by Wilson and Kraft (1993), which was carried out on students in dating relationships. In control conditions, they had to introspect about some unrelated topic. During the first weekly session, the participants under an experimental condition reported that the introspection made them aware of certain thoughts that were not consistent with their earlier feelings that they had about their relationships and, thus, there was an attitude change in the direction of those reasons. Furthermore, this change in attitude remained consistent across the duration of the study. The participants under control conditions displayed increased change in attitude during every weekly session and as the study culminated, the change experienced by these participants was at the same level as the change experienced by the participants under the experimental condition.

Self-perception

As discussed earlier, most often, introspection is not adequate and that is when it can be supplemented with the help of self-perception.

Self-perception theory was proposed by Bem where attitudes can be inferred in a way a third person would infer. Thus, the theory involves observation of one's own behaviour. Self-perception theory has been described by Barrett (2017, p. 119) as 'idea that peoples sometimes infer their own attitudes in the same way that a third party might infer their attitudes by watching their behaviour'.

The self-perception theory has also been discussed in Chapter 7 on attitude that also mentions the study carried out by Chaiken and Baldwin (1981), which indicated that the participants who displayed weak and unclear attitude, inferred their attitudes based on their own behaviours. A study carried out by Frank and Gilovish (1988) revealed that the participants wearing black uniforms displayed more aggression when compared with participants wearing white uniform. Thus, as an observer would perceive those wearing black uniform as 'tough, mean and aggressive' (p. 83), the participant wearing the black uniform perceived themselves in similar manner. It can also be said that individuals may also learn about themselves through their observation of how others behave (Barrett, 2017).

Further, a study by Yee and Bailenson (2007) discussed about the 'Proteus Effect' that occurs when 'users in online environments may conform to the expectations and stereotypes of the identity of their avatars (avatar here means the digital representation of an individual)' (p. 271). Thus, consistent with the self-perception theory, the user in an online environment displays behaviour that they feel is expected from them by others. Yee and Bailenson (2007) carried out two experimental researches to test the hypothesis whether behaviour of an individual is in compliance with their self-representation online without the influence of how they are perceived by others, that is, the study was carried out to test the 'Proteus Effect'. The findings of the first research indicated that when the participants were assigned to avatars that were less attractive, in immersive virtual environment, they were less intimate with the confederates in terms of self-disclosure and interpersonal distance tasks when compared with participants who were assigned to avatars that were more attractive. The second research indicated that participants who were assigned shorter avatars displayed behaviour that was less confident during a negotiation task when compared with participants who were assigned taller avatars.

Furthermore, intrinsic and extrinsic motivation also need to be discussed in the context of self-perception theory. Intrinsic motivation can be defined as 'the desire to engage in an activity because we enjoy it or find it interesting, not because of external rewards or pressures' (Aronson et al., 2014, p. 138). Thus, for example, a person will exercise regularly only when he has an internal desire to exercise. Extrinsic motivation can be defined as 'the desire to engage in an activity because of external rewards or pressures, not because we enjoy the task or find it interesting' (Aronson et al., 2014, p. 138). Thus, for example, a person will exercise regularly because his/her doctor cautioned about health-related issues that the person could face owing to overweight.

During the growing-up process, an individual receives a number of rewards, like getting a favourite toy for securing higher marks in school examination or being felicitated for following safety regulations at work. And it is important to focus on the effect of these rewards on how people think about themselves and their self-concept (Aronson, Wilson, & Akert, 2014). When a behaviour is rewarded, the likelihood of that behaviour occurring again increases. And thus, when individuals who carry out a certain activity, like exercise, due to intrinsic motivation, are rewarded, then this extrinsic motivation should further encourage them to carry out that activity. However, as per self-perception theory, rewards can have a negative effect on intrinsic motivation, and when the extrinsic motivation replaces intrinsic motivation, the individuals could lose their interest in the activity. This is termed as the over justification effect (Aronson et al., 2014). Overjustification effect can be described as an outcome of perception of people that their behaviours are driven by reasons that are extrinsic, leading to underestimation of the degree to which the behaviour is determined by reasons that are intrinsic.

Self-perception theory can also be applied to understanding emotions. Here we can discuss about the facial feedback hypothesis that states that individuals make inferences about their feelings from their facial expressions (Barrett, 2017). A study was carried out by Strack, Martin and Stepper (1988) to test the hypothesis that affective responses are influenced by their facial activity. The participants had to hold a pen in their mouth, in one condition, between their teeth that created a facial expression similar to a smile, and in the second condition, they had to hold the pen between their lips that created frown-like expression. The participants were then showed cartoons and asked to evaluate these cartoons based on how funny they were. The results indicated that participants who held the pen between their teeth found the cartoons to be funnier when compared to the participants who held it between their lips.

OTHER CONCEPTS RELATED TO SELF

This section of the chapter will shed light on some others concepts that are related to self. These are discussed herewith.

Self-awareness

Self-awareness can be described as awareness about one's own feelings, behaviours and characteristics. It can also be described as 'realisation of oneself as an individual entity' as stated by Crisp and Turner (2010, p. 2). Self-awareness develops over a period of time and is not inborn. In a research carried out by Lewis and Brooks (1978), infants of 9–12 months were not able to recognise their own mirror image. However, self-awareness developed after around 18 months. This mainly occurs as a result of fast growth in the spindle cells that can be described as a specialised neurons present in the anterior cingulate, which is located in the frontal lobe of the Brain (Allman & Hasenstaub, 1999). Self-awareness can be of two types.

1. **Private self-awareness:** When an individual becomes temporarily aware about one's self, its private and personal aspects, it can be termed as private self-awareness. This can occur when individuals see themselves in the mirror or when they reflect on the emotions because of physiological arousal (Crisp & Turner, 2010). Private self-awareness leads to escalated emotional responses; there is clarity in knowledge and such individuals follow personal standards of behaviour.
2. **Public self-awareness:** Public self-awareness, as described by Crisp and Turner (2010, p. 7), occurs when 'a person is aware of public aspects of themselves that can be seen and evaluated by others'. This mainly occurs when the individual is in a social set-up, for example, at a wedding when they are aware that people are observing them. There could be a problem here when there is a gap between the actual public image of the individual and the desired image. Further, in this context, the individual follows the social standards of behaviour as opposed to the personal standards of behaviour in private self-awareness.

In this context, it would be interesting to discuss about Johari window given in Box 3.1.

BOX 3.1 *Johari Window*

Johari window was developed by American psychologists Joseph Luft and Harry Ingham in the 1950s was named by combining their first names, Joe and Harry. Johari window is relevant owing to its application in soft skills, intergroup development, team development, interpersonal relationship and promoting self-awareness. The Johari window model is also referred to as a 'disclosure/feedback model of self-awareness'. It actually represents information, feelings, experience, views, attitudes, skills, intentions, motivation and so on within or about a person, in relation to their group. It categorises people into four categories based on the windows; these are as follows:

	Known to self	**Not known to self**
Known to others	Arena	Blind
Not known to others	Closed	Dark

1. **The open receptive person** falls in the arena window. Such people are confident and have high self-awareness.
2. **The blabbermouth** falls in the blind window. Such people know less about themselves, indicating low self-awareness, and others tend to know more about them.
3. **The pumper** falls in the closed window. Such people keep to themselves and do not divulge much information to others, but are keen to know about others.
4. **The hermit** falls in the dark window. It is difficult to understand such people and their behaviours tends to be unpredictable.

Self-monitoring Behaviour

The concept of self-monitoring behaviour was identified by Snyder and his colleagues (Gangestad & Snyder, 1985; Snyder & Ickes, 1985). Certain external and internal factors as well as reactions of others influence the extent to which an individual will regulate his/her behaviour. External situations can be the presence of others whereas internal factors have to do with interests, attitude and so on of an individual. For example, an individual will regulate his/her own behaviour when in the presence of his/her superiors. Self-monitoring can be defined as 'the degree to which individuals regulate their behaviour on the basis of the external situation and the reactions of others (high self monitors) or on the basis of internal factors such as their own beliefs, attitudes and interests (low self monitors)' (Baron & Byrne, 1995). It can, thus, be said that the high and low self-monitors differ in their conception of self (Leone & Hawkins, 2006). The high self-monitors perceive identities as outcome of social interactions, whereas low self-monitors perceive identities as a product of personal disposition. Furthermore, the high self-monitors can be categorised into two, those who regulate their behaviour on the basis of the presence of the audience and those who regulate their behaviour on the basis of the assumptions with regard to what is to be done in certain situations. DeBono (2006) indicated that high self-monitors and low self-monitors were responsive to image-oriented advertising and advertisements based on product quality, respectively, thus indicating the influence of self-monitoring on consumer behaviour, although the need for more research in this direction was also expressed by DeBono. The research also highlighted that low self-monitors based their judgement with regard to quality of the product on product performance, whereas the high self-monitors based their judgement on the image-enhancing capabilities of the product.

Self-monitoring also plays an important role in interpersonal relationship. Low self-monitors pay attention to themselves, whereas high self-motivators pay attention to others. Further, high self-monitors are more likely to speak in third person, whereas the low self-monitors tend to speak in the first person. With regard to interpersonal choices, low self-monitors tend to select a companion (e.g., a partner to carry out an activity assigned at work) based on the extent to which they like the person. On the other hand, high self-monitors are likely to select a companion based on his/her performance (Baron & Byrne, 1995). Thus, high self-monitors adopt an avoidant pattern of attachment as they may not feel comfortable when they are psychologically close to the significant persons in their lives because of the fear that the significant others may expect more intimacy from the high self-monitors. Furthermore, the high self-monitors may display unwillingness to seek forgiveness from their close partners when they have committed a mistake. The low self-monitors also want their social network to be like them and need enough freedom and security so that there is an expression of their dispositional attributes without facing any interpersonal conflict. Thus, low self-monitors create a social network in which they are intimate with significant others and have no fear about the expectations of the significant others with regard to intimacy. They are also more willing to seek forgiveness from their partners when they commit a mistake (Sandage et al., 2000).

Self-monitoring mainly finds it application to consumer behaviour and interpersonal relationship, especially to understand dating behaviour or close and intimate relationships. Self-monitoring behaviour can be measured with the help of a self-monitoring scale that was developed by Snyder in 1974 (Baron & Byrne, 1995).

Self-focusing

Self-focusing can be described as centrality with reference to an individual's sense of self (Baron & Byrne, 1995). This denotes the extent to which the self-focus is either inward (towards oneself) or outward (environment). Both memory and cognition play an important role in self-focusing, mainly because one needs to be able to not only recall from past experiences but also process the available information in order to focus on oneself. A positive relationship also exists between self-focusing and self-insight (Hixon & Swann, 1993), and self-focusing can also have an impact on the behaviour of the individual. Thus, a person with high self-focusing may try to reduce the gap between his/her self-concept and behaviour or will try to avoid such situations that lead to development of such gaps. Further, persons with weak self-focusing do not display consistency in their behaviour in different situations when compared with persons who have strong self-focusing (Baron & Byrne, 1995).

Mood of the person can also have an impact on self-focusing and the self-content that is focused and will have an impact on the mood of the person (Sedikides, 1992).

In a study carried out by Sedikides (1992), participants with positive and negative self-conceptions were asked to rate their mood under two conditions—when they had self-focused attention (done by asking the participants to write a story about themselves) and when they had other focused attention (done by asking the participants to write a story about an acquaintance). The results indicated that under the condition where they had to focus on themselves, participants with positive self-conception reported being happier when compared with participants who had negative self-conception. And, in the condition where the participants had other focused attention, no difference was found in mood reported by participants with negative or positive self-conception.

Self-focusing was also seen to differ in young and older adolescents. Ullman (1987) carried out a study on 84 participants who were high school students between the age group 12–18 years. The results indicated that for young adolescents being genuine constituted disclosure about facts that are accessible to others, whereas being genuine for older adolescents meant recognition and expression of their true nature.

With reference to situational influence on self-focusing, one may pay more attention to oneself and less towards the environment when one is familiar as well as comfortable with the environment. However, the cues in the environment become more relevant, when the environment is threatening and not familiar (Baron & Byrne, 1995).

Self-motives

Self-motives can be described as drives within ourselves. They can be described in terms of three main motives (Crisp & Turner, 2010). The first is self-assessment that can be described as evaluation of oneself. Such an evaluation can be positive or negative. Self-assessment helps us develop a better understanding about ourselves. It can be described as a desire to have a clear idea about our skills, abilities and opinions. Self-verification is the second motive in which the self-concept we hold about ourselves is conformed. Self-verification has an impact on our self-perception as if the information gathered by us conforms with our perception of ourselves, then we are reassured that our self-perception is correct and vice versa. Self-verification mainly focuses on the information about oneself that is negative. The third motive is self-enhancement. Contrary to self-verification, in self-enhancement, positive information about self is sought. In self-enhancement, an individual presents himself/herself as possessing characteristics that are socially desirable. Self-enhancement in itself is an important term and there are various methods to enhance one's self; some of them are as follows:

- There could be downward comparison, where the issues and problems faced by others are seen as more serious compared to what this individual is going through. For example, a person who did not get a job that he actually wanted may say that his/her situation is much better than that of a neighbour who is unemployed.

- Yet another technique is self-serving bias (discussed earlier) in which one's success is attributed to the factors that are personal and one's failures are attributed to the situational factors. For example, if a person gets good marks in an examination, he/she attributes it to the hard work put in by him/her. But if he/she fails in the exam, then he/she attributes it to strict or unfair evaluation by the examiner.
- Self-handicapping is another technique that can be defined as 'the tendency to sabotage one's performance to provide an excuse for possible failure' (Weiten et al., 2012, p. 196). You must have come across people who provide an excuse of falling sick to cover for their poor performance in a task or activity. But in self-handicapping, the person deliberately makes an attempt to sabotage his/her performance so that later he/she can justify if they fail. For example, while preparing for a presentation at work, the individual puts off the work till the last minute and if the presentation is not up to the mark (which is likely), he/she will explain this poor performance by stating that he/she did not prepare. Thus, the poor performance is attributed to lack of preparation rather than lack of ability.
- There is also false consensus effect. This can be described as a tendency of an individual to believe that others agree or think as he/she does. In many cases, it leads to self-enhancement of the person as he/she thinks that others agree with him/her. This particular tendency depends on availability heuristics. False consensus effect can occur in two ways: First, people tend to remember situations when others agreed to them rather than when others disagreed with them. This kind of faulty processing of social information can give way to faulty consensus effect. Second, it is possible that the people we are close to, significant people in our lives, actually share our point of view. Thus, they agree with what you believe or think. Thus, the situations during which we were agreed to are higher, which can again lead to the false consensus effect.

SELF IN CYBERSPACE

Internet and social networking has today become part and parcel of our lives, and individuals are involved in use of cyberspace at work, for education and for leisure-related activities. In this context, it is necessary that we understand self in cyberspace.

The example referred to here will assist in building an understanding about self in cyberspace.

Sushil was a different person online. In reality, he was a shy boy who would not even attempt to interact with others, but online he was 'machoman96', who had his own way and could confidently engage in long chats. People who knew Sushil in person could never relate to the image he had created online, and people who knew him online had no idea about how Sushil was in person. There was a clear distinction between these two Sushils.

Turkle in 1995 described cyberspace as 'life on the screen'. The term cyberspace was first coined by Willian Gibson in 1984. He used the term in his novel, *Neuromancer*, which is a science fiction. The term cyberspace is derived from the term 'cybernetics'. Cyberspace was described by Gibson as a 'space that exists within the computer networks' (Chester, 2004, p. 51).

Cyberspace does provide opportunities for the individuals to express their self in a unique manner owing to various reasons (Whitty & Young, 2017). This is especially possible because of the anonymity provided by the Internet, which makes it possible for the individuals to be disembodied, that is, it helps them in creating and experiencing an identity that is not limited or dependent on their physical appearance (Whitty & Young, 2017). In the words of Turkle (1995b, p. 180), cyberspace is 'a significant social laboratory for experimenting with the constructions and reconstructions of self that characterise post-modern life'.

One of the first theorists to study the idea of disembodied self in cyberspace was Sherry Turkle, who considered computer as a 'second self' and asserted the opportunity provided by the Internet to reinvent one's self (Whitty & Young, 2017). Turkle (1999) also states that Internet has played a significant role in linking the people all over the world and, thus, has contributed to a shift in the way people think about identity. Further, an interaction that is online also provides an opportunity to remain anonymous (Turkle, 1995) and there is also an opportunity to display, experience and communicate an aspect of self that was earlier not explored (Turkle, 1999). The boundaries between self and the role may also become vague because of multi-user domains (McCorduck, 1996).

Most often when one wants to join a chat channel, they have to select a screen name and these are the names that are chosen by the individual, unlike the offline names that are most often given. This can be termed as the first opportunity to create an impression online as well as attract others to chat. Screen names can also be misleading and may conceal the reality, and further they are also easy to change. Thus, there could be just one person chatting with two or more screen names. Further, the information provided in the profile can also be manipulated and could be fact or fiction. Thus, cyberspace does provide an opportunity for anonymity and can also involve deception. A study carried out by Waskul and Douglas (1997) indicated that a 'cyberself' emerged as a result of interaction during online chat and the identity is not limited by the physical form of the person. Thus, most often than not, the self in cyberspace is different from the self offline. There are other researches that indicate that cyberspace, in fact, provides an opportunity to reveal one's true self. This was observed in experiments carried out by Bargh, McKenna and Fitzsimons (2002) that have been discussed in detail in Chapter 6 on interpersonal attraction. Thus, individuals could be more open online than they are offline. A study by Joinson in 2003 also indicated a higher self-disclosure when online as compared to offline interactions (Chester, 2004).

GENDER IDENTITY

Sheena was expecting a baby and as her due date approached, she was admitted to the hospital. Her parents and in-laws also reached the hospital and eagerly and anxiously waited for the good news. As Sheena delivered the baby, the nurse came out and declared, 'It's a girl'. In the next few days, Sheena received a number of baby clothes and stuff in pink and most of the toys were dolls. Apparently, Sheena's baby was already initiated into the identity of a female (as perceived by the society).

Gender identity refers to 'the sex that the person associates with himself/herself' (Baron & Byrne, 1995, p. 197). Thus, it is possible that a person may not identify himself/herself with one's own sex but may identify with the opposite sex, which is termed as transsexualism.

In this context, we need to clarify the terms gender and sex. Baron and Byrne (1995, p. 196) have the following to say about sex and gender:

> Sex can be defined in terms of biological factors, the anatomical and physiological differences that are genetically determined and present at birth. Gender will refer to essentially everything else associated with one's sex in a given society, including the roles, actions, preferences and other attributes that are—or that the society assumes to be—typical of women or men.

Thus, in the aforementioned example, Sheena's baby was termed as a girl based on physiological and anatomical aspects. However, the baby would be brought up (based on her sex) in such a way that her roles, actions and preferences will be in accordance with what is expected or typical of a woman as expected by the society.

The awareness about one's sex or gender develops as the child is around 2 years old. And, gender consistency, the awareness that gender is a fundamental characteristic that is consistent over a period of time and that it is not influenced by factors that are external (for example, the clothes that are worn or the hairstyle), is realised by children in 4–7 years of age (Baron & Byrne, 1995).

Gender can be termed as one of the fundamental categories in social world. When we come across people, we tend to easily categorise them as male or female. There are many reasons why this may occur, although one of them could be that in most of the languages we do have pronouns that are gender based. For example, in English we have 'he' and 'she' and 'him' and 'her' (Sears et al., 1991).

Gender typing can be discussed here, which can be described as a process in which people and things are categorised as either masculine or feminine (Sears et al., 1991). This is often based on the physical attributes that provide cues with regard to gender such as hairstyle, clothes and so on. Parents also play an important role in this as the child may be dressed in a particular manner based on the sex of the baby. Thus, there are not many situations in which such a categorisation is not possible and when such rare situations emerge, it is resolved by seeking more information. Besides persons, activists and objects are also categorised into masculine or feminine. Firefighting, for example, is seen as masculine and being a nurse is seen as feminine. Cooking is seen as feminine, smoking is seen as masculine, toy guns are meant for boys and dolls are meant for girls and so on. This also continues to other developmental stages. Thus, from sharing of household work by couples to occupations, there is categorisation.

Theories of Gender Identity

Four main theories of gender identity have been stated by Bem in 1984 (Baron & Byrne, 1995); these are discussed here.

1. **Psychoanalytic theory:** Proposed by Freud, this theory states that the perception of one's own gender develops in a child through the process of identification with the same-sex parent. This identification also helps the child deal with issues and problems that arise as a result of desire in the child to possess the parent with the opposite sex (Baron & Byrne, 1995).
2. **Cognitive development theory:** Here, cognitive development is seen as a determinant of gender identification. And as children have a realisation about their own gender, whether masculine or feminine, they learn to recognise the roles that are appropriate and consistent with the gender that is chosen.
3. **Social learning theory:** The focus of this theory is on learning. The theory states that children will learn by observing their parents, and certain behaviours are matched with each parent. For example, mummy wears a sari because she is a woman and daddy wears trousers because he is a man and so on. Over a period of time, the matched behaviours are generalised to other individuals and the child also learns the cause and effect relationship between gender and behaviour. Further, gender-appropriate behaviours are also encouraged and reinforced. For example, a boy is often told not to cry, because he is not a girl.

4. **Gender schema theory:** Proposed by Bem in 1983 (Baron & Byrne, 1995), this theory is a combination of cognitive developmental theory and social learning theory. The theory states that Children possess 'generalised readiness' that assist them in organisation of information related to the self that is based on the cultural definitions of behaviour that is sex-appropriate (Baron & Byrne, 1995).

Bem developed a sex role inventory, called the Bem Sex Role Inventory (BSRI), that consists of a list of traits or characteristics that could be perceived as distinct for females and males and individuals taking the test have to agree or disagree whether a particular trait applies to them (Baron & Byrnes, 1995). The traits for the test were selected based on their rating with regard to whether they were seen as desirable to one sex or other. Thus one-third (20 items) of the items in this test were related to the traits that were perceived as masculine and one-third (20 items) were related to the traits that were perceived as feminine. The remaining items (20 items) were neutral items. If the individual taking the test agreed to most of the items related to masculine traits, they earned points on masculine dimension and vice versa. Thus, individuals could be termed as masculine or feminine based on their high and low scores on these two dimensions.

Thus, an individual is termed as masculine when that individual has high masculinity and low femininity. The individual is termed as feminine, if the individual has high femininity and low masculinity. The individual is termed as undifferentiated if a low score is obtained by that individual on both masculinity and femininity. In addition, the individual is termed as 'androgynous' when the individuals has high on both masculinity and femininity. Androgyny can be defined as 'the tendency to describe oneself as behaving in ways typical of both gender roles' (Baron & Byrnes, 1995, p. 201). Various studies have indicated that individuals who are androgynous are liked better, adjust well, easily adapt to situational demands, display comfort with their sexuality and experience increased interpersonal satisfaction (Baron & Byrne, 1995).

Gender stereotype also needs to be discussed in this context, which has been covered in detail in Chapter 7 on attitude.

SUMMARY

This chapter was initiated with a focus on the three main features of self, including how aware we are with ourselves, how self is understood in the context of social situation when we relate with others and how our behaviour and decisions are largely determined by self. An attempt was also made to understand the concept of self by defining it and understanding its relevance. The term self-concept was then discussed. Self-concept can be described as the collection of beliefs that we have about self. These beliefs are organised and are also referred to as self-schemas. The development of self-concept in terms of self-regulation, self-description and autobiographical memory was also discussed. The theories of self-concept management and maintenance were then highlighted and factors that influence self-concept were described. The chapter then explained the concepts of self-esteem and self-efficacy. Self-esteem, in simple terms, can be described as one's attitude towards oneself. It deals with the evaluation of his or her self-worth. It is mainly a reflection of how an individual feels about who he/she is. Self-efficacy can be described as perception and belief about whether an individual can achieve his/her goal and whether he/she has capabilities and necessary skills to deal with activities at hand. Introspection and self-perception were also elucidated. The chapter then discussed other concepts related to self, including self-awareness, self-monitoring behaviour, self-focusing and self-motives. Internet and social networking have today become part and parcel of our lives, and individuals are actively involved in the use of cyberspace at work, for education and leisure-related activities; in this regard, self in cyberspace has also been discussed. The chapter ends with a detailed discussion on gender identity, including theories of gender identity.

QUESTIONS

1. Discuss the concept of 'self'.
2. Define self-concept and discuss its development.
3. Explain the theories of self-concept management and maintenance.
4. Compare between self-esteem and self-efficacy.
5. What is introspection?
6. Describe in detail the concept of self-perception.
7. Explain self-focusing.
8. Explain self in cyberspace with a focus on research carried out in this area.
9. Define gender identity and describe its theories.

REFERENCES

Baumeister, R., Bratslavsky, E., Muraven, M., & Tice, D. (1998). Ego depletion: Is the active self a limited resource? *Journal of Personality and Social Psychology*, *74*(5), 1252–1265.

Crisp, R. J. and Turner, R. N. (2010). *Essential social psychology*. New Delhi: SAGE Publications Asia-Pacific.

Gallup, G. (1997). On the rise and fall of self-conception in primates. *Annals of The New York Academy of Sciences*, *818*(1), 73–82.

Turkle, S. (1999). Cyberspace and identity. *Contemporary Sociology*, *28*(6), 643.

Wellman, H. M., & Gelman, A. A. (1988). Children's understanding of the nonobvious. In R. J. Sternberg (Ed.), *Advances in the psychology of human intelligence* (Vol. 4). Hillsdale, NJ: Lawrence Erlbaum Associates.

Yee, N., & Bailenson, J. (2007). The Proteus effect: The effect of transformed self-representation on behavior. *Human Communication Research*, *33*(3), 271–290.

FURTHER READINGS

For more information on self, refer to the following:

Baumeister, R. (1999). *The self in social psychology* (1st ed.). Philadelphia, PA: Psychology Press.

Bennett, M., & Sani, F. (Eds.). (2004). *The development of the social self*. Hove: Psychology Press.

Mifsud B. J. (2008). *Self-regulation in cyberspace* (1st ed.). The Hague: TMC Asser Press.

CHAPTER 4

Social Cognition

Living in a place like Delhi, you learn to be cautious or even overcautious, especially when you have migrated from a different place and are new in the city. Further, there is also this strong social perception about how unsafe Delhi is for women. After Meena shifted her base to this city, one day she was travelling back home late in the evening by an auto-rickshaw. With all the apprehension and the words of wisdom that she had received from her near and dear ones who wanted her to be safe in this city, she looked at the auto driver with suspicion and was extremely cautious. But as Meena safely reached her destination and paid the auto driver off, she realised that she had left her smart phone in the auto. Meena thought to herself that her bad experience with the city had started. She realised at that moment that she had lost all her data, contacts, pictures and so on. But in about half an hour, her mother got in touch with her. Meena's mother's number was topmost on her list of contacts and the auto driver had contacted her with regard to Meena's phone. Next day, Meena got her phone back. And she realised that not all people are as bad as probably you expect them to be. Many of you may have experienced similar encounters, where you completely misjudged the situation or the person.

The above situation is an example of the way we interpret the situations and people around us.

In the first chapter, we discussed about the traditional 'Inuit' greeting called 'kunik' amongst some groups of Eskimos, who greet each other, mainly close relatives and friends, by rubbing their nose. Social cognition can play a role in the way in which we perceive this tradition, as we see 'namaste' or shaking hands as a general way of greeting each other, and our lack of awareness about such a ritual makes us perceive two people rubbing nose with apprehension. However, once our awareness is updated about the tradition, we learn to understand and appreciate the act. And the next time we see people greeting in such a way, our interpretation is going to be much different.

Social cognition, thus, plays a major role in the subject area of social psychology as an individual's behaviour can be attributed to the way the social situation and people in it are perceived by him/her. Many a time, our behaviour in social situations is not just determined by external stimulus alone, but it is as a result of mental representations that we already have about those situations. Our social cognition to a greater extent is also based on our experiences. Thus, in certain cases, it is possible that we develop a mental set or be judgemental while perceiving situations and people and make wrong interpretations.

Learning Objectives

After reading this chapter, you will be able to

- Explain the concept of social cognition
- Describe automatic and controlled processing

- Discuss the aspects of social thought
- Discuss the term schema that is also described as mental representations
- Describe heuristics, often explained as mental shortcuts
- Discuss social categorisation
- Explain the relationship between cognition and emotions

THE CONCEPT OF SOCIAL COGNITION

Social cognition is a combination of two words, that is, 'social' that, of course, speaks about the social context or set-up and 'cognition' that has to do with mental processing. Cognition does cover the greater part of what we studied in general psychology, such as sensation, perception, memory and learning.

Social cognition deals with the mental representation or interpretation of our social set-up or surrounding. It can be described as an area of study that focuses on how inferences are drawn from social information. The information that we receive from our environment can be incomplete, ambiguous and incongruous. The main focus of social cognition is on how we infer or make judgements on the basis of such an information.

Social cognitions can also be described as a scientific approach in order to understand the social situations from a cognitive dimension. It focuses on how information from social settings is processed and represented by individuals and how this information is then used to understand and interpret the world around us. Moscowitz (2005, p. 3) defined social cognition as 'the study of mental processes involved in perceiving, attending to, remembering, thinking about and making sense of the people in our social world'. Social cognition can be further described as a perspective or a tool that can be used in order to study the phenomena under social psychology. For example, a morgue or cemetery will always have an eerie feeling not because it is a morgue or cemetery but because socially we perceive death and things and places related to death in a particular fashion. There is a feeling of mystery around it. The same is applicable to people; if I ask you to describe a criminal, you may picture him (women may not be the first image of a criminal you may have unless you had a bad experience in your life) in a manner as depicted in some of our Hindi movies—tall, dark, probably muscular and with a mole or scar on his face. However, facial features do not determine whether a person is a criminal or not, but actions of the person do. Physical appearance cannot be correlated with criminal actions.

In a similar manner, how do we perceive crime or violence against women? There are numerous people (even women) who perceive domestic violence as a part and parcel of a family life and that it is absolutely normal for a husband to batter his wife as a way of disciplining her. When there is such a flawed interpretation, despite having numerous regulations and laws, the focus should also be on changing the social cognition of the people. Many a time, teenagers and youngsters also indulge in risky behaviour with a faulty interpretation of dangers involved.

Thus, our behaviour in a social set-up is to a greater extent determined by the way we perceive and interpret the world around us. And social psychologists shoulder a great responsibility in this regard as they play an important role in the development of suitable interventions that will contribute to bringing about a change in cognitions of people in society.

Further, there is also difference between how individuals think about other people and how they think about non-people such as objects (Barrett, 2017). The first point to be considered here is that when we think about others, they also think about us. And our thinking can get affected by our thoughts regarding what the other person is thinking about us, and the other person also goes through the same process. This can be termed as 'looking glass self', a term proposed by Cooley in 1802. Thus, if you look at a vase or a car and think about it, the vase or the car will not think about you. But when you interact with other individuals, you are aware that they are thinking about you and interpreting your behaviour.

In this context, it is important to highlight that not all but only certain individuals are relevant with reference to our goals. For example, an individual is intending to apply for a new opening in another company, and, at a party, he/she accidentally meets a person who happens to be a human resource manager in that company. This individual will be concerned about the impressions he/she creates on that person as it is related to his/her goal of getting the job in the other company. Further, thinking about others also involves causal explanations. For example, if one of your friends sees you but ignores you and walks the other way, then you are going to wonder about the reason why this friend behaved in such a manner. Also, human beings tend to think about people more than non-people and the brain processes involved when we think about people and non-people also differ (Barrett, 2017).

Stages of Social Information Processing

Social cognition can also be described as a group of processes that are interrelated and includes perceiving, paying attention, thinking and deriving meaning about oneself and others.

For any information to be processed, it is necessary that the information is perceived by the individual. Perception involves not only the use of senses but also the interpretation of information received from the senses on the basis of existing information, learned from past experience, which is encoding. The information received from the senses becomes meaningful only when it is in the context of the existing knowledge. This is then followed by the interpretation and conclusions that are derived based on perception and encoding. The last stage is that of response or reaction.

For example, if you are trying to understand a term as explained in this book, you will first read the particular paragraph (or listen to it). The information thus obtained by you through your senses will then be interpreted (perception) and based on the existing information you have or your experience, this information will be encoded. The information is then further interpreted in the light of the existing information you have and your experience and then conclusions are made. Once all the stages are complete, the last stage is that of response where you will react in one way or the other; you may refer to the Internet for further information or may need to clarify a doubt.

As such, social cognition appears to be simple in nature, mainly because an individual is not making an effort and the process necessarily seems automatic. But it is a complex as well as a dynamic process. Human beings are continuously involved in perception, attention, trying to remember things, events, people and so on in the context of social situation which again is constantly changing. This can have an impact on the accuracy of social cognition, and individuals could make a number of errors while making judgements about others.

Social cognition can be termed as having two main goals, one has to do with accuracy and the other to do with conservation of mental resources (Barrett, 2017). Further, these two goals are also interrelated and at the same time incompatible, because for a processing to be accurate, more mental resources are required, and a faster processing may require less mental resources but could leave a scope for errors and mistakes. Besides these two goals, yet another goal of social cognition is social enhancement that can be described as a tendency to maintain a self-image that is positive.

It is also to be noted here that a distinction can be drawn between what is believed and what is understood. A study was carried out by Gilbert (1991, p. 116) which stated how individuals display a proneness to accept what they hear and see as true. The explanation that he provided was, 'people are Spinozan systems that, when faced with shortages of time, energy, or conclusive evidence, may fail to unaccept the ideas that they involuntarily accept during comprehension'. In 1993, Gilbert et al. carried out a study that constituted of a total of three experiments. In experiments 1 and 2, the participants were provided false information about a criminal defendant as they were under load, and in experiment 3, the participants were provided false information about a college student as they were under time pressure. The participants were then asked to make judgements about the target. The results revealed that load as well as time pressure lead to participants believing false information as well as utilising it to make consequential decisions with regard to the target. Thus, the participants automatically believed the false information about the targets as they were under load or time pressure.

Social Inference

Social cognition is about how people make inferences. Thus, we also need to focus on this related term, social inference. Social inference involves the following steps:

1. **Information gathering.** Information gathering is one of the important steps in forming inferences. It can be influenced by prior expectations of the perceiver, and although this can be of great help in certain cases, it can interfere with our inferences, especially when the prior expectations are faulty, biased and when such expectations discourage an individual from considering any information at all. Once the information is collected, it is then important to select the piece of information on the basis of which the inferences will be drawn. An inference drawn from small amount of information can be biased and disastrous.

   Information can be available to us in forms of statistical information or case history information. The case history information influences our judgements better when compared to the statistical information, despite statistical information being far more objective (Sears et al., 1991).
2. **Integration of information.** Once the information is gathered, we need to make a decision about what information can be used. This also involves integrating the information. Our stereotypes and favouritism can interfere with the process of integration. Many a time, our decision-making process is not consistent with the rational model of inference. And, in a way, computers are better than us while taking a decision as they do so on the basis of fixed criteria and information is analysed in a fixed and standardised manner unlike human beings.
3. **Making judgements based on integration of information.** The last step in making inferences is that of making judgements based on the integration of information. In this context, we can discuss about the term judgements of covariance that has to do with the association between two or more things. For example, we often say that the eldest child is far more responsible compared to the younger siblings. Thus, we are associating the ordinal position with taking responsibility. But such an association can also be faulty as there can be eldest children who are irresponsible and younger ones who are responsible. While integrating the information in order to make judgement, care should be taken to ensure that a good amount of information is available, which is correct and not integrated haphazardly.

AUTOMATIC AND CONTROLLED PROCESSING

Human beings possess two processing systems, automatic processing (referred to as X system) and controlled processing (referred to as C system), that coexist in our brain and try to control the mental system. The main difference between these two processing systems is that the automatic system is not conscious and lacks, or has low, conscious awareness as it operates. Controlled processing, on the other hand, displays higher level of conscious awareness. The automatic system is shared by others including animals in accordance with evolutionary perspective and controlled processing is developed only later and is found only in human beings and to some extent in primates (Barrett, 2017). When compared with the automatic processing, the controlled processing is slow and involves effort, though it is sequential, intentional and logical. On the other hand, the automatic processing is unintentional, intuitive and efficient.

Controlled processing deals with problems that are abstract and general, whereas the automatic processing is restricted to problems that are narrowly defined. The automatic processes are based on implicit memory and are dependent on the context, whereas the controlled processes require concrete working memory and can be dissociated from the context. An example of automatic processes would be an individual trying to miss a hit by a football that comes his/her way on a playground. An example of controlled processes would be writing an article or working on an important document.

Both these processes can also be differentiated on the basis of emotion. For example, often in India, when one is down with common cold, a very common 'grandmother's concoction' is often given which is a mixture of herbs and most often is bitter in taste. The very first reaction to this concoction, when it is offered, is that of disgust and unwillingness to ingest it, but when one is told about its medicinal effect and the relief that it would provide, after some convincing on the part of mostly a mother or an aunt, the individual would overcome the earlier reaction of disgust and will try to have the concoction. The example also denotes that automatic processes can be overruled by controlled processes (Barrett, 2017).

The regions in brain that these two systems are based on also differ. As stated in Barrett (2017, p. 85),

> According to Lieberman et al., 2002, the X system (also referred to as System 1) engages in parallel processing and consists of the amygdala, the basil ganglia, the lateral temporal, ventromedial prefrontal and dorsal anterior cingulate cortexes. Involved primarily with conscious processes, the C system (also referred to as System 2) is composed mostly of lateral prefrontal, posterior parietal cortexes besides the hippocampus and medial temporal lobe region.

It is very difficult to completely distinguish between the automatic processes and controlled processes, and behaviours as such cannot be compartmentalised as being one or the other, though the degree to which the behaviour is automatic or controlled can be determined. In this context, the term automaticity can be discussed. Automaticity can be defined as an 'extent to which a given event is unintentional, occurs without conscious awareness, is accomplished efficiently and once begun cannot be controlled' (Barrett, 2017, p. 85).

There are also various types of automatic processes, including the processes that are first explicitly learned and then they become automatic. For example, as one learns to type, initially one is conscious about how one is typing, though once we have learned the typing thoroughly, it becomes automatic and we know exactly where the keys on a keyboard are. Yet another type of automatic processes is the one in which a behaviour is influenced by concepts that are implicitly learned. For example, one may have prejudices that are implicit with regard to a single women. Third type of automatic processes is priming. It has been discussed under schemas in this chapter.

ASPECTS OF SOCIAL THOUGHTS

In the process of understanding others, it is highly possible that we make errors. We can fall prey to biases, stereotypes, judgements and so on that can lead to certain serious consequences, though our social thoughts can be adaptive as they can help us pay attention to relevant information and develop an understanding about our social set-up without investing a great amount of effort.

The aspects of social thoughts are described as follows.

Information that Is Inconsistent

Suppose you have a colleague who is very successful in his/her job and loves to do what he/she does. He/she is even being considered for promotion and you perceive him/her to be not only lucky but also happy and satisfied with his/her life. One fine day, during a lunch, this colleague is sharing about all his/her achievements and positive experiences. You have your divided attention on what he/she is saying and on the food that you are eating. And then suddenly he/she says that she is quitting his/her job. You almost drop your spoon and are completely shocked. It is clear from your response that you are all attention to this inconsistent piece of information. You did not expect him/her to say such a thing and it was inconsistent with your schema about him/her.

In the aforementioned example, the response is very natural as we tend to pay more attention to something that is inconsistent or unexpected. Also, such information is processed better and can find its place in the long-term memory and thus may influence our future judgements in social set-ups. However, it not necessarily changes or modifies our perception or viewpoints.

Hilton, Kleine and Von Hippelin in 1991 used dichotic listening technique to study the amount of attention provided to consistent and inconsistent information (Baron & Byrne, 1995). In dichotic listening, the listeners are provided with different information in both the ears. This leads to the listeners simultaneously listening to the information provided. The participants were, thus, made to listen to the responses of two children with regard to a test of intellectual performance. One of the child (control) performed consistently, while the other showed either of the contrasting patterns of performing better at the start and then deteriorating or performing badly at the start and then doing well in the test. The participants were given additional information about this child, either he/she came from an advantageous background and was a good student or he/she was from disadvantageous background and was a poor student. The results indicated that the participants did pay attention to the child who was doing well and later deteriorated or was doing badly initially but picked up with performance later on. This happened because the participants did not expect the performance of the child to change drastically and thus it was inconsistent with their information and expectation.

Automatic Vigilance

Automatic vigilance can be described as our tendency to pay more attention to the information that is negative. Read the following paragraph carefully.

> Sumit is an honest person and is doing extremely well with his studies. He aspires to a be surgeon one day and has been working in that direction. His interests are reading books, listening to music, gambling and trekking. He is also socially active and helps with teaching children in slum area.

After reading the above paragraph, did any particular word catch your attention? If your answer is 'gambling', then you just experienced automatic vigilance. This can be helpful as when we are cautious to something negative, that probably will save us from some danger or something that may be harmful. However, it is also possible that we ignore other relevant information while we attend to the negative information.

Motivated Scepticism

Motivated scepticism occurs when information is inconsistent with what we already know or believe, and when the information is consistent with our preferred conclusion or belief, then we are less careful or sceptic. This also indicates that in order to make decisions that are consistent or inconsistent with our earlier preference, we take different criteria into consideration. Further, this scepticism may also depend on whether the information is desirable or undesirable (Ditto & Lopez, 1992). For example, there are two candidates (A and B) for local elections. And though you have not decided whom to vote for, you do have some preference for candidate A. During a debate between the two candidates organised by a local news channel, you come across information about the position and opinions of both the candidates. In this context, given the fact that you have preference for candidate A, not much information (i.e., consistent with your point of view) will be required for you to decide that you will vote for this candidate. On the other hand, the information (i.e., consistent with your point of view) required for you to change your preference (and vote for candidate B) will be much more. Thus, the information that is consistent with your views will be easily accepted and the scepticism in this regard will be negligible. Furthermore, the information that is consistent with what we believe is also less carefully or sceptically examined by us, when compared to information that is inconsistent with what we believe.

Counterfactual Thinking

Counterfactual thinking occurs when we think about alternate events or outcomes. Thus, a usual or normal behaviour that results in a negative outcome is seen with less sympathy compared to an unusual behaviour with negative outcome. Consider the following example.

Shireen is always cautious about wearing her seat belt while driving, even when she is going a short distance. However, today when she had to go half a kilometre, she did not wear her seat belt and met with an accident and was hurt. Natasha never wears her seat belt as she finds it unnecessary and uncomfortable. Today, when she was going to office, she met with an accident and got hurt.

Whom would you sympathise with more, Shireen or Natasha? Your answer most probably will be Shireen as her behaviour today of not putting the seat belt was unusual, whereas Natasha displayed her usual behaviour of not wearing a seat belt. Thus, we sympathise with Shireen more than Natasha by employing counterfactual thinking.

Meer Ownership Effect

This is a tendency where the objects and things owned by us are viewed more favourably than those that we do not own. Further, we are also prone to evaluate these objects and things positively. This is also relevant because we relate what we possess with our self-image. And our self-image can be enhanced by making a positive assessment of our possessions and vice versa. Further, the mere ownership effect is higher when self-image is threatened and it is lower when self-image is enhanced.

Owning a cell phone amongst students, even in schools, has become a part and parcel of their self-image. A person not owning a cell phone is seen as lacking a positive image as compared to a person who has the latest smart phone.

In the next section of this chapter, two concepts that are relevant in social cognition will be discussed, they are schemas and heuristics. These can be described as shortcuts or ways to infer information while minimising the use of cognitive resources. Although similar, in a way, they are used in different contexts and also operate differently. The concepts will be clear when we discuss them in detail.

SCHEMAS: THE MENTAL REPRESENTATIONS

Schemas can be explained as 'mental structures people use to organise their knowledge about the social world around themes or subjects and that influence the information people notice, think about and remember' (Aronson et al., 2014, p. 59). They can be described as the expectations that we have about a particular situation or person. According to Fiske and Taylor (1991), schemas are a set of cognitions about a particular concept that is organised and structured. They are cognitive representations in which there is a comparison between the features or characteristics of the new situation or stimulus with the abstract representations that we have in our memory. For example, if we see one of our friends cutting a cake, we know that most likely it is her/his birthday. This is as a result of information stored in our memory about cutting of cakes on birthdays. We apply the similar process to objects and even people. In a party, for example, if you meet a person who is jovial, fun-loving, makes great communication and is comfortable with people, you are likely to term him/her as social by nature or extrovert. This kind of categorisation also helps us remember others.

Some of the important aspects about schemas are as follows:

- Individuals will interpret new information related to social situations, social roles, objects and people based on schemas.
- They also help in identifying the important aspects of the social situations and stimulus.
- They help make information received by us more structured and organised.
- They also help in quick processing of information that may be relevant for schemas.
- They also help in not only remembering information but also interpreting it and making inferences. Thus, they enhance our memory.
- They also assist by providing guidelines that can determine the interaction with others.
- One of the important features of schemas is that they, most of the times, have hierarchical organisation.
- They also assist in dealing with missing information by filling the gaps with the help of schema-consistent information.
- They help an individual in using his/her past experiences in new situations.
- Schemas also help in altering the way in which the information is processed.
- Expectations about what may happen next are also dealt with by schemas. These expectations determine whether we are going to find the situation or an individual pleasant or unpleasant. If our experiences and expectations are consistent, then we will be pleased and if there is an inconsistency between our expectations and experiences, then we will be displeased. For example, an individual's schemas may make him/her believe that due to hard work that he/she

has put in, he/she will be considered for a higher position in the organisation. If the expectations of this person are fulfilled, then he/she will be pleased, and if not, then he/she will be displeased.

- Schemas also consist of an emotional component, that is called as schema-driven affect.
- Although many a time, an individual may share same schemas with others regarding people and social situation, there are schemas that are personal (to that individual), that are influenced by values and interests of the individual. Thus, individual differences do exist with regard to schemas to some extent.

Schemas seems to be of great help and relevance going by the features we discussed; however, they can also interfere with perception of situations and people. Development of stereotypes on the basis of schemas can be very dangerous as individuals may make wrong inferences. If we develop a stereotype about a particular individual or a group of individuals, then it can lead to a very unhealthy situation where the well-being and lives of people are at stake. Assumptions based on faulty schemas can lead to inferences that are faulty and misleading. In this case, it is important for us to not jump to conclusions but pay more attention so as to get more information that will help us infer in a better manner and correctly. There are certain situations when, we may pay less attention towards schemas and more towards the information. These are discussed as follows:

1. **Dependency on the outcome:** This occurs when another person's actions determine the outcome. Thus, more attention is paid to that person rather than the schemas. Attention in this case is also paid to information that is inconsistent with the schemas, mainly because they are relevant.
2. **Accuracy:** When we seek to be accurate or when we need to take important decisions, we pay less attention to the schemas that probably will give us quick and easy interpretation.
3. **Accountability:** When we are required to be accountable or are answerable for our decisions, we need to focus more on the information before we take these important decisions; thus, we pay less attention to the schemas.

There are also situations when we are prone to using schemas, they are discussed as follows:

1. **Impression formation.** Schemas greatly influence our process of impression formation. Often there are instances when we make inferences about a particular person quickly on the basis of their appearance and based on our first interaction.
2. **Decision-making under pressure.** When we need to take immediate decisions in a limited period of time, we may rely on our schemas.

Factors that Determine Which Schema is Used

After a discussion on the concept of schemas, it is also important to understand the factors that determine which schema is used in various situations. Sometimes the selection of a particular schema will depend on the nature of information, whereas, in certain cases, it does not depend on the information provided by the situation. The factors that determine which schema is used are discussed here.

1. **Natural contours.** This can be termed as one of the most relevant determinants while selecting a schema. Schemas get naturally activated based on the information that one gets from the

environment. While discussing about natural contours, we also need to speak about the term 'breakpoints'. Breakpoints mainly occur between two different actions and determine where a particular action ends and another starts, for example, when you look at a particular person at a construction site who is mixing the concrete, then filling a container with it and carrying it away. This action is seen by us in chunks, for example, mixing the concrete, filling the container and carrying it away. The points where each of these chunks of action ends and the other starts are breakpoints. These breakpoints are a part and parcel of any behaviour and thus follow the natural contours with reference to the information received by us. This chunking of information will also depend on the prior experience and expectations of the perceiver. Breakpoints are relevant because they provide information about the sequence of a particular behaviour. Also, it helps remember the information in a better manner. Breakpoints occur due to the following reasons:

- They are as a result of change in behaviour. This is mainly related to movement of body parts.
- They occur as a result of changes in the state of objects that are associated with the person.
- Individuals employ more breakpoints when unexpected actions are experienced or when less information about the action is available. Breakpoints mainly help in making the actions more meaningful.

Thus, when we talk about the natural contours as one of the factors that determine the use of a particular schema, we need to remember that the information received from the environment or situation is not taken as a whole while making inferences. But this information is ingested by us in a structured manner and in a meaningful way.

2. **Salience.** It is also possible many a time that we base our inferences on environmental salience. Salience implies a particular or specific feature. Physical features many a time are more impressing in determining schema. These features can be related to age, gender, facial features and even physical attractiveness of a person. This invoking of schema based on salient features can be unhealthy, especially when information is quickly processed based on some stereotype or prejudice. Such an application of schema can be harmful and dangerous and will interfere with behaviour and interaction of the perceiver.
3. **Roles.** It is many a time easy to remember information or individuals based on their roles. For example, try to remember a teacher in your school or college who was very strict. Role schemas are even more useful when compared to personality traits. In fact, individuals are first perceived through role schemas and then by their personality traits. Role schemas are also more distinct when compared to traits.
4. **Primacy.** Which schema will be used by the perceiver will also depend on the primacy of the information. The prior information that is gained by the perceiver will determine the schema and the inference of later information will depend on this prior information.
5. **Priming.** A schema that has been recently used is more likely to be used again by the perceiver even in an unrelated situation. Thus, the subsequent cognitive process can become rapid and effective with the help of priming. This can be termed as priming effect. This mainly happens because the schema recently used is easily available, it can be easily retrieved and can be used for quick inference of information. However, it is to be noted that, a schema that was previously activated will be invoked in order to explain the new information only when the schema is relevant to the information. If the new information is not relevant to the recently used schema, then these schemas are not invoked. For example, if a person was shown a list of words including the word 'apple' and later is asked to name a fruit, the first fruit that is more likely to come to this individual's mind is 'apple'. This mainly happens because the information is readily available; thus, it was

possible to easily retrieve it. Also in certain situations, the information is retrieved in this way in order to make quick conclusions. Priming can occur without the individual being aware of it; this is termed as automatic priming.

6. **Importance.** The relevance of the information and inferences to be drawn will also determine which schema is invoked. This will also determine the amount of time that is invested on thinking with regard to the situation and information. The inferences drawn will also be complex and will be based on more than one schema. For example, if you want to take an important decision about which programme to select for further education, you will take the decision by utilising many schemas, such as your interest, career goals, expectations of parents and other significant people in your life, and even the value and career prospects of the programmes and so on.
7. **Individual differences.** Individual differences will exist in determining which schemas are employed and invoked. Same information will be inferred by different people in different ways. This is also true because the experiences and expectations of the people differ. And these experiences and expectations to a greater extent are determined by cultural factors.
8. **Goals.** Goals of the perceiver will also determine which schemas are used. The perceiver is actively involved in structuring and organising the information that he/she gets from the environment and the goals of the perceiver will have an influence on how this is done.

The Schematic Processing

According to Bargh (1983), most of the time, schematic processing is automatic. Such a processing does not require an individual to pay attention. The processing, thus, requires minimal effort and time. The schematic processing can be explained with help of the following example.

Rita, an 11th standard student, was new in her class. She can be described as an extrovert, a fun-loving and a lively girl who had interest in music, theatre and making new friends. She recently shifted to a small town from Mumbai as her father, who was an IAS officer, was posted here. She was upset that she had to relocate to this small town and had to leave her friends and school. She was also apprehensive about her new school and classmates. She was quiet on her first day and interacted less with her new classmates. Sameera who was in the same class saw this new girl and when she came to know about Rita, she was quick to make inferences and conclusions that being a daughter of an IAS officer and being from a metropolitan city like Mumbai, Rita was arrogant and did not care to interact with small-town girls like herself. Such an inference about Rita on behalf of Sameera is a result of her schemas about girls from metropolitan cities, though interaction over months with Rita did make Sameera realise that Rita was not like the person she expected her to be. In this case, it was not Rita who created such an impression, but it was Sameera who made wrong inferences about Rita.

When we are in a situation or are interacting with someone, we make assumptions that need to be confirmed, that is termed as confirmatory hypothesis testing. We try to collect more and more information that can be used to support or reject these hypothesis. And in this process, we may either realise that inferences made by us based on our schemas were either correct or faulty. The degree to which people selectively confirm hypotheses will be reduced if there is an opposite hypothesis or when there is a need for valid information.

Individuals as such do not passively receive information and they may act or behave in such a way that change the extent to which the schemas are contradicted or supported. In the aforementioned example, it is possible that the indifferent behaviour of Sameera and other classmates can make Rita behave in an arrogant manner. This is as a result of self-fulfilling prophecy, which occurs when an individual's faulty expectations and inferences about another individual result in that individual imbibing those expectations and inferences.

An experiment with regard to self-fulfilling prophecy was carried out by Mark Snyder and William Swann (1978). In this experiment, pairs of participants were formed where one was given the role of an interviewer and the other was given the role of an interviewee. The interviewers were then provided with descriptions of extravert: outgoing, sociable, energetic, confident, talkative, enthusiastic, warm and friendly), and of introvert: shy, timid, reserved, quiet, distant, retiring, cool and aloof. Some of the interviewers were asked to test the hypothesis that the person they interviewed (the interviewee) was an extravert and others were asked to test the hypothesis that the person they interviewed (the interviewee) was an introvert. A list of 26 questions to be asked was also provided to the interviewers. Of these (pretested) questions, 11 questions were those that were more likely to be asked to extraverts, 10 questions were those that were more likely to be asked to an introvert, whereas 5 questions were likely to be judged as neutral. The interviewers were given freedom to ask any 12 questions that they wished to. The results indicated that the interviewer chose their questions based on their expectation, that is, based on the hypothesis that they were testing.

Furthermore, the tapes related to only the interviewees' responses to the questions were shown to certain judges who were asked to decide whether the interviewee was an extravert or an introvert. It revealed that the interviewees who were interviewed by interviewers with a hypothesis that the interviewee was an extravert were judged as displaying the behaviour of an extravert and the interviewees who were interviewed by interviewers with a hypothesis that the interviewee was an introvert were judged as displaying the behaviour of an introvert. Thus, it was concluded that the interviewer's behaviour and questions had influenced the interviewee and their behaviour was altered to match the expectations of the interviewer.

Self-fulfilling prophecy can lead a dissonance between the perceiver's viewpoint about the individual and the individual's concept of himself/herself. In the example previously discussed, there is a dissonance between Sameera's viewpoint about Rita and the concept that Rita has about herself. Whether self-fulfilling prophecy will take place or not will depend on the certainty of the expectations by the perceiver and the certainty of the self-concept of the other individual. If the other person has a strong self-concept, then it will not be possible for the perceiver to influence the other individual's behaviour and actions. However, if the individual is uncertain about his/her own self-concept, then he/she will be influenced by the perceiver's expectations and inferences.

COGNITIVE HEURISTICS: THE MENTAL SHORTCUTS

The term heuristics has been derived from a Greek word, 'heurisco', that means 'discover'. And in the field of social cognition, heuristics can be used to make quick and efficient judgements, though these judgements may not always be accurate. Heuristics can be termed as decision-making rules that are simple and often used in order to draw quick and easy conclusions. These can be described as specific rules of processing and can be termed as mental shortcuts used to reduce or minimise mental efforts. Any problem-solving activity, for example, may require a large investment of time and attention. But with the help of heuristics, the problem-solving activity can be reduced to mere judgements that are not complex and thus require much less time and attention. These shortcuts also help in eliciting the schemas for information processing.

As stated by Tversky and Kahneman (1974, p. 1124), 'People rely on a limited number of heuristic principles which reduce the complex tasks of assessing probabilities and predicting values to simpler judgemental operations. In general, these heuristics are quite useful, but sometimes they lead to severe and systematic errors'.

Some of the heuristics often used are discussed as follows.

Representativeness Heuristic

This heuristic carries out the process of matching the information obtained from the environment with the schemas so as to confirm whether the match is correct. For example, Anuj is shy and prefers to keep to himself. He is often deep in his thoughts. He is very unorganised, forgets stuff and is not very well dressed most of the time but is very creative. From this description of Anuj, what would you say—is he a management professional or an artist. It is more likely that you say that he is an artist as you compare the description of Anuj to the information you already have. However, the truth is that an artists can be organised and opposite of how Anuj is being described. Representativeness heuristics can be described as the mental shortcuts where certain instances are categorised based on how similar they are to a typical member of a particular category (Barrett, 2017). Although in most cases, representativeness heuristics can also be accurate, it is possible that certain relevant information is ignored and conclusions are made without giving a second thought.

A pilot study was carried out by Payne and Crowlesy (2008) on assessing the use of cognitive heuristic representativeness in clinical reasoning. Two main aspects of the representative heuristic were focused on in the study–judgement based on the perceived frequency and representativeness with regard to causal beliefs. The results indicated that the participants applied both the aspects of representative heüristic as they carried out reasoning and also committed errors related to misapplication of the heuristics.

Availability Heuristic

The term availability heuristics was put forth by Daniel Kahneman and Amos Tversky in 1973. In availability heuristics, the inferences are based on the information or examples that are easily remembered. Availability heuristic is described by Barrett (2017, p. 92) as 'mental shortcuts in which people judge the frequency or likelihood of an event based on how easily relevant examples come to mind'. The cognitive effort involved in this is minimal as is in representativeness heuristic. There can be errors in availability heuristics as information that is easy will be easily remembered. Thus, such information is likely to be frequently used while making judgements about others and about one's self. In a study carried out by Schwarz et al. (1991), the participants were asked to provide 6 (easy tasks) or 12 (difficult tasks) examples of assertive or unassertive behaviour displayed by them. They were then asked to rate themselves with reference how assertive they were. The results displayed that when the participants recalled 6 examples of assertive behaviour rather than 12, they rated themselves as assertive and as the participants recalled 6 examples rather than 12 examples of unassertive behaviour, they rated themselves as unassertive. In another study carried out by Fox (2006), the participants who were students were asked to fill up an evaluation form where they could list 2 (easy task) or 10 (difficult tasks) ways in which the course could be made better. The results indicated that the participants who had to list 2 ways to improve the course rated thè course less favourable compared to the participants who were asked to provide 10 ways to improve the course. Thus, it can be said that the participants who had to come up with 10 criticisms of the course found it difficult to come up with so many criticisms and thus made conclusions that as they could not recall so many criticisms about the course, the course must be good and thus rated it favourable.

Simulation Heuristic

The simulation heuristic can be described as a tendency of an individual to think that the events or situations that can be easily simulated mentally or imagined, are more likely to occur. Simulation heuristic can be used for various tasks, including prediction, causality and affective responses (Sears et al., 1991).

A study was carried out by Wells and Gavanski (1989) on mental simulation of causality. Two experiments were carried out in this study. In the first experiment, the participants were asked to read one of the two versions of a story in which a young lady goes to a restaurant along with her boss. The boss is not aware that the lady is allergic to wine and orders a dish that has wine sauce in it. After consuming the dish, the lady dies due to allergic reaction. The two versions of the story differed as in one version of the story, the boss initially considered ordering an alternative dish for the lady that did not have wine sauce in it, and in the other version, the boss considered ordering an alternative dish for the lady that also had wine sauce in it. The results indicated that participants were more likely to judge the causal role of the boss in the death of the lady when they were given the second version where the alternative meal also had the wine sauce.

In the second experiment, the participants were asked to read a story that involved a paraplegic couple and a taxi driver. In the story, the taxi driver refuses to take the couple and as a result the couple has to take their own car. They drive off a bridge that has collapsed just before and they both die. There were two versions of this story that differed. In the first version, the taxi driver drives off the bridge before it collapses and thus crosses it safely and in the second version, the taxi driver drives off the bridge but narrowly manages to escape his taxi as it sinks in the water below. The results of this experiment indicated that the taxi drivers refusal to take the couple was perceived by the participants as a stronger cause of the couple's death.

The results of both the experiments confirm that the effects on causal judgements can be predicted by the mental simulation framework.

Anchoring Heuristic

Anchors are mainly useful when we are trying to understand the meaning of ambiguous information. These anchors can also be described as reference points that may be adjusted in a way before you make final conclusions. Anchoring heuristics is used to a greater extent in marketing as well to influence the decision-making of consumers. Tversky and Kahenman (1974) carried out a study in which they asked the participants to make an estimate with regard to the number of African countries that were part of the United Nations, though this was done after the wheel of fortune was spun. The wheel of fortune had numbers on it from 0 to 100 and was rigged to stop either at 10 or 65. The wheel was spun and as it stopped, the participants were asked to make an estimate about the percentage, whether it was higher or lower than the number on the wheel of fortune. The participants who had number 65 displayed on their wheel reported that 45 per cent of African countries were part of the United Nations and the participants who had number 10 displayed on their wheel reported that 25 per cent of African countries were part of the United Nations. Thus, anchoring effect was displayed by the participants.

SOCIAL CATEGORISATION

Categorisation can be defined as 'the process of understanding what something is by knowing what other things it is equivalent to, and what other things it is different from' (McGarty, 1999, p. 1). Crisp and Turner (2010, p. 72) describe categorisation as 'a way of classifying some collection of objects, events, opinions, attitudes, concepts or people'.

For example, how would you categorise elephant, dog, strawberry, saree, cow, lion, mango, banana, trousers and shirt? A guess is that you may have categorised the following into three main categories as follows:

Animals: elephant, dog, cow, lion

Fruits: strawberry, mango, banana

Clothes: saree, trousers, shirt

What made you categorise these as animals, fruits and clothes? You mainly did so on the basis of how they are similar or not similar. This is what categorisation is about.

Categories are not determined only on the basis of certain definite features or attributes, but on the basis of the typicality, that is, whether the variable is typical or atypical of a certain category. This typicality can be explained by understanding prototype. Prototype has been explained as members that are most representative of a certain category. For example, if you are asked to think of pets, what may first come to your mind is a dog or a cat than say a horse (i.e., comparatively atypical), as a cat and a dog are more typical with regard to the category of pets. Thus, a dog and a cat come easily to your mind when compared to a horse or a monkey or a snake that are also kept as pet but are increasingly atypical. There could also be an error in categorisation.

In the context of social categories, prototypes can be referred to as stereotypes (we will discuss in detail about stereotypes in Chapter 7). Development of stereotypes can be attributed to illusory correlation besides other factors. Illusory correlation can be explained as a belief that a relationship exists between two variables when in fact there is insignificant or no relationship at all between the two variables. The term illusory correlation was coined by Loren J. Chapman in 1927. In a study carried out by Chapman (1967), the participants were presented with two arrays of words and they were asked to inform about how frequently a word from one array was paired with a word from the other array. The participants reported a higher frequency for word pairs that visually appeared different from other words (like words that were very long) and the word pairs that had same semantic meaning. Such results were obtained despite of the fact that the words were presented with equal frequency.

Variations in categories can be found not only with regard to the content of the category but also on the basis of its structure, whether it is homogeneous or heterogeneous. Heterogeneous denotes that the group consists of members who are of various different sorts or types, whereas homogeneous denotes that the group consists of members who are of fewer types or are to a greater extent similar to each other. This will also be touched upon when we discuss about in-group and out-group in Chapter 11.

Categorisation mainly serves two purposes—it helps save time and enables less investment in cognitive processes, and it brings about a clarity and refinement in how the world is perceived by the individuals (Crisp & Turner, 2010).

Three main factors determine whether categorisation will be used or not. The first factor is temporal primacy, that is, categorisation on the basis of factors that we come across first. The second factor is perceptual salience that occurs when the difference becomes noticeable. The third factor is chronic accessibility that occurs when the categorisation is based on race, gender, caste, religion and so on, that is done so commonly that it becomes exceedingly automatic.

COGNITION AND EMOTIONS

Cognition can have an impact on our emotions, as much as our emotions can have an impact on our cognition. Emotions can be described as physiological changes that are accompanied by feelings which are powerful and most often uncontrollable. These can also be defined as 'a complex pattern of bodily and mental changes that includes physiological arousal, feelings, cognitive processes, visible expressions (including face and posture) and specific behavioural reactions made in response to a situation perceived as personally significant' (Gerrig & Zimbardo, 2005, p. 418).

Three main approaches can be used to explain emotion. The first is the Cannon–Bard Theory of central neural processes. This theory states that physiological changes and experiences that are subjective in nature (such as joy, fear, anger and guilt) are experienced when an individual is exposed to an event or situation that provokes emotions. For example, you return home from school/college/work and are not aware that your younger sibling who stays away from home is behind your bedroom door to surprise you. And he/she suddenly jumps in front of you. What will your reaction be in this case? You will experience physiological changes with increase in blood pressure and heart rate and will also experience certain subjective experiences such as shock and joy.

The second approach is the James–Lange Theory of body reactions that states that the physiological reactions to certain events or situations that are automatic in nature lead to our emotional experiences (that are subjective in nature). Keeping in mind the example discussed earlier, you feel shock and joy because of the physiological changes that occurred in you.

The third approach to emotion, the Schachter's two-factor theory, states that arousal results in initiation of a search for the cause of the feelings. The causes thus identified are significant in determination of how we term the arousal. For example, if an employee is playing game on his/her office computer and suddenly looks up and sees the boss standing in front, he/she will experience an arousal, that may then be labelled as fear. This theory can be categorised under cognitive appraisal theory. And, in fact, Schachter believed that emotional experiences are a result of combined effect of cognitive appraisal and the arousal that is physiological in nature (Gerrig & Zimbardo, 2005).

Cognition and emotion are much related and can have an influence on each other. The cognition will determine the way we experience feelings and emotions. If a schema includes powerful affective components, our emotions will get affected. Cognition can impact our reactions to certain situations that evoke emotions. Such reactions are also based on the way the situation is interpreted by us. Expectations about our reaction about a particular situation will also determine the way we interpret a situation.

Emotions can also have an influence on cognition. Emotions can have an impact on our cognition to such an extent that our perception of the world and things around us changes. While experiencing positive emotion, we will perceive people and things and even ambiguous stimuli around us, in a more favourable manner and vice versa.

Further, emotions can also have an impact on our memory. Whether it is encoding, organisation of information in memory or retrieval, the emotional states experienced by the person will influence each of these steps. Most often, the information that is consistent with our emotional state is remembered better than the information that is inconsistent with our emotional state. Even our creativity gets affected by the emotional state experienced by us. Persons in neutral mood are not as effective in problem-solving and creative tasks as compared to people who are in positive emotional state. Frogas while explaining the motivated processing strategy states that individuals are motivated to uphold the positive emotional states that they experience, and any cognitive effort that may interfere with retention of such emotional states are avoided. Whereas with regard to negative emotional states, individuals will strive to get information, which will enhance their emotional state (Baron & Byrne, 1995).

Emotions also play a significant role in motivation and attention and are also relevant in social context as they play an important role in regulation of social interactions. For example, in the morning as you reach office and find that your boss is not actually in good mood, you may avoid any significant interaction with him/her like asking for a half day or a day off. Further emotions may also play a significant role in determining altruistic behaviour, that is, an individual will be more giving or kind when in good mood than when not.

When discussing about emotions, we also need to describe the facial feedback hypothesis and vascular theory of emotional efference. Facial feedback hypothesis states that the changes in our emotional experiences can be as a result of changes in our facial expressions. Thus, facial expressions are not just means of reflecting emotions, and according to this hypothesis, if an individual smiles, he/she will experience happiness. There are studies as well to support this hypothesis. A study was carried out by McCanne and Anderson (1987) in which female participants were asked to imagine negative and positive situations, and while doing so, they were asked to suppress or increase tension in certain facial muscles. The findings indicated that the participants experienced diminished enjoyment of the positive situations when they suppressed the facial muscle (used while smiling) and less distress to negative events when they suppressed the facial muscle (used while frowning). Although the hypothesis has some support, the mechanism behind this hypothesis is not known.

In this context, the vascular theory of emotional efference put forth by Zajonc, Murphy and Inglehart. (1989) can be discussed. An older version of this theory was put forth by Waynbaum in 1907 (Baron & Byrne, 1995). This theory states that the vascular system present in head is affected by the changes in facial expressions. The facial expressions result in cooling down of the venous blood supply of the brain by pressing of these veins or by the regulation of the amount of air entering the nasal cavities that can cool the blood in the veins. This change can then further affect the temperature of the brain as well as the neurochemicals-related events that are mainly related to feelings that are positive or negative. Thus, the theory confirms that some connection does exist between the facial expression and emotions.

SUMMARY

This chapter on social cognition is indeed an important milestone in the course of this book, as it gives us an idea about how we understand the world around us. To sum up, in this chapter, we discussed about the concepts of social cognition and the stages in the processing of social information. We also discussed the term social inference. The chapter also covered automatic and controlled processing. Human beings possess two processing systems, automatic (referred to as X system) and controlled processing (referred to as C system), that both exist in our brain and try to control the mental system. The main difference between these two processing systems is that the automatic system is not conscious, lacks conscious awareness or has low conscious awareness as it operates and the controlled processing displays higher level of conscious awareness. Further, we focused on the aspects of social thought. The five main aspects that we discussed are information that is inconsistent, automatic vigilance, motivated scepticism, counterfactual thinking and mere ownership effect. We then discussed about the terms schema and heuristics that help us in bridging the gaps in the information received by us and make it more meaningful in a quick and easy manner. Understanding these terms must have made you realise how we make judgements and jump to conclusions. The chapter also elucidated social categorisation that can be described as a way of classifying some collection of objects, events, opinions, attitudes, concepts or people. Ultimately, the chapter discussed about the relationship between cognition and emotions.

This chapter is relevant not only to understand how individuals behave but also to understand your own social cognition. As psychologists, you will probably get into counselling, interacting with people, designing interventions and helping people make decisions and solve problems. The concepts learned by you in this chapter will be of great help when you engage in such activities.

QUESTIONS

1. Describe the concept of social cognition.
2. Explain the stages of social information processing.
3. Discuss the various aspects of social thought.
4. Elucidate the factors that determine which schemas to use.
5. Differentiate between schemas and heuristics.
6. Describe the relationship between cognition and emotions.

REFERENCE

Wells, G., & Gavanski, I. (1989). Mental simulation of causality. *Journal of Personality and Social Psychology*, *56*(2), 161–169.

FURTHER READINGS

For further information on social cognition, the following link can be referred to:

http://psychology.about.com/od/socialpsychology/g/social-cognition.htm

For further information on social cognition, the following books can be referred to:

Bless, H., Fiedler, K., & Strack, F. (2003). *Social cognition: How individuals construct social reality*. New York, NY: Psychology Press.

Fiske, S. T., & Taylor, S. E. (2013). *Social cognition: From brains to culture* (2nd ed.). Boston, MA: McGraw-Hill.

Gerrig, R. J., & Zimbardo, P. G. (2005). *Psychology and life*. New Delhi: Pearson Education and Dorling Kindersley Publishing Inc.

Moskowitz, G. B. (2004). *Social cognition: Understanding self and others*. New York, NY: Guilford Publications.

CHAPTER 5

Social Perception

Our life is not only determined by social situations but also by people in it. Our life becomes more and more meaningful because of the people around us, especially the people who play significant roles in our lives. Time and again, while learning human behaviour, you must have been told that human being is social in nature and individuals are interdependent. It is important to focus on social perception, as the perceptions that people have about each other will determine interpersonal relationships and behaviours.

The following example will help understand the term social perception:

A humble looking elderly woman, clad in a simple cotton sari, waited outside the office of the manager of a leading hospital. She waited for long hours, but the secretary would not allow her to meet the manager. As he was busy in a meeting with a leading industrialist who would help him construct a new wing in his hospital, the manager had no time for this woman. The manager instructed his secretary to inform the woman that he was busy and she could meet him the next week. Ultimately, he had to agree to meet the woman because she was persistent and would not go away.

As the elderly lady entered the manager's cabin, he concluded that the lady probably wanted some concession in treatment for her relative. However, when woman expressed that she would like to donate some amount for construction of a new wing that can be named after her late husband, the manager laughed in disbelief and boasted about how costly the whole affair is and that she could not afford it. He mentioned the amount the industrialist, with whom he had meeting earlier, would be paying for the new wing in the hospital.

The lady left disappointed. A couple of years later, the manager applied for a job with a new hospital that had gained immense recognition in society for its services. In the hallway, he saw the picture of the person, in whose name the hospital was started. Next to him was the picture of the wife and main financial donor of the hospital. This was the same woman that the manager had disappointed a couple of years back.

The manager, in this example, with his schemas and heuristics working overtime, had made quick but faulty inferences about the woman. He relied on the first impression and did not even bother to validate his first impression.

Social perception can be termed as an aspect of social cognition. But the term will be discussed in detail, in this chapter, so as to understand how impressions are created and how people judge each other's behaviours. Social perception can be described as a perception that mainly helps people understand other people in their social set-up. It can also be described as an area of study that focuses on impressions that we form about others and how we make inferences about other's behaviour.

Learning Objectives

After reading this chapter, you will be able to

- Explain the concept of person perception
- Describe impression and impression formation
- Discuss the term attribution
- Discuss communication with a focus on non-verbal communication

PERSON PERCEPTION

Imagine the first day of your college. There will be few classmates that you probably know. However, there will also be a lot of others whom you meet for the first time. What would your first encounter be like? You will probably use yours schemas and heuristics (that we discussed in Chapter 4) and make quick inferences about these people. Their clothing, non-verbal behaviours and the interpretation that you make of the information available at that moment will determine the way you perceive these classmates. It is possible, that some of these classmates, who created a positive impression on you, are not the way you perceived them initially. There would be others whom you labelled as less friendly, but they proved to be otherwise.

The aforementioned example is related to person perception that can be described as a process of forming an impression about others. While in social cognition we talk about cognition in a social set-up, person perception, as the name suggests, is mainly about people around us.

Person perception focuses on how impressions are created, information used while impressions are created, biases that affect the impressions and the accuracy of the impressions. In person perception, we form impressions about others. In this, people are categorised in a meaningful manner based on physical and psychological factors. We may categorise people based on their height and weight ('he is fat' or 'she is tall'). We may even categorise them as being honest, sincere, or mean and so on, based on psychological factors.

We, thus, interpret based on any observable information we get about the people. It can be their physical appearance, clothing, behaviour or even personality traits.

Some of the main sources that helps us derive information are discussed here.

1. **Physical appearance:** We frequently judge other individuals based on physical appearance, height, weight, complexion and even the dressing style. A woman wearing a sari will be perceived in a different manner compared to a woman wearing trousers. This will also depend on the attitudes of the perceiver. We are in a way prone to jump to conclusions based on the information we get on the basis of physical appearance.
2. **Verbal behaviour:** This is another source of information. We can make numerous conclusions based on what people say and how they communicate. During interview, the first impression that we try to create is definitely by dressing smartly. However, the way we speak also gives away a lot about us. Based on one's conversation, individuals can be termed as critical, approachable, friendly, reserved and so on. However, we again have to be cautious not to jump to conclusions. For example, on the first day of the college, we see a girl arguing with the office staff, we may conclude that this is one girl who is a troublemaker. Nevertheless, when you come to know later

on that the girl was in fact arguing with the staff because they were not providing suitable services to her visually impaired friend, you would see her in a different way.

3. **Actions or behaviours:** This is one source of information that we may safely rely on, as actions always speak louder than words. Thus, the behaviours of a person in varied situations provide us with information that can be used to make inferences about him/her.
4. **Non-verbal behaviour:** This includes the facial expressions, body language, posture, eye contact and gestures. The way you sit and the way you maintain eye contact is relevant, for example, during an interview.
5. **Environmental set-up or context:** An individual's behaviour can be interpreted based on his/her environmental set-up or context at that time of the behaviour.

Impressions that we derived from the aforementioned sources of information will also depend on whether they are made based on a snap judgement or systematic judgements. Snap judgements rely on less information that may not be accurate. On the other hand, systematic judgements involve investment of time in order to gather adequate information that is accurate. Systematic judgements also include attributions.

IMPRESSION AND IMPRESSION FORMATION

Impression is an important term when we talk about person perception. When we are about to appear for an interview or even a viva voce for our practicum examination, we do our best to create the right impression and this we try to display through our behaviour, both verbal and non-verbal. When we interact with others, formation of impression takes place and we all try to categorise each other. Impressions are nothing but how we organise information about a particular person. Impressions can be termed as meaningful as we are able to understand certain constant characteristics or trait in an individual. These impressions can then be utilised to not only predict an individual's behaviour in future but also understand his/her behaviour in the past.

There are three main dimensions that determine the impressions that we generate about certain personality traits (Hansen, 1984b); these dimensions are discussed here in detail.

1. **Evaluative:** This has to do with how we evaluate people. It can be in terms of good or bad. For example, interviewers may discuss about a particular candidate being good. This is also one of the most relevant of the three dimensions. When we meet a particular person for the first time, we are going to categorise him/her based on this dimension.
2. **Potency:** This mainly deals with the potentiality of the person that we are forming impression about. This can be in terms of weak or strong.
3. **Activity:** The third dimension has to do with activity, that is, whether the person is active or passive.

The information that we collect about others is combined by us in order to form general impressions about individuals. The evaluative dimension is the most important in this regard, as they have implications that are related to behaviour, when compared with other dimensions. This information about how people form impressions based on evaluative dimension can also be helpful in understanding how people use the information with regard to the other two dimensions of potency and activity.

Significant research in this context was carried out by Asch. In 1946, Asch (Barrett, 2017) carried out a study to investigate how the initial impressions of other individuals, are formed. Moreover, he suggested two main processes in this context, one of them is the additive model and the other is the configural model. The additive process, involves addition of all the trait evaluations that we carry out about a particular person. For example, if one of your friends achieve the following scores on certain traits—Friendly +3, Sincere +2, Honest +3, Jovial +1, Trustworthy +2, then as per the additive rule, the overall evaluation will be +11. In a configurable model, the individual is perceived as a configuration of various characteristics and as a psychological unit and this has an influence on how individual elements are interpreted. These models were also tested by Asch in a total of 12 studies that he carried out. In these experiments, the participants were presented with different sets of personal objectives and then based on these adjectives, they were asked to form an overall impression about the target. In the main experiment, one of the following list of adjectives was given to the participants (list as cited in Barrett, 2017, p. 152):

(a) intelligent–skilful–industrious–**warm**–determined–practical–cautious

(b) intelligent–skilful–industrious–**cold**–determined–practical–cautious

As can be noticed in the list, they differ only on the basis of the fourth word 'warm' and 'cold'.

The results indicated that this simple switch in one word changed the general impression and the description differed significantly in both the groups. Based on these experiments, Asch concluded that most of the impressions were formed based on the configurable model rather than the additive model and certain traits seem to have more influence when compared with other traits. This was apparent when he substituted the switch from 'warm to cold' to 'polite to blunt' and found the impressions to be weak in 'polite to blunt' when compared with 'warm to cold'. Thus, he further concluded that the variations in peripheral traits (polite–blunt) had less influence when compared to variations in the central traits (warm–cold).

One question that can be ask here, though, is why 'warm–cold' could be considered as central traits. A possible answer to this was given by Wishner (1960) where he indicated that central traits are those traits that display a high correlation with other traits that are assessed. It is, thus, possible to make 'polite–blunt' as central traits if impressions on scales that have high correlation with these traits are taken.

In this context, we can also discuss about implicit personality theory that states that certain traits appear to go along together, whereas others do not. For example, a warm person is also seen as approachable; thus, based on one trait, inferences are made about other traits that the person may possess. A trait that is central carries much more weight and thus has an impact on the impression of that person which does not occur with regard to a peripheral trait because one cannot draw inferences from these traits.

The study by Asch was also replicated by Harold Kelley (1950) and the results indicated that not only the evaluation of targets of others by an individual, but his/her behaviour towards them was influenced by central traits. Further, a study carried out by Zanna and Hamilton (1972) indicated that impression ratings with regard to a dimension could be changed based on the descriptions of trait, without affecting the other dimensions.

Anderson (1965, 1974) discussed that in the process of predicting the overall impression about the target, the meanings of traits on certain dimensions were averaged. The averaging rules state that 'the overall evaluation can be predicted by dividing the sum of the trait evaluations by the number of traits used in forming the overall evaluation' (Hansen, 1984, p. 28). Using the example we discussed in additive rule, the overall evaluation for the friend (with additive model evaluation of +11) in terms of averaging rule will be 2.2. According to the averaging rule, the overall impression does not become positive or negative merely by adding positive or negative traits, respectively. However, the overall impression will become favourable only when the additional trait is more positively evaluated when compared with the average evaluation of the traits that were known earlier and an overall impression will become negative only when the additional trait is more negatively evaluated when compared with the average evaluation of the traits that were known earlier. Norman Anderson felt that the averaging rules were very simple, though fundamental and, thus, he introduced another rule called the weighted averaging. Weighted averaging is a comparatively complex rule and was derived by adding two components to the averaging rule. One of these components is trait weights or weighting traits and the other is first impression. Weighting traits state that traits can also be seen as either important or having more or less weightage from the point of view of the perceiver, besides them being negative or positive. There can be certain traits that we may feel are more important than others. Some of us may value family orientation as one of the most important traits in our life partner, others may value trustworthiness as more important than other traits in a life partner. Thus, traits do carry some weightage for the perceiver. With reference to first impression, many of us are influenced to a greater extent by the first set of information we receive about a particular person. Further, the initial information that is received with regard to a person has a stronger impact (when compared with later information) on the impression that one forms about a particular person and the way the later information is interpreted will also depend on the first information that is received. Thus, first impression is an important component in the context of averaging rules. And on the basis of trait weights and first impressions, the weighted averaging rule can be employed to make accurate predictions with regard to how traits are combined in order to form an overall impression about an individual.

Impressions are also to a greater extent influenced by social cognition. Impressions are influenced by certain frameworks that are mental representations and termed as schemas that we discussed in the previous chapter.

The impression formation process can be explained with the help of two main models, the dual processing model by Bewer and the continuum model by Fiske and Neuberg. Both the models state that impression formation constitutes of two processes that are distinct, namely, categorisation and individuation. According to the dual processing model, both processes are utilised while deriving impressions about others. This shift in the perception, whether it is based on categorisation or individuation, depends on whether the conditions are favourable or unfavourable to either of the processes.

On the other hand the continuum model provides the concept of a continuum with categorisation at one end and individuation at the other. Thus, individuals may be perceived as belonging to a certain group or they may be perceived as not possessing the membership of certain category (Crisp & Turner, 2010). According to the continuum model, in the process of information processing, attempts are made by an individual to categorise the target individual, but when this is not possible and a fit between the target individual and the category is not achieved, then there is a shift towards individuation.

The shift from categorisation to individuation discussed earlier can be termed as de-categorisation, which denotes that the target individual will now be perceived as an individual rather than as member of a certain group, thus leading to removal of bias based on category and decrease in stereotype.

It is possible for us to measure impressions by using techniques like semantic differential. In semantic differential, individuals are asked to categorise certain objects, concepts or even people based on a seven-point scale. Example of a semantic differential is as given here; you can rate one of your friends on the following dimensions:

Friendly	___ ___ ___ ___ ___ ___ ___	Unfriendly
Honest	___ ___ ___ ___ ___ ___ ___	Dishonest
Hard-working	___ ___ ___ ___ ___ ___ ___	Lazy
Jovial	___ ___ ___ ___ ___ ___ ___	Serious
Strong	___ ___ ___ ___ ___ ___ ___	Weak

Thus, you can evaluate your friend by placing a mark on each scale provided in the above example.

ATTRIBUTION

What possibly could be the reason for Sunil to leave his job with a leading multinational corporation (MNC) and go back to his native village?

What could be the reason behind Reshmi walking out of her marriage and moving out of her comfortable home and relationship?

What could be the reason behind the fight between Jai and Jagdeesh?

Why was Deepa screaming at the person on the street?

Individuals are often curious to know about the causes and reasons behind behaviours of people. Attributions can be described as the interpretations or inferences that we make about the causes behind behaviour of others, our own behaviour and also events. It can also be described as a process through which information is sought by us. Though more formally it can be described as effort of an individual to understand the reasons or causes behind behaviour of other individuals and, in certain cases, also one's own behaviour (Baron & Byrne, 1995). For example, when your friend seems to be really upset, you may start attributing his/her behaviour. You may think he/she had fight with his/her parents or siblings, or someone said something bad to him/her and so on.

Heider significantly contributed to the field of attribution. He proposed that not only psychologists but all human beings involve in understanding behaviour of other individuals and in order to make these prediction, some basic and general theory of human behaviour is needed, that he referred to as 'naive psychology'. He stated that the need to develop a clear understanding and the need to have a control over the environment are two main motives in any individual and one way in which these motives can be achieved is the ability to predict behaviour of other individuals (Sears et al., 1991). One of the major driving forces while making social inferences is attribution of causality as that assists in making the world more meaningful and contributes to reducing the unpredictability (Crisp & Turner, 2010).

Dimensions of Causality

Various dimensions of causality are discussed in detail here.

- **Locus of attribution:** Locus of attribution can be internal or external. Internal attributions highlight the role of personal characteristics, traits, abilities and feelings of an individual that determine behaviour. On the other hand, external attribution focuses on the external factors such as the demands and constraints in the situation or environment (Weiten et al., 2012). Examples of internal attribution include personality, health, moods, abilities, efforts put in by the individuals and so on and examples of external attribution include pressures from significant others, money, luck, nature of the context and so on.

  Thus in case of internal attribution the locus of attribution is internal and in case of external attribution, the locus of attribution is external. For example, if a student fails in an examination and the failure is attributed to his/her not studying hard enough, this can be termed as internal attribution and if he/she attributes the failure to strict or unfair evaluation by the examiner, then this can be termed as external attribution.

- **Stability and instability:** Attributions can also be categorised based on stability and controllability (discussed next) of the inferences made by the individuals. Stability can be described as the extent to which the causes are termed as being comparatively stable and permanent as opposed to being unstable, temporary and fluctuating (Crisp & Turner, 2010). Thus, a cause could be a comparatively permanent aspect of an external environment or internal characteristics of an individual. For example, abilities of an individual are relatively permanent; similarly, in external environment, rules and regulations are comparatively permanent. On the other hand, there could also be certain causes, whether related to the external environment or internal dispositions of an individual that are unstable. For example, weather (external environment) is not permanent and can change. Similarly, effort and mood (internal characteristics) are not constant and may change. Thus, causes could fall in four quadrants, internal and stable (example, ability), internal and unstable (example, effort), external and stable (example, rules of a game) and external and unstable (example, weather).
- **Controllability:** Controllability can be described as the degree to which others influence the causes as opposed to degree to which these causes are random or cannot be controlled. For example, efforts put in by an individual are under control of that individual, but the difficulty of the task assigned to him/her is not under his/her control. Controllability can be perceived in accordance with the locus of attribution and stability and instability of the inferences.

Theories of Attribution

The theories of attribution highlight how the conclusions are reached by a person and what are the thought processes involved in it.

- **Correspondent inference theory:** This theory was proposed by Jones and Davis (1965) and according to this theory, when social inferences are made by an individual, the stable personality characteristics determine the behaviours of that individual. The preference is given to the internal characteristics rather than external or situational attributions. This holds true also because the internal, dispositional attributions are perceived as more stable when compared to those that are situational or external. Three main types of information are processed while assessing the correspondence between behaviour and personality or while arriving at correspondence inference; these are social desirability, choice (intentional or not) and non-common effect. Social desirability information denotes whether the behaviour that is observed conforms to the social norms. An individual who counters social norms (behaviour that is socially undesirable) is more likely to display behaviour that corresponds to an underlying personality when compared to a person who conforms to the social norms. The second type of information has to do with choice, that is, whether the behaviour that is observed is chosen freely or not. A behaviour that is chosen freely is more likely to be an outcome of an underlying personality when compared to behaviour that was induced or was not freely chosen. Yet another type of information that is important in this context is the non-common effects principle. A behaviour can be termed as having a non-common effect when it has consequences that are unique. A unique behaviour is more likely to be as a result of internal, dispositional attributes (Crisp & Turner, 2010).
- **The co-variance model:** This model was proposed by Harold Kelley in 1967 in which the covariation denotes a tendency to seek an association between certain cause and certain effect with reference to different situations (Sears et al., 1991). Thus, if a certain cause appears to be

associated with certain effect in different conditions and if the effect does not occur when that cause is absent, then the effect is attributed to that cause. Thus, there is a covariation between the cause and the effect. For example, if Ishan gets nervous before his dance performance but is not otherwise nervous in his day-to-day life, could we term Ishan as inherently nervous? Apparently no. The effect that is nervousness in this case will be attributed to the cause, that is, dance performance. And in the absence of dance performance, Ishan will not display any nervousness.

This is similar to what is done by scientists where they study causality based on how it is associated with the effect in different conditions of the experiment. This model is also called as 'naive scientist model'.

According to Kelly, three types of information are used while making causal attributions and attention is paid to whether the effect is same across the stimulus object, actors (individuals) and contexts (Sears et al., 1991). This is based on whether the behaviour is specific to a certain stimulus object or not, whether the behaviour is specific to a certain actor (individual) or not and whether the behaviour is specific to a certain situation or not. The three types of information that are used in order to make causal attributions are discussed as follows:

1. *Distinctiveness information*. This is with reference to the extent to which the individual displays certain behaviour with a particular stimulus object and not other objects. For example, a professor is critical only of presentations made by a certain student, thus indicating that the distinctiveness is high. However, if the professor is always critical, then the distinctiveness of the behaviour is low.
2. *Consensus information*. This is with reference to the extent to which other individuals display the same behaviour in this situations. For example, if other professors in this particular educational institute are also critical when presentations are made by this student, then consensus is high and if only one professor is critical, then consensus is low.
3. *Consistency information*. This is with reference to the extent to which the individuals display the same behaviour during other situations and during other times. For example, if the professor is always critical when this student is presenting, the consistency is high and, if the professor is not always critical, then the consistency is low.

Thus, it can be said that attributional decisions are made by individuals based on this model when all the information and time to make the decision is provided to them. However, individuals may not pay equal attention to the information provided to them and they may focus more on one aspect of the information rather than the other aspects. In certain cases, it is also possible that certain information is missing, but individuals are still able to take attributional decisions. It indicates that there are other ways in which judgements such as these are made by individuals (Crisp & Turner, 2010).

Attributional Biases

Biases could crop in when attributions are made by individuals because not all attributions are made in a systematic and complex manner as stated by certain models. In addition, most often social judgements are made through shortcuts rather than through complex processes. Thus, there could be certain attributional biases that we make on regular basis.

- **Fundamental attribution bias:** Individuals may display a general tendency to make attributions that are based on internal factors rather than external factors and this is termed as fundamental attribution bias. Ross, Amabile and Steinmetz (1977) carried out a study (two experiments) in a laboratory set-up, where individuals were assigned a role of either questioner or contestant in a game that was similar to a game called 'Jeopardy'. The questioners were instructed to think of questions based on general knowledge that were answerable as well as challenging and, thus, they had an advantage as they had framed the questions, to which they already knew the answers. The contestants, on the other hand, had no information about the sort of questions that will be asked and thus were at a disadvantage. As the questioners already knew the answers and the contestants did not, it was clear that the judgements could not be made based on the intelligence of the questioners or the contestants. The people watching the game were also made aware about this. The results though indicated that the people who were watching the game, despite being aware of the roles assigned to the questioners and contestants, questioners were termed as having higher intelligence and the contestants were termed as having lower intelligence. Another study carried out by Riggio and Garcia (2009) indicated that the students who were asked to read a passage about a person's bad day, attributed the bad day to internal factors without any consideration to the external factors that could have contributed to the person having a bad day. Further, to study the effect or priming, the students in another group were made to watch a video that demonstrated the potential of social influences and environmental factors in determining an individual's behaviour, and they were then asked to read the same passage that was given to the earlier group of students. The students in this other group attributed the bad day to situational factors. The fundamental attribution bias is not universal and cross-cultural differences have been observed (Crisp & Turner, 2010).

- **Actor–observer bias:** This can be described as a tendency to attribute one's own behaviour to external factors and the behaviour of others to internal factors. For example, if a person himself/herself fails in an examination attributes the failure is attributed to tough or unfair evaluation but if some other person fails in an examination, the failure is attributed to lack of effort on the part of that person. In a study carried to by Storms (1973), two observer participants looked at two actor participants who engaged in a conversation that was vague and unstructured. A questionnaire was then used to measure the attributions (internal or external) by actors of their own behaviour. The observers were also asked to attribute the behaviour of the actors that they were matched with. In the experimental condition, the actors and the observers got to see the videotapes of the conversation and, in control condition, no such tape was shown. The results indicated that the actors were more likely to attribute their behaviour to external or situational factors, whereas observers were more likely to explain the behaviours of actors as a result of dispositional factors.
- **Self-serving attributions:** This states that our success is attributed to internal factors and failures are attributed to external factors. For example, an individual will attribute his/her promotion at work to his/her hard work and efforts and his/her failure to get a promotion is attributed to the external factors like bad luck.

In this context we can also discuss about intergroup attributions, that are similar to self-serving attributions and can also be termed as group-serving attributions (Crisp and Turner, 2010). It is mainly seen at group level, where the success of one's own group is attributed to internal factors and failures are attributed to external factors. For example, if the Indian cricket team wins, we attribute the success of the team to hard work put in by the players. However, if they lose, their loss is attributed to bad pitch. This can cultivate prejudice and discrimination in society, as positive behaviour by a certain social group is attributed to external factors and negative behaviour is attributed to internal factors.

NON-VERBAL COMMUNICATION

Muthhu wanted to inform his boss about the leave he would be taking the next day due to a family function at home. He arrived early to his office and waited for his boss so that he can seek permission of the Boss. However, as his Boss arrived, he could notice that she was in a very bad mood; she swiftly moved to her cabin without wishing anyone and closed the door of her office with a bang. Mutthu knew that this was not the right time to ask the Boss about his leave.

Various temporary factors or causes such as emotions, moods, fatigue, illness and so on can have an impact on our social behaviours and thoughts. For example, people are more likely to be favourable towards others when they are in a good mood than when in a bad mood. However, a valid question in this context would be: How do we gather knowledge about these temporary factors? How do we know whether an individual is in a right mood or is experiencing joy or anger? One way in which such a piece of information can be obtained is by asking directly, but most often individuals are not willing to bring forth their internal feelings and reactions in a social domain, and, therefore, this approach (i.e., asking directly) may not be effective. In such a situation, one can rely on, or pay close attention to, the non-verbal behaviour displayed by the individual, which can give relevant information about the inner feelings and reactions of that individual.

Going back to the aforementioned example, how did Muthhu know that his boss was in a bad mood—apparently from the non-verbal behaviour displayed by his boss.

Non-verbal behaviour constitutes facial expressions, gestures, use of touch, tone of voice, postures, eye contact and other actions that are expressive. Based on the changes in these, one can gather information about the inner feelings and emotions of a person. Non-verbal behaviours are also difficult to control and conceal and therefore they may provide valuable information. The meanings that are conveyed by the non-verbal behaviours and the effort that are put in by individuals in interpreting them is termed as non-verbal communication. Non-verbal communication can be defined as 'the way in which people communicate, intentionally or unintentionally, without words' (Aronson et al., 2014, p. 92).

- **Facial expressions:** Facial expressions can be termed as a good source to learn about the mood and feelings of an individual. For example, a good news will bring a smile to one's face and that can be an indication that the person is happy. Cicero, a roman orator, had the following to say about face, 'The face is the image of the soul', and contemporary research has also been pointing in the same direction (Baron & Byrne, 1995). There are six main emotions that can be clearly seen on a face, anger, fear, sadness, disgust, happiness and surprise and these appear from quite an early age in life, though there could also be combinations of these emotions and an individual could reflect anger and disgust at the same time and the reactions may also vary in the degree of their strength. Though it would be interesting to note whether all emotions as felt by an individual gets reflected on the face or are they able to regulate these emotions and, also, what is the role played by culture in this context. In this context, it can be said that, a connection does exists between the emotions, experiences and facial expressions. As stated by Baron and Byrne (1995, p. 45), 'When individuals experience various emotions, electrical activity in specific facial muscles increases and when they move these muscles into the patterns of specific facial expressions, they show distinctive shifts in physiological reactions and report experiencing the emotions in question'.

  The universality of facial expressions was first suggested by Darwin in 1872. The expression of emotions was studied by him in an attempt to support his theory of emotions (Ekman, 1977).

Research carried out by Ekman, Friesen and Ellsworth (1972) indicated that culture did have an influence on facial expressions. Facial expressions were also found to be culture-specific and as each culture had its own verbal language, they also had a language with regard to facial expressions (Matsumoto & Hwang, 2011). Study by Fridlund (1992) indicated that context-specific social motives determine facial expressions of emotions. Ekman (1993) carried out a cross-cultural study on facial expressions and the study indicated that different aspects related to expressions were found to be universal as well as specific to culture.

In a study carried out by Levenson, Ekman and Friensen (1990), a total of four experiments were conducted to study voluntarily produced emotional facial configurations and their association with differentiated patterns of autonomic activity, and if there is any association, how these are mediated. In the experiments, the participants were provided with muscle-by-muscle instructions as well as coaching to produce facial configurations of emotions such as anger, disgust, fear, happiness, sadness and surprise. There was also monitoring of heart rate, skin conductance, finger temperature and somatic activity as they produced the facial configurations. The findings of the study revealed that significant levels of subjective experience of associated emotions were produced by voluntary facial activity. Further, the autonomic distinctions among emotions were found that were negative as well as between emotions that were negative and emotions that were positive. Consistency was observed in the autonomic distinctions among emotions between the data obtained from group and individual participants. Further, when voluntary facial configurations very closely resembled actual emotional expressions, the autonomic distinctions among emotions were stronger. They were also stronger when the participants reported experience of associated emotion. The results also showed that the capacity with regard to voluntary facial activity in generation of emotion-specific autonomic activity did not require the participants to see facial expressions either in a mirror or on the experimenter's face and it could not be explained by variance in the difficulty of making expressions or variance in the concomitant somatic activity.

Studies have also indicated that the simple geometric shapes that underlie facial expressions can play a role in conveying meaning of emotions. This is especially true with regard to a downward pointing 'V' that resembles an expression of anger. A study carried out by Larson, Aronoff and Stearns (2007) indicated that downward pointing 'V' was detected faster and also more accurately when compared with other shapes that were identical and pointed upwards.

- **Body language:** This is yet another aspect of non-verbal communication. In a lecture, the speaker can easily identify the people who are really interested in the lecture and those who are not. This can be done by simply observing the body language of the people. Body language includes, gestures, postures and even movements and through these, information can be generated about the people. Studies have also been carried out on link between emotions and body movement. In a study carried out by Harrigan et al. (1991), the participants had to watch a videotape that had one person interviewing another person. The person who was being interviewed either displayed no body movements (i.e., self-touching) or displayed one of the various patterns of hand activities that included one hand touching the other hand, touching their nose or touching the arm. The participants who observed these videotapes had to rate the persons who were interviewed. The results showed that the ratings were affected by the specific movements of hand. The person who was interviewed was also termed as less expressive when no movement was involved and more expressive when he/she touched one's own nose.

  In a study carried out by Aronoff, Woike and Hyman (1992), the results indicated that warmth was conveyed by body patterns that were round and threat by body patterns that were diagonal and angular. Thus, indicating that larger patterns of body movement also provide information in an attempt to understand social behaviour of individuals. In another study carried out by Montepare et al. (1999), the researchers investigated the use of body movements and gestures as cues to emotions in younger and older adults. The study was carried out on 82 younger and older adults and was carried out in two parts. In the first part of the study, the participants were made to watch videotapes of young adult actors who portrayed emotional situations and the participants had to identify the emotions that were depicted in the videotape. In each of these videotapes, the faces of the actors were electronically blurred and they were silent. This was done in order to facilitate the isolation of body cues with regard to emotions. The results indicated that both young and older adult participants displayed accuracy in emotion identification, although the older adult participants made overall more errors when compared with the younger adult participants, especially with regard to emotions that were negative. In the second part of the study, the participants had to rate the display in the videotapes with the help of a scale that reflected various body movement dimensions, such as form, tempo and so on. The results of this study indicated that the ratings provided by both the group of participants were similar. The results also provided information about the specific body cues related to emotions. The errors made by the older adult participants were found to be linked with the reactions to exaggerated or ambiguous body cues.

Thus, in the context of body language, gestures, postures, emblems and even gait of the person can provide relevant information about the social behaviour of a person.

- **Eye contact:** This is another very relevant aspect of non-verbal communication. Eyes can also reveal significant information about feelings of an individual. The way in which the eye contact is maintained, or not maintained, provides us relevant information about the person. Studies have also indicated that identification and interpretation of eye gaze plays a significant role in development of social cognition as well as in social interaction (Macrae et al., 2002). However, this could also vary in different cultures. In a study carried out by Uono and Hietanen (2015) on eye contact perception in the West and East, the Finnish and Japanese participants were asked to indicate whether the Finnish and Japanese neutral faces that displayed various gaze directions were looking at them or not. The results indicated that the cultural differences did exist in the way eye contacts were perceived.
- **Touching:** Touching is interpreted in different manners based on who does the touching. An individual would not mind a significant person, such as a parent or friend, touching him/her but would react against a touch by a stranger; however, what if the stranger is a doctor, in which case the touching may be permitted. Further, various other factors may also play a role here, such as the gender of the person, age, the context and so on. Thus, touch can mean different things based on these factors and based on the way touch is perceived, the reaction will be negative or positive. The reaction will be positive when the touch is considered as acceptable and vice versa. Culture also plays an important role here, as there could be cultural differences in the way in which the touch is perceived.

With reference to gender difference in touch, a study was carried out by Hall and Veccia (1990). The study was carried out on 4,500 pairs of individuals that were judged to be together and were above 14 years of age. The participants were observed in public spaces (20 different locations). The results indicated that the frequency with which each sex touched the other was equal (across all ages and initiating body parts). However, among younger pairs, the male touching female prevailed, whereas amongst older pairs, female touching male prevailed. With reference to touches with hand, males touched females more and females touched males less. Further, it was found that females were more likely to use 'arms linked' and males were more likely to use 'arms around' and this was observed across all ages. Further, with reference to touching pattern, non-hand touches were used more by females and hand touches were used more by males.

SUMMARY

Social perception plays an important role in understanding social behaviour. It can be described as a perception that mainly helps people understand other people in their social set-up. It can also be described as an area of study that focuses on impressions that we form about others and how we make inferences about other's behaviour. The chapter first focused on person perception, which deals with how impressions are created, information used while impressions are created, biases that affect the impressions and the accuracy of the impressions. Some important sources that help us derive information in this context are physical appearance, verbal behaviour, actions or behaviours, non-verbal behaviour and environmental set-up and context. Further, the chapter also discussed impression and impression formation, with a focus on experiment carried out by Asch. The concept of attribution was then explained. Attributions can be described as the interpretations or inferences that we make about the causes behind behaviour of others, our own behaviour and also events. The dimensions of causality, namely, locus of attribution, stability and instability and controllability were also discussed. With regard to theories of attribution, the correspondent inference theory and the co-variance model were explained in detail. The attribution biases including fundamental attribution bias, actor-observer bias and self-serving attributions were also described. Lastly, non-verbal communication that plays a significant role in understanding social behaviour was also highlighted, including discussions on facial expressions, body language, eye contact and touch.

QUESTIONS

1. Explain the concept of person perception and discuss the main sources that helps derive information.
2. Discuss impression and impression formation.
3. Elucidate attribution and describe the dimensions of causality.
4. Discuss the theories of attribution.
5. Explain attribution bias with suitable examples.
6. Describe non-verbal communication with a focus on facial expressions and eye contact.

REFERENCES

Anderson, N. H. (1965). Primacy effects in personality impression formation using a generalized order effect paradigm. *Journal of Personality and Social Psychology*, 2(1), 1–9. Retrieved from http://dx.doi.org/10.1037/h0021966

Anderson, N. H. (1974). Cognitive algebra: Integration theory applied to social attribution. In L. Berkowitz (Ed.), *Advances in experimental social psychology* (Vol. 7). New York, NY: Academic Press.

Ekman, P. (1977). Facial expression. In A. Siegman & S. Feldstein (Eds.). *Nonverbal behaviour and communication*. New Jersey: Lawrence Erlbaum Association. Retrieved from https://www.paulekman.com/wp-content/uploads/2013/07/Facial-Expression.pdf

Jones, E. E. & Davis, K. E. (1965). From acts to dispositions: The attribution process in person perception. In L. Berkowitz (Ed.), *Advances in experimental social psychology* (Vol. 2). New York, NY: Academic Press.

FURTHER READINGS

For more information on culture and facial expressions, following article can be read:

Rachael, E. J. (2013). Culture and facial expressions of emotion. *Visual Cognition,* 21, 1248–1286. http://dx.doi.org/10.1080/13506285.2013.835367

For culture and non-verbal behaviour, the following can be referred to:

Matsumoto, D. (2006). Culture and nonverbal behavior. In Manusov, V., & Patterson, M. (Eds.), *Handbook of nonverbal communication* (pp. 219–235). Thousand Oaks, CA: SAGE Publications.

CHAPTER 6

Interpersonal Attraction

Naina was born and brought up in a small town in Andhra Pradesh and shifting to Mumbai was a major transit for her. She was staying in a working women's hostel and as she came back from her first day at work, she met this girl from Gujarat. On that day, she had no idea that this girl would become one of her best buddies.

Sabina and Harshal lived in the same locality and have known each other since childhood. As they grew up, they fell in love with each other and decided to engage in a committed relationship.

Reema met Ashok on a social networking site. As their relationship developed further, they decided to meet. Though the day Reema met Ashok, she felt that he was much older than she imagined and was not very comfortable while interacting with him, unlike what she felt while interacting with him online.

Rahul and Anjali have been married for four years now but due to their personality differences, they have not been able to adjust with each other. So they mutually decided to get a divorce.

These are some of the examples related to relationships that exist between the people, that also raise questions with regard to why we like or love someone or why someone likes or dislikes us? What are the consequences of this liking or disliking? What are its influences? And so on.

Interpersonal attraction covers a wide range of issues right from attraction, friendship to intimate relationship. The first example denotes how often friendships develop with total strangers. The second example gives a hint about proximity and role it plays in attraction and development of close relationship. The third example highlights online attraction and hints at online deception. The last example is that of a married couple in close relationship that have now decided to dissolve the relationship. All these are related to the topics that will be covered in this chapter.

Learning Objectives

After reading this chapter, you will be able to

- ❐ Describe the concepts of affiliation and interpersonal attraction
- ❐ Discuss the theories of attraction
- ❐ Explain the determinants of attraction with focus on similarity and proximity

- ❐ Discuss online attractions
- ❐ Describe friendship and close relationships
- ❐ Explain homosexual couples and relationships
- ❐ Elucidate troubled relationship and breakups

AFFILIATION

As is mentioned time and again, human beings are social in nature, and thus, tendency to affiliate is present in them in high degree. Buunk (2001, p. 372) defined affiliation as 'the tendency to seek out the company of others, irrespective of the feelings towards others'. Affiliation can be explained as the desire of an individual to be with others, and this is seen even in infants. This need for affiliation becomes more and more complex as the person grows up, and he/she may affiliate with others for various reasons such as to enjoy, gain power, feel intimate and so on. Lack of affiliation, thus, can have a long-term negative impact on individuals.

Why do we seek affiliation can be explained in more than one way. It can be stated here that seeking affiliation and forming close relationships is a trait that is inherited, aids in survival and reproduction, and creates a support system that can be relied upon when in need. Affiliation can also be attributed to the evolutionary development of human beings, where the survival chance was higher when with others, especially while facing dangers from different predators.

The privacy regulation theory can be discussed here. The privacy regulation theory states that two main principles, dialectic and optimisation, determine the fluctuations that occur over a period of time in one's ideal level of privacy. The dialectic principle is related to the need for privacy (as opposed to affiliation) in which one can be open or closed with others during a certain period of time. On the other hand, in optimisation principal, an attempt is made in which the desired and actual levels of contact with others are aligned. Thus, there is a regulation so that the person does not feel too lonely or too crowded. These feeling of loneliness or crowdedness experienced by a person will fluctuate based on the level of contact that is desired by the person at a given point of time.

Yet another model that can help explain affiliation is a social affiliation model, with its focus on homeostasis. The principle of homeostasis states that the level of contact with others is controlled by persons in order to keep it balanced and closer to the level of contact desired by them. In a study carried out by O'Conner and Rosenblood (1996), it was observed that the interaction that was carried out by the participants of the study were at the levels desired by them, thus also indicating effective regulation of need for affiliation (Crisp & Turner, 2010).

Three main motives can be attributed to why individuals seek affiliation, especially under stressful conditions; they are discussed here.

1. **Social comparison:** Social comparison as a motive to seek affiliation can be explained with the help of social comparison theory. Social comparison theory can be used to explain why individuals prefer to affiliate. According to this theory, 'individuals assess their attitudes, abilities and emotions by comparing themselves with similar others and that they do so especially when they are uncertain about themselves' (Buunk, 2001, p. 374). Thus, seeking affiliation during stressful conditions can be explained as providing an opportunity for the individual to carry out

a comparison between his/her response and that of others so as to determine whether the feelings in the given situation are appropriate or not.

2. **Reduction of anxiety:** Individuals, in a stressful situation, may affiliate with others because they can express their sympathy with others in similar situations and also receive support, comfort and reassurance from them. This tendency has been explained by attachment theory that mainly focuses on the attachment during childhood, between the mother (or caregiver) and the infant, which determines the ability to engage in relationships during adulthood that are stable and intimate in nature.

   Attachment during childhood serves two main function: It provides a sense of security and facilitates obtaining information about the environment. There are three main styles of attachment.

   - **Secure attachment style:** This style develops when the parent or the caregiver is available to the child when in distress and is responsive to the needs of the child. Individuals with this style of attachment perceive others as supportive, dependable and are willing to affiliate with others.
   - **Avoidant attachment style:** As opposed to secure attachment style, this style develops when the parent or the caregiver is not available to the child when in distress and is unresponsive to the needs of the child. Individuals with this attachment style tend to perceive others as not trustworthy and may distance themselves from others.
   - **Anxious/ambivalent attachment style:** This attachment style develops when the parent or the caregiver is not consistent with regard to how he/she responds to the needs of the child. Sometimes he/she is responsive and available but sometimes he/she is not. This may lead to the individual to have desire to be with others but also have a fear that they may be rejected or that they may not get any response to their desire.

   Based on the avoidant attachment style and the anxious attachment style, there are three more attachment styles that need to be discussed. Persons who have high anxiety attachment and low avoidant attachment can be termed as having a preoccupied attachment style. Such persons have low self-esteem although they perceive others positively. Such persons may worry that they may not be loved by others because they are not good enough. There is also dismissive-avoidance attachment, denoting persons who are low on anxiety attachment and high on avoidance attachment. Such persons display high self-esteem but may have trust issues and thus are not comfortable with intimate relationships. Lastly, there is also the fearful-avoidant attachment style, denoting persons who are high on both anxious attachment and avoidant attachment. Such persons have low self-esteem and also have trust issues. They also perceive others negatively which further confirms their distrust in others.

   Thus, attachment styles determine whether a person may prefer to affiliate with others and that, in turn, leads to individuals seeking affiliation in order to reduce their anxieties when in stress-provoking situations. Further, individuals with the secure attachment style will easily seek affiliation in order to reduce anxiety in stress-provoking situations when compared with individuals having the other two attachment styles.

   Although it is also possible that increased anxiety leads to decreased desire for affiliation as the individuals may feel that affiliating with others and sharing their anxieties may further aggravate it (Buunk, 2001).

3. **To seek information:** Affiliation can also be attributed to the motive of seeking information. As stated by Shaver and Klinnert (1989), children through their attachment with their parents are

able to obtain information regarding any threat during certain situations. This is applicable to adults as well; when in threatening situations, they may seek affiliation with others so as to obtain information regarding the threat and its implications.

Negative Effects of Lack of Affiliation

It was briefly mentioned before that the lack of affiliation can have long-term consequences on the individual. The lack of affiliation can negatively affect the health of an individual. In a study carried out by Berkman and Syme (1979), mortality was linked with lack of affiliation. It is also possible that some individuals are not able to fulfil the desire or need to affiliate (Buunk, 2001). This can give rise to problems such as social anxiety and feelings of loneliness. When the desire or need to affiliate is not fulfilled, the person may develop social anxiety and, thus, the person may avoid social interactions and social set-ups. Though, in general, people do experience some sort of social anxiety in their lives, the people who have been deprived from affiliation may actually develop chronic social anxiety, which will interfere with their day-to-day functioning, where they may start stammering or stuttering while speaking. Such persons not only expect rejection from others but are also more attentive to negative feedback from others. This affects their behaviour and they may display nervous mannerisms, anxiety and such behaviours that may truly lead to attracting negative feedback (self-fulfilling prophecy). As stated by the two-factor theory of emotion proposed by Schachter, when an individual experiences anxiety in a social set-up, he/she may assume that others are evaluating him/her negatively, and this is seen as a factor that leads to him/her experiencing anxiety.

Lack of affiliation can also give rise to loneliness in an individual. Loneliness can be described as 'a complex affective response stemming from felt deficits in the number and nature of one's social relationships' (Buunk, 2001, p. 380). Loneliness can also be attributed to quality of relationship rather than quantity (Williams & Solano, 1983). One's interpretation and reaction to loneliness will determine whether it will be for a temporary period of time or will grow to become chronic. As described by Shaver and Runinstein (1980), loneliness can also be described in terms of four groups of feelings (Buunk, 2001).

- **Desperation:** denoting feelings of helplessness, desperation, fear and anxiety, and rejection.
- **Depression:** denoted by feeling related to depression, sadness, nothingness, meaninglessness and estrangement.
- **Impatient boredom:** denoted by feelings of uneasiness, and lack of concentration and patience.
- **Self-deprecation:** denoted by feelings of being unattractive and lack of security.

Loneliness can also be emotional as a result of lack of intimate relationship with partner or it could be social, which indicates lack of supportive friends or any supportive network (Buunk, 2001). Emotional loneliness can occur even when social loneliness is not experienced.

WHAT IS INTERPERSONAL ATTRACTION?

In simple terms, interpersonal attraction can be described as attitude towards others. Thus, if you like someone, you have a positive attitude towards them and if you dislike them, you have a negative attitude towards them. While affiliation has to do with a desire to be with others, interpersonal attraction is aimed at interacting with others. This also serves as a basis of how relationships such as friendship and other intimate relationships develop. The term attraction will become clearer as we further discuss its principles.

Principles of Attraction

There are two main principles of attraction.

1. **Association:** This term has been borrowed from classical conditioning which states that we tend to like persons and have positive attitude towards people whom we associate with positive experiences and vice versa. For example, if an individual is criticised by his/her boss in front of a colleague, this individual will dislike the colleague as he/she associates this colleague with criticism by the boss (negative experience). This will also be reflected under the theories of attraction that will be discussed in the next section. A study on the principal of association was carried out by May and Hamilton in 1980 (Sears et al., 1991). The objective of the study was to investigate the effect of background, pleasant and unpleasant on interpersonal attraction. The participants were college-going females. The researchers first identified the music that college-going females in general liked and disliked. The participants were asked to rate the photographs of male strangers while listening to music they liked, while listening to music they did not like and without any music. The results indicated that these male strangers were rated unfavourably when they were associated with music that they disliked and vice versa. Thus, it can be said that liking or disliking for someone can be influenced by conditioned emotional response (Sears et al., 1991).
2. **Reinforcement**: Reinforcement is a term that comes from learning theories and finds its application in interpersonal attraction. We tend to like persons who reward us or who evaluate us positively. This will be discussed in the theories of attraction that are predominantly based on reinforcement. Why people like people who reward them in some way or the other can be explained with the help of social exchange theory, which focuses on costs and benefits. Thus, when we see that our interaction with a person is beneficial and there are negligible costs, we tend to like them and vice versa. Further, there is also a comparison between the benefits that we get from different persons.

Gender difference also exists in attraction. One of the explanations in this context can be found in parental investment theory, which states that strategies used by males and females to attract vary mainly because of reasons related to the evolution. Women, in a way, have more to invest when it comes to reproduction, as they go through the process of pregnancy, childbirth and childcare; thus, they are more careful while selecting a partner. Also, because of the same reason, they are also more contained and cautious in communication of attraction as otherwise it can hamper their worth and status as a potential partner.

THEORIES OF ATTRACTION

Most of the theories related to attraction are based on reinforcement theories, though there are differences in how these theories are conceptualised (Sigall, 1984).

Reinforcement Model

Bernice Lott and Albert Lott proposed a reinforcement model, which states that the reason behind interpersonal attraction is that when a person is rewarded in the presence of another person, the one who was rewarded will develop liking for this another person. For example, if a manager praises an employee in front of another manager, the employee will develop liking for the other manager as well. This can also be termed as an application of secondary reinforcement. A study was carried out by Griffitt and Guay (1969) in which the participants were evaluated for their creativity by a person in the presence of some other person. When the evaluation was positive, the person being evaluated expressed liking for both the person who evaluated them and the person who was just present during the evaluation. On the other hand, when the evaluation was negative, the evaluator and the person who was present during the evaluation were both disliked by the participants. Further, no difference was found between the attraction felt by the participants towards both the persons, although only one of them provided the reinforcement in terms of the evaluation with regard to creativity of the participants.

Reinforcement-affect Model

This theory was proposed by Donn Byrne and Gerald Clore. Though in a way similar to the model proposed by Lott and Lott, discussed previously, this model focuses on feelings. The principles of this model are as follows:

- Stimuli can be identified by individuals as being rewarding or punishing, and the rewarding stimuli are sought and punishing stimuli are avoided by the individuals.
- Positive feelings are triggered as a result of rewarding stimuli, whereas negative feelings are triggered by the punishing stimuli.
- The feelings triggered by the stimuli determine how the stimuli are evaluated. Thus, the evaluation will be positive if it triggers positive feelings and vice versa.
- Stimuli that are neutral but are related to reward will lead to positive feelings. Whereas neutral stimuli that are related to punishment will lead to negative feelings. Thus, a person will be liked or disliked based on his/her association with the feeling (or affect) that is positive or negative.

Exchange Theory

Interpersonal attraction can also be explained with the help of instrumental conditioning. Exchange theories can be discussed in this context that focus on costs and benefits. Although there are a number of exchange theories, the one that has been discussed here is the one proposed by John Thibaut and Harold Kelly. When we discuss about interpersonal attraction, there are necessarily two persons involved, who are both involved in costs and benefits analysis with regard to the interaction. Thus, when two persons are interacting with each other, each of them will be involved in costs and benefits analysis of this interaction. Rewards and costs are seen from a broader perspective, including monetary reward, boost in self-esteem to costs such as boredom, monetary loss and so on.

In this context, the comparison level can be discussed, which is related to the expectancy that people have with regard to the interaction or relationship. This comparison level is determined by similar relationships, past experiences and personal factors (Sigall, 1984). And whether another person is liked or not will depend on whether the rewards that are obtained from this relationship fall below the comparison level. There is also a comparison level for alternatives, which is related to the lowest level of reward that a person may accept during the exchange, given that other opportunities are present.

The main highlight of this theory, as proposed by Thibaut and Kelly, is on the perception of cost and reward and also on instrumental nature of relationship that seems to exist between the individuals and reward or punishment that is received. The cost and benefits are also compared with possible costs and rewards in an alternative relationship. This could be one explanation why individuals remain in abusive relationship.

In this context, equity theory can also be discussed, which is based on exchange theory, although it specifically deals with the expectations of the individuals with regard to the exchanges and equality or inequality in these exchanges. If equity in exchanges is perceived then the relationship will develop. However, if inequity is perceived, the relationship could suffer.

A distinction can also be made between exchange relationships and communal relationships.

- **Exchange relationships:** In such relationships, there is a concern with regard to what is given in a relationship and what is received and whether there is equity or not. Such relationships exist in an organisational set-up between the employer and employee. For example, if an employee waits beyond his/her office hours and puts extra effort for the company, he/she will expect recognition or a remuneration in exchange.
- **Communal relationships:** Here the focus is on the welfare of others, and examples of such relationship are between family members and friends. A sibling who comes over to take care of a person during illness will have no expectation but is more concerned with the welfare of that person.

These relationships also help determine pro-social behaviour.

Balance Theory

Here, the cognitive consistency theory by Heider will be discussed that focuses on the mental process of an individual such as perceptions, attitudes, expectations, thinking and so on. The theory is based on assumption that the individuals will thrive to achieve balance or consistency when the cognitions are inconsistent or imbalanced and lead to the experience of a psychological tension that is negative.

The model also highlights the triads that include P (person), O (another person) and X (an attitude object or yet another person). The relationship between P, O and X is perceived from the point of view of P and in this context, two relationships are possible:

- *Unit relation*, which is related to belonging. For example, a husband and wife can be said to have a unit relation as opposed to two strangers, who do not share anything in common. A unit relation can also exist between an individual and his/her house or a vehicle.
- *Sentiment relation*, which is related to evaluation. For example, if partners in close relationship like each other, they have a positive sentimental relationship and if they do not like each other, they have a negative sentimental relationship.

There has to be a balance between the unit relation and sentiment relation. There is a balance when the relationship between the elements is harmonious and without stress. But if there is no balance, then attempts will be made to establish the balance.

In case of partners who are married, if they like each other, there is a balance between the unit relation and sentiment relation. However, if they dislike each other, there is an imbalance that can be dealt with by either breaking up with each other (thus, ending the unit relation) or the partners can work on their feelings towards each other to make them more positive so as to achieve the balance.

This can also be applied to the triad of P, O and X. If P likes O (+), P likes X (+) and O likes X (+), then the relations are positive and there is balance. But, if P likes O (+), P likes X (+) and O dislikes X (–) or P dislikes O (–), or P dislikes X (–) and O dislikes X (–), the relation is negative in both the situation and there will be an imbalance. Triad will be balanced when there is an odd number of positive relationships; that is the reason why in the latter two situations the relation is not balanced as in the first case there are two positives and in the later, there are none.

Thus, if P likes O (+) and P also likes being traditional, that is X (+), and thinks that O also likes being traditional (+), then there is a balance. But if P thinks the O dislikes being traditional (–), then there is an imbalance and attempts will be made to restore the balance. It can be made positive when P dislikes O, thus making one positive in place of two positives.

The balance thus restored is done in a way that requires least effort. Thus, P will judge if it is easier to dislike his/her values of being traditional or dislike O, whichever is easy will be chosen by P.

DETERMINANTS OF ATTRACTION

The determinants of attraction can be categorised into target centred (including physical determinants, warmth, competence, characteristics that are complementary and also similarity), that is, related to the person that this individual may or may not get attracted to, or perceiver centred (including proximity and anxiety), denoting the subjective perception of this individual.

Physical Determinants

The first thing about a person that we come across is his/her physical characteristics that also create a first impression on us. People who are seen as attractive (having this good quality) may also be seen as possessing other good qualities (resulting in the Halo effect). For example, persons who are perceived as attractive are also assumed to be well educated and having high status.

Although the perceptions with regard to what is termed as physically attractive and what is not can differ to a greater extent, and one of the factors contributing to this difference could be culture. Also there are certain similarities with regard to what is found to be attractive, including the smaller waist to hip ratio, facial symmetry (both the sides of the face are matched) and even facial maturity, females with immature features are preferred as are males with matured features (Crisp & Turner, 2010).

Most often than not people who are seen as physically attractive are also treated better and also seen as having personality traits superior to those who are not physically attractive. A study was carried out by Feingold (1992) in which a meta-analysis, on 90 studies related to relationship between physical attractiveness and personality, was carried out (cited by Crisp & Turner, 2010). Although the analysis indicated no relationship between physical attractiveness and factors such as intelligence, dominance, self-esteem or mental health, the analysis indicated that people who were attractive were less lonely and less socially anxious and displayed better social skills when compared with people who were less attractive.

Further, the radiating effect of beauty may also play a role, that is, an individual's public image may be enhanced when he/she is in the company of an attractive person, who is neither a stranger and nor a friend in closer relationship with the individual (Kernis & Wheeler, 1981).

Warmth

Persons who are perceived as warm are also seen as attractive. This could be mainly attributed to the positive attitude that such people have towards others that promotes their perception as being warm, friendly and approachable. On the other hand, people who keep complaining, or dislike things and are most often critical, are seen as cold and thus not attractive. Further, whether a person is perceived as being warm or not will also depend on their non-verbal behaviour. People who smile and are expressive and attentive are perceived as warm.

Competence

Persons who are perceived competent are also seen as attractive. One reason for this could be that individuals who are incompetent are less rewarding when compared with individuals who are competent. For example, a good speaker with effective communication skills will be perceived as more attractive. However, there is one exception in this case, if the person is too perfect, he/she may not be seen as that attractive.

Characteristics that are Complementary

It is also possible that individuals get attracted to people who have complementary characteristics rather than similar characteristics. An individual who has a trait that is valued by this person (or the trait he/she would like to have) but not possessed by this person will be seen as attractive by this person in this context. Thus, on one hand, this is not related to the factor of 'similarity' (that has been broadly discussed in the next section of this chapter) but is also not in accordance with the concept of 'opposites attract' (Crisp & Turner, 2010). In this context, looks-for-status exchange can also be discussed, where men get attracted to beautiful and youthful women and women get attracted to men with higher status (Crisp & Turner, 2010). This again can be attributed to the evolutionary past where attraction is linked with increasing the probability of reproduction and ensuring that the genes are passed on to the next generation, though this viewpoint has been criticised for justifying gender inequality. The socio-cultural perspective states that power and dominance that has been enjoyed by men through ages led to women being perceived as exchange objects with a focus on their beauty. As a result, women who were left without skills due to lack of power had no other way but to seek men with high status so as to achieve that status.

Reciprocity Principle

This focuses on the tendency of the individuals to like persons who like them and vice versa. Thus, individuals get attracted to persons who like them and are not attracted to those who dislike them, although this also depends on the self-esteem of the individual. In a study carried out by Dittes (1959), participants with low self-esteem liked the group they interacted with when the group members behaved positively and disliked them when they behaved negatively. On the other hand, the group behaviour has no impact on the participants with high self-esteem. The results thus indicated increased reciprocity in people with low self-esteem as opposed to individuals with high self-esteem (Crisp & Turner, 2010).

Anxiety

The aforementioned determinants were mainly target-centred. The next determinant that will be discussed is perceiver-centred determinant, that is, anxiety. We discussed, under affiliation, that anxiety can lead to people seeking company of others. Further, lack of affiliation may also lead to social anxiety. People who experience anxiety may get attracted to others under similar situations (who are also experiencing anxiety) due to social comparison (that was again discussed under affiliation). Thus, their reactions are validated and confirmed when they interact with persons who are going through similar situations. This can again be related to social support that will be discussed in Chapter 9 on pro-social behaviour.

Besides the aforementioned determinants, two other prominent determinants of attraction are similarity and proximity. These are discussed in the following section.

SIMILARITY AND PROXIMITY IN ATTRACTION

Individuals also have a tendency to get attracted to individuals who are similar to them. This similarity can be in terms of attitude, personality and even interests and values. Similarity plays an especially important role with regard to relationships such as friendship and other close and intimate relationships. A study was carried out by Newcomb (1961) in which the students were allotted rooms (in a large house) with some roommates having similar attitudes or roommates having dissimilar attitudes. Results indicated that students with similar attitude liked each other and developed friendship, and roommates with dissimilar attitude disliked each other and did not develop friendship. Studies have also indicated that the likelihood of participants getting attracted to strangers sharing common attitude is higher than them getting attracted to strangers with whom they shared less common attitudes (Byrne, 1961; Byrne et al., 1970).

Further, it also needs to be considered whether the similarity is perceived or actual. A study in this regard was carried out by Tidwell, Eastwick and Finkel (2012) who investigated the impact of perceived and actual similarity during face-to-face initial romantic speed-dating encounters, which revealed that perceived similarity rather than actual similarity predicted attraction. However, perceived similarity was a weaker factor while predicting similarity with regard to specific traits when compared with general traits.

Significance of similarity in attraction is not limited to attitudes and can be extended to other factors such as ethnic and religious background, educational level, age and even social class (Sears et al., 1991). Attraction can also be influenced by whether the similarities were in terms of physical or psychological characteristics. Research carried out by Duck and Craig (1975) indicated that the actual similarities in terms of psychological qualities such as confidence and cleverness were less predictive of initial attraction when compared with external qualities such as hairstyle or age.

In this context, we also need to discuss about matching principle that plays a role in intimate relationships such as marriage. This can be described as a tendency where the individual chooses a similar partner (Sears et al., 1991). In the Indian context, marriages, to a greater extent, are based on similarity with regard to status, class, religion, caste, education and so on. This can also be attributed to a similar (to matching principle) term called matching hypothesis (Walster et al., 1966) that can be described as shared belief at social level, and states that during the process of initiating romantic relationships, individuals seek persons who have more or less similar social desirability as theirs. Individuals are attracted to individuals with similar attractiveness mainly because that increases the likelihood of sharing similar opinions about oneself and would also lead to decreased risk of rejection (Crisp & Turner, 2010).

There are various explanations with regard to significance of similarity in the context of attraction; these are discussed as follows.

- **Similarity is perceived as being rewarding:** Most often, when people agree with us, we feel more confident and also further confirm our ideas and opinions, whereas when someone dislikes our ideas and opinions and challenges them, our confidence could take a setback and the experience is not as such pleasant.
- **Theory of cognitive dissonance:** This theory can also be used to explain the relevance of similarity in attraction. According to this theory, individuals seek consistency and balance in their attitudes and avoid dissonance. Thus, their likes and dislikes are organised in a way that are consistent and harmonious. Given this theory, it would be exceedingly difficult to like a person and differ with them on certain basic issues. Thus, the persons who agree with our views and opinions are liked by us and vice versa.
- **Deliberate decision:** This states that most often persons deliberately select such partners who are similar to them, whether in terms of social desirability or attitude. This can be explained with the help of expectancy-value theory related to decision-making which not only focuses on the value of the reward or gains of being with that person but also expectancy with regard to how successful they would be with the selection of the partner. For example, an individual will approach an attractive person not only because of the fact that the person is attractive (value) but also based on the expectancy with regard to whether the person will agree to go on a date with them. Thus, individuals make realistic and deliberate choices with regard to the most desirable person and therefore select individuals who are similar to them.

There are also certain exceptions to attraction due to similarities. In certain cases, people who are similar to us may be disliked by us and even avoided. This can be attributed to differences, also being rewarding as similarity. Although it is often said that 'birds of a feather flock together', it is also said that 'opposites attract'. Differences bring newness in our lives, and people often like to associate with persons who are dissimilar to them. Further, when persons are not similar, they also bring their own sets of skills and diverse opinions. This is extremely important when working in groups and teams. Also, when similarity can be perceived as threatening in certain cases where persons may feel that if someone who is similar to them had an unfortunate experience, they can also be vulnerable to such experience and therefore avoid people who are similar to them.

Besides similarity, proximity (or propinquity) is also an important determinant in interpersonal attraction. Proximity denotes the physical distance between the persons. As a result of rapid developments in communication technology and easy access to Internet and even transportation, people do develop relationships with persons at long distance, but nonetheless the role of proximity in interpersonal attraction cannot be undermined. Thus, a person is more likely to become friends with a person in his/her area rather than a person in some other country. This can mainly be attributed to the fact that most often strangers are avoided by us unless we come in some contact with them because they are in our proximity, our area of residence, or classroom or at workplace and so on (Baron & Byrne, 1995). Further, repeated exposure also plays a role here, where when we are exposed to certain stimulus, persons in this context, then it is more likely that we end up evaluating these stimuli (or person) in a positive manner, provided that there was no initial negative experience. For example, if an individual meets a person who happens to work in the same building where he/she works and tends to meet this person almost every day, then it is more likely that there will be attraction with this person and friendship and an interpersonal relationship can develop. Advertising firms also make use of this, where the audience is repeatedly exposed to the products.

Whether proximity will lead to attraction or not will also depend on the emotional state of the person. If the emotional state is negative, likelihood of developing attraction decreases and vice versa, and further attraction will take place only when persons feel motivated to affiliate with these persons. Thus, a number of factors can play a role in how proximity leads to attraction. A research carried out by Festinger, Schachter and Back (1950) studied the pattern of friendship in married students housing complex. The results indicated that likelihood of friendship developing between the couples on the same floor was more than that with couples staying on other floors and also indicated increased social interaction with the immediate neighbours.

ONLINE ATTRACTION

Given the increased use of Internet and social networking, it would be interesting to understand online attraction. Internet has, in a way, led to meltdown of geographical boundaries, and one can easily connect with persons even on the other side of the globe. Thus, more often than not, individuals meet persons online through the social networking sites and chatrooms and so on. There are also dating- and marriage-related websites, which are equally popular in India. Online attraction is also very intriguing as the situation is definitely not the same as in face-to-face interaction. It would be interesting to understand how one gets attracted to a person whom he/she may not have even seen or may have seen through the photographs (mainly selfies) and is not in his/her proximity. These are often strangers but still attraction develops between them.

There are two main aspects that play a role when it comes to online attraction (Crisp & Turner, 2010); these are discussed as follows.

1. **Presenting the true self:** Self can be categorised in this context as true self and actual self.
   - *True self*. Indicated by traits and characteristics possessed by the individual that he/she find difficult to express or share while interacting with others.
   - *Actual self*. As opposed to true self, these are the traits or characteristics possessed by the individual that he/she could express and share with others.

When an individual is interacting online, he/she is in a better position to present or display his/her true self than when interacting in person. Thus, the traits and characteristics that were otherwise found by the individuals difficult to disclose in a face-to-face interaction are easily disclosed in an online interaction. In a study, Bargh et al. (2002) carried out three experiments in a laboratory set-up to study the effect of differential self-expression in the Internet relationship formation. The study was carried out on university graduates. The results of Experiments 1 and 2 indicated that during Internet interactions, the true self was found to be more accessible in memory, and during interactions that were face-to-face, actual self was found to be more accessible in memory. The results of experiment 3 indicated that when participants were assigned randomly to interact with others through Internet, they were able to express their true self-traits in a better way to their partners. This is also possible because of the scope provided by the Internet that in a way promotes self-expression, primarily due to anonymity provided by the Internet. Further, the costs of revealing one's own true self is lesser when interacting through Internet than during face-to-face interaction.

Expression of true self also helps develop strong relationships that are based on empathy and understanding between the partners. Thus, it is possible that interactions over Internet may develop into stronger and closer relationships (Bargh et al., 2002).

2. **Self-presentation:** Online attraction provides scope to control the way an individual presents oneself. This mainly includes how the online profile is constructed, misrepresentation and evaluation of potential partner's online profile (Crisp & Turner, 2010).

Most often, the online profile that is constructed is done in such a way that the person appears to be attractive. This is mainly displayed through a photograph. Thus, physical characteristics play an important role in online attraction as they do during face-to-face interaction. Further, making the profile attractive also includes how the information about one's self and one's interest and so on are displayed. Most often, this information is displayed in a unique and distinctive way (Crisp & Turner, 2010).

As individuals are able to control their self-presentation during online interaction, they are also provided with an opportunity for misrepresentation (Cornwell & Lundgren, 2001), besides online deceptions (Bowker & Tuffin, 2003; Donath, 1999; Donn & Sherman, 2002). A study carried out by Brym and Lenton (2001) on online dating participants indicated that misrepresentation was used quite commonly, especially with regard to age, marital status and appearance. Besides, misrepresentation also occurs with regard to previous relationships, children, weight and socio-economic status (Crisp & Turner, 2010).

Further, how the online profile of potential partners is evaluated is also significant. Physical appearance, interests, values, socio-economic status and personality were seen as significant factors while the individual searched for potential partners online (Crisp & Turner, 2010).

FRIENDSHIP AND CLOSE RELATIONSHIPS

Friendship

Friendship brings to our mind the perfect friends Viru and Jay from *Sholay* or the group of friends from *Rang De Basanti*. Although it may not be as deep when compared with a romantic relationship, it does have a major impact on our lives. Right from our childhood to as we grow up, friends play an important role in our lives, whether in terms of socialisation, peer influence or in providing social support. Friends play such an important role in an individual's life he/she can share his/her thoughts, feelings, ideas, and even issues and problems with them. Friendship also has a significant impact on the quality of life of an individual (Berkowitz, 1986).

Development of friendship can be attributed to similarities in attitude, values, interests and even age and gender. Why and how friendship develops can be explained with the help of social penetration theory. This theory highlights the role of self-disclosure. Self-disclosure denotes sharing information about one's self with others. Self-disclosure helps increasing self-awareness, developing closer, deeper and more meaningful relationships, improving communication, reducing sense of shame or guilt and increasing self-acceptance and resolving conflicts and interpersonal problems.

Initially, when two strangers meet, there is not much sharing of information between them, but as they become more comfortable with each other, they may share more personal information about themselves with each other. More the self-disclosure, more the chances that an intimate relationship will develop between the persons. Reciprocity (termed as self-disclosure reciprocity) also plays a role here and as one of the persons reveals information about himself/herself, the other will also do the same. Thus, the level of self-disclosure by each individual matches and relationship continues to develop in a suitable manner and as the relationship becomes more intimate, self-disclosure gives way to give and take of support and understanding between the individuals (Crisp & Turner, 2010).

Self-disclosure also plays a role when the relationship is dissolved, in which self-disclosure decreases and de-penetration occurs. Thus, the phases of relationship constitutes gradual increase in self-disclosure as the relationship begins, followed by the middle phase of the relationship where disclosure is at a regular pace (thus, penetration take place) and as the relationship starts to dissolve, there is de-penetration, where the disclosure decreases and the relationship ends. Further, if the disclosure is too fast at the beginning of the relationship, then the chances are that the relationship will not progress further, though this may not be always true and some individuals may rapidly disclose information and still develop friendships or close relationships.

Gender differences could also exist in friendship that can be explained in terms of intimacy and physical contact. Women tend to be engaged in friendship that is more intimate in nature as compared to men (Crisp & Turner, 2010). Studies also indicated that women tend to be more involved in self-disclosure when compared with men (Dindia & Allen, 1992).

Further with regard to physical intimacy, women engage in more physical contact with friends of the same sex when compared with men (Crisp & Turner, 2010). Gender differences in friendship can be attributed to heterosexual masculinity that men are socialised since childhood to conform to. In heterosexual masculinity, the feminine traits related to vulnerability and tenderness are less valued when compared with masculine traits such as power and control (Crisp & Turner, 2010). As we know, men are often discouraged from crying or expressing their emotions and this also includes avoiding self-disclosure and physical contact with same-sex friends.

Romantic Relationship and Love

This can be termed as a more intense form of interpersonal relationship. The factors that determine our attraction also play a role in this context. Initially, the topic was almost neglected by social psychologist as it was not found to be appropriate for empirical enquiry, but later it generated much interest amongst the researchers.

Zick Rubin defined the concepts of both liking and loving and also developed scales for their measurement (Raven & Rubin, 1983). Rubin defined love 'in terms of feelings of attachment, caring, and intimacy as distinguished from liking which is characterised by general favourable evaluation, respect, admiration, particularly in such qualities as intelligence, respectability, maturity, responsibility and so forth' (Raven & Rubin, 1983, p. 254). While assessing the validity of his scale on love, Rubin administered both the scales on 158 dating couples who were undergraduate students. The girlfriends and boyfriends were made to sit next to each other as they answered both the scales, once for their girlfriend/boyfriend and then for their close friend of the same sex. The results indicated that the scores on the love scale were higher for one's dating partner compared to the close friend, although there was no considerable difference in the scores on the liking scale. Significant difference was also found in liking by girlfriends and boyfriends, where the girls liked their boyfriends more than the boys liked their girlfriends. Further, the female participants also had higher scores on the love scale with regard to their same-sex close friends when compared with male participants. This was attributed to the difference in socialisation experiences of males and females that determine their expectations as well as friendship and love pattern. Rubin also found positive relationship between scores on the love scale and the time they spent in gazing in each other's eyes. When the couples were followed up after six months, the couples who had scored higher on the love scale were more likely to be together and reported being in relation as intensely as before. These findings highlight clearly that difference exists between love and mere liking.

Love can be categorised into various types. Love, in one way, can be categorised into passionate love, game-playing love and friendship love, which can further be combined to form further categories of love, namely, possessive love, that is a combination of passionate love and game-playing love, pragmatic love, that is a combination of friendship love and game-playing love and lastly, altruistic love, that is a combination of passionate love and friendship love. Further, as stated by Sternberg (1986), in his triangular theory of love, based on the amount and level of intimacy, passion and commitment, love can be categorised in different ways (Crisp & Turner, 2010). In this chapter, two main types of love will be focused on, passionate love and compassionate love.

Passionate love: Passionate love has been described as a longing for a person that is intense in nature and is often observed during the initial stages of a romantic relationship. It is characterised by behaviours such as deep emotions, longing for and thinking about the person, desire to spend time with that person rather than friends and so on. The personalised experience of passionate love can also be attributed to the changes that take place in brain chemistry (Crisp & Turner, 2010).

Hatfield and Walster (1981) stated that passionate love can occur under three conditions (cited in Crisp & Turner, 2010):

1. The person needs to comprehend the idea of love and needs to have expectation that he/she will fall in love sometime in his/her life.
2. The person needs to meet a potential partner who matches the expectations. Expectations could also be related to the gender and level of attractiveness of that person.
3. The person needs to experience physiological arousal in the presence of this person or while thinking about him/her. And the physiological arousal experienced by this person can be associated with this potential partner or the lover.

How love can be attributed to physiological arousal can be explained with the help of the three-factor theory of love proposed by Hatfield and Walster. Physiological arousal can be experienced in different settings and are labelled accordingly as fear, anxiety and so on. This labelling can be attributed to the external cues in the situation and, thus, a physiological arousal in the presence of a person who is perceived as attractive will lead to this arousal being labelled as romantic or related to love. The term excitement transfer needs to be clarified in this context. As stated by Zillman (1984), excitement transfer denotes a physiological process in which arousal that is as a result of a particular stimulus is transferred and added to another stimulus (Crisp & Turner, 2010).

Compassionate love: The initial stage of romantic relationship denoted by passionate love is often short and when the relationship crosses this stage, it goes on to become compassionate love. Compassionate love is comparatively long-lasting but less passionate than passionate love. This compassionate love can lead to overlapping of mental representations of the two persons in love or in romantic relationship and, thus, the persons in love with each other perceive themselves more in terms of their shared characteristics than their individualised traits (Smith, Coasts, & Walling, 1999). The progression from passionate love to compassionate love has been explained from the evolutionary perspective, where during initial stage of a relationship related to the sexual mating system, the objective is to reproduce and ensure that the genes are passed on to the next generation. However, during the later stages of relationship, the main focus is on attachment between the partners as well as towards the offspring, which maximises the chances of survival. Partners who have a bond or compassionate love between them are in a better position to help the offspring grow and survive through the childhood.

Simon, Eder and Evans (1992) stated four main social norms in the development of cultural knowledge of love (cited in Crisp & Turner, 2010). These were based on their study on female adolescents in the individual age group of 11–14 years in the United States. These four norms are as follows:

- *Moderation in love*. The first norm is about moderation in love, indicating that other aspects of life such as academics, sports and so on are also important and that an individual should not focus only on love. In fact, girls who were overly interested in boys were criticised for having no other concrete interest in their lives.
- *Suppression of feelings directed towards others who were already attached*. This was yet another social norm indicating that once a girl had expressed her interest and feeling with the group for a particular boy, then the boy was considered as off-limits for other girls. Violation of this norm invited negative gossip about those who violated it.
- *Monogamy*. Girls were expected not to have feelings for more than one boy. Violation of this norm invited confrontation from other girls as well as gossip.
- *Continuity in love*. There was an expectation of some sort of continuity in love, especially after the first encounter with romantic love. In this, however, it did not matter if it was not with the same boy with whom the girl had her first romantic relationship. Thus, the focus was on status and popularity rather than the target of love, that is, the boy.

Physical intimacy in romantic relationship: Physical intimacy between partners involved in romantic relationship is a crucial aspect, especially due to new emerging patterns of physical intimacy. There have been gross changes in the sexual behaviours and attitudes over the period of time, and sexual interactions between individuals have become a significant feature of interpersonal relationship and over a period of time, there has been a somewhat shift towards permissiveness. However, cultural differences do exist in this regard. For example, in Indian societies, premarital sex is still out of bounds, although, to some extent, courtship before marriage is permitted, and despite youngsters dating and being involved in intimate relationships, it is not encouraged. In a study carried out by Kumar and Tiwari (2003) on knowledge, attitude and behaviour towards premarital sex, 469 unmarried youths from city slums in Delhi and Lucknow were studied. The results indicated the prevalence of premarital sex in 23.1 per cent of youth in Delhi (total sample 255) and 12.1 per cent of the youth in Lucknow (total sample 214).

In a study carried out by Viral Dave et al. (2013) on high-risk premarital sexual behaviour of college-going male students in Gujarat, the results indicated that out of the total 450 participants, 13.78 per cent had one or more than one exposure to premarital sex. The sex partners included girlfriends, homosexuals and commercial sex workers. In another study carried out by Prasad et al. (2014) on premarital sex and age at first sex among male college students in Pondicherry, the results indicated that the percentage of prevalence of premarital sex amongst the participants was 30.08 per cent and the average age at first sexual encounter was 18.3(± 2.8) years. As indicated in the aforementioned studies, there is an increase in youngsters in India who indulge or approve of premarital sex. As revealed by a survey, HT-MaRS Youth Survey (2015) (as mentioned in an article in *Hindustan Times*), 61 per cent of those who took the survey reported that they did not believe that premarital sex was a taboo, though 63 per cent believed that they would like their partners to be virgin (Bawa, 2015). In the same article, Dr Sanjay Chugh, a Delhi-based psychiatrist, has also been quoted on how the male mindset in India with regard to sexuality is unchanged when compared with women who are more open to their sexuality. He also indicated that though there has been a sort of de-stigmatisation with regard to premarital sex and casual relationships, but the youth still displayed the fear of being caught.

In this context, we also need to discuss about socio-sexuality, that was proposed by Simpson and Gangestad (1991, 1992). Socio-sexuality can be described as a dimension with restricted socio-sexual orientation at one end and unrestricted socio-sexual orientation at the other. Socio-sexuality helps understand any individual differences in sexual relationship. Restricted socio-sexuality orientation denotes a sexual relationship that is based on an emotional bonding, intimate in nature and involving commitment. The unrestricted socio-sexual orientation, on the other hand, denotes a sexual relationship that is not based on intimate and emotional bonding or commitment. These were attributed by Simpson and Gangestad, using an evolutionary perspective, to the two different reproductive strategies that were adopted by our ancestors. (1) The chances of passing ones genes and ensuring that the offspring will be cared for were higher with a partner or mate when there was commitment and emotional bonding. (2) And having fitness, that is, the ability of reproduction and possession of necessary resources. However, most often, it would be difficult to find such a partner who had both these qualities and that lead to individuals developing the two different strategies of socio-sexual orientation.

Commitment in a relationship is very important and is denoted by willingness to remain in the relationship. However, commitment is not correlated to whether one is happy or not in the relationship.

Commitment can be explained with the help of the investment model stated by Rusbult (1980 and 1983). According to this model, there are three main factors that determine commitment:

- Satisfaction needs to be high in a relationship.
- More the investment in terms of time, efforts, sacrifices, shared activities and so on, more the commitment in a relationship.
- The perceived quality of alternatives needs to be low. It could be an alternative partner, desire to live alone, successful career and so on. If there is an attractive alternative, for example, another alternative partner who is better than the one with whom he/she is in a relationship, then commitment would be low.

Though when committed in a relationship, individuals use strategies that are directed towards maintaining the relationship and that helps deal with any attractive alternatives.

Further, personal dedication (how positively attracted the person is to the present relationship, moral commitment, commitment based on values, social and religious obligations and responsibilities, etc.) and constraint commitment (costs of leaving the relationship, for example, no availability of attractive alternative, huge investment in the relationship in terms of effort, time, etc.) can also influence commitment (Adams & Jones, 1997).

Whether a relationship is found to be satisfying or not can also be determined with the help of various factors:

- Contributions of each partner to the relationship and whether these contributions are perceived as equal or not. This can be explained with the help of social exchange theory and equity theory, which again is based on social exchange theory. Thus, if the contributions of the partners is perceived as not equal, based on the degree of this inequity and its direction, there could be an impact on the relationship.

- How caring and understanding the partner is also contributes to whether there is satisfaction in the relationship or not. Empathy and ability to communicate the support and acceptance of one's opinions and perspectives also contributes to satisfaction in a relationship.
- Yet another factor is the extent to which the partners feel that there is disclosure (or concealment) of information. Disclosure of information denotes openness, intimacy and close relationship and, thus, in this case when information is concealed, that can have an impact on the relationship.
- The attribution pattern with regard to problems that occur in relationships can also be one of the factors that determine satisfaction experienced. Most often, in happy relationships, problems are blamed on self, whereas their solutions are credited to their partner, and vice versa in unhappy relationships (Crisp & Turner, 2010).
- Relationship satisfaction is also higher in couples who perceive themselves as better than most of the other couples.
- When the social support networks of the couple are integrated, the relationship satisfaction is also high.
- Self-disclosure also plays a role in satisfaction in relationship. A study carried out by Sanderson and Cantor (1997) on dating couples indicated that partners who had a focus on intimacy and involved in self-disclosure were more satisfied in the relationship and experienced relationship stability.

HOMOSEXUAL COUPLES AND RELATIONSHIPS

Homosexual couples are people with same-sex partners and, as we discuss about interpersonal relationships and romantic relationships, it is inevitable that close or romantic relationships between same-sex couples are discussed.

Before homosexual couples and relationships are discussed, the developmental theory of sexual orientations that provide a perspective on what determines the homosexuality or heterosexuality of individuals will be focused on.

Exotic becomes erotic—A developmental theory of sexual orientation. This theory that was proposed by Daryl Bem (1996) describes the antecedents of a person's romantic or erotic attractions to opposite or same-sex persons. The theory provides a temporal sequence that leads to sexual orientation for males and females in a culture with gender polarisation. The sequence begins with A and ends with F.

A: Biological variables (including genes and prenatal hormones). These variables determine the childhood temperament.

B: Childhood temperament. The temperament will determine the activities liked or disliked by the child, and the children would show preference towards peers who like the activities that they like.

C: Sex typical or sex atypical activity and preference of playmate. Children who indicate preference for sex-typical activities and playmates of the same sex are termed as gender conforming children and children who indicate preference for sex atypical activities and playmates of opposite sex are termed as gender nonconforming.

D: Feeling different from the opposite sex or same-sex peers (feeling similar, different or exotic). Gender confirming children will feel that they are dissimilar to peers of the opposite sex and gender nonconforming children will feel different from peers of the same sex.

E: Non-specific autonomic arousal to opposite or same-sex peers results from the feeling of dissimilarity discussed under D. Thus, a boy (male typical child) may feel contempt in the presence of girls and similarly, girls (female typical child) may feel apprehensions when boys are present. As in gender conformity, in gender nonconformity as well, children will experience non-specific arousal when with peers to whom they feel they are dissimilar.

F: The autonomic arousal during childhood gets transformed to erotic or romantic attraction to opposite or same-sex persons (indicating sexual orientation).

Thus, the theory explains attraction between same-sex partners as a result of behaviour that is gender non-conforming. Children who grow up with feelings that they are dissimilar to same-sex peers will grow up to be homosexuals. Similarly, children who grow up feeling that they are dissimilar to peers of the opposite sex will grow up to become heterosexual and will be attracted to individuals of the opposite sex.

One way in which homosexual relationships can be explained is sexuality and love. The homosexual partners do experience love and also involve in sex (Peplau & Cochran, 1990). However, there are problems with this perspective, mainly with regard to how sexuality can be defined in this context and whether it denotes genital acts or also encompasses other forms of physical affection/latent sexuality; this perspective also oversights other aspects such as communication, commitment and so on (Peplau & Cochran, 1990). Most often, homosexual relationships have been operationally defined by researchers in terms of character relationship (including living together and sexual relationship) and based on self-definitions by the homosexual individuals as gay or lesbian. In this context, the major questions is how to understand homosexual couples, whether it denotes more of a close friendship with an element of romance or there is any other approach that can be used to explain this relationship.

It is often a misconception that homosexual couples are similar to heterosexual couples, with one partner playing a feminine role that of a wife and the other playing a masculine role that of a husband. In fact, majority of the contemporary homosexual couples displayed flexibility and would take turns in roles played by them and, thus, the model with regard to heterosexual couples cannot be applied to homosexual couples (Peplau, 1982). A small fraction of homosexual couples do engage in the feminine–masculine role playing and reasons in this regard also needs to be investigated further. Also, most often, there are certain common variables that predict the quality and stability of a relationship, amongst homosexual or heterosexual couples (Kurdek, 2004, 2005). Further, the processes studied under socials exchange theory that hold good with regard to cross-gender relationships also hold good in same-gender relationships and the rewards, costs and outcomes of the relationship are considered in similar ways by comparing with past relationships and alternative situations (Peplau & Fingerhut, 2007). A study carried out by Felmelee, Orzechowicz and Fortes (2010) on attractions and stereotypes in same-gender relationships, in which 120 male and female participants were studied, indicated that agreeableness and extroversions form significant bases for attraction besides physical attractiveness. Similarities between same-gender and cross-gender couples were also indicated as relevant by the findings of this study.

Research carried out by Bell and Weinberg (1978) indicated that, most often, homosexual individuals desire and prefer a love relationship that is steady as compared to a casual relationship. Further, gay men, and lesbians as well, perceive their relationships as satisfying, and similarities were found between the love and satisfaction experienced by homosexual and heterosexual couples (Peplau & Cochran, 1990).

A study carried out by Bailey et al. (1997) on partner preferences of gay men and lesbians indicated that when compared with heterosexual persons, homosexual persons were more receptive to the sex typicality of the potential romantic partner. The study also indicated that lesbians displayed preference towards partners who looked feminine, as gay men displayed preference towards partners with masculine looks. Research also indicated that the likelihood of homosexual couples of valuing and achieving equality in their relationship is higher when compared with heterosexual couples (Dunne, 1997).

Further, we also need to understand what determines the structure of such a relationship, how the division of activities is carried out and how the power is balanced between the partners. In a study carried out by Kurdek (1993), comparison was carried out with regard to how lesbian, gay and married heterosexual couples carry out the division of household labour. The results indicated that lesbian couples involved in sharing and gay couples, on the other hand, used balancing in allocation of household labour. The married heterogeneous couples were found to be involved in segregation, in which wives were mainly involved in carrying out most of the household labour.

It is also important to note that the homosexual individuals frequently experience stigma in terms of internalised homophobia and discrimination, at both individual and couple level, thus affecting the quality of the relationship (Otis et al., 2006) and, therefore, homosexual individuals may not get involved in a relationship that is intimate. Similar results were also found in studies carried out by Balsam and Szymanski (2005). Stigmatisation also leads to depression, interpersonal withdrawal and inhibited sexuality that can further have a negative impact on the relationship (Green & Mitchell, 2002).

Thus, some of the studies discussed in this section of the chapter do give an idea about homosexual couples and relationships, but further research can be carried out in this direction. Further, various other aspects such as conflict and violence in homosexual relationships also need to be investigated.

TROUBLED RELATIONSHIPS AND BREAKUPS

Any relationship will go through different phases comprising beginning, middle phase and end. Although some relationship may end due to external causes such as natural calamities or due to ageing or death, other relationships may end due to internal causes such as lack of attention or difference in opinions and expectations of the partners (Raven and Rubin, 1983).

Relationships have both positive and negative aspects, and couples in committed relationships such as marriage could have their ups and downs and phases of adjustments. Sources of conflict between partners range from faithfulness issues to overprotectiveness and being ignored. It is also possible that behaviour of one of the partners is such that it leads to conflict between the partners. The realisation of being dissimilar to each other in terms of attitudes, values and beliefs may also lead to troubled relationships. The passionate love phase may also weary, with couples realising that they might not be best for each other and as this phase wears off, the couples could develop troubled relationships. It is also possible that the partners change over time and dissimilarities develop between them. For example, a husband who was otherwise a proponent of independent women before marriage may feel that after birth of their child the wife should leave her job and focus on the family. When the differences between the two people become difficult to handle or manage, the dissatisfaction with the relationship also increases, which may lead to breakup. Boredom can also be one of the reasons for breaking up of relationships. The routine life after marriage, if not managed in time by the couple, could also lead to dissatisfaction in relationship. Communication is also an important aspect here. Thus, there could be a number of factors from dissimilarity to communication issues that may lead to troubled relationship between the partners.

In any relationship, a kind of psychological distance is maintained between the individuals (Raven & Rubin, 1983), which is in a way similar to physical distance maintained by people. This psychological distance is more when you don't know the person and gradually decreases as you become more and more familiar. Gradually, trust develops between the persons and they would also be able to involve in self-disclosure and develop a close relationship. This leads to a psychological distance that is comfortable for both the partners or a psychological distance that is ideal. This distance can be maintained and re-established by either of the partners. Thus, if due to some argument or withdrawal by one of the partners, the psychological distance increases, then it can be re-established by the other partner. Similarly, if it decreases because one of the partners becomes too intimate, then the other partner will re-establish the distance and bring it to its normal or ideal level.

However, in relationships that do not work, the partners fail to adjust to the changes that take place in the psychological distance and the partners may experience a breakup. Although effective coping and willingness to cope with the deteriorating relationship and intervention from friends, family or even a therapist can help save the relationship.

Relationship dissolution model proposed by Duck can be explained in this context. According to this model, the couple or partners go through four phases as they head towards a breakup (Crisp & Turner, 2010); these are discussed as follows:

Phase 1, Intrapsychic phase. An attempt is made to identify the sources of the problem and an internal cost and benefit analysis is also carried out. The problem is either repressed or shared with the friends.

Phase 2, Dyadic phase. The situation or the problem is discussed by the couple or partners in order to come up with reconciliation. The couple may involve in negotiation, reconciliation attempts or arguments (that may further aggravate the problem).

Phase 3, Social phase. At this stage, the couples or the partners accept that the relationship is breaking up and they seek social support and at the same time, seek ways in which they can save their social image.

Phase 4, Grave dressing phase. Involves accepting that the relationship is over and working on the division of the property or belongings and also deciding about the custody of children (if any). The individuals may also involve in informing others about their version of why the relationship ended.

After the breakup, though the anger may disappear, but the sadness may remain and the individuals may take time to cope with it (Crisp & Turner, 2016). To what extent the individuals are affected by the breakup can be determined by the following factors:

- **Attachment pattern.** Individuals with secure attachment style and fearful avoidant attachment style cope with sadness experienced as a result of breakup better when compared with individuals having dismissive avoidant attachment style.
- **Partner-initiated breakup.** As the name suggests, this is the breakup that is initiated or brought about by one's partner. Such persons find it difficult to cope with the breakup and are likely to experience anxiety and depression and take longer to cope with the breakup when compared with the partners who initiated the breakup. This can be attributed to the unexpected nature of the breakup and also the lack of control (Crisp & Turner, 2016).
- **Rejection sensitivity.** The extent to which the persons expect rejection and their reaction to rejection can also have an impact on how they cope with the breakup.

Breaking up can have a negative impact on both or one of the partners. Besides the partners, even their friends and family, children (if any), may be affected, especially if it was a committed relationship such as marriage. Divorce, for example, is still a social stigma and couples are expected to try to find out ways and work towards maintaining the relationship. Whatever be the reason for the breakup or the divorce, individuals involved do need time and skills to cope with the situation and may also require help and support in the process.

SUMMARY

This chapter focused on interpersonal attraction and covered topics that ranged from affiliation to close relationships. It also focused on troubled relationships and breakups. In the process of understanding interpersonal attraction, affiliation, that is, the desire to be with others, was also discussed. While understanding why individuals seek affiliation, especially under conditions that are stressful, social comparison theory, reduction of anxiety and seeking information were discussed. The section on affiliation also focused on negative effects of lack of affiliation that leads to social anxiety and loneliness, besides having a negative effect on the overall well-being of the individual. The chapter further explained interpersonal attraction with a focus on principles of attraction, including association and reinforcement. Theories of attraction were also discussed with focus on reinforcement model, reinforcement affect model, exchange theory and balance theory. Determinants of attraction were then elucidated with an emphasis on physical determinants, warmth, competence, characteristics that are complementary, reciprocity principle and anxiety. Similarity and proximity in attraction were also dealt with in detail. Given the increased use of Internet and social networking, online attraction was also covered, where presenting the true self and self-presentation were highlighted as playing a significant role. Further, the chapter also discussed two relevant topics, namely, friendship and close relationships. Friendship has a significant impact on the quality of life of an individual, and romantic relations and love could be termed as intense form of interpersonal relationship. And although initially the topic was almost neglected by social psychologist as it was not found to be appropriate for empirical enquiry. Further, passionate love and compassionate love, besides physical intimacy, in romantic relationships were also discussed. Further a discussion was also carried out on homosexual couples and relationships. In this context, the developmental theory of sexual orientations that provides a perspective on what determines individuals to become homosexual or heterosexual was also explained. The chapter lastly focused on troubled relationships and breakups and touched on its impact on the individuals.

QUESTIONS

1. Define affiliation. Discuss the three main motives that can be attributed to why individuals seek affiliation.
2. Explain the principles of attraction.
3. Describe various theories of attraction.
4. Elucidate the determinants of attraction.
5. Discuss the role of similarity and proximity in attraction.

6. Write a note on online attraction.
7. Explain romantic relationship and love and discuss the types of love.
8. Explain troubled relationships with a focus on phases of breakup.

REFERENCES

Bell A. P., & Weinberg, M. S. (1978). Homosexualities. *Psychological Medicine, 9*(3), 599. Retrieved from http://dx.doi.org/10.1017/s0033291700032396

Berkman, L. F., & Syme, S. L. (1979). Social networks, host resistance, and mortality: A nine-year follow-up study of Almeda county residents. *American Journal of Epidemiology*, *109*, 186–204.

Dittes, J. E. (1959). Attractiveness of a group as function of self esteem and acceptance by group. *Journal of Abnormal and Social Psychology*, *59*, 77–82.

O'Connor, S., & Rosenblood, L. (1996). Affiliation motivation in everyday experience: A theoretical perspective. *Journal of Personality and Social Psychology*, *70*, 513–522.

Rusbult, C. E. (1980). Commitment and satisfaction in romantic associations: A test of the investment model. *Journal of Experimental Psychology*, *16*, 172–186.

Rusbult, C. E. (1983). A longitudinal test of the investment model: The development (and deterioration) of satisfaction and commitment in heterosexual involvements. *Journal of Personality and Social Psychology*, *45*, 101–117.

Shaver, P., & Klinert, M. (1982). Schechter's theories of affiliation and emotion: implications of developmental research. In L. Wheeler (ed.), *Review of personality and social psychology* (Vol. 3, pp. 37–72). Beverly Hills, CA: SAGE Publications.

Sternberg, R. J. (1986). A triangular theory of love. *Psychological Review*, *93*, 119–135.

Zillman, D. (1984). *Connections between sex and aggression*. Hillsdale, NJ: Erlbaum.

FURTHER READINGS

For further reading on online relationships and dating, the following book can be read:

Whitty, M. T., & Young, G. (2017). *Cyberpsychology*. Singapore: John Wiley and Sons.

Following books can also be referred:

Sollie, D., & Leslie, L. (1994). *Gender, families, and close relationships* (1st ed.). Thousand Oaks, CA: SAGE Publications.

Riggio, R. E., & Feldman, R. S. (Eds.). (2005). *Applications of nonverbal communication*. New York, NY: Psychology Press.

CHAPTER 7

Attitude

Provide your opinion for the following:

- *What do you think about euthanasia?*
- *What is your view about the latest car in the market?*
- *What do you think about caste-based reservation?*
- *What is your opinion about same-sex marriages?*
- *Which music do you like?*
- *What do you have to say about a particular washing powder, a lotion or a perfume/deodorant?*
- *How do you rate the pizza delivery and quality?*

The way you feel about the aforementioned issues, whether favourable or unfavourable, will determine your attitude towards these issues.

Most of you must have answered some or the other poll in your life. In addition, more such questions come your way in day-to-day life. Not only manufacturing companies, organisations, even media is often interested in what you want to say. However, they may be more interested in the general attitude of the public rather than an individual attitude. Nonetheless, in general, there is major focus on attitude towards products, government policies and programmes, political parties and so on. This focus on attitude is not a futile exercise given the fact that attitude has a major influence on behaviour of the individuals, and attitude towards certain product will determine whether that product will be bought or not, attitude towards political parties will determine whether individuals will vote for it or not and so on.

Attitudes can be directed towards varied objects that could be tangible objects such as cars, bags, perfumes and so on or group of people, for example, a political party or people belonging to certain caste, religion or region. It can also be towards an idea that is abstract in nature, such as honesty or democracy, and it can be towards a behaviour, for example, aggression, adventurism even sexual orientation or alcohol consumption.

Besides understanding the concept of attitude, it is also important to understand how attitudes are formed and whether they can be changed; if yes, how? Negative attitude and resulting discriminations also need to be studied. And, that is what will be covered in this chapter.

Learning Objectives

After reading this chapter, you will be able to

- Explain the concept of attitude
- Discuss attitude formation
- Describe how attitudes guide behaviour
- Elucidate attitude change
- Discuss the concepts of stereotype, prejudice and discrimination
- Explain the ways to overcome stereotype, prejudice and discrimination

WHAT IS ATTITUDE?

Attitude in simple terms can be described as how one thinks or feels about a thing, person, place or even event. It can also be described as an evaluation of the attitude object and can be positive, negative, mixed or neutral (Barrett, 2017). There are various perspectives through which we can try to understand the concept of attitude.

Although initially attitude was described mainly based on whether the attitude object is favoured or not, it is not possible to define attitude along a single dimension because an individuals' attitudes towards certain attitude objects could also be ambivalent. Further, there could also be inconsistent attitudes towards a single object. For example, Kavitha may like a Pizza for the way it tastes, but she may also be concerned about the calories that she may gain after its consumption. Thus, Kavitha's evaluation regarding pizza is both positive and negative. How attitudes are expressed may also depend on the situation and, in the context of indicating her favourite food, Kavitha may mention how good a pizza tastes, whereas when engaging in talk about healthy diet, she may mention about how pizza could add to fat in the body.

Most often, when you are asked to express your attitude towards an object, you may not be able to provide a single attitude and your response could include more than one attitude with regard to various aspects of that object. Attitudes could be positive, negative, ambivalent or neutral based on the following (Barrett, 2017):

- A positive attitude could be as a result of low negative and high positive.
- A negative attitude could be as a result of high negative and low positive.
- An ambivalent attitude could be as a result of high negative and high positive.
- A neutral attitude can be as a result of low negative and low positive.

Attitude can also be classifies as implicit, explicit and dual.

- **Implicit attitude:** These are the attitudes that individuals may not be conscious or aware about.
- **Explicit attitude:** These are the attitudes that individuals are aware about.
- **Dual attitude:** These are the attitudes that are inconsistently implicit or explicit.

Further, attitudes can also be categorised into general and specific. A general attitude is overall evaluation about the attitude object, whereas a specific attitude is related to certain features of the attitude object. For example, a person may have a strong negative attitude about his/her friend's smoking habits (specific attitude), but in general he/she may have a positive attitude about this friend because of his/her fun-loving character, trustworthiness and style.

Allport, in 1935, defined attitude as 'a mental and neural states of readiness, organised through experience, exerting a directive or dynamic influence upon the individual's response to all objects and situations with which it is related to' (Sears et al., 1991, p. 137). This definition focuses on the role of past experiences of the person that determines his/her attitude, and it is also seen as a predisposition that is learned.

Yet another definition of attitude was provided by Krech and Crutchfield (1948, p. 152). They defined attitudes as 'an enduring organisation of motivational, emotional, perceptual, and cognitive processes with respect to some aspect of the individual's world'. This definition focuses on the present subjective experience rather than how attitude originated. The emphasis is also on the cognition rather than overt behaviour.

Eagly and Chaiken (1993, p. 1) defined attitude as 'a psychological tendency that is expressed by evaluating a particular entity with some degree of favour or disfavour', thus, describing it in terms of favourableness towards a particular object, person or event.

Although there are a number of definitions of attitude, it can be described in three main ways.

1. Attitude as a feeling reaction or evaluation. Here, attitude is described in terms of an individual's favourableness or unfavourableness towards an object. This is the simplest way to describe attitude.
2. Attitude as a readiness to respond to an object or issue in a particular manner. The definition given by Allport can find its place here.
3. Attitude as a composition of cognitive, affective and behavioural elements. This can also be referred to as the tripartite model of attitude (discussed in detail in the following section).

Components of Attitude

There are three main components of attitude, that are discussed as follows:

1. **Cognitive component:** This denotes the thoughts of an individual with regard to a particular object. These thoughts could be related to facts, knowledge, ideas, opinions and even beliefs with regard to the object. When an individual utilises the information available to him/her in forming an opinion about the object, whether favourable or unfavourable, that represents the cognitive element of the attitude. Cognitive component can also be termed as storage component where the information about the attitude objects are organised. For example, suppose when an individual has an unfavourable opinion or negative attitude about smoking because it can have a negative impact on one's health, then he/she derived this attitude as a result of information he/she has about ill effects of smoking.
2. **Behavioural component:** This denotes the tendency of the individual to act with regard to the attitude object. The behaviour will, thus, be based on the attitude, whether negative or positive. Behaviour (overt actions), though, needs to be differentiated from behavioural tendency, which may not actually predict one's actual behaviour. This behavioural tendency or intention to behave in a particular manner is more in accord with the cognitive and affective component of attitude

rather than the actual behaviour. For example, a person may believe that he needs to wear helmet while riding but may not actually wear it; although the person may have intentions to wear the helmet, it may not translate into actual behaviour of wearing it.

3. **Affective component:** This is related to the emotions or feelings of the person towards the attitude object, for example, feelings people have towards music or people and so on. Further, these feelings may also vary in terms of their intensity. A person may have strong favourable feelings about freedom of speech but may have a casual favourable feeling about rainwater harvesting. Thus, this person will be more involved in activities related to freedom of speech and not so much in activities related to rainwater harvesting.

Emotions and cognitions are interrelated and the intention to behave can be determined by the harmony between cognitive and affective components. This has even found its application in advertising where emotions are used in persuasive appeal.

Emotions also play an important role in the formation of attitude besides contributing to attitude change.

Amongst all the three components of attitude, cognitive and affective components are stronger compared to the behavioural component. Further, it is not necessary that an attitude has all the three components. For example, an individual may not have any belief or knowledge about a product, but may still have a positive attitude about it and, in fact, the individual may never involve in actually purchasing that product.

We will now look at an example of attitude, explained with the help of Figure 7.1.

Figure 7.1 shows the attitude of Shreeja towards marriage (the attitude object) and it is surrounded by various aspects that are perceived as significant by Shreeja. These also represent various cognitions

Figure 7.1 ***Example of Attitude***

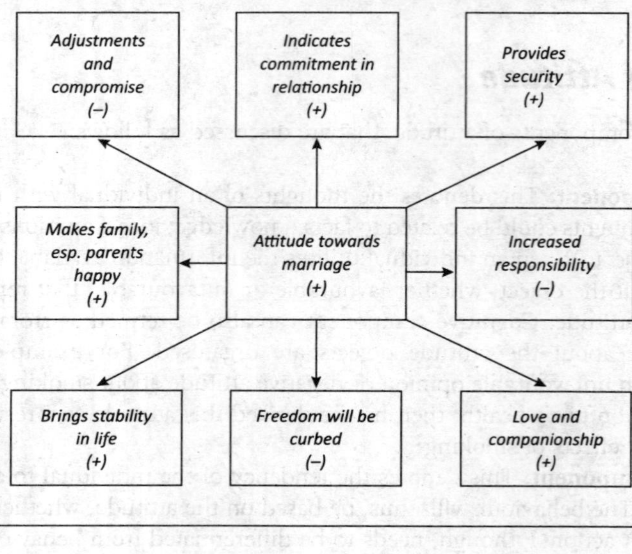

Source: Author.

that Shreeja has about marriage. Each of these cognitions will again have certain feelings, either positive or negative, that are connected with it. Thus, negative and positive signs have also been given under each cognition. The positive signs represent favourable affect and negative signs represent unfavourable affect. The main attitude object also has been given a sign and that represents the affect related to that object. In this case, it is positive, indicating a favourable affect. As seen in the Figure 7.1, Shreeja has negative feelings towards marriage mainly because of aspects such as adjustments and commitments that are required to be made, increased responsibility and curbed freedom. She has positive feeling about marriage owing to aspects such as it makes family/parents happy, indicates commitment in relationship, love and companionship, brings stability in life and provides security. Keeping in mind all these cognitions and their evaluations, her overall attitude towards marriage is positive.

The example thus helps us identify the cognitive and affective components of attitude. However, there is yet another component, that of behaviour. In the present example, based on the favourable evaluation about marriage by Shreeja, she would be open to getting married and may also meet prospective partners.

It is also to be noted that most often the cognitions involved in attitude are very complex. In the example of attitude that Shreeja has towards marriage, we just saw few cognitions; however, in a realistic situation, there would be numerous cognitions related to an attitude object. There could be various thoughts and beliefs about the object but they may or may not be factually correct. Also, the cognition related to 'love and companionship' (as can be seen in Figure 7.1) can again be interpreted in the context of what attitude Shreeja has about love or companionship, and this will again lead to many other related attitudes. Thus, there would be a cluster of thoughts related to marriage. Further, the cognitions also vary in their significance; for example, the cognition 'makes family/parents happy' could be more significant compared to the cognition 'brings stability in life'.

Though the attitudes may display cognitive complexity, they are simple with reference to their evaluation. All the feelings of Shreeja towards marriage are organised and dominated by her overall positive evaluation of marriage. As can be seen in Figure 7.1, most of the attitudes related to marriage are perceived as positive by Shreeja as is her overall attitude, which is again positive. Thus though there could be many cognitions related to an attitude object, the evaluation is quite simple.

Characteristic Features of Attitudes

The characteristic features of attitude are mentioned as follows:

1. **It is learned or acquired.** As will also be discussed under how attitudes are formed, attitudes are acquired or learned by the individuals, and experiences and socialisation of the individuals do play a role here.
2. **They provide direction and can motivate people.** Behaviour of an individual can be directed by his/her attitude. For example, if an individual has a positive attitude towards exercising regularly, he/she is more likely to be motivated to exercise and engage in exercising.
3. **They are relatively permanent.** Attitudes are consistent and stable over a period of time; although they could be changed, it is a gradual process.
4. **Attitude is with reference to an attitude object.** Attitude is with regard to a certain attitude object that can be a thing, a person, an idea or an issue.

Functions of Attitude

The focus, while discussing functions of attitude is on extent to which attitude leads to satisfaction of different psychological needs. Four main functions of attitude are discussed here.

1. **Utilitarian function:** Attitudes play a role in helping individuals have a better relationship and an overall better life. For example, a positive attitude towards one's spouse will help maintain the relationship, or a negative attitude towards smoking will lead to less health-related hazards that come with smoking. Conformity also plays a role here, where we may have an attitude that is in agreement with others. This, in a way, helps us maintain the membership of a group. Thus, one's public attitude could be different from one's private attitude. For example, a person may actually have a negative attitude towards working women but his/her public attitude will be positive towards working women because significant people around him/her have that attitude.
2. **Knowledge function:** Attitude also makes life more meaningful and coherent as it contributes to the organisation as well as prediction of the social world and, thus, it can also be explained as a cognitive schema (Crisp & Turner, 2010). For example, stereotypes denote one's expectations with regard to various social groups.
3. **Ego defensive function:** This function of attitude helps individuals protect themselves from certain truths about themselves that could be threatening and, thus, help them develop a positive attitude about themselves. This helps in maintenance of self-esteem of the individual. For example, a student may develop a negative attitude towards a classmate who has scored more marks than him/her.
4. **Value expression function:** Attitude also functions as an expression of certain values that are considered as important by the individual. For example, if an individual values handmade products by traditional artisans then he/she will be involved in buying and promoting handmade products by traditional artisans.

Attitude, Beliefs and Values

As we discussed about attitudes, it is also important to focus on the concepts of beliefs and values.

There is a close association between attitude and beliefs and, in fact, some of the theorists purpose that the three components of attitude are evaluations, behavioural intensions and beliefs (Raven & Rubin, 1983).

Beliefs can be described as 'what we know about an object or what we think we know about it' (Raven & Rubin, 1983, p. 130). Beliefs may also indirectly lead to evaluation of attitude objects. For example, if we associate cigarette smoking with health hazards and evaluate it negatively, we will also have a negative attitude towards cigarette smoking.

Belief and attitude have a characteristic in common, that is, centrality, meaning the focus is on, or the importance is given to, the individual. Further, they both have a cognitive component. Individuals will often have few central beliefs or attitude that are extremely difficult to change and if these central beliefs or attitudes are changed then there are serious consequences as it also involves restructuring of the cognitive system that is based on those beliefs and attitudes. Major psychological and behavioural changes are required if a shift has to be brought about in beliefs that are central as compared to beliefs that are peripheral. Although in certain cases, resistance is also found to change in peripheral or moderately central beliefs (Raven & Rubin, 1983).

Centrality in beliefs is determined by a number of factors including logic and experience that is direct in nature. Further, beliefs with regard to one's identity or concept about one's self are also central.

Despite certain similarities, belief and attitude do differ, as attitude in general has all the three components, that is, cognitive, affective and behavioural. However, belief has just two, cognitive and behavioural. Further, belief may also not have the property to direct a behaviour or motivate an individual. Changing attitudes is comparatively a faster process when compared with changing beliefs of a person.

Values can be described as central attitudes about what is right or wrong and form core of beliefs, attitudes and behaviours of individuals (Raven & Rubin, 1983). They influence individual's behaviours and actions to a greater extent and are, therefore, focused on by social psychology researchers. However, social psychologists have also hesitated from conducting research on this topic, as values are very personal and strongly held by individuals. They are also very difficult to change.

Values can be categorised as terminal value or instrumental value. Milton Rokeach (1973) developed the Rokeach Value Survey that consists of 18 terminal values and 18 instrumental values. A terminal value, as defined by Rokeach, is 'an end state of existence which is personally and socially worth striving for' (for example, a comfortable life, freedom, happiness and so on). Instrumental value is (as defined by Rokeach) 'a mode of conduct which is personally and socially preferable in all situations with respect to all others'. For example, honest, helping, obedient, polite and so on (Raven & Rubin, 1983, p. 136).

Values can be considered central, but the beliefs that we have about our self-concept or ourselves are even more central and relevant to us. These beliefs can be related to our ethnicity, sexuality and abilities that we have or do not have and can be related to our physical, intellectual and emotional strengths and weaknesses (Raven & Rubin, 1983).

Though most of the time it is considered that values cannot be changed, Rockeach (1973) derived a technique called self-confrontation that can be used in order to change values. Self-confrontation involves bringing about an inconsistency between the values and the self-concept that results in changing the values in order to bring it on par with the self-concept.

Thus, it can be used in order to bring about change in one's values. However, ethical issues in this regard need to be focused on because if certain values like honesty and punctuality can be changed to being more significant, then they can also be changed to be less significant. Further, different individuals may have different values and as social psychologists, we cannot make decisions about which values are more relevant and which are less. Thus, we are in a dangerous game when we talk about bringing about change in the value system of a person or group of people.

When we talk about values in the Indian context, they are contextual in nature as values for Indians may vary according to situations (Sinha & Tripathi, 1990). Moral values, however, have a high status in the Indian context but they may or may not be manifested in their behaviours as this again is determined by situational factors.

Further, there are two different sets of values that are contradictory to each other but still coexist. The first is related to one's own group and second for other's eyes (Sinha & Tripathi, 1990). Thus, the behaviour with in-group members is different from that with out-group members.

As social psychologists, we have to understand how values develop and manifest in the Indian context. Any attempt to modify and change them should also be done with utmost caution by taking into consideration the ethical issues involved.

MEASUREMENT OF ATTITUDE

There are various ways in which attitude can be measured. These necessarily differ when measuring explicit and implicit attitudes. Various measures of attitude are described as follows.

Self-report Measures

A simple way in which attitude of individuals can be measured is by asking them directly about it. Self-report measures, thus, can be effectively used in this context. These are questionnaires designed to measure the strength of attitude displayed by an individual towards an attitude object. This can be termed as an overt measure of attitude, as the person answering them is aware about what is being measured. Other measures that can be termed as overt measures are surveys and interviews.

The items in self-report measures could be close-ended or open-ended. In close-ended items, a statement is given and certain options are provided to the respondents that they have to choose from based on which option they feel is most applicable or determines their opinion with regard to the statement.

There are various types of attitude scales. One such scale is the summated rating scale. Likert type scale is a type of summated rating scale and can be described as 'a set of attitude items, all of which are considered of approximately equal "attitude value" and to each of which subjects respond with degrees of agreement or disagreement (intensity)' (Kerlinger, 1992, p. 453).

The respondents are asked a statement and they have to select one of the five options given to them, which will indicate the extent of their favourableness or unfavourableness. For example,

A product XYZ is cost-effective

1	2	3	4	5
Strongly disagree				Strongly agree

From the aforementioned five options, the respondent is expected to select or circle any one option and that will indicate the strength of his/her attitude with regard to this statement. If there are ten statements with regard to the product XYZ, a respondent who has a favourable opinion about the product will circle or mark '5' on each of the statements. Thus, the total score would be 50. If the opinion is unfavourable and the respondent marks '1' for each statement, the score would be 10. If a respondent has favourable opinion about certain aspects of the product and unfavourable opinion about other aspects, the total score would fall between 10 and 50, denoting moderate attitude.

However, care needs to be taken in determining whether agreement or disagreement denotes favourableness. In the aforementioned statement, agreement denotes favourableness. However, if the statement was asked as follows, then the agreement denotes unfavourableness.

A product XYZ is costly.

5	4	3	2	1
Strongly disagree				Strongly agree

In the process of development of summated ratings questionnaire, a large number of statements related to the attitude that is being measured are gathered by a researcher and are administered to a large number of respondents to which these respondents have to respond with agreement or disagreement. Based on the responses, only the statements that discriminate between individuals, who scored high and who scored low, are retained and included in the final questionnaire. Thus a statement will be included in the final questionnaire only if the respondents who agreed with it also agreed with other statements that were favourable, or the respondents who disagreed with a statement also disagreed with other statements that were unfavourable. Statements that are neutral can also be accommodated in this scale.

Yet another scale that can be used in measurement of attitude is Thurstone's equal appearing interval scale, in which 'each item is assigned a scale value and the scale value indicates the strength of attitude of an agreement response to the item' (Kerlinger, 1992, p. 454).

Thus, attitude towards any object can be measured by having a series of statements that range from extremely unfavourable to extremely favourable, as shown in the example of the scale below:

Extremely unfavourable | Neutral | Extremely favourable

An example of the equal appearing interval scale is the attitude towards the Church that was developed by Thrustone and Chave (1930). The scale consists of 45 items with scale values ranging across the whole continuum. Also in the scale, the higher the scale value, the more negative the attitude towards the attitude object, that was Church.

Besides the method of summated ratings and method of equal appearing intervals, yet another method that can be used is the semantic differential method in which the respondents are presented with people, object or concept and are required to characterise them on various 7-point bipolar scales. An example of this was discussed under impression formation. One advantage of the semantic differential method is that same adjectives can be used to measure different attitudes.

There are open-ended items as well that can be included in a questionnaire. Such items provide a scope for the respondents to provide their evaluation of an attitude object in their own words. Responses to open-ended questions provide the researcher with a large amount of information related to the evaluation of attitude object that otherwise would have remained untapped if close-ended statements were used. Responses to the open-ended questions can be interpreted based on themes reflected in the responses given by the respondent and, in fact, close-ended questions can also be developed based on the responses given in the an open-ended questionnaire.

One of the disadvantages of self-report inventories is that respondents may give responses that are socially desirable; thus, their actual attitude may not be reflected. They might do so to create a favourable impression of themselves. This is most likely to occur in the absence of anonymity or when the topic for which attitude is measured is sensitive or highly emotional.

One way in which this can be avoided is by employing 'bogus pipeline'. It is a technique in which there is a machine that the participants are hooked up to and are told that the machine records the physiological aspects of their true feelings; however, in reality, the machine does not reveal any true feelings. The participants are then asked to report their favourableness or unfavourableness towards the attitude object. As the participants believe that the machine will assess their attitude accurately, they provide responses that are not influenced by social desirability and are not filtered, revealing their true attitudes.

Physiological Measures

Various physiological measures, such as skin resistance, heartbeat, heart cycle, pupil dilation and so on, can also be used to measure attitudes (Pallak et al., 1984). This can be done by comparing the physiological indicators in response to a neutral object with those in response to the attitude object. For example, pupil dilation can be studied by first showing a neutral product to the participants and then showing a certain product (attitude object). The readings thus obtained can be compared to measure the intensity of the attitude towards the attitude object. On one hand, where physiological measures are effective as the participants are not able to change or modify their responses, on the other, there are disadvantages as well, because physiological changes could be as a result of other variables rather than the actual attitude object. Further, they provide information only about the intensity of the attitude and may not differentiate between the attitudes of individuals who have contrasting attitude towards certain issues or attitude objects.

Covert Measures

Attitude can also be measured with the help of covert measures, in which the participant is not aware that his/her attitude is being measured and, thus, will not make any attempts to change or modify his/her response. This again will help deal with the issue of social desirability. One technique that can be termed as an indirect measure of attitude is lost letter technique developed by Milgram (1977). A lost email method also has been added besides the use of paper mail (Bushman & Bonacci, 2004). A study was carried out by Kern and Yeaton (2010) using the lost letter technique, in which 192 letters were placed on windshields of vehicles that were parked in the parking lots of restaurants and departmental stores. The addresses (to be delivered to) written on the envelopes was 'Admissions' at Institute of Medicine (traditional medicine) or Institute of Chiropractic Care (non-traditional medicine) that were fictitious. The return addresses were of either a male or a female. The people who found these letters thus had to make a decision whether to return or not to return the envelope from a male or female to either the Institute of Medicine or Institute of Chiropractic Care. The results indicated that the likelihood of returning the letters to the Institute of Medicine and Institute of Chiropractic Care was same. The likelihood of letters with return address of a female was same when compared with the letters with return address of a male. Thus, the study revealed that there was no difference in the attitude related to Institute of Medicine and Institute of Chiropractic Care. Also, no difference in attitude was found with regard to attitudes related to gender role with reference to the two professions as reflected by the institutes.

Thus, the lost letter technique can be used to measure attitude towards attitude object.

However, doubts have been raised with regard to the validity of this technique. In a study carried out by Bolton (1974), the validity of lost letter technique by Milgram was tested as it was compared with the findings based on the questionnaire that measured the same attitude in the same community. There was a significant difference between results obtained by lost letter technique and those obtained by the questionnaire, thus questioning the validity of this technique.

ATTITUDE FORMATION

Attitudes are important because without attitude we would have a very neutral view of the whole world, the people things around us. We would have no idea about whom to approach and with whom we need to maintain a distance. Thus, formation of attitude is a significant part of an individual's life.

There are various ways in which attitudes can develop, and these are discussed in the following sections.

Biological Perspective

This traces the roots of attitude to a biological and evolutionary perspective. Some attitudes can be attributed directly to heredity, while others are attributed indirectly to personality and arousal tendencies. Various studies have indicated that job satisfaction, vocational attitudes, attitudes towards consumption of alcohol can be attributed to genes (Tesser, 1993). The role of genes was also found in attitudes such as support towards death penalty and preventing and prohibiting racial discrimination (Olson et al., 2001), and further, partial influence of genes was also found in attitude towards same-sex relationships and religious behaviour and attendance (Button et al., 2011; Verweij et al., 2008). Attitudes that are complex in nature and moral attitudes are more likely to have genetic basis when compared with simpler attitudes and non-moral attitudes (Barrett, 2017). However, the influence of biological factors does not stand alone; it is in combination with learning as well as environmental influences.

Individuals Experiences

Attitudes also develop as a result of individual experiences, and these can be understood from the perspective of learning theories. Classical conditioning can explain how individuals could develop positive or negative attitude towards an attitude object that is neutral. In a study carried out by Staats, Staats and Crawford (1962) certain neutral words were paired with noise and shock. The results indicated that the words that were conditioned were evaluated negatively by the participants compared to the words that were not conditioned. This can be attributed to the association that takes place between the words and the noise and shock, as the pairing between them is repeated over a period of time.

Mere Exposure Effect

Though the basic requirement in classical conditioning is pairing of the stimuli that are positive or negative with the attitude object, the development of positive attitude can take place even in the absence of a pairing through repeated exposure or contact with that attitude object. This has been referred to as the mere exposure effect (Barrett, 2017). Thus, when you are in frequent contact with a person, object or an idea, you may develop a positive or favourable attitude towards that person, object or idea. In a study carried out by Zajonc in 1968, the participants were presented with Chinese-like characters or symbols (total 10) that appeared on the screen for just two seconds each, though they varied in the frequency that they were presented in (Crisp & Turner, 2010). Some were presented with more frequency than other characters (some were presented 10 times, other 25 times and so on). The participants were then informed that the characters shown to them were adjectives and they had to guess whether these adjectives had positive or negative connotations. The results indicated a positive linear correlation between the frequency of exposure and positive evaluation of the character by the participants, thus indicating that repeated exposure could lead to a positive attitude towards the object. However, it is also possible that mere exposure leads to a negative evaluation, especially when the first impression has been negative, and overexposure to a stimulus may also lead to boredom (Barrett, 2017). All this finds its application in the field of advertising.

Formation of attitudes can also be explained with the help of instrumental conditioning, where reinforcements could be used to develop positive or negative attitudes. A behaviour or attitude that is followed by negative consequences is less likely to be repeated when compared with a behaviour or attitude that is followed by positive consequences. Instrumental conditioning can be differentiated from classical conditioning based on the role played by the person so that the association is formed. In classical conditioning, as such, the person is not involved in any action, but in instrumental conditioning, the person carries out certain actions that lead to reception of either reward or punishment.

Yet another learning theory, that is, social learning theory, states that attitudes could be learned through observations, especially by observing which attitudes of others receive reward or punishment. For example, children could learn attitudes towards certain product by observing their parents. Though attitudes can be learned through observing just anyone, observational learning is selective in nature and children tend to observe persons who are in control or provide care and security. Keeping this in mind, parental attitudes do have a strong influence on the child followed by the influence of teachers and peers as the child grows up (Pallak et al., 1984).

Contextual Influences

Attitudes can also be formed as a result of contextual influences ranging from religion, caste, culture to schools and even media. Attitudes in this regard can form implicitly or explicitly. With regard to attitudes that are formed implicitly, the attitudes are formed in the absence of any intention in that direction. Exposure to messages through advertisements and media may lead to development of certain attitudes; for example, people may develop a more favourable viewpoint towards fair complexion. Attitudes can also be formed explicitly, where intentionally attempts are made to influence the attitude of people. During election campaigning, one political party may attempt to develop an unfavourable attitude towards the opponent party amongst the public (Barrett, 2017).

Self-perception Theory

Self-perception theory (also discussed in the Chapter 3 on self) can also be used to explain how attitudes develop. According to this theory, as proposed by Bem, attitudes develop as a result of observation of one's own behaviour rather than due to association or exposure. Thus, opinions are expressed by us on certain issues, which are then attributed to causes that are internal or external. Thus, individuals may not have any knowledge about certain attitudes displayed by them but these are inferred based on their behaviour and the situation or circumstances in which the behaviour occurred. For example, when offered different kinds of cookies, Reena takes a butter cookie. When asked why she chose a butter cookie, Reena thinks that she chose to take a butter cookie while nobody forced her to do so. Therefore, she must be liking butter cookies. Thus, Reena may accordingly inform that she likes butter cookies. As can be seen in this example, Reena inferred her attitude based on her behaviour and the situation or circumstances in which the behaviour occurred.

Self-perception process is less likely to occur when one's attitude are clear and more likely to occur when they are ambiguous and not clear. This theory can, thus, be applied when individuals lack prior attitudes that are clearly defined. A study, in this regard, was carried out by Chaiken and Baldwin (1981). The participants of this study were 85 undergraduate students. The participants were separated based on whether they displayed consistent and strong attitude or displayed inconsistent and weak attitudes towards environment. Then perception of the participants whether they perceived their own behaviour as pro- or anti-environment was varied. This was done by manipulating the perceptions with regard to their own behaviour by making the participants respond to certain specific questions related to difficult or easy behaviours. For example, when an individual is asked a question such as 'have you ever recycled a soft drink can?', the likelihood of the answer being yes was higher and the participant's perception about one's self would be pro-environmental. However, when the question asked was 'do you always recycle your soft drink cans?', the likelihood of answer being no was higher and, thus, the participants' would perceive themselves as being anti-environmental (example of questions quoted from

Sears et al., 1991 p. 167). The results indicated that participants who were made to perceive their behaviour as pro-environmental perceived themselves as pro-environmental in their attitude as well, when compared with those who were made to perceive their behaviour as anti-environmental. Thus, it can be concluded that the self-perception theory holds good here as individuals who did not display clear and well-defined prior attitudes with regard to attitude object relied on their own behaviour as they inferred their attitudes. The lack of clear and well-defined prior attitude can be attributed to less experience, possessed by the individual, with reference to the issue or he/she may lack immediate sensory data regarding the issues (Sears et al., 1991).

HOW ATTITUDES GUIDE BEHAVIOUR

In general, you will not expect a person to drink milk if he does not like milk, indicating that there is a consistency between one's attitude and behaviour. Although there could be exceptions that will be clearer as we discuss the example given here.

Samina graduated with a degree in law and was determined to use what she studied for the betterment of the community. She initially started volunteering for a non-governmental organisation that worked with people in a slum area to make them aware about their rights. One day when she met her teacher and told about what she was doing, her teacher felt very proud of what she was doing. Years passed and at the college reunion, the same teacher met Samina again after a period of five years and was surprised to know that Samina was now working with a construction company that was working towards building a shopping mall in the same area where the slum was situated.

In the aforementioned example, do you think that Samina's behaviour is consistent with her attitudes? The answer is no. If it was consistent, then Samina would not have worked with this construction company. However, as she was working in the slum area, she realised that she was not earning much and with increasing financial problems at home, she had to take a decision and accept a job at the construction company.

Thus, attitudes do guide behaviours to a great extent. As was seen in the example discussed earlier, initially Samina did work with a non-governmental organization that worked with people in a slum area and that behaviour was consistent with her attitude. However, changes in circumstances lead to changes in her behaviour.

At this point, it is also important to describe the concept of behaviour. 'Behaviour is a change in physical state of the individual such that he[/she] responds physically/emotionally as well as intellectually to a perceived situation' (Mostyn, 1978, p. 20). Behaviour can further be categorised as overt or covert. Overt behaviour can be described as behaviour that can be observed and covert behaviour are not observed directly but could be termed as a response of muscle and glands that are implicit, for example, heart rate, sweating, eye blinking and so on (Mostyn, 1978).

With regard to how attitude guides behaviour, a study was carried out by Richard LaPierre in 1934, in which the relationship between the verbal statements of intention and actual behaviour was studied (Pallak et al., 1984). The focus of the study was to investigate the intergroup attitudes and study whether behaviour can be predicted based on attitude. In the initial phase of the research, LaPierre visited hotels and restaurants in United States along with Chinese couples to understand behaviours towards Chinese couples, given the racial prejudice that prevailed in the 1930s in US against Asians. The results indicated that only one hotel/restaurant (out of around 251) actually refused to serve the couples, thus indicating lower levels of discrimination. After around a period of six months, the same hotels and restaurant were then sent a questionnaire that included questions related to whether they would be willing to serve Chinese couples in their hotel/restaurant. The results indicated that 92 per cent of those who replied the questionnaire said that they would not serve the Chinese couples and the rest 8 per cent replied that they were uncertain. The overall findings indicate an inconsistency between attitude and behaviour.

There are a number of difficulties that the researchers have to face while carrying out research on relationship between attitude and behaviour; one of them is related to the reliability of the measures used to measure attitude as well as behaviour. Further, there could also be issues related to the difficulty of the items in the questionnaire, that is, it is easier to provide an answer as 'no' when asked if they would accept a guest who was Chinese in their hotels/restaurants (thus indicating prejudice) than to refuse service and manifest discrimination in reality or behave in a prejudiced manner to a person in front of you.

Yet another difficulty is related to the changes in the object. That is, the questionnaire in the study carried out by LaPierre was related to the members of Chinese race that is not same as attitudes with regard to a certain Chinese couple. Thus attitude that was studied with the help of the questionnaire and the one that reflected in the behaviour could be different from each other. The study carried out by LaPierre displayed a major problem where the respondents involved in answering the questionnaire and respondents in the behaviour phase were not the same, as the persons who answered the questionnaire were mainly managers and owners of the hotels and restaurants and the person who actually behaved with the Chinese couple were the hosts, waiters and desk clerks (Pittman et al., 1984).

Some of the factors that influence the relationship between attitude and behaviour are discussed as follows:

- **Specificity:** Behaviour can be predicted based on attitude only when they refer to the specificity that is at the same level. Thus, a general attitude would not predict behaviour as would a specific attitude. For example, in the study carried out by LaPierre, a specific behaviour was studied, that is, whether they would serve these particular Chinese couple, whereas attitude measured was general in nature, that is, whether they would serve Chinese people in general.
- **Time:** Time is yet another factor that can have an influence on the relationship between attitude and behaviour. The inconsistency between attitude and behaviour can also be as a result of the time gap between their measurements. The longer the time gap, the higher the chances that there will be inconsistency between the attitude and behaviour and higher the possibility that there will be change in the attitude.
- **Self-awareness:** Here, a differentiation can be made between private and public self-awareness. A person who has high private self-awareness will behave consistently with his/her attitude and a person who has high public self-awareness will behave consistently with the attitude that is held by majority of people, especially in the presence of others. For example, a person may privately believe that one should not consume alcohol in public, indicating a high private self-awareness and this will lead to this person acting in sync with his/her attitude and will never consume alcohol in public. However, a person who is high on public self-awareness, may indulge in alcohol consumption in public (though he/she may believe that alcohol should not be consumed in public), when with friends, a majority of whom believe that there is nothing wrong in consuming alcohol in public. Thus, it can be said that attitudes predict behaviour when there is private self-awareness rather than public self-awareness (where as a result of conformity pressure the person will behave in sync with the public attitude).
- **Accessibility of the attitude:** Private or public self-awareness can be determined by the extent of accessibility of the private or public attitudes. This can be related to the availability heuristics

that was discussed in Chapter 4. In availability heuristics, the inferences are based on the information that is easily remembered, and the cognitive efforts involved are also minimal and, thus, the likelihood that something that comes to our mind easily will have an impact on our behaviour is high. Thus, attitudes could be more or less accessible. The attitude accessibility can be measured in terms of the time taken by a person to respond to attitude-object-related questions. The behaviour that follows can, thus, be predicted based on the speed with which the responses are given (Crisp & Turner, 2010).

- **Attitude strength:** The stronger the attitude, the more the influence that it will have on behaviour of the individual and this is independent of whether the attitude is accessible or not. Attitude strength and the consistency between attitude and behaviour can be influenced by:
    - o amount of information available with regard to the object (more the information more the attitude strength and consistency);
    - o the extent to which the person is involved in the issue at personal level (the more the personal involvement the higher the likelihood that there will be consistency between the behaviour and the attitude);
    - o attitudes that are developed as a result of direct experience are high in attitude strength and also display attitude–behaviour consistency.
- **Mindlessness:** Besides attitude, there could also be certain non-attitudinal factors, such as habits, affect and reflexes, that can have an influence on human behaviour (Pittman et al., 1984). Thus, human behaviour, many a times, could be mindless, that is, it could be habitual in nature as opposed to responsive to the actual attributes of the environment. Thus, attitudes may fail to determine behaviour when persons are behaving habitually without realising the relevance of their attitude. For example, an individual's behaviour as he/she experiences an emotion like anger may not be determined by his/her attitude.
- **Balance theory:** The desire to maintain cognitive consistency can determine (to a greater extent) the effect that attitude can have on behaviour. In this context, two main theories can be discussed, that is, cognitive dissonance theory (to be discussed under attitude change) and balance theory. Proposed by Heider, balance theory focuses on consistency between the elements of the mental system of a person. The theory explains how individuals have a tendency to maintain consistency in their pattern of liking or disliking towards other individuals or objects. According to Heider, a system is in balance when there is no pressure to bring about a change in any of its elements due to inconsistency (Barrett, 2017). That is, the structures are stable when the patterns of liking and disliking are balanced; however, when these patterns are not balanced, then the structures would be unstable and thus there would be pressure to change so that the structures are balanced again. Balance theory was discussed in detail in Chapter 6 on interpersonal attraction with a focus on the triads that include P (person), O (another person) and X (an attitude object or yet another person).
- **Theory of planned behaviour:** Theory of planned behaviour by Icek Ajzen can be used in order to help understand how attitudes determine behaviour. The focus here is on behavioural intension. According to this theory, behaviour is a result of behavioural intentions that, in turn, are determined by attitudes towards behaviour, subjective norms and perceived behavioural control.
    - o The attitude towards behaviour is determined by the individual's beliefs with regard to certain outcomes of performing a particular behaviour and his/her evaluations of these behavioural outcomes.

- o Subjective norms include expectations of significant others as perceived by the individuals as well as the extent to which the individual is motivated to conform to the expectations of the significant others.
- o Perceived control has to do with perception with regard to the difficulty level of the performance of behaviour.

These three factors, thus, interact to determine the behavioural intensions. Perceived behavioural control can also have a direct influence on behavioural intentions, though attitude towards behaviour and subjective norms cannot determine behaviour independently. Example of theory of planned behaviour has been given in Figure 7.2.

In Figure 7.2, the behaviour with regard to whether the person will exercise regularly or not will depend on his/her intentions to exercise regularly that, in turn, will depend on the attitude 'I want to exercise' which is positive. Subjective norms are again positive, as in this case, the family of the person also wants him/her to exercise. Lastly, the perceived control, in this case, seems to be low, as the person does not have enough time to actually exercise.

ATTITUDE CHANGE

Various ways to bring about attitude change in a person are discussed in detail in this section.

Cognitive Dissonance Theory

Cognitive dissonance theory was proposed by Festinger (1957). The theory states that feelings of discomfort are created when behaviour contradicts existing attitudes. Thus, when individuals act in ways that are not consistent with their attitude they will feel uncomfortable. For example, a person

Figure 7.2 ***Example of Theory of Planned Behaviour***

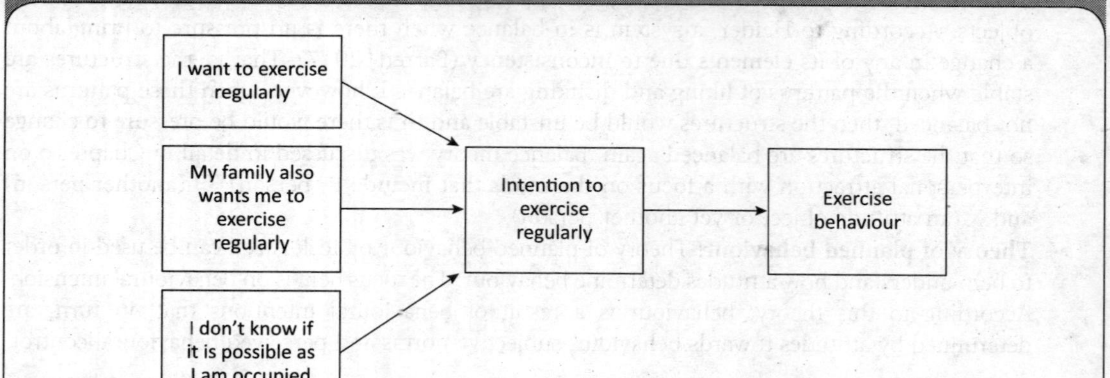

Source: Author.

who is pro-environmentalist will feel bad or uncomfortable when he/she wastes water. The knowledge of such an inconsistency between behaviour and attitude will lead to an internal imbalance or dissonance in that person which creates a psychological pressure on that person to reduce or remove this imbalance or dissonance. The person will, therefore, attempt to deal with the dissonance or imbalance in different ways. The person though will change his/her attitude when none of the ways seems apparent.

A study was carried out by Festinger and Carlsmith (1959) in which the participants were asked to perform two tasks that were boring, which involved emptying and refilling of tray with spools and repeatedly turning 48 pegs on a board (cited in Crisp & Turner, 2010). The participants were initially informed by the researcher that they were in control group and, therefore, were not given information about the experiment. They were also informed that there was another condition where the participants were informed about the task to be performed being interesting.

Later the researcher requested these participants to help them with the other participants who were going to be in the group that will be informed that the task is enjoyable. The participants had to inform the next participant that they had participated in the experiment and that the tasks given to them were enjoyable and fun. The participants had to lie to the next participant and thus had to behave in a way that was inconsistent with their attitude that the task was in fact boring.

At this stage, there were three manipulations that were carried out, where different amount of money, $1 and $20, were offered to the participants for lying about the task and there were other participants who were not asked to lie and were not paid any money (control group).

The results indicated that the tasks were rated least favourably by the participants in the control group. The participants, who received $1, reported the task to be significantly enjoyable when compared with the responses of the participants in the control group. However, no significant difference was found in the responses of the participants who received $20 and the participants in the control group.

Instrumental conditioning (discussed earlier) states that individuals who are rewarded for certain behaviour would develop positive attitude towards that behaviour. Keeping this in mind, participants who received $20 should have developed a stronger positive attitude for the behaviour that was rewarded as did the participants who received $1. However, the results were not in accordance with this. Going back to what has been stated by the cognitive dissonance theory, the inconsistency between behaviour and attitude leads to dissonance and an internal state that is uncomfortable and needs to be resolved, and if there are no ways that are apparent to resolve the uncomfortable internal state, then the attitude will be changed.

In this experiment by Festinger and Carlsmith, the participants were introduced to different levels of justification in form of $1 and $20 given to them. The participants who received $1 to lie had to come up with ways to reduce the discrepancy and the uncomfortable internal state; however, the justification of receiving $1 would not be sufficient in this regard, thus they changed their attitude having no other apparent way and, therefore, termed the task as enjoyable. In addition, participants who received $20 had a justification that was sufficient to deal with the inconsistency and to reduce the uncomfortable internal state; thus, they did not feel the need to change their attitude and therefore they reported that the task was not enjoyable.

The following factors can have an effect on dissonance.

1. **Justification:** This is with regard to whether persons have any justification with regard to their certain behaviour or not. When they have a justification, they can explain the same and thus change in attitude is not required. However, if there is no justification, then the attitude needs to be changed.

2. **Choice:** This denotes that if the person had a choice or was forced to behave in a particular manner, then he/she can explain accordingly and dissonance will not take place, but if they had a choice but still behaved in a particular way, then dissonance would take place.
3. **Investment:** The more the investment that the individuals makes in his/her opinion or point of view, the more it is significant for the self-concept of that individual and thus the effects of dissonance will be stronger. However, if the investment in the opinion or point of view is less, then they are not as significant for the individual's self-concept and thus the effects of dissonance will also be lower.

When compared with self-perception theory (discussed earlier), on one hand where self-perception holds true for individuals who do not have clearly defined prior attitudes towards the object, cognitive dissonance holds true when individuals do have clearly defined prior attitudes towards the attitude object.

Persuasion

We are constantly exposed to external messages where we are told to buy a particular shampoo or deodorant through advertisements in newspaper, radio and television or appealed to contribute to certain charitable organisation and so on. These are examples of external messages that are trying to persuade us in a particular manner.

In persuasion, attitude changes take place as a result of messages that are external rather than due to internal inconsistencies as in cognitive dissonance theory.

There are various approaches to understand persuasion.

1. **Traditional approach:** Also known as the Yale approach (as early research in this regard was carried out at Yale University), this approach to persuasion indicates the following elements that are involved in efforts to persuade.
   - *Source*, from where the message originates. This can also be referred to as the communicator.
   - *Communication*, the type of message.
   - *Audience* or the *target*, towards whom the message is directed and whose attitude needs to be changed.

The findings of research carried out in this regard could be highlighted as provided here (Baron & Byrne, 1995).

- Individuals who are experts could be termed as more persuasive when compared with individuals who are not experts. This could be the reason why dentists are shown to advertise toothpaste and actors are involved in cosmetic products, as they are perceived as experts.
- Messages that seem to be deliberate or especially designed in order to change attitude are less successful compared to messages that do not seem to be deliberate.
- Attractive communicators tend to be good persuaders when compared with communicators who are less attractive.
- In the presence of distraction by an extraneous event, individuals become more prone to persuasion as compared to when they are paying complete attention to what is being said.
- It is easier to persuade individuals having low self-esteem when compared with individuals having high self-esteem. Although this has also been challenged and may not always be true.

- A two-sided approach (than one-sided approach) that presents both the sides of an arguments are more effective with an audience with attitudes that are incompatible with the attitudes of the persuader. However, one side of the argument can be strongly stressed while highlighting certain positive points of the other side.
- Individuals who speak slowly are less persuasive when compared with individuals who speak rapidly. However, this seems to be true only when there is a difference in the views of the audience and that of the speaker.
- Messages that generate strong emotions lead to better persuasion, especially when message also includes suggestions with regard to how attitudes or behaviour could be changed in order to avoid any negative consequences. This can be incorporated while attempts are made to bring about a change in attitudes and behaviours related to health.

Thus, it can be said that the traditional approach does provide some insight in persuasion, though it does not provide us with information regarding why attitudes change as a result of persuasion.

2. **Cognitive approach:** The focus of this approach is on understanding the cognitive process that determines how persuasion results in attitude change. The focus is also on cognitive response analysis that includes understanding the thought process of people when they receive an exposure to messages that are persuasive and how attitude changes because of the thought and cognitive processes.

In this context, we will discuss about the elaboration likelihood model, which states that there are two different routes with regard to how persuasion takes place, the central route and peripheral route. Though both these routes lead to change in attitude, the quality of the attitude may differ.

In central route, individuals are motivated and able to think with reference to the message content, this is also termed as high elaboration conditions and they are also influenced by the quality and strength of the argument presented to them (Crisp & Turner, 2010).

With regard to peripheral route, the individuals are either not motivated or unable to analyse or think with regard to the content of the message. However, they may pay attention to certain irrelevant cues (for example, how attractive the communicator is and so on) related to the content and quality of the communication. This is also termed as low elaboration conditions (Crisp & Turner, 2010).

There are a number of determinants with regard to which a route will be taken, central or peripheral; these are discussed as follows.

- **Speed of speech:** A rapid speech may make it difficult to process the message content and, therefore, this may lead to choice of the peripheral route and abandonment of the central route.
- **Mood:** Individuals who are happy are more likely to take the peripheral route and individuals who are not happy are more prone to take the central route. This can be attributed to the signal that 'something might be wrong' that is triggered by a mood that is negative (Crisp & Turner, 2010).
- **Self-relevance:** The selection of route will also depend on the degree of relevance of the issue to self. The more the relevance to self, more the likelihood that the central route will be selected.
- **Individual differences:** People are different from each other and thus the routes taken by them differ as well. Persons with increased need for cognition are more likely to opt for central route than people who have decreased need for cognition. Differences in self-monitoring also play a role here, where persons with higher self-monitoring (those who are concerned with what others

think about them) tend to take central routes when compared with persons having lower self-monitoring (those who are not concerned with what others think about them).

- **Humour:** When the humour is relevant, the central route is taken and when humour is irrelevant, then the peripheral route is taken.

It is clear that when the central route is taken, the focus is on the quality and strength of the argument that determines whether the attitude change will occur or not. However, when the peripheral route is taken, there are a number of factors that need to be discussed.

- **Physical attractiveness:** The physically attractive source is more likely to lead to successful persuasion when compared with sources that are not physically attractive.
- **Similarity to self:** Similarity has been discussed in details in Chapter 6 on interpersonal attraction and this too plays a role here. The similarity with the source in terms of attitude, appearance and so on can enhance persuasiveness with regard to the message (Crisp & Turner, 2016).
- **Credibility:** The credibility of the source can also have an impact on the likelihood of change in an attitude. Credibility can be denoted by the characteristics of the source, such as expertise, unbiasedness and trustworthiness. And the more the credibility, the more the possibility that persuasion will take place. A study carried out by Hovland and Weiss in 1951 in which the participants (students of a college in the USA) were more persuaded about an article with regard to nuclear submarines being safe when the article author was Robbert Oppenheimer than when the article was attributed to Pravada, a Soviet news agency (Crisp and Turner, 2010). The study also indicated that this difference in persuasion as a result of difference in credibility decreases over a period of time, which was referred to as the sleeper effect, thus indicating that even persons who are not credible can persuade over a period of time. And this has been attributed to the deterioration of source memory. When the information related to the argument is encoded, the information related to the source of argument is also encoded. However, the source memory may decay over a period of time and that also leads to decreased effect of the credibility (facilitating or inhibitory) of the source. Thus, there could be a decrease in high credibility persuasion and increase in low credibility persuasion.

Resistance to Persuasion

As has been mentioned earlier in this chapter, attitudes are not that easy to change and even efforts to persuade may meet with resistance. There are various factors that need to be discussed here.

- *Reactance*. Baron and Byrne (1995, p. 154) described reactance as 'the negative reactions we experience when we conclude that someone is trying to limit our personal freedom by getting us to do what they want us to do'. In such a situation, the change of the attitude would be in the opposite direction, which has been termed as negative attitude change. The attitude here is seen as direct threat to the personal freedom and, therefore, there is a strong resistance to this attempt to bring about attitude change.
- *Forewarning*. When individuals are aware that the message that they are exposed to is mainly designed to change their attitude, then this forewarning or advance knowledge of intention to persuade will contribute to resistance towards the persuasive message. However, lack of knowledge that the message is designed in order to change the attitude of the individuals increases the likelihood that the views of the individuals will change. This can be attributed to

the formulation of counterarguments that take place when persuasive messages received are contradictory to the current views possessed by the individuals. Forewarning also plays an important role in providing time to recall significant information that can then be used to counter the persuasive message.

3. **Selective avoidance:** This refers to 'a tendency to direct our attention away from information that challenges our existing attitudes' (Baron & Byrne, 1995, p. 155). There could also be increase in attention that is paid to information that supports our existing views. The tendency to seek information that is consistent with our attitude and avoid information that is inconsistent with our attitudes can be termed as two sides of selective exposure, that is, efforts that are intentional and directed towards seeking information that supports our existing attitude (Baron & Byrne, 1995).

STEREOTYPE, PREJUDICE AND DISCRIMINATION

Before we go on to discuss about stereotype, prejudice and discrimination, a term that we will briefly highlight is diversity. We live in a world that constitutes of people who are different from us as well as different from each other—people belonging to different gender, sexual orientations, races, religions, castes, economic statuses, disabilities and so on. Thus, comes the term 'diversity', which aptly describes the environment or situation in which we exist. This diversity socially influences our behaviour and thus it becomes necessary to focus on psychology of diversity.

Diversity can be described as the existence of differences. However, it can be interchangeably used with the term social differences. Individuals differ from each other mainly on physical, psychological and intellectual basis. However, individuals can be termed as socially different when they belong to different social categories, for example religion (whether Hindu, Muslim or Christian), marital status (whether married, single or divorced) and so on. These social categories also help us understand the individuals in a better way, though they may also lead individuals to become judgemental or have false perception about certain categories. For example, a woman who is married and is a homemaker brings a particular image to our mind. Thus, these categories provide us with immense information about how we perceive and experience the world and people around us. Diversity can be described as having two main principles; firstly, individuals tend to modify and distort the objective social differences through their thoughts, behaviours and judgements and secondly, our behaviour and identities are influenced by our social context that is diverse in nature.

Two cognitive processes are involved in the way individuals think about people who are different from them, one way is categorisation and the other is stereotype (Blaine, 2013). Categorisation was discussed in Chapter 4 on social cognition and stereotype will be discussed in this section of the chapter. Further, individuals not only think but also feel about diversity. Thus, social differences are not only identified and described, but they are also evaluated and as a result prejudice can emerge (Blaine, 2013), which in turn could be manifested as discrimination.

Stereotype

In a simple exercise, some individuals were asked to describe their image of a scientist, a model, a teacher and a musician. The responses were quite typical with scientist described as a male having white long hair and wearing a lab coat, a model was perceived as thin and tall wearing fashionable clothes and high heels, a teacher was described in a sari and wearing spectacles and a musician was described as having long hair, holding a guitar and wearing trendy clothes. Well, this was just an exercise, and the way these persons are described, by other individuals, may differ. We often have specific images with regard to different types of people that may also contribute to the development of stereotype.

The term stereotype was first proposed by Walter Lippmann in 1922. Stereotypes can be defined as 'a generalisation about a group of people, in which certain traits are assigned to virtually all members of the group, regardless of actual variation among the members' (Aronson et al., 2014, p. 437).

As stated by Sears et al. (1991 p. 398), stereotypes are 'beliefs about the typical characteristics of group members'.

Stereotypes can also be described as a cognitive process and can be negative or positive. Negative stereotype occurs when we dislike a certain group and positive stereotype occurs when we like a certain group.

Going back to the example discussed earlier, most of us know that scientists could be females and they could have neatly combed hair, and teachers are not necessarily females who always wear sari and spectacles or musicians could be classical musicians who may wear a completely different attire and play a different instrument. Nevertheless, we may categorise persons based on what is regarded as being normative and this could be similar within certain cultures and could be due to the role played by media. Stereotype, of course, goes beyond categorisation and does not consider the realistic variations that exist amongst the members in a particular group.

Stereotype is also termed as a technique that is mainly used to simplify the way the world is perceived and, in fact, Allport, in 1954, described stereotype as 'the law of least effort' (Aronson et al., 2014, p. 437). Human beings often use shortcuts and rules of thumb when they try to understand other human beings and, therefore, the information that is in accordance with one's own ideas and beliefs about a certain group receives more attention and is also rehearsed and recalled more when compared with information that is not in accordance with one's ideas and beliefs about a certain group.

Stereotypes are often termed as inaccurate and also unfair, though there is yet another viewpoint that there could be some accuracy in stereotypes. In this context, we can discuss about 'the Kernel of truth hypothesis' that can be used to explain stereotype. This hypothesis emphasises that the stereotypes could be based on scientific realities, though they may be exaggerated in the way certain target groups are characterised (Schneider, 2004). A study carried out by Jussim et al. (2009) indicated that various stereotypes related to race, ethnicity and gender across an array of domains were accurate.

Stereotypes are also difficult to contradict once they are formed, mainly because as stereotypes are used, they determine the type of information that is remembered by us. And information that is not consistent with the stereotype is not remembered (Taylor, 1984). A study was carried out by Katz and Braly in 1933 on students of Princeton University. The participants in this study were asked to select any five characteristics from a list of 84 characteristics provided to them that they had to apply to 10 ethnic/national groups including 'North Americans, Chinese, English, Germans, Irish, Italians, Japanese, Jews, Blacks and Turks' (Taylor, 1984, p. 329). The participants assigned similar characteristics to these groups despite having very limited knowledge about these groups. Blacks were assigned the most negative characteristics by the participant and were termed as 'ignorant, happy-go-lucky, lazy, musical and superstitious' (Taylor, 1984, p. 329). Studies that were carried out even years after this study indicated that there was some amount of agreement in how the groups were described based on characteristics though with lower consensus, and there was emergence of certain new stereotypes as well (Taylor, 1984).

Stereotype can have a negative effect as members of that group are perceived as alike though in reality they may be distinct. The internal variety of the members of the stereotyped group is overlooked.

The stereotypes are often termed as negative due to the focus of the content that is also negative rather than positive when directed towards a certain group and also because they overlook individuals' characteristics in a group. Further, they are based on a reasoning that is, to a greater extent, faulty. Stereotypes are also not flexible and are not easy to change.

In the context of stereotype, we can discuss about illusory correlation that can be described as 'a tendency to see relationship or correlation between events that are actually unrelated' (Aronson et al., 2014, p. 438). Thus, two variables are seen as related even when they are not. For example, during a cricket match, one might believe that India will win if he/she does not get up from his/her seat during the match or if they wear a particular shirt or cap. In this case, though sitting in certain place or wearing a particular shirt or cap is actually not related to India winning the match, one expects that these two things are actually related. Such illusory correlations are more likely to occur when the events or persons are different from what is typical. Thus, persons belonging to minority groups, that can be based on religion, race, ethnicity and so on, can be termed as distinct when compared with majority. Distinctiveness of such groups leads to development of illusory correlation in terms of the relationship between the distinctive target person and his/her behaviour.

Gender Stereotype

To reemphasise what is stereotype, Barrrett (2017, p. 351) described stereotype as 'beliefs about the characteristics, attributes and behaviours of a group and its members'. There are also certain attributes and characteristics that are assigned to men and women and these can be termed as gender stereotypes. Thus, men and women are perceived based on the images that are typical of being a male and being a female. In this context, we can discuss about cultural and personal stereotypes. Culture plays an important role in providing us an exposure to the images with reference to gender. Movies also often show the leading actress in distress and the lead hero fighting the goons and rescuing her. Not only advertisements and media but even certain religious teachings, art, literature and even textbooks at school level may include certain contents that convey what is feminine and what is masculine (Sears et al., 1991). A study carried out by Thorne (1993) indicated that the gender role stereotype are internalised by children from books, songs, television as well as movies. In fact, a study also indicated decreased gender role stereotype in children who had not watched television (Kimball, 1986) and children displayed gender role perceptions that were not traditional when they viewed programmes having non-traditional gender roles (Rosenwasser, Lingenfelter, & Harrington, 1989).

This kind of stereotype can have an influence not only on women, but on men as well as most of the men are expected to be 'macho', well built, responsible and professional. This is an ideal image of a man and others who do not have these characteristics may feel the stress and pressure, as they do not conform to these high standards laid down in front of them.

Personal stereotype can be defined as 'our own unique beliefs about the attributes of groups of people such as women and men' (Sears et al., 1991, p. 434). The personal stereotype can be as a result of the following:

- Gender is perceived in accordance with how each sex is characterised based on general personality traits. Thus, men are seen to have certain personality traits, as are women. For example, a typical man could have personality traits such as aggressive, unemotional, self-confident, ambitious, dominant and so on, where as a typical woman will have personality traits such as gentle, talkative, dependent, interested in own appearance and so on (Sears et al., 1991).

- Gender is thought about by individuals in terms of images that they have about different types of females and males. Thus schemas are formed with regard to the type of males and females. For example, women are seen as mothers, single women, career-oriented women and so on. In a similar manner, men are also seen as fathers, firefighters, sportsman and so on. Each of these embody certain cluster of traits that are distinctive. Mother is seen having certain distinctive cluster of traits such as caring, nurturing and so on and a career-oriented women is seen as having certain other distinctive cluster of traits such as independent (that are categorised as masculine traits), attractive and neatly dressed (feminine traits). It is also to be noted here that certain traits attributed typically to other sex can also be incorporated in a stereotype (Sears et al., 1991). Gender stereotype can have an impact on the way males or females are perceived and treated.

While discussing about gender stereotype, we could also focus on the third gender. As per 2011 census, there are 488,000 transgenders in India (Gautam, 2017). Although they had equal legal rights (as a result of a landmark judgement by the Supreme Court), they often face discrimination at home and in society and have no other option but to survive by begging, through prostitution or by performing at ceremonies. Most of them lack education due to discrimination as well as harassment. They are also not able to land a decent job and if employed, they face difficulty due to discrimination and non-cooperation from the co-workers. As the article by Gautam (2017) highlights, what the transgender need is not mere sympathy from the society but opportunities and jobs so that they can lead a life of self-respect with dignity and feel equal.

Prejudice

To explain the term prejudice with the help of an example, Ravi was popular amongst his co-workers and was liked by most including his superiors. He had a jovial nature and people often enjoyed his company. During an annual health check-up, Ravi was found to be HIV positive and despite confidentiality the news somehow leaked and spread throughout the office. The same popular Ravi became an eyesore. Post this news, people developed a negative attitude towards Ravi. This negative attitude can be termed as prejudice.

The word prejudice has been derived from a Latin word *praejudicum* which means to pre-judge (Taylor, 1984). Prejudice can be defined as 'a negative attitude or feeling held towards members of an out group' (Crisp & Turner, 2010, p. 189). Prejudice can also be defined as 'a hostile or negative attitude towards people in a distinguishable group, based solely on their membership in that group' (Aronson et al., 2014, p. 436). Prejudice can have an influence on an individual's judgement and can also determine one's political attitude and behaviour (Sears et al., 1991). Thus, it can be said that when an individual has a prejudice about a certain social group, the members of that group are evaluated negatively because they belong to that group and their individual characteristics do not play any role. Since Ravi is now HIV positive and persons who are HIV positive are often viewed by the society in a negative manner (not only due to presumptions about how they must have acquired the illness but also due to a fear and misconceptions about how HIV is transmitted), Ravi is not perceived on the basis of his personal characteristics but as HIV positive.

Prejudice can also be said to have three components cognitive, affective and behaviour, as attitude. As discussed earlier in this chapter, it is often possible that there is no sync between the thoughts, feelings and behaviour displayed by individuals, as was apparent from the study carried out by LaPierre. Attitude could also be termed as one of the significant factors that could lead to prejudiced behaviour (Ajzen & Fishbein, 1977).

Explicit and Implicit Prejudice

Prejudice can be categorised based on whether the attitude is explicit or implicit. Explicit attitudes are ones that an individual is conscious about, they are deliberate in nature and, thus, can also be controlled. A simple questionnaire can be used to measure the explicit attitudes of people. For example, a questionnaire on attitude towards the dowry system can be used to measure the explicit attitudes of the people, though the explicit attitudes can be influenced by social desirability, this is, the person will display a negative attitude towards the dowry system despite having favourable attitude towards it as that is seen as socially desirable (i.e., being perceived by others in a positive light). Implicit attitudes, on the other hand, are not intentional and are activated even when the attitude object is symbolically or actually present (Crisp & Turner, 2010). Thus measuring implicit attitude will help deal with social desirability. Implicit and explicit attitudes influence behaviour differently and implicit attitudes are also more difficult to change when compared with explicit attitudes.

In-group and Out-group

In the context of prejudice, we also need to focus on what is in-group and out-group. In-groups can be described as categories that are necessarily social in nature and are the groups to which a person belongs. Other persons who also belong to this category are members of in-group from the perspective of this person. For example, you may belong to a certain religious group or a nationality and that is your in-group. Other persons belonging to your religious group or nationality can be termed as members of this in-group.

On the other hand, out-groups are categories that are social in nature and are groups to which the person does not belong. Thus, the person cannot be termed as a member of that group. For example, the other religious groups besides yours or other nationalities besides yours will be termed as out-groups.

Further, we can also discuss about ethnocentrism that can be defined as 'the belief that the in-group is the centre of everything and is superior to out-groups' (Sears et al., 1991, p. 400). Prejudice can, in fact, stem from ethnocentrism. In-group and out-group can also lead to development of discrimination

When one is in an in-group, there could be a number of outcomes, discussed as follows:

- **Assumed similarity effect.** The other members in an in-group are perceived as being similar to one self. Thus, people belonging to a certain region will feel other persons belonging to the same region as similar. For example, when in a foreign country, Indians, whether from Punjab or Maharashtra, will find each other similar, as they perceive themselves as belonging to one in-group that is being Indians.
- **Out-group homogeneity effect.** The members of out-group are perceived more as a group than as individuals and are termed as lacking diversity and more alike to each other. For example, Indians may perceive themselves as a more diverse group and would term Chinese or Japanese as being a more homogeneous group, as being alike, not diverse.
- **In-group favouritism effect.** More often than not an in-group bias can be observed in how people interact with each other. In-group bias can be described as a bias that favours or sees one's own groups (in-group) in more positive or favourable manner when compared with the out-group. This is also referred to as in-group favouritism or intergroup bias (Crisp & Turner, 2010).

Development of Prejudice

Various factors and theories that explain prejudice are discussed here in detail.

- **Socialisation:** Prejudice can develop as a result of socialisation. Socialisation can be termed as a learning process through which the attitudes are learned. For example, children may learn to respect elders through socialisation. Thus, negative attitudes towards certain social groups are also learned. Though parents and significant others in a person's life (during childhood) do play a role, but prejudice can also be learnt outside the home set-up, necessarily because it can be a social norm in a particular group of which the individual is a member. For example, people belonging to certain group may be prejudiced about persons belonging to another group because that is a social norm and has been learned as a part of the socialisation process that occurs mainly during early childhood.
- **Influence of media:** Media also plays a significant role in development of prejudice amongst children, and advertisements and movies watched by children can have an influence on the way prejudices are developed. Further, the increased coverage of attention given by media to certain sections of the society when compared with other sections can also lead to development of prejudice in children as they may receive certain cues from what is shown in the media.
- **Psychodynamic theories:** Prejudice can also be explained with the help of psychodynamic theories that mainly focus on prejudice as an extension of internal motivational tensions in an individual (Sears et al., 1991). Prejudice, thus, can be explained as displaced aggression. As described by Sears et al. (1991, p. 405), displacement occurs when 'the source of frustration or annoyance cannot be attacked because of fear or simple unavailability'. Thus if a person loses his/her job and is not able to blame anyone due to fear or because there is no one he/she can blame, then they look for persons whom they can blame and thus may say that it was due to migration from other states or countries that they lost their job.

  Adorno, Frenkel-Brunswick, Levinson and Stanford in 1950 proposed that prejudice could also be explained as a personality type (cited in Crisp & Turner, 2010). Thus, individuals could more or less prejudiced depending on the way they were brought up. Here, we can discuss about authoritarian personality that develops as a result of strict and dominant parenting style leading to a defensive reaction. As the child is not able to react to the parents who are overly strict and dominating, these feelings of hostility are transferred to weaker or easier targets, more likely towards groups with lower status or minority groups and this tendency is carried forward during adulthood as well. However, this explanation of prejudice is not as popular and has been greatly criticised.
- **Realistic group conflict:** Development of prejudice can also be explained in terms of realistic group conflict. According to this theory, two groups that compete with each other for certain resources that are limited can lead to emergence of hostility between the groups thus leading to evaluations that are negative and mutual. For example, two groups may conflict with each other over river water.
- **Relative deprivation:** Yet another theory that can explain prejudice is relative deprivation that can be explained as a feeling of being deprived in relation to others. This feeling is also subjective in nature and can lead to development of antagonism between the groups. Reservations for example can lead to feelings of deprivation in certain sections of the society and thus antagonism may develop against the section of society that is benefited by reservation. Relative deprivation can be categorised into two categories.

i. *Egoistic deprivation*. This occurs mainly in comparison with people that one knows and can be members of an in-group. It can be described as 'the feeling that we ourselves are deprived relative to other people with whom we compare' (Sears et al., 1991, p. 407).
ii. *Fraternal deprivation*. This occurs when the feeling is that one's own group is deprived when compared with another group. Thus, the threat is felt as a group rather than as an individual.

- **Cognitive approach to prejudice:** Prejudice can also be explained in terms of cognitive biases associated with how individuals are perceived. Most often, when individuals are perceived, they are categorised into different categorise that could be based on caste, religion, region, gender and so on. Thus, when we look at a person we will first categorise that a person as man or woman, young or old and so on. In information processing, the person is first categorised and then attention is paid to more information only based on whether it is consistent with the category that we have placed the person into. This helps in faster processing of information without much effort, though it could also lead to development of stereotypes. When we categorise individuals into categories, we do so on the basis of certain salient cues, which could be the colour of one's skin, hair or even based on the clothes worn by the person. Schemas can also be used to explain prejudice.
- **Social identity theory:** Social identity theory proposed by Tajfel can also help explain prejudice. There are three main assumptions of this theory that need to be considered (Sears et al., 1991).

i. The social world is categorised by individuals into in-group and out-group.
ii. People seek positive self-concept and their social identity as a member of a certain group will help them develop a sense of self-esteem.
iii. The evaluation of an in-group by individuals, in relation to the out-group, partially determines their self-concept.

Thus, the individuals will try to enhance the status of one's own group so that their self-esteem is also enhanced.

Also, as self-esteem is linked with the feelings that one's in-group is superior and social identity is largely based on how one categorised one's self into an in-group, this self-categorisation as well as in-group favouritism, discussed earlier, will lead to higher self-esteem in an individual. Further, the need to enhance one's own self-esteem can lead to development of in-group favouritism; thus, in-group favouritism will be higher when the self-esteem is low or is perceived as under threat, and in this situation, prejudice could also be high.

Discrimination

The term discrimination has been derived from a Latin term *discrimino* which means to separate or divide (Schneider, 2004). Discrimination can be termed as a behavioural manifestation of prejudice (Crisp & Turner, 2010) and can be observed (Schneider, 2004). Thus, persons who have a prejudice towards a certain group are more likely to display discriminatory behaviour towards that group. Discrimination can be defined as 'an unjustified negative or harmful action toward the members of a group solely because of their membership in that group' (Aronson et al., 2014, p. 441).

For example, Sheetal and Varun were both in line for promotion as general managers. When their seniors were discussing about who deserves to be promoted, most of them had a prejudiced view that

Sheetal being a woman will not be able to be as dedicated as Varun. Despite Sheetal being more hard-working and deserving than Varun, Varun managed to get the promotion, mainly because of the prejudice that the seniors had lead to discrimination.

As can be seen in the aforementioned example, the action (i.e., promotion of Varun and not Sheetal) is unjustified as it is based on gender of these individuals and not on certain other significant parameters of performance. In a similar manner, individuals are discriminated based on colour of their skin or their weight and so on.

Most of us engage in some kind of discrimination or other. For example, one may not like when a person with criminal history moves into your neighbourhood. This kind of discrimination is most often approved as well. However, there are other kinds of discrimination that cannot be justified or approved. For example, there should be no discrimination based on gender, caste, religion or region as far as employment is concerned and this is even covered by policies and laws, though other discriminations could also take place that are as such not illegal. For example, a company may not hire married couples; thus, either husband or the wife could get the job.

There are other discriminations as well; for example, most often widows are not allowed to participate in festivities or during auspicious occasions, or most of the public spaces in India are not barrier-free and this can restrict the free movement of people with physical disability. Such discriminations, of course, could be debated but they do not fall under the purview of law.

Discrimination can also be subtle in nature, that is, not articulated in a conscious manner by either the perceiver or the target. Thus, there could be discriminations that are indirect in nature and can have an impact on the target, who may not be in position even to react to the discrimination due to lack of power. For example, women in certain families may not be vocal even when most important decisions are taken about their own lives. Further, individuals belonging to minority may face indirect discrimination on regular basis in their lives. A transgender my face stares from people or may be ignored on regular basis in their day-to-day life.

When the target group is discriminated, they may react by being defensive and by behaving cautiously. The target groups may also receive feedbacks that are positive but condescending at the same time (Schneider, 2004). For example, managers may go easy on the way women employees are evaluated during performance appraisal, just because they are women.

Discriminations could also be institutional where the prejudice that is overt becomes a part of policies that are public or institutional or when there are policies in existence that actually restrict the opportunities, access and choices available to individuals belonging to the targeted group (Schneider, 2004). For example, in certain organisations, only males are employed or people belonging to certain groups are not employed. Single women, for example, find it difficult to get flats on rent even in metropolitan cities. There could also be discrimination based on culture that points towards cultural racism, where the cultural heritage of one race is seen as superior to that of another (Jones, 1997).

Whether discrimination exists or not can be determined based on self-reporting of discrimination, which is based on experiences of people with reference to discrimination. However, it is important to focus here on the extent of accuracy with which the discrimination is perceived. Further, individuals who belong to such groups that have been victimised or discriminated at some point are more likely to pay attention to cues that hint at bias. Laboratory experiments can also be used to study if discrimination occurs. Another way in which discrimination can be examined is through job-related audits.

Discrimination, thus, can be termed a major societal problem and can have a negative impact on the individuals of the target group.

WAYS TO OVERCOME STEREOTYPE, PREJUDICE AND DISCRIMINATION

There are various ways in which attempts can be made to reduce stereotype, prejudice and discrimination; these are discussed in details here.

Contact Hypothesis

The intergroup biases and prejudice can be reduced when intergroup contact under suitable conditions is promoted. In this context, the various conditions necessary were proposed by Allport in 1954 (cited in Crisp & Turner, 2010).

- The social norms and social condition should emphasise on equality and integration. This is also necessary to avoid any dissonance. And the attitude and behaviour needs to be in accord with each other.
- Equal social status should also be ensured during the contact. The groups whether minority or majority need to feel equal in status when compared with other groups.
- Cooperation is required during the contact to achieve the common objective.

Though contact hypothesis has been widely used to deal with prejudice, it has also been criticised mainly due to lack of information about how the effect generated by the contact will be carried forward, beyond the situation in which the contact takes place, to other situations and also from persons involved in the contact to the whole out-group (Crisp & Turner, 2010). Yet another criticism is the complex nature of contact hypothesis that requires number of conditions to be followed so that the intergroup contact actually leads to reduction in prejudice.

One of the intergroup contacts is Jigsaw classroom designed by Aronson and others, which can be used to reduce the intergroup bias (Barrett, 2017). In jigsaw classroom, a problem is given to the children belonging to different racial or ethnic backgrounds and they have to solve it by cooperating with each other.

Indirect Contact

Contact hypothesis can be used in settings where the group members have an opportunity to contact each other, which is possible when they work or study together and so on. However, unless such a situation is available, the members of different groups will not be able to form a contact with each other. In this case, indirect contact can be helpful. Indirect contact can be categorised into extended contact and imagined contact, discussed in detail here.

- **Extended contact:** This can be referred to as a phenomenon in which mere knowledge that one of the in-group members is in a close relationship with individuals belonging to an out-group will lead to reduction in negative intergroup conflicts. A study was carried out by Wright et al. (1997) in four phases and the findings indicated that after phase one, the participants displayed intergroup competition after categorisation was introduced by the researchers. In phase two, as intergroup competition was introduced, there was an increase in intergroup bias. However, in phase three, decreased negative out-group attitude was found after the participants learned about positive inter-group contact with a member of an out-group. In phase four, the participants who observed a clear in-group–out-group friendship displayed lower negative out-group attitudes.

- **Imagined contact:** This can be described as a mental simulation with regard to an interaction between member(s) of the out-group (Crisp & Turner, 2010). Such mental simulations can lead to decrease in the feelings of apprehensions and make individuals more comfortable with regard to any contact with member(s) of out-group in future. In a study carried out by Turner et al. in 2007, young participants in the experimental group were asked to imagine an interaction with an elderly stranger, as young participants in the control condition imagined about an outdoor scene. They were then asked to write down what they had imagined and then were informed about a study that would be carried out in future that involved interaction with either an elderly person or young person. The participants, who imagined the interaction with an elderly stranger, were positive about interacting with an elderly person, whereas the participants in the control condition showed preference to interact with a young person (Crisp & Turner, 2010).

Re-categorisation

This is yet another way in which intergroup bias can be reduced. Re-categorisation includes 'viewing in-group and out-group members primarily as members of a larger, mutually inclusive group, thereby diminishing the importance of intergroup differences' (Barrett, 2017, p. 385). For example, we could belong to different states, Delhi, Tamil Nadu, Kerala, West Bengal, Maharashtra and when we categorise ourselves according to these states we have an in-group and out-group. However, if we re-categorise ourselves as Indians, then the intergroup differences reduce. Re-categorisation is based on the common in-group identity model that states that categorisation of persons into in-group and out-group lays the foundation for intergroup bias (Barrett, 2017). Thus, if the differences between the groups are shown in less light and similarities or commonalities are highlighted, then the bias between the groups can be decreased.

SUMMARY

To summarise, attitude in simple terms can be described as how one thinks or feels about a thing, person, place or even event. It can also be described as an evaluation of the attitude object and it can be positive, negative, mixed or neutral. Attitude can also be classified as implicit, explicit and dual. The three main components of attitude are cognitive, behavioural and affective components. Attitudes are learned or acquired, provide direction and can motivate people. They are also relatively permanent. Various functions of attitude are utilitarian function, knowledge function, ego defensive function and value expression function that were discussed in this chapter. The chapter also covered the formation of attitude with a focus on biological perspective, individual experiences, mere exposure effect, contextual influences and self-perception theory. The chapter also covered how behaviours are guided by attitudes. The factors that influence the relationship between attitude and behaviour, such as specificity, time, self-awareness, accessibility of the attitude, attitude strength, mindlessness, balance theory and theory of planned behaviour, were also discussed. Further, attitude change was also discussed with a focus on cognitive dissonance theory that was proposed by Festinger (1957). The theory states that feelings of discomfort are created when behaviour contradicts existing attitudes. Persuasion was also discussed in this context. The chapter then described the concepts of stereotype, prejudice and discrimination. Stereotypes can also be described as a cognitive process and can be negative or positive. Prejudice can be described as an attitude or feeling that is negative and is directed towards members of out-groups. Discrimination can be termed as a behavioural manifestation of prejudice. Lastly, ways to overcome stereotype, prejudice and discrimination were also discussed.

QUESTIONS

1. Define attitude and describe its components.
2. Discuss the characteristic features of attitude.
3. Discuss various functions of attitude.
4. Describe various perspectives with reference to how attitude develops.
5. Explain the influence of attitude on behaviour.
6. Discuss theory of planned behaviour with suitable example.
7. Explain cognitive dissonance theory.
8. Explain the concept of stereotype with a focus on gender stereotype.
9. Discuss in detail prejudice and discrimination.
10. Describe the ways to overcome stereotype, prejudice and discrimination.

REFERENCES

Festinger, L. (1957). *A theory of cognitive dissonance*. California: Stanford University Press.

Rokeach, M. (1973). *The nature of human values*. New York, NY: Free Press.

Schneider, S. J. (2004). *The psychology of stereotyping*. New York, NY: Guilford Press.

Sinha J. B. P. (1990). The salient Indian values and their socio-ecological roots. *Indian Journal of Social Sciences*, 3(4), 477–488.

FURTHER READINGS

For more definitions and information on stereotype, you can refer to the following:

Schneider, D. J. (2004). *The psychology of stereotyping*. New York, NY: The Guilford Press. Available at http://web.fmk.edu.rs/files/blogs/2010-11/Psihologija/Socijalna/THE%20PSYCHOLOGY%20OF%20STEREOTYPING.pdf

The following books can also be read:

Maio, G., & Haddock, G. (2012). *Psychology of attitudes* (1st ed.). London: SAGE Publications.

Dawes, R. (1972). *Fundamentals of attitude measurement* (1st ed.). New York, NY: Wiley.

SECTION III

The Individual and the Society

CHAPTER 8

Social Influence

It was a new academic year and Sameer and his friends were the in corridor of his college. His friends insisted that they had to rag the freshers, and though Sameer did not believe in ragging and knew that it was bad, he indulged in ragging, was caught and as a result was rusticated from the college.

Jamuna was a simple labourer who worked at a construction site. He worked hard to make ends meet and provide his family with food and shelter. Gradually, in the company of some other construction workers, Jamuna started consuming tobacco and also got into the habit of alcohol consumption. His wife tried her best to make Jamuna get rid of these bad vices and, as much as possible, tried to keep him away from his friends who obviously were a bad influence. But when Jamuna's friend came to know about this, they teased him and challenged him to show his wife who the boss in the house was, and on that day, Jamuna beat up his wife.

These are examples of what is referred to as social influence, where others influence and determine our behaviour. Many a time, we indulge in such behaviours that we may not completely agree with, for example, buying a dress or clothes that we probably did not like so much but we still buy them, because our best friends liked it. On the other hand, it is also possible that we influence someone else's behaviour and decision-making. These are some of the aspects covered under the umbrella of social influence that we will be discussing in this chapter.

In this chapter, the concept of social influence will be discussed and the chapter will also describe conformity and highlight normative and informational social influence. The concepts of minority influence, compliance and obedience will be discussed. The chapter will also explain social influence and social reality besides focusing on the term social norms.

Learning Objectives

After reading this chapter, you will be able to

- Discuss the term 'social influence'
- Explain normative and informational social influence
- Discuss minority influence
- Describe conformity, compliance and obedience
- Discuss social influence and social reality
- Explain the term 'social norms'

WHAT IS SOCIAL INFLUENCE?

Social influence can be described as an individual's effort to change the behaviour or attitude of another individual. It is one of the most important processes in social psychology and a clear understanding of the term is required in order to determine the negative and positive influences of this phenomenon.

Three definitions of social influences are discussed as follows:

Avermaet (2004, p. 404) defined social influence as 'a change in the judgements, opinions and attitudes of an individual as a result of being exposed to the views of others'.

Social influence has also been defined by Barrett (2017, p. 190) as 'an internal or external change in a person caused by the real or imagined pressure from others'.

Baron and Byrne (1995, p. 350) define social influence as 'efforts on the part of one person to alter the behaviour or attitudes of one or more others'.

These definitions denote that there is a change in the behaviour, attitude, judgement or opinion of the individual, which is as a result of the social influence or influence of others in our social set-up. The definition by Barrett mainly emphasises on the pressure that could be real or imagined. A real pressure can be described as requests that are overt and directed towards bringing about a change in the receiver's attitudes, beliefs or behaviours. On the other hand, imagined pressure is experienced when an individual believes, accurately or inaccurately, that others expect him/her to display certain attitudes and beliefs or engage in certain behaviours (Barrett, 2017).

Social influence is not only studied by social psychologists but also by sociologists. It has wide application, whether it is studying adolescent behaviours or advertising and marketing.

Social influences can be deliberate, direct and clear or indirect and concealed. The previously stated example of a group of friends influencing Jamuna's behaviour is an example of a direct social influence, whereas an advertisement that probably influences you to try a new deodorant or buy a particular chocolate is more subtle and indirect. Advertisements in a way are also subtle social influences.

Leadership, bargaining, negotiation and persuasion are ways in which individuals can influence each other's behaviours. An employer, as a leader, can influence his/her employees' behaviour and performance. We might bargain with a vegetable vendor to give us cauliflower at a lower rate or to give some coriander and green chillies free of cost. An adolescent may negotiate with his/her parents to raise his/her pocket money. Bargaining and negotiation can also take place at much higher levels, even international levels. A mother may use persuasion to feed yet another morsel to her child. Students may request their teachers to postpone the date of assignment submission.

Principles of Interpersonal Influence

Six main principles of interpersonal influence have been proposed by Cialdini (Barrette, 2017). These are discussed as follows:

1. **Scarcity:** This principle denotes that when options and items are not easily found or are available in a limited manner, they are given more value by the individuals. In this context, the compliance with actions and behaviours that are related to obtaining such an item or going with such an option will increase. For example, in advertisements, one may come across 'limited' gold coins that are distributed along with a product on first-come-first-serve basis or an advertisement may

indicate that only 10 limited edition products are available. This will lead to behaviour directed towards getting these products.

2. **Liking/friendship:** This principle denotes that adherence to requests from individuals who are evaluated positively is high. Thus, requests that are made by friends and significant others in our lives whom we like or perceive positively are more likely to be adhered to by us. This again is applied in advertisements where popular actors and sportsperson are involved in promoting certain products to influence the behaviours of the consumers.
3. **Commitment/consistence:** This is yet another principle and has been described as 'increased likelihood that people will enact a behaviour that is consistent with their own past behaviour and allows them to follow through on prior commitments' (Barrett, 2017, p. 194). A person who has been displaying pro-environment behaviour is more likely to be convinced to adopt new techniques of garbage disposal.
4. **Reciprocity:** This principle denotes that the likelihood of compliance is high when the request is from an individual who behaved in a favourable manner in the past. Thus, if a person who has helped you in the past asks you to buy a certain insurance policy, you are more likely to comply.
5. **Social validation:** The likelihood of an individual enacting a certain behaviour is high when others are thought to be enacting or engaging in that same behaviour. Social validation is also termed as social proof. For example, an individual will use a certain product because others are also using it.
6. **Authority:** The sixth principle proposed by Cialdin is the authority principle, which denotes that the likelihood of individuals behaving in the way that was suggested or requested by a perceived authority is high. Obedience can be explained with the help of this principle. To take an example, when a teacher asks a student to read a certain paragraph, the student will behave in the way that was suggested by the teacher.

Social Impact Theory

Social impact theory was developed by Latané. The theory focuses on the strength of an influence (that can be either positive or negative) that others can have on an individual. Social impact theory can be termed as a general theory of social influence that can be utilised to understand conformity and obedience (Crisp & Turner, 2010).

According to Latané, the strength of the influences will depend on the characteristics of the observer or source of the influence, their number and immediacy (Sears et al., 1991). The theory also helps us to determine the behaviours and actions of people in the presence of others. For example, during a presentation, individuals might not be so nervous when presenting a paper in front of their friends. But when it comes to presenting the same paper in front of a larger audience constituting of faculty members and other classmates, they might feel butterflies in their stomachs and may not perform to their best. The number of people exerting influence also determines the strength of the influence. The more the individuals exerting influence, the greater the strength of the influence. Thus, the number of observers present (few friends or a large audience), their characteristics (friends or faculty members) and their strength in terms of their status, age and relationship with the individual will also make a difference. Immediacy is also important and denotes 'how close the group exerting power is in time and space' (Crisp and Turner, 2010, p. 183).

Latané further explained how, in certain cases, the presence of others results in social facilitation, and in other cases, it leads to social loafing (Sears et al., 1991). In social facilitation situation, the individual is the only target of social impact by others, and as the number of people exerting impact on this individual increases, the social impact also increases. However, in social loafing situations, several individuals work on a single task and each of these individuals is a target of influence by an outsider and, thus, the social impact exerted by this outsider is divided amongst several targets.

CONFORMITY

To discuss with the help of an example, there is a group of five young boys/friends who like to hang out together. One of them feels that it is cool to try smoking and drugs as these are supposedly signs of manhood. He influences others to try it and is quite dominant. One of the boys in this group knows that it would be wrong to be involved in smoking and trying out drugs but has to give in as otherwise he will not be accepted in the group and will also be termed as 'not having enough guts to try out challenging things'. This boy knew in the bottom of his heart that what he and his friends are about to do is wrong but he gives in, as he wants to feel the sense of belonging.

In the example given, the boy conformed with his group as he probably wanted to fit in with them and belong with them and did not want to feel left out. This is what conformity is about.

Conformity can be described as pressures to go along with other people around you, to behave in the same manner as other persons in one's group or society (Baron & Byrne, 2006). It can also be described as conforming to the societal expectations about how one should behave in varied situations. Though it may be difficult to understand how individuals can be influenced to act in a manner that they do not want to act in, are expected to act in, and that is sometimes even forced on them by others, in the absence of conformity there would be great confusion and chaos in social situations. Certain norms are relevant for our smooth functioning in society. Respect for elders, for example, is essential and individuals can be expected to conform to such a social norm. However, conformity that appears in the context of examples, discussed at the beginning of this chapter, can be unhealthy.

Solomon Asch (1951) carried out an experiment that contributed to this area of knowledge. Asch carried out a study on a group of around nine (male) participants who were college students. In the experiment, the participants were told that they would be comparing lines on the basis of their length. During the experiment, two white cards were presented to the participants. One of the white cards had a single vertical line on it that was the standard, and the other white card had three vertical lines on it. Out of these three lines, the participants were asked to choose one that was same as that of the standard line (Figure 8.1). The participants were asked to give their opinion in front of the whole group and in the order that they were made to sit in the classroom. However, the main participant was not aware that the rest of the members of the group were in fact confederates of the researcher. This main participant was made to sit last; thus, he had to provide his opinion at the end after he had heard all the other opinions. In certain trials, the confederates were asked by the researcher to unanimously provide an incorrect answer. There were around 18 trials in each series of judging the line, out of which, for 12 trials, the majority of the participants gave an incorrect answer. The results indicated that on 37 per cent of the trials, the participant gave an incorrect answer, going by the answers given by the majority. When interviewed after the study, the non-conformers (those who did not go with the majority) said that they believed in what they saw and went with it. The people who conformed felt that they might be wrong in some way or the other and, therefore, went with the majority. Though replicated and even criticised, the experiment provides us a glimpse of how social conformity can take place.

In a later research, when Asch asked all the participants to write their answers on a paper, the conformity dropped. Thus, we can distinguish between public compliance and private acceptance (Baron & Byrne, 2006). In public or in the presence of others, there is less possibility that we will

Figure 8.1 ***The Standard Line and Comparison Lines Used in Asch's Experiment***

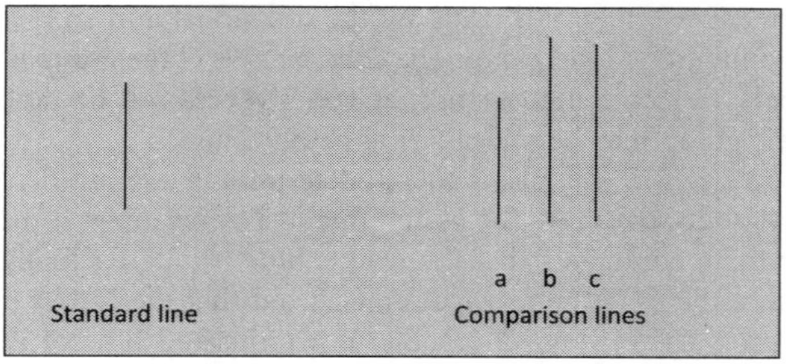

Source: Author.

contradict, but that does not mean that we change our fundamental beliefs views, attitudes and principles; we just do not express them.

Influences on Conformity

Conformity can be influenced by social norms. We might not like wearing traditional clothes, but we are expected to wear them when we are attending an Indian wedding or taking part in a religious activity. And though there is no written rule that you have to dress in a particular manner for a wedding or during a religious activity, you end up dressing traditionally as that is the norm. Our behaviour in social context is determined by these social norms. In India, children are expected to greet the elders respectfully. Similarly, certain behaviours are expected from men and women. Social norms apply to all aspects of our behaviour, from how we talk, to how we eat, to how we lead our lives and the choices that we make. Though there are also people who do deviate from these social norms, these are the exceptions. Besides social norms, other factors such as cohesiveness (how attracted we feel towards the group or individual influencing us), existence or lack of social support and even other characteristics such as gender can have an impact on conformity. Studies show that females are more likely to conform than males (Reitan & Shaw, 1964).

The following factors were also found to have an influence on conformity, as displayed by the experiment carried out by Asch:

1. The extent of conformity will depend on the attractiveness of the group members. The more attractive the group members, the higher the conformity.
2. Conformity will also depend on the difficulty of the task. The more difficult the task, the higher the conformity.
3. Lastly, conformity also depends on the cohesiveness amongst the group members. The higher the cohesiveness, the more the conformity.

The following can be described in the context of influences on conformity:

- **Commitment to the group:** Commitment can be described as forces that work in the direction of retaining an individual in a group or in a relationship. These forces could be positive or negative.

Some of the examples of positive forces are liking the members in the group, identification with group values, belief in goal-oriented activities of the group, deriving sense of identification with group and so on. On the other hand, the examples of negative forces are lack of alternatives, great amount of investment in the group made by the individual and so on. These forces make an individual more committed to the group. The cohesiveness of the group is also related to whether the group members are committed or not, as cohesiveness can be described as the degree of commitment of the group members (Sears et al., 1999).

- **Group size:** Group size will also play a role in determining commitment and, in fact, the more the members in a group, the more the commitment. For example, if there are two people in a room and one of them comments that the wall is blue (though actually it is green in colour), it is more likely that the other person will point it out that the colour of the wall is green and not blue. However, if there were ten people in a room and nine of them comment that the colour of the wall is blue (though in reality it is green), then this tenth person will have a doubt on his/her own perception and may go along with what has been said by others. Thus, the person will conform to the opinion or point of view held by the majority. Asch (1955) stated that a majority size of three members could also have an impact on the opinion or point of view of the group. Thus, just three members are sufficient to make other members conform to the opinion of these members.
- **Group unanimity:** Yet another factor that can determine conformity is the group unanimity in terms of its opinion. When a member faces a group that has taken a unanimous decision, it would be exceedingly difficult for him/her not to conform. However, if there is no unanimity amongst the group members, the conformity will decrease. This is the case even if one other of the group members does not agree with what has been said by the other members in the group. In this context, it does not matter who the dissenter is, he/she could be an expert or not an expert, a member with high or low prestige. The timing of the dissent also seems to play a role here, as conformity will decrease if the dissent occurs after the opinion has been expressed by the majority and the conformity decreases further when the dissent is before the majority has expressed its opinion. This decrease in conformity as a result of ruination of unanimity can be due to various factors such as decrease in trust/confidence in the correctness of the majority, support from any other group member that strengthens the self-confidence of the person who dissented and so on.
- **The desire for individuation:** The desire for individuation can also influence conformity. Persons with high individuation are less likely to conform and maintain their stand even in face of a different opinion from the majority, and persons with low individuation are more likely to conform. Further, individuals with high desire for control are less likely to conform as opposed to people with low desire for control (Burger, 1987).

As there are individuals who conform, there are individuals who can be termed as anti-conformist as well. The term is used to describe people who do not conform. There is also a possibility that certain individuals do not conform with their group and refuse to behave in the manner suggested by others. Such people choose to stand firm on their opinions and values. This is referred to as individuation, which occurs when one wants to maintain one's individuality or uniqueness or wants to distinguish oneself from others (Baron & Byrne, 2006). Another reason why individuals do not conform is because they want to have certain control over their lives and do not want to relinquish that control to others. Further discussion in this direction will be carried out with regard to minority influence.

NORMATIVE SOCIAL INFLUENCE AND INFORMATIONAL SOCIAL INFLUENCE

There are two types of social influences, normative and informational social influence.

1. **Normative social influence:** Normative social influence can be defined as 'the influence of other people that leads us to conform in order to be liked and accepted by them; this type of conformity results in public compliance with the group's beliefs and behaviours but not necessarily in private acceptance of those beliefs and behaviours' (Aranson et al., 2014, p. 246).

Social norms play an important role here (later in this chapter, social norms will be discussed in detail) as individuals may display certain behaviours just to conform with the social norms, whether implicit or explicit.

In certain cases, we choose to confirm also because we want to be liked by the group members and want to be accepted by them. Thus, many a time, we agree with our parents, teachers and significant people in our lives, as we want to be accepted and liked by them. This can be termed as normative social influence as we change our behaviours so as to fulfil others' expectations. It can also be described as a predisposition to be influenced by others with an objective to get some reward from them or to avoid punishment.

Every group has certain expectations from its members with regard to how they behave. All the group members are required to conform to the norms and rules set down by the group. The members who do not conform are seen as different and may also be termed as deviant. The deviant members could be subjected to rejection, punishments and may also be ridiculed. And though some of the individuals are able to cope with such social exclusion, most human beings seek affection, love and support and thus may not be able to cope well with being excluded or being ridiculed by their group. Thus, they may choose to conform to the group though they may not agree with the opinions or the stand taken by the group.

2. **Informational social influence:** Sometimes, we conform as we measure our responses and behaviour with those of others, as that is the reality for us in the social context (social reality). This is also called informational social influence. It can be described as a predisposition to accept facts obtained from others as confirmation about reality.

Informational social influence can be defined as 'the influence of other people that leads us to conform because we see them as a source of information to guide our behaviour; we conform because we believe that others' interpretation of an ambiguous situation is more correct than ours and will help us choose an appropriate course of action' (Aranson et al., 2014, p. 240).

In 1936, Muzafer Sherif carried out an experiment that is widely known as the autokinetic effect experiment. In this experiment, the participants were made to sit in a dark room with their attention focused on a dot of light that was at a distance of 15 feet from the participants. The participants were asked to report the movement of this dot of light in terms of inches. Several such trials were carried out where the participants had to report any movement in the dot of light. Most of the participants in this experiment reported that the dot of light was moving, though in reality there was no movement. The movement in the dot of light was as a result of a visual illusion that is referred to as autokinetic effect. This can be attributed to a lack of a reference point in which the position of the dot of light can be anchored, which leads to the dot being perceived as moving. It has to be noted here that there was a variation in the estimations that was made by the participants with regard to movement of the dot of light in inches. Whereas, some reported that the movement was about an inch, some reported it to be as much as 10 inches.

In the second phase of the experiment carried out by Sherif after a few days, the participants from the earlier phase were made to sit with two other participants. All the three participants had now to provide their responses aloud. It is to be noted here that in the earlier phase of the experiment, these participants had displayed variations in their reporting of movement of the dot of light in terms of inches. But in the second phase, over the several trials, it was observed that a common estimate was reached by the participants, to which every participant in the group (of three participants) conformed. Thus, the participants relied on the information provided by the other participants. The participants thus believed that the estimations made by the group were correct.

In this context, the term private acceptance can be discussed that denotes genuine belief that others are correct, which leads to conformity with behaviours of others, though there could also be public compliance that occurs when individuals conform to behaviour of others publicly, without necessarily believing in what is being said or done by others.

MINORITY INFLUENCE

Most often it is seen that a group has an influence on an individual, and the point of view held by the majority is complied with, though it is not always that the non-conformists are silenced or the deviants in a group are suppressed. Otherwise, there would be no social change; there would be no one going against the flow. In this context, thus, the concept of minority influence can be discussed. Minority influence can be defined as 'the case where a minority of group members influences the behaviour or beliefs of the majority' (Aronsosn et al., 2014, p. 258). In minority influence, one of the main aspects is consistency, that is, the same view should be expressed by the minority members over a period of time. Further, members of minority also need to agree with each other as otherwise, their voices will not be heard and, thus, the opinions of the minority will be dismissed.

A distinction can be made between diachronic consistency and synchronic consistency. A diachronic consistency denotes consistency that is over a period of time, whereas a synchronic consistency denotes a consistency that exists between the members, where each one is supported by the other.

Consistency can play an important role in minority influence in the following ways:

- Consistency will help in making the individual with certain opinions noticeable to the majority, and that in turn may lead to the members of majority to rethink with regard to the position adopted by them.
- Consistency also creates an impression about how convinced the minority is with regard to their own opinion. It also highlights their commitment towards their viewpoint.
- Consistency also interferes with well-established norms and paves the way for conflict and doubt, and thus their point of view will be noticed and will be taken seriously by the majority.

Besides consistency, confidence is also important. A minority that is confident and dedicated towards their opinion and stand demonstrates that they have a strong point to make.

A study was carried out by Moscovici and Zavalloni (1969) to study the effect of a consistent minority on majority. The study was similar to that carried out by Asch. In the study, the participants were put in groups of four participants with two confederates. The participants were then showed 36 slides that had different shades of blue. The participants had to state the colour of each slide aloud. In the first part of the experiment, the confederates provided their response as 'green' for all the 36 slides that were displayed. In the second part of the experiment, the confederates provided their response as 'green' for 24 slides and response as 'blue' for 12 slides. Thus, in the first part, they displayed consistency, and in the second part inconsistency was displayed by them. The results indicated that the effect of minority was higher in the first part of the experiment as compared to the effect of the minority in the second part of the experiment. Thus, the experiment indicated that consistency on part of the minority could have an influence on the majority. In another study carried out by Moscovici and Personnaz (1980), female participants were showed blue slides that were labelled as green consistently by female confederates. The confederates though were either presented as members of minority or members of majority. During every trial, the participants were asked not only to indicate the colour of the slide shown to them, but also to report the colour of the after-image that they perceived on the white screen that followed when the slide was removed. The results indicated that when the influence agent was a minority, the participant's judgement with regard to the chromatic after-image changed, and the modifications were less pronounced when the source of influence was present than when the source of influence was absent.

As minority cannot influence others through the means of normative social influence, they have to indulge in the use of other methods like informational social influence that can help them seek private acceptance. On the other hand, majority mainly rely on public compliance that is achieved with the help of normative social influence. Further, as majority make use of social comparison process in order to make others conform to their point of view, divergent thinking is used by minority to influence others.

Nemeth (1986), who carried out a study on the differential contributions of majority and minority influence, emphasised that public influence is exerted by majority, whereas minority influence mainly exists at a latent level. Nemeth further indicated that the influence by minority includes cognitive processing when compared with the influence by majority and that the consideration of point of view expressed by minority may or may not lead to attitude change but it may lead to elaborate thinking with regard to issues by the majority that leads to better judgements.

COMPLIANCE

In conformity, it was discussed that we want to be liked by others; however, we are also aware that others would do things for us if they like us, that is, when compliance comes into the picture. Examples of compliance are as follows.

After waking up early in the morning, making her bed and getting ready for school in time, Sara greeted her parents cordially, touched her grandparents' feet and was at the breakfast table having milk and even fruits. This was an ideal behaviour displayed by Sara. Her behaviour was in stark contrast to her normal morning rituals where she had to be woken up by her mother and coerced to get ready for school. Making Sara have milk and fruits would be an early morning challenge for her mother. Her parents must have guessed that there was something that Sara wanted. Sara indeed needed their permission to go for an overnight picnic and this was her way of seeking their permission.

An individual seeking compliance attempts to change the actions and behaviours of one or more individuals by means of direct requests or other strategies. The individual uses any strategy or means to influence other individuals to do things or behave in his/her favour. Children, for example, may cry, throw tantrums and act up in order to get their favourite toy or video game. Similarly, in a group of people, an individual may use various tactics in order to make the other members comply with him/her.

He/she may plead, be dominant, be critical, challenge the members and so on. In certain cases, the other individual may comply with certain requests without any reason or without giving any serious thinking to it. This has been termed as mindlessness by Langer. The term was briefly touched upon in the chapter on attitude.

Bases of Social Power

There are six bases of power that could be used in order to influence individuals.

1. **Reward:** One way in which others can be influenced is by providing rewards. The ability to provide rewards or positive outcomes to others can be termed as one of the basis of social power. Rewards could range from a simple smile, to acknowledgement and recognition and to monetary benefits. Rewards may or may not be explicit. For example, parents may make an explicit bargain with their child, where the child would get a bicycle if he/she scores good marks in the examination. There could also be reciprocity with regard to rewards in certain relationships, where one person is expected to behave in a certain way and the other is expected to reciprocate.
2. **Coercion:** Yet another basis of power is coercion. Coercion can also range from subtle disapproval to punishments and use of physical force in convincing a person. In an organisational set-up, a manager may reprimand an employee for always being late to work. Coercion as such is not opposite of rewards, but can be differentiated from it, as rewards motivate individuals to display good behaviour or display desired behaviour, whereas in coercion the individuals indulge in behaviour as expected by the influencer. Further, coercion may require surveillance, which is not required in rewards.
3. **Expertise:** Experts could be termed as individuals with some kind of special knowledge and skills. And this expertise can also serve as a basis of power. A doctor, for example, is perceived as an expert, and if he/she prescribes a certain vitamin then individuals are more likely to comply.
4. **Information:** An individual's behaviour can also be influenced by providing him/her with information or rational arguments. Providing information about the ill effects of tobacco consumption may prompt an individual to quit tobacco consumption.
5. **Referent power:** Individuals may display a desire to be like persons they admire and identify with. This leads to the development of referent power, where the behaviours of others is voluntarily copied because the individual wants to be like that person. Thus, an individual may want to wear the clothes of a certain brand that are worn by a famous actor or a sportsperson. However, there could also be negative referent power also, where an individual wants to distance from an individual that he/she dislikes and does not want to identify with.
6. **Legitimate authority:** Certain individual may have authority to ask another individual to act in a certain manner. For example, a teacher may ask a student to solve the sum given on the blackboard. A manager may ask an employee to carry out a certain task. The teacher and the manager here are persons with legitimate authority. Such legal authority is guided by social roles that lay down legitimate rights and responsibilities in relationships such as parent–child, teacher–student, manager–employee and so on.

In this context, the 'power of helplessness' can also be discussed, which can be described as a special kind of legitimate power. For example, a paraplegic person may seek help from others to open a door, or a child may seek help to take a toy from a shelf that he/she is not able to reach. In these situations, the paraplegic individual and the child are seen as powerless and, thus, others may comply with their request for assistance. This can also be related to the norm of social responsibility which denotes that persons who are less fortunate need to be helped. Though it is also possible that persons who receive such help (through legitimate power of helplessness) may develop feelings of incompetence and as a result may display low self-esteem (Sears et al., 1999).

Techniques of Compliance

- **Ingratiation:** Ingratiation is one of the techniques used in compliance. In this, the individual tries to improve their attractiveness to make others more prone to complying with them (Baron & Byrne, 2006). In the example, discussed earlier, Sara behaves in an ideal manner in order to make herself look good so that others comply with her demands and requests. This also involves focusing on the person who is in position to gratify the request (the target person) so as to create a positive impression on them.
- **Foot-in-the-door technique:** One of the techniques of conformity is foot-in-the-door technique. In this, the person will first gain compliance for smaller requests and then put forth his/her larger request. This technique is used especially in the marketing field. In malls and shopping complex, you may come across people requesting you to try out certain samples of their products. Once you do so, then they try to sell the product to you. This technique is based on two factors. First, that individuals see the situations as less threatening and, second, there is a change in self-perception, as they see themselves as altruistic in fulfilling requests of others.
- **Door-in-the-face technique:** Another technique is the door-in-the-face technique. This is reverse of the earlier technique. In this, first, the individual will ask for a larger request and then when it is denied then smaller requests are introduced. For example, an employee may initially ask for a leave the next day and once the employer refuses, he/she may then ask if he/she can at least leave early that day. The reason behind success of this technique is that when individuals deny larger requests they may be obliged to at least agree with smaller requests. This is also termed as reciprocal concessions (Baron & Byrne, 2006). The second reason is that individuals want to have a positive impression about themselves and do not want to keep denying requests. This is called as self-presentation where they do not want to create an impression of being an insensitive person who refuses all requests.
- **That's not all (TNA) technique:** The next technique is the 'that's not all' (TNA) technique. For example, when you visit a travel agency to plan your travel, before you even finalise anything, they may offer you free breakfast during your travel. Similarly, while you buy a four wheeler, free accessories and even insurance are provided. In this, the deal is in a way sugar-coated to make it seem more attractive and difficult to resist.

Reciprocity works in this context as we feel that the other person is making so many concessions that you have to comply. At a store, you might be forced to buy an item, even though you did not wish to, as the salesperson shows you all the options of the product along with a lucrative discount.

Other Techniques of Compliance

- **Flattery:** Certain individuals can use flattery with their superiors to get a positive performance assessment or to get a lucrative assignment.

- **Agreements:** Agreements can also be used to seek compliance. For example, Sara would have agreed to whatever said by her parents to get permission to go for the picnic.
- **Non-verbal behaviour:** Even our non-verbal behaviour of sitting in an attentive manner, nodding with smile and other non-verbal behaviours are displayed to get compliance.
- **Self-enhancement**: Self-enhancement involves improving one's appearance and behaviour. During an interview, we put our best foot forward by dressing formally and carrying ourselves in a formal manner that would create a positive impression on the interviewers.
- **Self-depreciation:** Self-depreciation includes giving unfavourable information about oneself to convey modesty.
- **Self-disclosure:** Self-disclosure includes providing information about oneself to paint a picture of honesty and transparency.
- **Complaining:** Yet another way in which one can seek compliance is by complaining. A mother may complain about her child lying on the sofa all day watching TV and not studying. This constant complaining may influence the child to actually switch off the TV and study for a while.

However, if these tactics are overdone or overused then there could also be negative consequences.

OBEDIENCE

Many a time, in many situations, we have to obey others, as we have no other choice. In India, for example, we are told to respect and obey others, especially our parents. For example, Ishan was looking forward to a weekend with his family. He and his family were supposed to visit his grandmother over the weekend to celebrate her 75th birthday. However, on Friday, Ishan's boss told him that he has to go to the head office of the company the next day for an important meeting. Ishan could not refuse and had to follow the orders of his boss.

In obedience, an individual will give command or direct others to behave in a particular manner or change their actions. Such persons have some power vested in them as a result of their status or position in the group or society.

There are various forms of obedience; there can be obedience to law, to social norms and to government and religious institutions. There can also be obedience to God. There is obedience to self-imposed restrictions (like deciding not to eat non-vegetarian food). There is also obedience to one's family, friends and significant others and obedience to our employers.

An experiment was conducted by Milgram with regard to obedience that also highlighted issues of ethics in research, besides showing the negative consequences of obedience. In the experiment, the participants (who were males) were told that they were participating in an experiment on effects of punishment on learning. These participants had to deliver an electric shock to another participant (who was an accomplice and sitting in another room) if he made any errors in the simple learning task. An equipment with 30 switches was provided to deliver the shock. Also, participants were asked to move to a higher switch every time an error was committed by the other participant. The first switch delivered a shock of 15 volts and obviously, the higher switches delivered higher shock. The maximum shock was up to 450 volts. However, in reality, the participants (the accomplice) never received any shock but were asked to act that they were indeed receiving the shock. During the experiment, the other participant (accomplice) made numerous errors and the participants had to administer the shock that they did as they had received the command from the experimenter and were also pressurised to give shock. The results indicated that almost 65 per cent of the participants obeyed the experimenter completely. The same was not seen in the control group where commands were not given, nor were they pressurised. In fact, the participants even protested when they had to administer the shock. The experiment clearly showed that an individual's behaviour can be influenced by obedience, though the experiment has been criticised for various ethical issues.

Obedience will also depend on the personality of the person obeying. One of the characteristics in this regard is the authoritarian submission, which deals with a predisposition to submit to an authoritative figure. Locus of control is yet another characteristic. Individuals with external locus of control are more prone to be obedient than individuals with internal locus of control.

Obedience may also depend to a greater extent on the upbringing of the person and the social norms prevalent in the society. In Indian society as well, obedience is valued and children are expected to be obedient, especially towards their parents and even teachers.

Many a time, individuals obey to behave in manners that might even negatively affect others because, they don't consider themselves as responsible for the actions. They feel that the actions were taken by them under someone's order and that they were just obeying and thus they cannot be held responsible for the consequences. Also, in certain cases, they might find it difficult to resist as they themselves might face negative consequences. Further, such individuals may also comply because initial actions may be milder. Nevertheless, they gradually become harmful, which the individuals do not realise.

There are various ways of refuting orders or refusing to obey. The following strategies can be used to help individuals to disobey destructive orders:

1. The individuals can be reminded that ultimately they are the ones who are responsible for inflicting pain/distress.
2. They may also be made aware that submissive behaviour beyond a certain point is not necessary and is harmful.
3. The authority of the person giving orders can be challenged and awareness must be carried amongst the individuals about ill effects of power and authority and negative effects it can create.

SOCIAL INFLUENCE AND SOCIAL REALITY

Understanding the term 'social reality' is relevant when social influence is discussed. The following examples can help in understanding the concept of social reality.

Suppose you go for a movie with a group of friends and when you come out you express that you did not like it, that it was not worth the money and time and that the best part of it was the popcorn that you had. But most of your friends disagree with you and say that they liked the movie very much. Certainly, in this situation you are going to doubt yourself.

This doubt occurs because you realise that there is a lack of social reality. The social reality of other group members is also shaken, especially if there were two other friends who supported your opinion.

This will lead to a discussion amongst you and your friends about whether the movie was good or bad, and this is mainly done in order to restore social reality in the group.

Social Comparison Theory by Festinger attempts to assess how the validity of a belief is determined. According to Festinger (1950), when the social reality is absent, the group members will try to reinstate it by communicating with each other (cited in Kahn & Donnerstein, 1984). However, this will also depend on the cohesiveness of the group. If the group is cohesive, the following three outcomes will ensue:

1. You change your belief and agree that the movie was not that bad. This of course will reinstate the social reality.
2. You may refuse to budge from your belief that the movie was indeed bad and convince others about your belief that the movie was not worth watching. This again will restore social reality. But since you were a minority, it would be termed as 'minority influence'.
3. Neither you nor your friends compromise on the belief. In this case, social reality can be restored only if you were excluded from the group. In such a situation, you can expect not to be invited for the next movie outing. You may though continue to confirm your belief through reviews on the movie and views of some other friends.

An experiment was carried out by Stanley Schachter (1951) in order to validate the theory put forth by Festinger about social reality. In this experiment, the participants (mainly male college students) were assigned to four different clubs:

1. High cohesive and high relevant: The participants were placed in the club that they wanted to join and discussed an issue that was relevant.
2. High cohesive and low relevant: The participants were placed in the club that they wanted to join and discussed an issue that had low relevance.
3. Low cohesive and high relevant: The participants were placed in the club that they did not like and discussed an issue that had high relevance.
4. Low cohesive and low relevance: The participants were placed in the club that they did not like and discussed an issue that had low relevance.

A case study about a juvenile delinquent was then provided to all the participants, which was such that the participants would sympathise with and felt bad about the juvenile delinquent.

However, amongst the participants in all the four groups were three confederates:

1. The mode: The mode agreed with majority of the group through the discussion.
2. The deviate: The deviate disagreed with the group and felt that the juvenile should be strongly punished, and he did not budge from his position till the end.
3. The slider: The slider initially agreed with the deviate but later went with the group, ultimately assuming the position of the mode.

The results of the experiment supported the theory of Festinger, and the group got involved in more communication with the deviate than with other accomplices. However, it was also observed that in high cohesive and high relevant club, there was not much communication with the deviate. In the low cohesive and low relevance club, the communication with the deviate increased.

Further, when the club members also displayed an unfavourable attitude towards the deviates, they were allotted roles that were less prestigious in subsequent discussion groups.

SOCIAL NORMS

The term 'norm' has been derived from the Latin word *norma* that means a carpenter's square that looks like an 'L'. This tool helps the carpenter in designing and creating furniture.

Paluck (2009) defined norms as 'socially shared definitions of the way people do behave or should behave'. Social norms can also be defined as 'shared ways of thinking, feeling, desiring, deciding and acting which are observable in regularly repeated behaviours and are adopted because they are assumed to solve problems' (Critto, 1999).

Social norms provide us with information about what is acceptable and what is not. These can also be described as standards of behaviour. For example, during a family gathering in India, all the youngsters are expected to seek blessings from the elderly members of the family. Most of the youngsters will do so as per the prior instructions provided by their parents. However, there might be some youngster who does not like it and may refuse to seek any blessing as he/she feels that it is a futile exercise. In this situation, the youngster is breaking the social norm and it will be noticed by others. Although social norm is in a way invisible, the moment they are violated, they surface automatically and become visible.

When we go for some party, we have to follow different norms related to greeting, eating habits, conversation and so on, and of course we are aware of these norms as they are prevalent in that society. It might be difficult for a stranger or an outsider though, who probably is not aware about the norms. He/she may, however, get gradually socialised and learn the norms.

Further, it is also important to note that norms are followed not because they are the only means but because they are a practice or a tradition. They are arbitrary and do not necessarily have a rational reasoning. For example, with regard to eating habits, it is not necessary to eat with a fork as you might as well use your fingers. But we may use a fork because that is the practice and we feel that if we eat with our fingers people are going to notice and talk about it. Similarly, during weddings, we follow certain rituals without questioning them as we are expected to follow them.

However favourable or unfavourable a norm may be, they are significant and very much required to maintain and regulate interactions in a social set-up. Further, in this context, we can also talk about sanctions or authorisations on following a particular norm. These sanctions or authorisations can be either positive or negative, and these can reinforce our behaviour especially with reference to following a particular norm. However, if we have already accepted a norm then our behaviour will be self-enforced and any sanction or authorisation may not be required (Kuppuswamy, 1973).

Norms can be of various kinds. Cognitive norms, for example, can be described as beliefs that individuals have about certain issues, objects, individuals and so on. These relate to social reality and not physical reality (Kuppuswamy, 1973). There are also evaluative norms, which mainly deal with how desirable an object, person etc. is. There are also behavioural norms, which mainly specify rules about behaviours.

Types of Norms

- **Group norms:** These are specific to certain groups. It can be a group of friends, for example. It is different from social norms that are defined on the basis of specific situation.
- **Explicit norms:** These are clear and adequately expressed norms. For example, traffic rules.
- **Implicit norms:** These are not spoken or written down and are implied. For example, greeting rituals in a particular society.
- **Injunctive norms:** These are based on an individual's perception about what is an appropriate behaviour according to others. For example, a child will behave according to expectations of his/her parents.
- **Descriptive norms:** These are one's perception about others' behaviour in various situations. For example, how you perceive your friend's behaviour.
- **Consensus norms:** If these norms were already prevalent among group members in a group, the group would come to a consensus or mutual decision without heeding to any contrary evidence.

- **Critical norms:** Group members with critical norms will evaluate all the evidences, give a critical thought and then take a decision.
- **Reciprocity norms:** These norms suggest that if you have been provided with some help then you have to reciprocate and provide help in return. It is like give and take.
- **Social responsibility norms:** These are with regard to our responsibility towards society. For example, not littering your city with garbage, but throwing it in proper dustbins is a social responsibility norm.
- **Situational norms:** These will differ from situation to situation. Norms at home will be different from those in a cinema hall or in college.

Research on formation and maintenance of social norms was carried out by Sherif and his colleagues. Muzzafar Sherif et al. (1961) mainly wanted to study the informal groups. Boys of age 11–12 years were included in the research after a selection process that involved interviews with teachers, school authorities and even family. Various records (such as medical, school, personality tests etc.) were also referred to during the selection process. The sample was thus homogeneous in nature and comprised of boys who were healthy, well-adjusted and had above average intelligence. A camp was created in which the boys were expected to participate. However, they were not aware that they were part of an experiment. During the camp, the boys were given various activities and challenges. First, the boys were put together in a bunkhouse where they were asked to choose a buddy. Later, they were divided into two groups and care was taken that their buddy was in the other group. The researchers clearly had observed the development of group structure during first phase of the research. One of the groups called themselves 'The Eagles' and the other 'The Rattlers'. Both the groups differed greatly in their structures. When in second phase, games that promoted conflicts were introduced, soon rivalry developed between the two groups and this also created a problem, as the researchers had no idea how to put an end to the conflict. Further, it was observed that as the two groups had conflicting aims, they displayed hostility towards each other. In the last phase, when the boys were given superordinate goals (goals that retract present goals), the boys started developing friendship with the members of the rival group and their ratings also were found to be less negative. This research helped understand in-group and out-group behaviour. Besides, it also contributed to understanding social issues like racism.

Yet another experiment was carried by Haney, Banks and Zimbardo (1973). Though it did not as such focus on obedience, it researched the group behaviour of the participants and focused on how orders are obeyed and even how roles that are abusive are adopted. In this study, through a newspaper advertisement, 24 participants were selected to participate in the research. The participants were normal and healthy males who were from middle-class families and were white. In this research, a simulated prison was created in the psychology department basement of Stanford University. The participants were then assigned roles of either guards or prisoners and they even signed contract in this regard which stated that $15 would be given to them per day with basic living facilities. They were also informed that certain civil rights might be compromised during the study. The role of the warden of the prison was played by Zimbardo. Though the prisoners were given no specific instructions, the guards were instructed to maintain order in the prison, though any kind of physical aggression on the prisoners was prohibited. Both the guards and the prisoners were given uniforms and had to play the respective role during the duration of the study. The experiment had to be ended within 6 days rather than 14 due to the drastic effect of the simulated prison on the participants, mainly because the participants had internalised the role. The guards displayed increased aggression and some of the prisoners had to be released from the experiment because of depression, rage and acute anxiety. This research is again criticised for ethical issues, but it highlights the effect of social roles in our lives.

SUMMARY

To summarise, in this chapter, we discussed how social influence plays an important role in determining individual and group behaviour. Social influence was described as an individual's effort to change the behaviour or attitude of another individual. Conformity was also discussed in detail with a focus on what influences conformity. Normative and informational social influences were also discussed in detail. The concept of minority influence was also explained, besides the concepts of compliance and obedience. The chapter further moved on to focus on social influence and social reality. Further social norms that can be described as standards of behaviour in a social set-up were also described.

QUESTIONS

1. Describe the term social influence with suitable examples.
2. Discuss the social impact theory.
3. Define the term conformity and explain the factors that influence conformity.
4. Describe the techniques of compliance.
5. Explain the experiment on obedience carried out by Milgram.
6. Define social norms and describe various types of norms.

REFERENCES

Haney, C., Banks, W.C., & Zimbardo, P. G. (1973). A study of prisoners and guards in a simulated prison. Naval Research Review.

Moscovici, S., & Zavalloni, M. (1969). The group as a polarizer of attitudes. *Journal of Personality and Social Psychology*, *12*, 125–135.

Paluck, E. (2009). What's in a norm? Sources and processes of norm change. *Journal of Personality and Social Psychology*, *96*(3), 594–600. Retrieved from http://dx.doi.org/10.1037/a0014688

Schachter, S. (1951). Deviation, rejection, and communication. *Journal of Abnormal and Social Psychology*, *46*, 190–208.

FURTHER READINGS

For more information on social influence, the following can be referred to:

Cacioppo, J. T., Petty, R. E., & Stoltenberg, C. D. (1985). Processes of social influence: The elaboration likelihood model of persuasion. In Kendall, P. C. (Ed.), *Advances in cognitive-behavioural research and therapy* (pp. 215–274). San Diego, CA: Academic Press.

Friedkin, N. (1998). *A structural theory of social influence*. Cambridge, MA: Cambridge University Press. Retrieved from http://www.tcnj.edu/~browntam/SocialInfluence.htm

For further information on conformity, the following can be referred to:

Baron, R. S., Vandello, J. A., & Brunsman, B. (1996). The forgotten variable in conformity research: Impact of task importance on social influence. *Journal of Personality and Social Psychology*, *71*(5), 915–927.

Hodges, B. H., & Geyer, A. L. (2006). A nonconformist account of the Asch Experiments: Values, pragmatics, and moral dilemmas. *Personality and Social Psychology Review, 10*(1), 2–19.

Schultz, P. W. (1999). Changing behaviour with normative feedback interventions: A field experiment on curbside recycling. *Basic and Applied Social Psychology, 21*(1), 25–36.

For further information on social norms, the following can be referred to:

Hechter, M., & Opp, K. D. (2001). *Social Norms*. New York, NY: Russell Sage Foundation.

Ullmann-Margalit, E. (1977). *The Emergence of Norms*. Oxford: Oxford University Press.

CHAPTER 9

Pro-social Behaviour

To start with this chapter, we will go through the stories of two seemingly ordinary persons, but not ordinary in their acts.

Married off at the age of 10 to a 30-year-old cowherd, she was 20 years old and 9 months pregnant when based on a rumour spread by a local landlord that the child she was expecting was his, her husband abandoned her. She was beaten up and was dumped in a cowshed where she gave birth to her daughter (her fourth child). She was almost on the verge of committing suicide due to hunger and not being able to feed her daughter. But she decided otherwise and initially started taking care of Adivasi (tribal) children mainly for livelihood. However, soon this became the mission of her life and today she is the mother of around 1,050 orphans. This is the story of Sindhutai Sapkal, called as 'Mother of Orphans', who even in her adverse situation found ways to help others—in this case, abandoned and orphaned children.

Born in a wealthy and prosperous family and nicknamed as 'Baba', he grew up in luxury and was in fact gifted a Singer sports car by his father. He was involved in successful law practice and also served as a defence lawyer for freedom fighters around 1942. His real calling came when he saw the plight of people suffering from leprosy. People with leprosy are outcast and ostracised not only because it is believed to be contagious but also because it is linked with sins of the past. To help such people he founded Anandwan Ashram in 1948, where patients with leprosy are taught to be self-sufficient, live with dignity and respect, and contribute to the community. This is the story of Baba Amte. His children have taken his work forward. His son Dr Prakash Baba Amte and his wife Dr Mandakini Amte, both medical doctors, are yet other examples of selfless lives devoted to the well-being of others.

Both these stories can be considered as examples of pro-social behaviour (or more precisely altruism) that we are going to discuss in this chapter.

In our day-to-day lives, as well, we may have come across such pro-social behaviours around us. A simple act of providing your seat to an elderly person in the bus or helping a neighbour carry his/her heavy luggage or helping a visually impaired person cross the road or even helping an injured animal, can be considered as examples of pro-social behaviour.

Learning Objectives

After reading this chapter, you will be able to

- ❒ Define pro-social behaviour
- ❒ Explain approaches and perspectives to pro-social behaviour

- Discuss the situational factors that determine pro-social behaviour
- Describe who is likely to receive help
- Explain bystander's apathy
- Discuss outcome of receiving help
- Describe social support

WHAT IS PRO-SOCIAL BEHAVIOUR?

In simple terms, pro-social behaviour can be described as one person helping another in absence of any obligation. Pro-social behaviour can be distinguished from helping behaviour, that is considered as a broader concept and altruism, which is a comparatively smaller concept under pro-social behaviour (Bierhoff, 2001).

Crisp and Turner (2010, p. 234) define helping behaviour as 'acts where people voluntarily and intentionally behave in a way that they believe will benefit others, although at the same time the behaviour may benefit them as well'. Helping behaviour does not include behaviours that are incidental or behaviours that are a result of some selfish motive. But the concept is broad enough to include such behaviours that result in benefits for others as well as self.

Altruism can be defined as 'an act performed voluntarily to help someone else when there is no expectation of receiving a reward in any form' (Sears et al., 1991, p. 367). This is a more specific term where there is no benefit for the self but it does benefit others. The term was introduced by August Compte in 1851 (Hodgetts et al., 2010) to explain the effects of moral acts of individuals directed towards helping other individuals.

This chapter, however, focuses on pro-social behaviour.

Pro-social behaviour is defined as 'any act that helps or is designed to help others, regardless of the helper's motives' (Sears et al., 1991, p. 367). Stang and Wrightsman in 1981 defined pro-social behaviour as 'voluntary behaviour performed with the intention of benefiting another person or group of persons' (Raven & Rubin, 1983, p. 309).

Pro-social behaviour mainly involves behaviour that is voluntary in nature and directed towards benefit of others. The voluntary and conscious nature of this behaviour is important to differentiate this behaviour from other behaviours incidental or forced that may result in benefiting others. For example, a tree planted by you may also provide shade to your neighbours or you paying tax regularly does help in nation-building and development, but these behaviours cannot be considered as pro-social behaviour because they are either incidental or forced and not voluntary. In this way, you contributing to the Prime Minister's Relief Fund during a natural calamity can be considered as a pro-social behaviour, but if it is done for tax benefit or for social recognition then the same cannot be considered as a pro-social behaviour.

Pro-social behaviour, as a concept, includes varied behaviours including volunteering, cooperation, conformity with social norms and even being polite (Barrett, 2017). Most often, a pro-social behaviour is termed as a mixture of sources egoistically and altruistically motivated. Furthermore, pro-social behaviour may also vary in terms of the degree of efforts put in by the individuals. This will range from helping a neighbour in changing a punctured tyre to actually saving the life of a person by even putting one's own life at risk. Thus, pro-social behaviour can be termed as non-serious or low-cost and serious or high-cost behaviours (Bierhoff, 2001). Though both serious and non-serious behaviours differ in the degree of investment in terms of the efforts and other resources, there are a number of characteristics that are similar to these behaviours.

APPROACHES AND PERSPECTIVES TO PRO-SOCIAL BEHAVIOUR

To understand pro-social behaviour in a much deeper and elaborate way, various approaches and perspectives can be discussed. These are discussed in detail further.

Biological Approach

This approach attributes pro-social behaviour to genetics. Two main concepts that are discussed in this context are kin selection and reciprocity.

Kin Selection

The basic assumption of kin selection is that individuals are able to recognise people better who are genetically related to them and help individuals who are similar to them genetically, than individuals who are not. This can also provide an explanation to behaviours involved in helping one's own offspring. This helping behaviour may also be extended to persons who may not be offsprings, but are genetically related to these individuals. And, in fact, this has been observed not only in human beings but also in animals.

Such a behaviour can be explained with the help of inclusive fitness, which Hamilton defines as 'the ability of one's genes to survive both in one's own offspring and in one's genetic relative' (Barrett, 2017, p. 276). Dolphins, for example, have often been seen to display such behaviours in rescuing other dolphins (Sears et al., 1991).

Reciprocity

The theory of reciprocal altruism that was developed by Robert Trivers explains pro-social behaviour that is based on reciprocity (Bierhoff, 2001). Reciprocity denotes that pro-social behaviour is reciprocal in nature, that is, we should reciprocate or return what others do to us. For example, kindness by others should be returned with kindness. The norm of reciprocity also plays a role here, where it is believed that individuals who have helped us should be helped and not harmed. However, it is possible that in certain cases (or even many cases in today's world), those who receive help may not return it when the other person requires it the most, thus threatening the very basis of reciprocal altruism. This is often dealt with through social norms and also shunning or punishing of those who do not involve in reciprocal altruism.

Individualistic Approach

This approach mainly focuses on the tendencies at individual level that determine their pro-social behaviour. These tendencies may or may not be determined genetically and could also be acquired through social experiences. This approach can be discussed in terms of mood states and personality characteristics (Bierhoff, 2001).

Mood States

Various studies have indicated that positive mood can be attributed to altruistic behaviour (Bierhoff, 2001). A meta-analysis carried out by Carlson et al. in 1988 indicated a positive relationship between helping behaviour and good mood (Bierhoff, 2001). This relationship, in a way, can also be attributed to the focus on rewards rather than costs when in good mood. Furthermore, helping behaviour may also lead to maintenance of the good mood that the individual is experiencing (Barrett, 2017). It is also possible that good mood leads to suppression of signals that indicate danger that would have otherwise suppressed the pro-social behaviour. This has been explained by the Affect as Information Model that was developed by Schwarz (Bierhoff, 2001). The model states that individuals' safety or danger in any situation is indicated by their mood and thus positive mood may indicate that the situation is safe and therefore the individuals may involve in pro-social behaviour.

Though contrary to what we would like to believe, negative mood can also be significantly associated with helping behaviour, besides good mood. In fact, negative mood can pave the way for helping behaviour, because it will make you feel good about it. The Mood Management Hypothesis also states that individuals may engage in helping behaviour because they want to manage their moods like sadness (Barrett, 2017). Interpersonal guilt is also a negative emotion that may lead to individuals behaving in a pro-social manner. Interpersonal guilt arises when an individual comes to know that he/she is responsible for the distress or negative situation that others are in (Bierhoff, 2001).

There is yet another model in this context. It is known as the Negative State Relief Model. The basic assumption underlying this model is that when individuals see others in trouble, they may feel sad about it and, therefore, engage in helping behaviour to reduce their own sadness or even guilt that they may experience in such a situation.

Besides the one previously mentioned, there is also arousal: cost–reward model, that states that individuals are negatively aroused when they see other individuals in distress and in that situation the individual will use the strategy that is least costly, to help the other individuals. This decision in turn will depend on the cost–reward analysis. Thus if Anil sees a person who has met with an accident, seeing the person in distress leads to a negative arousal in Anil and then he will adopt the least costly way (may be dialling 100) to help this person. In this case, as Anil carried out a quick cost and benefit analysis, he felt that the best way to deal with his negative arousal would be to dial 100 rather than rushing the injured person to the hospital, which would probably be of greater cost.

Personality Characteristics

There are certain main characteristics of a pro-social person which can be listed. These are described in detail in this section.

- *Social responsibility*. This denotes that people who are dependent on us need to be taken care of by us. For example, parents should take care of their children who are dependent on them or the grown children should take care of their elderly parents. A teacher is also expected to be responsible for his/her students. Social responsibility is in contrast to self-sufficiency that denotes that one should take care of oneself before others. People who exhibit pro-social behaviour necessarily have the characteristic of social responsibility when compared with people who are not pro-social.

- *Just world belief*. This denotes the expectation that individuals will receive what they deserve. Thus, a needy person is in such a situation because he/she deserved it. However, when sufferings or distresses of an individual are perceived as undeserved, then the just world belief is challenged and this in turn will promote people to display pro-social behaviour. This could be a reason why people make contributions towards treatment of young children suffering from grave illnesses as they are seen as not deserving to suffer, which challenges the just world belief and prompts some people to help them. Furthermore, it is also possible that in certain cases devaluation of the person in distress takes place. For example, a person who is HIV positive and does not have money for sustenance or treatment, may not receive necessary help because he may be devalued and will be perceived as deserving this bad fate. Research indicated that just world belief played a role in promoting pro-social behaviour only when a complete solution was possible to the problem and not otherwise (Miller, 1977).
- *Internal locus of control*. Internal locus of control in this context indicates that positive outcomes can be maximised and negative outcomes minimised by one's own behaviour and luck or fate does not play a role here. People with internal locus of control are more likely to provide help. Furthermore, social responsibility is positively correlated with internal locus of control that in turn is again related with pro-social behaviour (Bierhoff, 2001).
- *Personal distress*. Personal distress denotes one's own reaction to the distress experienced by others. When these individuals see others in distress they may feel sad, shocked, alarmed, concerned or even helpless and may experience physiological changes as well, such as palpitations, changes in facial expressions and so on (Sears et al., 1991). Though personal distress may encourage an individual to help the person in distress in order to reduce one's own personal distress, they may even try to escape or ignore the situation.
- *Empathy*. Empathy can be defined as an 'affective state that is triggered when an individual witnesses the emotional state of another person, which results from adopting the perspective of the other and understanding his or her emotions' (Bierhoff, 2001, p. 293). In simple terms, it is explained as 'putting oneself in someone else's shoes'. Studies have indicated a positive correlation between dispositional empathy and pro-social behaviour (Bierhoff, 2001). Dispositional empathy can be described as an emotion that is vicarious in nature, one that is induced when you come across an individual in need. When compared with people who are in personal distress, those people who empathise are more likely to engage in pro-social behaviour as the focus is on helping others and not on reducing one's own personal distress. Empathy altruism hypothesis could be discussed in this context. This hypothesis was proposed by Batson et al. in 1981 (Baron & Byrne, 1995), which states that motivation behind at least some of the pro-social behaviours can be attributed completely to the desire to help the person in need.
- *Egocentrism*. Egocentrism indicates more concern with one's self than others do. It is a reflection of self-absorption (Baron & Byrne, 1995). Individuals who are egocentric are less likely to provide help than people who are not egocentric.

Gender differences also exist in pro-social behaviour where studies have indicated that females are high on humanistic ideals when compared to males (Hoffman, 1975). A meta-analysis that was carried out by Eagly and Crowley in 1986 indicated no prominent gender difference in helping behaviour. The types of behaviour differed where males were more likely to help females but females helped both males and females. Males were more likely to help strangers than females, especially in a perceived dangerous situation. However, females were more likely to be helpful in day-to-day life when compared to males (Crisp & Turner, 2010).

Learning Perspective

How we behave, can be attributed to a larger extent to what has been learnt by us. Thus, pro-social behaviour can also be learned. Children from a young age are taught to help or share their stuff with others, especially their siblings. There is no doubt that family and then teachers and peers play a significant role here. Early childhood socialisation (could be the ideology followed by the parents or pro-social behaviour modelled by them) can have an impact on pro-social behaviour (Raven & Rubin, 1983). What is more important to focus on is application of the learning theories on how children learn to behave in a pro-social manner. Reinforcements, rewards and punishment do play a role in an individual's learning of pro-social behaviour. Studies have indicated that children tend to help and share more when they have been rewarded for that behaviour (Sears et al., 1991). Besides reinforcement, modelling also plays a role here. When the children saw a helpful model, helpful behaviour was learned by them. In a study carried out by Midlarsky, Bryan and Brickman in 1973 on girls in sixth grade, the participants were asked to play on a pinball machine, in which they could win chips that they could exchange for toys and candy. In one condition, before their turn to play on the machine, each participant watched an adult model put all her chips in a jar labelled 'my money', In another condition, the adult model put some chips in the jar labelled 'money for poor children'. The models then asked the participants to think about the poor children and how they could buy toys and candies for themselves with the chips. The results indicated that more donations of chips (19) were by girls who saw the model donating to poor children as compared to the children who saw the model keeping money for herself.

Pro-social behaviour of not only children but also adults can be influenced as they observe a helpful model. Television can also play a role in promoting pro-social behaviour. In fact, there was an increase in pro-social behaviour amongst children when they watched a helpful model on television. Further, though initially the pro-social behaviour may require external reinforcement, as a person grows up, the pro-social behaviour is internalised (Sears, Peplau, & Taylor, 1991).

Decision-making Perspective

Pro-social behaviour also depends on decision-making process, where the individual has to take a decision whether to help or not This decision-making process is a complex one, which involves various steps.

Step 1, Perception of need. For the decision-making process to start, first of all, there has to be a perception of need. In certain situations the need is clear, in others it might not be that obvious and people may look for certain cues that indicate need for help. For example, an elderly woman falling on the road is an obvious sign that help is required. But if you heard a child screaming in a neighbouring house, it can be because the child is being naughty or is reacting to being forced to eat food and you may actually not perceive it as child abuse. Therefore, the cues play an important role during this first step. In 1979, five characteristics of an emergency situation were identified by Shotland and Huston (cited in Sear et al., 1991, p. 369) They are as follows:

1. The event is sudden and is not expected For example, there is an unexpected fall along with a loud cry.
2. There seems to be some threat to the individual. For example, it seems as if someone is being attacked and so there is a perception of threat.
3. Unless someone intervenes, the possibility of harm to the individual could increase. For example, if the person who fell unconscious on the road is not helped the person may be hit by a vehicle or may die due to delayed first-aid/treatment.
4. The individual under distress is helpless. For example, a child who has fallen in a pothole on the road is not able to get out and is helpless.
5. It is possible to provide some intervention. For example, one can go and help the elderly woman, who has fallen down, and take her to the hospital or give her some water to drink.

During this first step, how the situation is interpreted is also important. If a child is being beaten by his/her parents one may not intervene thinking it is part of the disciplining process. However, if you see a stranger beating up a child then it is more likely that you will intervene.

Step 2, Personal responsibility is taken. The decision to help or not will also depend on the extent to which personal responsibility is taken. There are a number of factors in this context and one of them is commitment. Personal responsibility will depend on whether commitment has been established or not. For example, at airport, if a person asks you to keep an eye on her child as she uses the washroom, a commitment has been established and you will take personal responsibility for that child. Yet another factor is competence, whether the individual takes personal responsibility or not and whether he/she feels obliged to help or not will also depend on his/her skills. A doctor or a nurse will be more obliged to help a person who has been injured in an accident on the road.

Step 3, Cost and benefit analysis. Before a decision to help or not is taken the individual will carry out cost and benefit analysis. If benefits are more than costs then the person will engage in pro-social behaviour, but if costs are higher than benefits then the person will refrain from pro-social behaviour. This could be the reason why in India people often refrain from helping victims of road accidents as they analyse that the costs in terms of police enquiry, etc. are more than benefits. Cost and benefit analysis is also done in terms of safety or threat to oneself, besides profit or loss.

Step 4, Decision regarding how the help will be provided. This includes the final decision about how the help is to be provided. In case of an accident, it could be whether you should take the person directly to the hospital or call the police or an ambulance. This will again depend on a number of factors like type of help required by the individual, skills and even physical characteristics of the person who is helping.

Interpersonal Approach

This approach highlights the interdependent nature of relationship between human beings. In a doubles tennis match or a game of carrom, where a team of two has to compete, the members are interdependent on each other to reach the goal. They necessarily have to cooperate with each other to win the match. Kelly and Thibaut in 1978 proposed a theory of interdependence that was based on exchange theory (Bierhoff, 2001). The theory stated that individuals, who are interdependent, tend to modify a relationship that is based on costs and rewards, into a relationship that is pro-social in nature. This pro-social transformation is mutually beneficial for both the individuals, thus replacing egoistic decision role of doing what is best for his/her own self, to social decision role, that is, doing what is best for the other individual. The pro-social transformation depends on various factors including the duration of relationship, whether short or long and whether the relationship is close or not, indicating the cohesiveness and unity between the individuals.

Here a distinction can also be made between exchange relationships, that exist between strangers or familiar individuals and communal relationships, that exist between friends, family members and so on (Bierhoff, 2001). Where on one hand in exchange relationship the focus is on what is gained, in communal relationship, on the other, the focus is on the well-being of the individual. Thus, given that there is no benefit or gain, pro-social behaviour is higher in communal relationships than in exchange relationships.

SITUATIONAL FACTORS THAT DETERMINE PRO-SOCIAL BEHAVIOUR

There are situational factors as well that determine pro-social behaviour. In this section, the two main factors that will be focused on are environmental factors and time pressures.

Environmental Conditions

Environmental conditions such as weather, geographical area and its size, noise levels and so on. can influence pro-social behaviour. Studies indicated that people were less likely to help during rainy days than during sunny days (Sears et al., 1991). In a similar manner, people belonging to smaller towns are more likely to engage in pro-social behaviour when compared to people in big cities and in this, the present set-up plays a greater role rather than where the person was brought up. So even if a person hails from a small town he/she may end up not helping a person in need in a big city. This can be attributed not only to a higher number of bystanders that may be present in a big city but also to overload of stimulus received in such cities, which leads people to ignore the external information that is not relevant to them personally. Furthermore, noisy situations also decrease the likelihood that the pro-social behaviour will be displayed.

Time Pressures

Who is more likely to engage in pro-social behaviour—one who is rushing for a job interview or an examination or one who is on the way to get grocery? The focus here is on the time pressure that the person is under, to reach somewhere or get some work done and how that has an impact on pro-social behaviours. A study was carried out by Darley and Batson in 1973 on students of Princeton Theological Seminary (Barrett, 2017). In the study the participants were given instructions to walk from one building to another so as to give a talk on the biblical parable of the Good Samaritan or a topic that was not related to helping. The parable was regarding a priest who comes across a man who was robbed, beaten badly and half dead, as he was walking along the road. But the priest ignores this man and walks by without giving help. A Samaritan, who passes the same road, provides help and brings the wounded man to an inn so that he can recover and also pays for his care. In the study, as the participants passed from one building to another, they had to pass by a man who had fallen in the alley and seemed in pain. As such, it would be expected from priests and seminarians that they would help a person in need of help, especially when they were about to speak about the biblical parable. The results indicated that only 10 per cent of the participants who were in hurry actually helped, when compared to 63 per cent who were not in hurry and this was independent of the topic that they spoke on. Thus, more the time pressure, less the likelihood of engaging in pro-social behaviour. This can also be attributed to the narrowing of cognition and increased dependency on rapid processing of information that is not in-depth, when under time pressure.

WHO IS MORE LIKELY TO RECEIVE HELP?

This section focuses on the characteristics, of the individual who needs help, that determine whether help will be received or not by them.

1. **Whether the individual was responsible for the problem or not:** If the individual is responsible for his/her own problems, it is less likely that he/she will receive help. For example, if a person loses all his money and is in debt because of his habit of gambling and now he needs some financial help, he is least likely to get it because he is seen as being responsible for his own situation. However, a parent who has lost all his money for the treatment of his child may receive the much needed financial help even from strangers.

   Individual differences may also exist in the degree of readiness displayed by the individual who engages in pro-social behaviour. This is mainly because of the experience of threat that we encounter when we see someone in distress. As we see the person in distress, one of the immediate feelings is that this could happen to me as well (I could be in a situation where I desperately need money for treatment of my loved one). This threat is met with either of the two defences, repression (avoidance of threat) and sensitisation (thinking and intellectualisation of threat). Individuals who employ repression are less likely to engage in pro-social behaviour when compared to people who employ sensitisation.
2. **Attraction and similarity:** More the person who needs help is seen as attractive, the more likely that he/she will receive help. In this regard, similarity between the person who needs help and the person who could provide help may also count. In a foreign country, for example, people of same nationality are more likely to help each other in need.
3. **Group membership:** An in-group member (member belonging to one's own group) is more likely to receive help when compared with an out-group member (member not belonging to one's own group). This can also be seen in the context of ethnicity (Gaertner & Divido, 1977).
4. **Deservingness of the person:** A person who is perceived as deserving help is more likely to receive it than a person who is perceived as not deserving help. You might end up helping a poor child by buying food or medication rather than a child who wants a toy. The nature and the degree of legitimacy do play a role here. The evaluation of deservingness also involves application of attribution theory. Again, whether the person had control over the problem or not (as we discussed under responsibility of the individual in need) is an important factor. If the problem seems to be under the person's control, he/she is less likely to receive help and vice versa. Furthermore, whether the problem was under control or not also evokes certain feelings in us that direct our pro-social behaviour. When the person in need is perceived as being in distress due to situations not under his/her control, the feelings evoked are that of concern and care, whereas when the person in need seems to be in distress because of situations he/she could have controlled, the reaction is that of anger and discontent.

BYSTANDER'S APATHY

Though the newspapers and social network are often abuzz with the news of people who help and engage in pro-social behaviour at their own cost and sometimes even by risking their lives, there are also such news that we come across, for example, a young boy died on the road due to lack of medical attention even when there was a huge crowd witnessing him take his last breath or a woman who dies because of physical abuse by her own husband, without any interference from the neighbours.

These are examples of bystander's apathy. This can be described as decreased likelihood of receiving help when in presence of others. We are going to discuss about how performance is enhanced or deteriorates when in presence of others in Chapter 11. Whereas, in this chapter, we will focus on how presence of others reduces the possibility of help being provided. Not only the presence but the perception of presence of people can also lead to decrease in possibility that the help will be provided. Darley and Latane in 1968 stated that the bystander's apathy could be as a result of diffusion of responsibility, that is, many people are present and yet no one feels responsible to take action (Baron & Byrne, 1995). Darley and Latane also tested the hypothesis that as the number of persons increases the likelihood that the help will be provided reduces due to diffusion of responsibility. In this study, participants were undergraduate students. Deception was used in the study, as the participants were informed that they were actually participating in a study where they had to discuss about problems regarding attending college in urban areas. The interaction was not face to face and they were allotted a separate room and could communicate with the help of an intercom. Privacy was provided with an intention to avoid any embarrassment while they shared their personal problems. Some of the participants were told that there were just two discussants including them, others were told that there were three discussants and some other participants were told that there were six discussants. Participants had to speak for two minutes and then wait for comments from the listener(s). Further, deception was used as the rest of the discussants were not actual participant(s) but just tape recordings. In each session, the first one to speak was the voice in the tape recording who revealed in an embarrassed tone how he would experience seizures while experiencing stress. Then the other participant (in case of two persons) and participants (in case of three and six persons) spoke for two minutes each. After which the voice of the tape recorder spoke again indicating that he was having a medical emergency and could lose his life. Helpful behaviour was expected of the participant leaving the room, looking for the participant who was experiencing the medical emergency. The results were consistent with the hypothesis, where, as the number of bystanders increased the likelihood of the participants engaging in helping behaviour decreased. Further, the more the bystanders the more the delay in actual action was also observed. Besides these important findings, the study also highlighted the bystander's effect, that is, the participants who failed to take any action seemed confused, uncomfortable and even upset (Baron & Byrne, 1995).

Piliavin's bystander calculus model: This model stresses on the physiological reactions that are induced when an emergency situation is witnessed along with diffusion of responsibility. According to this model, there are three stages that a bystander goes through in such a situation.

- *Stage 1, Physiological arousal is experienced.* When an emergency is witnessed, the very first reaction that one may elicit is orienting reaction, which is lowered rather than heightened physiological response. This enables the individual to avoid panic and carry out an assessment of the situation and action that needs to be taken. This orienting reaction is immediately followed by heightened physiological responses, termed as defence reaction, for example, rapid heart rate. Individuals with such defence reaction (that follows the orienting reaction) are more likely to engage in pro-social behaviour.

- *Stage 2, The arousal or the emotional response is labelled.* Once the physiological arousal is experienced, a meaning needs to be attached to it. Different labels are given to these arousals, like anger or excitement and so on, and this is done based on the external cues reflected by the situation. As per the present model, the arousal in emergency is also a result of personal distress (that was discussed earlier in this chapter) and thus one may engage in pro-social behaviour to reduce this personal distress. Furthermore, besides personal distress, empathy also plays a role in determining whether pro-social behaviour is displayed or not.
- *Stage 3, The cost of helping and not helping is calculated.* Once the arousal experienced is labelled as personal distress, people try to come up with ways to deal with the personal distress. And this is done by weighing the costs of helping and not helping. This is further clear from Figure 9.1. As can be seen in the figure, if the cost of not helping is high the person may feel guilty for not helping or blame self for no action, whereas if the cost of helping is low and no risks in helping are perceived, then the person in need will receive direct help. For example, an elderly woman falling on the road will receive help because the cost of not helping is high and the cost of helping is low.

If the cost of helping as well as the cost of not helping is high, the person in need will receive some indirect help. For example, if a person witnesses another person being stabbed by knife, instead of actually going and helping the person, which would put his/her well-being at risk, the person may inform the police. Here attempts are also made by the person to reduce the cost of not helping. As stated by Piliavin and others, the cost of not helping is reduced in presence of others thus leading to bystander's

Figure 9.1 ***Cost of Helping and Cost of Not Helping, Based on Piliavin's Matrix***

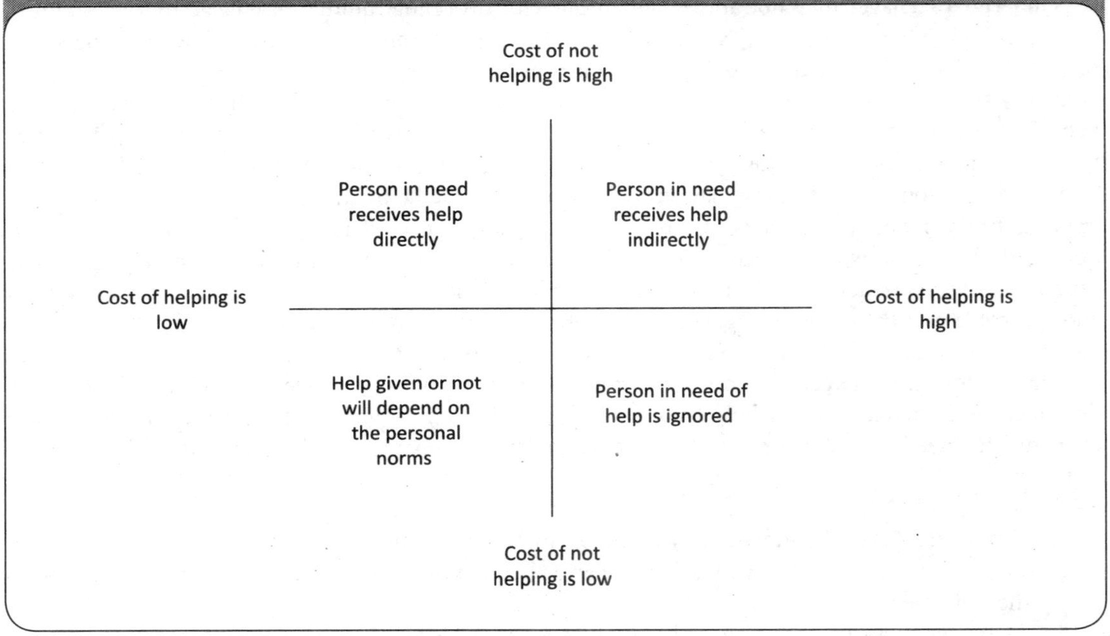

Source: Author.

apathy effect (Crisp & Turner, 2010). Thus, the person witnessing the stabbing may in fact do nothing if there were others present who witnessed the stabbing as well.

If the cost of helping and the cost of not helping are both low, pro-social behaviour depends on the personal norms of the person. For example, if a person miraculously misses being hit by a moving vehicle, another person, with a higher sense of social responsibility, may ask him/her if he/she is alright and may not do anything more as cost of helping and cost of not helping are both low in this case.

Lastly, when the cost of helping is high and cost of not helping is low, it can be said that the person in need will not receive any help. For example, if helping a stranger in need requires the person to shell out considerable amount of money or risk his/her own well-being, the person is least likely to display pro-social behaviour.

OUTCOME OF RECEIVING HELP

So far the discussions in the chapter were mainly from the perspective of the people who help, but the perspective of the person who receives help also needs to be considered. The same can be comprehended with the help of the example given here.

In a residential society when a woman was being beaten by her husband, one of the socially conscious neighbours called the police who arrived in time and arrested the husband. Satisfied with his own helpful act, the neighbour sighed with relief but was surprised when the woman blamed him for the arrest of her husband. What do you think happened in this situation? Should the neighbour have refrained from calling the police, in which case the husband could have harmed the wife further? Well, from the point of view of the neighbour, the decision taken to call the police was correct but this pro-social behaviour was not necessarily seen as beneficial by the person who was helped.

Similarly, a teenager may not appreciate an offer for dropping him/her at college by the parent on his/her old bike. A new mother may perceive the help received from her mother-in-law in caring for the baby as interference, rather than as helping behaviour.

In any pro-social behaviour, there are two parties: the one who gives help and the one who receives help. The chapter on pro-social behaviour would be incomplete without focusing on the person who receives help. This is also relevant in order to judge the success or failure of the pro-social behaviour. Though the person who is helping may strongly believe that the help did make a difference to the person in need, it may not be so and the person receiving help may have a different perspective. Furthermore, on one hand, the person who engaged in pro-social behaviour may derive satisfaction from helping, despite certain negative consequences, whereas, on the other hand, the person who receives help may feel inferior and incapable and thus they may give more weightage to contributions made by him/herself in dealing with the situation and undermine the role played by the person who helped.

The relationship between the individual who provides help and the one who receives help can be described as altruistic relationship. As stated by Fisher, Depulo and Nadler (1981), there are four elements that need to be discussed with reference to this relationship (cited in Bierhoff, 2001). They are as follows:

1. Characteristics of the individual who helps, including his/her intentions
2. Characteristics of the individual who receives help, including his/her self-esteem and concept of the self
3. Characteristics of the help provided such as amount, degree and nature of help
4. Characteristics of the situation, including opportunity to return the favour/help

These elements have an impact on the extent of self-threat and self-support that are intrinsic to the help provided to the recipient. If self-threat remains, then the help will receive a negative response from the recipient, and if self-support prevails, then the response from the recipient will be positive.

Varied reaction from the recipients of help can be explained with the help of the following theories:

- **Social exchange theory.** When help is provided by one person to another, an imbalance is created and the person who receives help may feel indebted. According to social exchange theory, any help received will be appreciated by the recipient only when he/she is able to reciprocate it. Thus, restoring the balance in this regard is important. Individuals who feel that they are less likely to return the favour or reciprocate are less likely to seek help. This also has to do with power balance, as the person who gives help will have greater influence on the recipient of help, if he/she is not in a position to reciprocate it.
- **Reactance theory.** This theory states that individuals seek maximisation of their freedom and react negatively if any threat is perceived to this freedom. Receiving help is often seen as a threat to one's freedom as then the recipient becomes obliged to the person giving help and it invokes negative reactions like hostility or displeasure.
- **Attribution theory.** When help is received by an individual, it can also have an impact on the self-esteem of the recipient. This also depends on the perception of the recipient. If the recipient perceives that the person is helping him/her because he/she cares, then the self-esteem of the individual will receive a boost, but if it is perceived as given because the recipient is seen as incompetent or incapable, then the self-esteem will decrease. Thus, it depends on attribution that the recipient attaches to why he/she is receiving help. Furthermore, in this context, if the need is associated with a factor that is external and cannot be controlled, then the self-esteem of the recipient is maintained and it will remain positive. However, if the help received is associated with factors that are internal like personal inadequacies that could have been controlled, then the self-esteem of the recipient will decrease.

SOCIAL SUPPORT

Suppose a person has recently gone through a very bad divorce or is recovering from an illness or is bereaving loss of a loved one, his/her pains and suffering will be mitigated to some extent in presence of social support from family and friends.

Buunk (2001, p. 378) defined social support as 'the feeling of being supported by others, usually divided into four components, that is, emotional support, appraisal support, informational support and instrumental support'. Social support deals with give and take of help in relationships while coping with life events or troubles in daily life. Social support generally plays an important role in helping individuals cope with certain distressing life events. It also has a sort of buffer effect, where persons who perceive the presence of social support are less affected by events that are stressful as compared to persons who perceive that they do not have social support.

Here one can also distinguish between cognitive social support, the perception with regard to availability of social support, and behavioural social support, that is, social support that is received.

Though the popular belief is that social support does help people cope better with their situations or distress, it is necessary that there is a match between the support received and the requirement of the individual. Furthermore, issues related to the reaction of the person (whether positive or negative) on receiving social support may also crop up in this context.

The persons giving social support may have their own insecurities about how effective help or support can be provided and may not have a long-term perspective in this regard. Their self-esteem can also get affected if they receive negative feedback from the people whom they are supporting. The social support relationship could be better where there is reciprocity. A social support that is one-sided may meet with negative consequences, especially in exchange relationships as opposed to communal relationships.

Social support can also be viewed from the point of affiliation that was discussed in Chapter 6 on interpersonal attraction. It can play a role in reducing anxiety and stress, which is one of the reasons why people affiliate with others.

Though overall social support is positive and important in a person's life, it can have certain adverse effects, especially when fear that the person is facing gets enhanced as he/she shares his/her feelings with others. Also, in case of individuals with anxious/ambivalent attachment style, social support may create further stress (Buunk, 2001).

SUMMARY

To conclude, the chapter discusses about pro-social behaviour. In simple terms, pro-social behaviour can be described as one person helping another in absence of any obligation. The term mainly involves behaviour that is voluntary in nature and directed towards benefit of others. The chapter describes various approaches and perspectives to pro-social behaviour, which include biological approach, individualistic approach, learning perspective, decision-making perspective and interpersonal approach. The situational factors that determine pro-social behaviour were also discussed with the focus on two main factors: the environmental conditions and time pressures. The chapter then highlighted the characteristics of the individuals who need help, which determine whether help will be received or not. This includes whether the individual was responsible for the problem or not, attraction and similarity between the person who helps and the person who receives help, group membership and deservingness of the person. The next topic covered was bystander's apathy that is described as decreased likelihood of receiving help when in presence of others. In this context, Piliavin's Bystander-calculus model was also discussed. The chapter also explains the outcome of receiving help that determines the success or failure of the pro-social behaviour. Various theories were discussed in this context which explain the reaction from the recipient of help. Lastly, social support, which deals with give and take of help in relationships while coping with life events or troubles in daily life, was also briefly discussed.

QUESTIONS

1. Define pro-social behaviour. Explain any two approaches to understanding pro-social behaviour.
2. Describe the situational factors that determine pro-social behaviour.
3. Discuss the characteristics of a person that determine whether he/she will receive help or not.
4. Elucidate bystander's apathy.
5. What are the outcomes of receiving help?
6. Explain social support.

REFERENCES

Bierhoff, H. W. (2001). Prosocial behaviour. In M. Hewstone and W. Stroebe (Eds.), *Introduction to social psychology*. Oxford: Blackwell Publishers.

Buunk, B. P. (2001). Affiliation, attraction and close relationships. In M. Hewstone and W. Stroebe (Eds.), *Introduction to social psychology*. Oxford: Blackwell Publishers.

Dovidio, J. F., Piliavin, J. A., Schroeder, D. A., & Penner, L. A. (2006). *The social psychology of prosocial behavior*. Mahwah, NJ: Lawrence Erlbaum Associates.

Eisenberg, N., & Mussen, P. (1989). *The roots of prosocial behavior in children*. Cambridge: Cambridge University Press.

Gaertner, S., & Dovidio, J. (1977). The subtlety of White racism, arousal, and helping behavior. *Journal of Personality and Social Psychology*, *35*(10), 691–707. Retrieved from http://dx.doi.org/10.1037//0022-3514.35.10.691

FURTHER READINGS

For more information on pro-social behaviour, following books can be read:

Bierhoff, H. (2002). *Prosocial behaviour*. New York, NY: Psychology Press.

Dovidio, J. F., Piliavin, J. A., Schroeder, D. A., & Penner, L. A. (2006). *The social psychology of prosocial behavior*. Mahwah, NJ: Lawrence Erlbaum Associates.

Eisenberg, N., & Mussen, P. (1989). *The roots of prosocial behavior in children*. Cambridge: Cambridge University Press.

CHAPTER 10

Aggression

An elderly couple was strangled to death in their own home, a four-year-old girl was raped and abused, a woman was brutally assaulted by her husband, in an argument on road over a minor car accident a person was shot. A single glance at the newspaper and we come across stories of brutal violence, rape, murder and a show of aggression.

Aggression today has become very much a part of our being in the society. Are human beings innately aggressive or has aggression increased recently? What is aggression? And how social psychologists, look at aggression and what role they can play to prevent and control it? These are some of the questions that will be probed into this chapter.

Looking at some of the examples provided here will provide a better idea about what aggression is.

Sheena was a very friendly girl. She was good at her studies and wanted to become a doctor. Her parents were very proud of her and felt that she could get help by attending coaching classes for maths and science to score good marks in her 12th standard. Sheena was very happy to join coaching classes. At her coaching classes, she made many friends. They were of her own age group and she enjoyed their company. However, she realised she was getting a little more attention from one particular boy. She tried to ignore him as most of the girls do, however, the boy would follow her and try to talk to her all the time. He would also come to her school. She reported this to her principal and the boy was punished. The next week, Sheena was admitted in the hospital with acid burns, she had an acid attack. The same boy, who claimed to love her, had thrown acid on her.

Rehan, was a 10-year-old boy who loved to play. He wanted to become a cricketer like Sachin Tendulkar when he grew up. His mother would have a tough time making Rehan study. She wanted him to study hard so that he can get a job and be financially secured. Their financial situation was not so good. Rehan's father was an auto-rickshaw driver and barely made any income. Monday morning, Rehan's father left home early. But his day did not go well, while taking his first customer to his destination, the tyre of his auto rickshaw burst, he had no spare tyre and had no money to replace it. The customer did not even pay him half of the fare, though they had almost reached the destination. He had to drag the auto to the mechanic who said that the tyre needs to be replaced. Rehan's father returned home with no money, broken tyre and a broken heart. When he reached home, he saw Rehan playing merrily. He was so angry at this sight that he dragged him into the house and beat him up black and blue. Rehan succumbed to his injuries three days later.

Vicky was very happy, it was his 20th birthday and his father had bought him a new car. He could not wait to meet his friends and go for a drive. He was waiting at a red signal when a labourer on his cycle scratched his brand new car. Vicky was furious. He got out of his car and beat up the labourer. Then he took out his pistol and shot the labourer in his head.

Do you see traces of aggression in the situations given above? What are the factors, do you think, that lead to such aggressive behaviours?

In this chapter, the concept of aggression will be discussed along with the concept of anti-social behaviour. Theories of aggression will also be explained. The chapter will highlight the determinants of aggression. The concept of anger will be dealt with and lastly the chapter will focus on the prevention and control of aggression.

Learning Objectives

After reading this chapter, you will be able to

- ❒ Elucidate what is aggression
- ❒ Discuss the theories of aggression
- ❒ Explain the determinants of aggression
- ❒ Discuss the concept of anger
- ❒ Discuss prevention and control of aggression

WHAT IS AGGRESSION?

In simple terms, aggression can be described as any behaviour that hurts someone. This description of aggression terms a behaviour as aggressive when the person towards whom the aggression was directed is hurt. But, if we just focus on whether the person was hurt or not, we will term a person who intended to hurt a person, but failed to do so, as not aggressive. Thus, we also need to focus on an important aspect of aggressive behaviour, that is, intention. For example, if a person driving a car accidentally hurts a person, it is not aggression, as he/she did not intend to do so. A person who tried to hit another person with a stick but failed to do so will still be called aggressive as he/she intended to hurt the other person. Further, it is also important to differentiate between hurtful behaviour and hurtful intentions (Sears et al., 1991).

Aggression, thus, can be described as a behaviour that is intentional in nature and is mainly aimed at inflicting pain, psychological or physical, to another person. Some of the definitions of aggression are discussed as follows:

Weiss (1969) described aggression as 'a behaviour directed against an object, and its primary intent or purpose is to injure'.

Sears et al. (1991, p. 335) defined aggression as 'any action that is intended to hurt others'.

Both the aforementioned definitions emphasise on the intention of the individual that is directed towards hurting another person or the object.

Baron (1977, p. 7) described aggression as 'any form of behaviour directed towards the goal of harming or injuring another living being who is motivated to avoid such treatment'. The two main key points, which can be highlighted in this definition, firstly, there is an infliction of harm on another person or being and secondly, the behaviour that is deliberate with the intention to harm.

According to Bushman and Anderson (2001, p. 274) 'aggression is any behaviour directed towards another individual that is carried out with the proximate intent to cause harm. In addition, the perpetrator must believe that the behaviour will harm the target and that the target is motivated to avoid the behaviour'.

Aggression can be perceived as universal and aggressive impulses and tendencies also seem natural (Baumeister & Bushman, 2008). Factors such as culture could play a role in curbing aggressive behaviour. Thus, in any society there are laws and rules that restrain aggressive behaviour, though there are also certain exceptions such as war, where aggression is a means of self-defence.

Forms of Aggression

Various forms of aggression are discussed here in detail.

1. **Hostile aggression:** This can be described as behaviour that is directed towards harming another individual. This type of aggression mainly stems from anger and is also termed as emotional aggression or reactive aggression. For example, when angry, a person may slap another person. Hostile aggression is a reaction or response that is typical in nature.
2. **Instrumental aggression** This can be described as a behaviour that is again directed to harm another individual but the behaviour is an instrument to achieve a non-aggressive goal. This is also termed as proactive aggression. Such an aggression is intentional and future oriented (Barrett, 2017). For example, in a game of football, aggression that is directed to make a goal or win the game.

   Both hostile aggression and instrumental aggression are not distinctive in nature and each can have certain elements of the others. For example, when during a football game, a player of the other team is pushed, it can be either because this player wants to win the game or it can be an expression of anger as well, as in hostile aggression. Hostile and instrumental aggression are high in terms of anger, though the degree of anger is greater in reactive aggression.
3. **Direct and indirect aggression:** In direct aggression, the target towards whom the aggression is directed is physically present and in indirect aggression, the target towards whom the aggression is directed is not physically present.
4. **Violence:** Yet another form of aggression is violence. Though most often it is used interchangeably with the term aggression, violence can be defined as aggression that is extreme and is also directed to seriously harm others. For example, stabbing a person with a knife.

It is also important to differentiate between anti-social and pro-social aggression. Aggression is perceived as bad when it is directed towards hurting another person, but certain aggressive actions are also perceived positively and in fact are commended. For example, soldiers are applauded, praised and also awarded for shooting a terrorist, who was responsible for taking innocent lives. Thus, aggression is also determined by whether the social norms are violated or not by the aggressive actions. Certain aggressive actions, though, may fall in between pro-social and anti-social aggressions—these are termed as sanctioned aggression. These are aggressive actions that fall within the boundaries of social norms though as such not required by the social norms. For example, a person hits another person in self-defence or parents may use disciplining techniques with a child who is being disobedient.

Distinction can also be made between aggressive behaviour and aggressive feelings, referred to as anger, as internal feelings may not always be revealed in terms of overt behaviour. The concept of anger will be discussed later in this chapter.

Furthermore, aggression can also be physical or verbal. Examples of physical aggression are pushing, shoving, biting or punching a person and examples of verbal aggression are insulting, teasing or even gossiping about a person.

Aggression and Anti-social Behaviour

Moving on to understand the term 'anti-social behaviour in group', though most often equated with aggression, the term is defined as 'behaviour that either damages interpersonal relationships or is culturally undesirable' (Baumeister & Bushman, 2008, p. 264). The term 'aggression' can be differentiated from the term 'anti-social behaviour' as aggression involves strategies that are social as well as anti-social, and thus there could be certain behaviours that are anti-social but may not be aggressive.

Various forms of anti-social behaviours are discussed as follows:

Cheating. Cheating could occur in exams, during sports performance and so on. And though perceived as anti-social behaviour, it is still prevalent in our society. Studies have indicated that persons with low academic ability, low self-control and persons who are pessimistic are more likely to indulge in cheating (Baumeister & Bushman, 2008). Cheating can be reduced not only by curbing the opportunities for cheating, such as by stricter supervisions, plagiarism checks and random checking but it can also be curbed by enhancing the self-awareness of the persons who indulge in cheating.

Stealing. Stealing or theft is yet another form of an anti-social behaviour. One of the significant factor that contributes to stealing and other anti-social behaviours as well is deindividuation, which takes place when one is in a group. People are more prone to indulging in anti-social behaviour when they are in groups.

Littering. Littering is yet another anti-social behaviour that we commonly observe in India. Many of us have come across situations where the window of the vehicle in front of you slides down and an empty packet of chips or a cold drink bottle is thrown out of it. There are also instances where people clean their houses spick and span and throw all the garbage on the road. Such anti-social behaviour affects the ambience of the area and also adds to the existing garbage problem and pollution. It could also lead to health related issues in humans as well as animals. To deal with such anti-social behaviour, again, stricter rules and norms are required.

Collective Aggression

Aggression can be at individual level or group level. When it occurs at group level, it can be termed as collective aggression that is discussed in this section.

We often come across news of confrontation between the police and protestors or we hear about how a mob went on a rampage and destroyed public property and attacked people. These incidences could be termed as examples of collective aggression. Collective aggression can be described as aggression that is carried out by a large group of people. This could be planned, for example war, or it could be unplanned, for example riots (Mummendey & Otten, 2001). Another way to explain such behaviour is in terms of deindividuation (discussed in Chapter 11) that takes place when an individual is part of a group. Thus, individuals may lose their rationality and behave impulsively when in a group. Individuals may also lose their self-control and display behaviour that is not consistent with normative standards. Factors that lead to deindividuation are anonymity (i.e., provided by the group), besides dissemination of responsibility and reduced time perspective (Mummendey & Otten, 2001).

Another perspective as to why people behave in such a way in groups was provided by 'emergent norm theory', that states that people behave the way they do in group, because when in groups, new norms get established and not because the individuals become less conscious about the norms. There is also a 'norm enhancement hypothesis' that states, 'groups behave more aggressively than individuals only when such behaviour can be defined as legitimate in terms of salient situational norms'

(Mummendey & Otten, 2001, p. 337). Thus, when in-group members reinforce each other's behaviour, they perceive their behaviour as appropriate.

There are various forms of collective aggression. One of them is genocide, that is sometimes termed as ethnic cleansing and is one of the worst forms of collective aggression. In genocide, the target or the victim group is subjected to atrocities by the dominating group that has more power when compared to that of the victim group which is being dominated. One of the most famous examples of genocide is the German Holocaust. The development of genocide may begin with behaviours that are less harmful, and there could be gradual psychological change in the perpetrators. The victim group is subjected to atrocities, which exist along with the justification that the dominating group has to protect itself against the target group.

THEORIES OF AGGRESSION

Various theories of aggression are discussed in this section in detail.

Biological Theories

Biological theories necessarily indicate a biological or genetic basis for aggressive behaviour. Under this approach, we shall discuss two main theories, the instinct theory and the psychodynamic theory.

Instinct theory: According to this approach, social behaviour has evolved over a period of time and the same applies to aggressive behaviour. Aggressive behaviour played a role in ensuring the survival of one's genes and to protect one's offspring as well. However, the theory can be criticised on the basis that there is lack of scientific evidence and human beings are aggressive for more reasons than just protecting their genes and offsprings.

According to Konard Lorenz in 1966 and 1974, aggression occurs a result of 'fighting instinct' (Baron & Byrne, 1995). This instinct has developed during evolution and is shared across species. Further, the field of sociobiology also holds the view that evolutions can explain social behaviours, including aggression, to a great extent.

Psychodynamic theory: Psychodynamic theory was dominant during the early 20th century. The two innate instincts that find their mention here are that of Thanatos and Eros. Thanatos can be described as instinct for death and Eros is opposite of Thanatos, that is, it is instinct of life. As stated by Freud, though the death instinct led to self-destructive behaviour, it could later get redirected towards others in the form of aggressive behaviour. As per psychodynamic theory, the natural build-up of tension in body could result in aggressive behaviours and actions, though no scientific evidence is available in this regard.

Frustration–Aggression Hypothesis

This mainly falls under social approach to understanding aggression. Dollard et al. in 1939 proposed that frustration can result in aggression. The frustration–aggression theory states, 'frustration—the perception that you are being prevented from attaining a goal—increases the probability of an aggressive response' (Aronson, Wilson, & Akert, 2014, p. 406).

Frustration can mainly occur when a person's goal-directed behaviour is blocked. It can be because of economic reasons as well as due to social and situational factors. Many a time, it is not possible to direct aggression at the source of frustration for various reasons. Then the aggression in such a case is directed at some other target. Also, such a target is vulnerable or weaker compared to the person who is inflicting aggression. Though the theory makes sense to a greater extent, it has been criticised due to little empirical evidence. Though a relationship may exist between frustration and aggression, it may not be spontaneous or direct.

Cognitive Neo-associationism

This theory was developed by Berkowitz, and it is based on the associative network models of memory. This theory proposes that there exists a direct link between the aversive event and aggression or flight behaviour and it is not necessary that specific emotions such as anger or fear are even experienced. According to this theory, anger and aggression do not occur in sequence but are processes that are parallel. The theory also refutes cognitive mediators as provoking aggressive behaviour. This theory also takes into consideration the environmental conditions.

Research in this regard was carried out by Berkowitz (1964, 1969, 1974), on his cue-arousal theory. He tried to introduce certain environmental conditions as cues for aggression. The research indicated that frustration resulted in an emotion such as anger but not aggression. The anger in turn can lead to aggressive behaviour.

Thus, aggressive behaviour can be said to be a result of the anger within an individual and due to the cues in the situation. Berkowitz in 1974 and Gustafson in 1986 and 1989, carried out further research in the area. This led to 'weapon effect', which determines whether aggression is determined by presence of a weapon in the situation and whether a weapon acts as a cue that can lead to aggression (Mummendry & Otten, 2004). A study was carried out by Berkowits and LePage (1967) to test the hypothesis whether frustrated or angry individuals display more aggression in the presence of a weapon. The research was mainly carried out to understand whether weapons serve as an aggression-arousing cue. It was carried out in two phases. In the first phase, the participants, who were male college students, had to carry out a task and their performance was evaluated by experimental confederates. The evaluation included a number of electric shocks that were not dependent on the actual performance of the participants and were used to generate the different strengths of aroused anger in the participants. The results indicated that more anger was reported by the participants who received higher number of shocks. In the second phase of this research, both angered and non-angered participants had to evaluate the performance of the confederates, again by giving electric shocks. In this phase, though, there were two experimental conditions. In one of the conditions, a shotgun and a revolver were present, and in the other condition, no weapons were present. The results indicated that angered participants administered more shocks when in the presence of the weapons as compared to when the weapons were not present, whereas the aggressive cues had no effect on the shocks administered by the non-angered participants.

Excitation Transfer Model

Excitation transfer theory states that arousal in a completely new situation can be a result of a residual arousal from a previous situation (Zillmann, 1971, 1988). Residual arousal is an arousal that is carried over from a previous situation. Thus, certain factors that are otherwise not directly related to aggressive behaviour can add to the arousal related to aggression, thus aggravating the aggressive response. This theory states arousal and aggression in a sequence where the latter follows the first. However, this can occur only when a person does not have clear information about the causes of arousal (Zillmann, Johnson, & Day, 1974).

Learning Theories

Aggressive behaviour can also be explained with the help of learning theories. These theories mainly indicate that our behaviour can be influenced by how others behave. In this context, we will discuss two main learning theories.

Operant Conditioning Theory

This theory was proposed by Skinner. Skinner spoke about operant reinforcement, that can be described as a process in which 'changes in behaviour result from the response to stimuli in a person's environment' (Crisp & Turner, 2010, p. 249). Thus, there is a stimulus–response pattern that can be strengthened when there is positive reinforcement. According to this theory, if an aggressive behaviour is provided with positive reinforcement, it will be encouraged and is more likely to occur in future. For example, if a child is praised by his parent for hitting back a boy who hit him, this aggressive behaviour of the child will be reinforced and the child will indulge in display of such retaliatory aggressive behaviour in future as well.

Social Learning Theory

This theory was proposed by Bandura. He proposed that behaviours can also be learned indirectly, by observing others. Thus, aggressive behaviour of a person can be a result of both direct and indirect experiences of aggression. In this context, the influence of media can also be discussed. Children can observe aggressive behaviour via media and imitate that behaviour. The famous Bobo doll experiment can be discussed here. In this study carried out by Bandura, Ross and Ross (1961), the participants were 24 preschool children who were assigned to three different conditions. The first group observed an adult model who was aggressive towards the Bobo doll by slapping the doll, striking it with a mallet, kicking it and also yelling aggressively at it. The second group was made to observe inhibited non-aggressive models, that is, they were exposed to models that were not aggressive. The groups were also divided based on male and female participants and they were exposed to same sex and opposite sex aggressive or non-aggressive models. Thus, there were actually eight experimental groups with six participants in each group and a single control group with 24 participants. The control group was not exposed to any adult model. The results indicated that the participants, who were exposed to models that were aggressive, displayed aggression that was similar to that displayed by the model. Male participants also displayed more aggression than female participants when exposed to a male aggressive model. The participants, who were exposed to male models that were non-aggressive, displayed lower levels of aggression in comparison to the control group.

General Aggression Model

This model can be termed as one of the comprehensive theories of aggression. 'The model focuses on a single episode or cycle of aggression that occurs during a particular social situation and accounts for both proximate influences (e.g., arousal) as well as more distal ones (such as genetic endowment)' (Barrett, 2017, p. 330). The model also includes the influence of interaction and subsequent episodes.

According to this model, the components of aggressive episode are personal and situational inputs, internal states and outcomes. Examples of personal inputs are gender and personality, and examples of situational inputs could be temperature, violence in media, frustration, pain and even provocation (Barrett, 2017). The internal state can be termed as a route or a roadway though which the personal and situational factors have an influence on the last component, that is, output. The internal state of an individual constitutes his/her effect, cognition and level of arousal. The outcome consists of appraisal and reappraisal of the situation, and also includes decision process that can lead to actions that are thoughtful or impulsive. The outcome of an episode can then further influence social interaction and aggressive episodes (Barrett, 2017).

The model has four stages (Eysenck, 2013) that are described as follows:

Stage 1: In the first stage, there are personal as well as situational variables. For example, the personal variable could be that an individual has a personality that is inherently aggressive and the situational variable could be that the person is frustrated and has been provoked by another individual.

Stage 2: Stage 1 leads to Stage 2. Where, based on the personal and situational inputs, in Stage 1, the individual will experience feelings that are hostile (related to the affect) and may have hostile thoughts (cognition) and he/she may get aroused due to activation of autonomic nervous system.

Stage 3: Stage 2 leads to Stage 3, that is, the process of appraisal, where the situation is interpreted and consequences of displaying aggression could also be considered.

Stage 4: Based on the consequences of the appraisal process that took place in Stage 3, a decision is taken with regard to whether the behaviour will be aggressive or not.

A diagrammatic representation of general aggression model is given Figure 10.1.

DETERMINANTS OF AGGRESSION

In this section of this chapter, the determinants of aggression will be discussed. The determinants of aggression can be categorised into person-centred and situation-centred determinants.

Person-Centred Determinants

Person-centred determinants of aggression can be categorised into the following:

Gender difference: Many a time, it is perceived that males are more aggressive compared to females. Studies (Bettencourt & Miller, 1996; Eagly & Steffen, 1986) indicate that women were less likely to show physical aggression than men and men also displayed unprovoked aggression more often compared to women.

This in a way can be explained with the help of hormonal differences between males and females, mainly testosterone that is higher amongst males compared to females. However, a greater role is also played by social influence and parenting. Besides the patriarchal system in the society can also play a significant role. The way girls and boys are socialised can make a difference in their behaviours and

Figure 10.1 *The General Aggression Model*

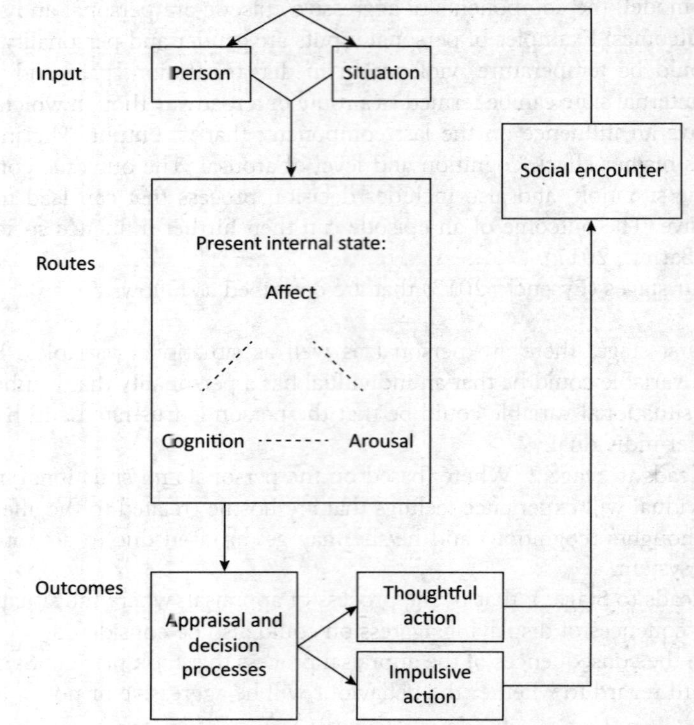

Source: Anderson and Bushan (2002).

display of aggression as well. Females are discouraged from being aggressive as part of their socialisation. Men, on the other hand, are not expected to be expressive and are not expected to 'cry'. This repression of emotions can have a long-term impact on them and thus the repressed emotions can be expressed as aggression. Furthermore, a difference also exists in the way aggression is expressed by men and women. Women may display more of verbal aggression. However, men are more likely to display physical aggression (Björkqvist et al., 1992).

Personality: Personality is yet another person-centred determinant of aggression. Traits such as irritability, rumination, emotional susceptibility were found to be consistent with aggression (Capara et al., 1994, 1996). People with Type A personality were also found to be more aggressive compared to Type B. Furthermore, individuals with low self-esteem are also found to be more aggressive. However, this view has been much debated, as some researchers believe that people with high self-esteem are more aggressive. This, in a way, can also be related to the power the person possesses or to what extent the person holds control of any situation and people. A person with such power and control will have higher self-esteem and can be aggressive as he/she can use the control and power for his/her own benefit.

Alcohol consumption: This is yet another determinant of aggression. Research has shown a display of aggression by people who have consumed alcohol (Bachman & Peralta, 2002). Alcohol has also been related with domestic violence (International Centre for Research on Women, 2000). A meta-analysis carried out by Bushman and Cooper in 1990 (Crisp & Turner, 2010) also revealed that men with drinking problems were more likely to be aggressive, compared to men without drinking problems. The main reasons why alcohol can be correlated with aggression are the physiological arousal that takes place after alcohol consumption and the impairment that occurs in the neuropsychological functioning as a result of alcohol consumption.

Alcohol expectancy theory also elaborates on the correlationship between alcohol consumption and aggression. This states that people are expected to be aggressive and less inhibited after consumption of alcohol. Thus, people may get into aggressive behaviour on this pretext that their behaviour will be excused by saying that they were aggressive due to consumption of alcohol and not otherwise and, thus, can get away with the argument.

Situation-Centred Determinants

Since we have now understood the person-centred determinants of aggression, we will now move on to the determinants in situation that can lead to aggression.

Physical environment: The aspects of physical environment in which we live can be termed as a determinant of aggressive behaviour. This mainly covers temperature, crowding and noise.

Higher temperature to a greater extent has been associated with aggression (Anderson & Anderson, 1984; Harris & Stadler, 1983). Furthermore, reactive aggression (as compared to proactive aggression) was more often linked to high temperatures.

The second aspect of physical environment that can cause aggression is crowding. The more crowded the place is, the more is the aggression. This can also be confirmed by the aggressive crowd behaviour that can be seen during protests or during games where people get into vandalism destroying public property and harming each other. Deindividuation is more likely to occur when in crowd and people may display aggression because they feel they cannot be identified or held accountable and thus their obedience to social norms is lower.

The next aspect of physical environment is noise. A very loud unpleasant sound can also lead to aggression. This can be due to increase in stress and physiological arousal as a result of loud noise.

In fact, events that are unpleasant or aversive can also lead to aggression. Besides, other physical discomfort caused as a result of pain, frustration, loud noise, foul odour, heat can also lead to aggression (Barrett, 2017). Aversive conditions along with aggressive cues can further increase the likelihood of aggressive behaviour. Aggressive cues lead to precipitation of aggressive thoughts that can lead to aggression, for example, words, objects and even images. Here we can also discus about the weapon effect (discussed earlier in this chapter), that is, the likelihood of aggression increases in presence of a weapon, whether a rifle or a revolver (Barrett, 2017).

Frustration

The topic of frustration was briefly touched upon in the discussion on theories of aggression, but will be discussed under this section in detail.

Frustration can be deemed as one of the major causes of aggression. Frustration takes place when an individual's goal-directed behaviour is thwarted. Thus, the individual is not able to achieve his/her goal and reach gratification and thus experiences frustration. For example, if an individual was expecting a promotion but is not given one, he/she may experience frustration.

A Marathi movie titled *Dombivali Fast* can also be used as an example here. The movie is about Madhav Apte who is a common middle-class man leading a routine life with his wife and two children. He is a man of principles and has strong values. But he is constantly pushed by his wife and colleagues that make it very difficult for him to firmly stand for what he believes in. One day he becomes so frustrated with the unfitting behaviour of the people around him that he just snaps and he goes on a rampage in an attempt to do what is right and ends up killing people and taking his own life ultimately.

Various studies have also determined this relationship between frustration and aggression. A study was carried out by Barker et al. (1941) on frustration in young children. The study was carried out on 30 children who were subjected to frustrating and non-frustrating play situations. In the non-frustrating situation, the children were allowed to play with toys for 20 minutes.

With regard to frustration situation, the children were led to a room full of attractive toys, but were not allowed to play with these toys as they were blocked by a wire screen.

The behaviours of the children in both the groups were recorded by the experimenter. The results indicated that the frustration experienced by the children in the frustrating play situation, not only reduced the constructiveness of the play, but also led to restless and destructive behaviour and unhappiness. Increased in-group aggression was also noted.

There are various factors that lead to experience of frustration and corresponding increase in likelihood of display of aggression. One of the factors that can be discussed is how close the person was towards achieving the goal. When the goal is close, the expectation of pleasure is high. If it gets thwarted, the more will be the aggression displayed. Yet another factor related to frustration is expectation.

Although research evidence indicates that frustration leads to aggression, there could be instances where frustration does not lead to aggression. This may also depend on various other factors including the size, strength and ability to retaliate, the person who is the source of frustration. Furthermore, the likelihood of aggression will also be low if the frustration is understandable and legitimate, not intentional.

Frustration also needs to be differentiated from deprivation. For example, in the research discussed earlier, aggression was observed in children when they expected the toys and they had reasons to expect to be able to play with the toys. This expectation was thwarted and in turn led to destructive behaviour. But in the case of deprivation, when children do not have any toys, they may not display aggression. Though absolute deprivation may not lead to aggression, relative deprivation seems to have links with aggression. In relative deprivation, a discrepancy is perceived between what they expect to have and what they have.

Social disadvantage and social rejection: Individuals belonging to socially disadvantaged groups may display aggression due to relative deprivation that may occur when the individuals believe that they are being unjustly treated in comparison to others.

Social rejection occurs when an individual is rejected by others, especially by the significant people in one's life. We often come across an acid throwing incident by a person whose romantic advances were rejected by a girl whom he liked. Social rejection leads to experience of a social pain that is similar to physical pain. Thus, it is aversive and can precipitate aggression.

Provocation: This is yet another determinant of aggression that occurs when 'one person intentionally elicits an aggressive response from another through the use of insults, physical aggression, blocking goal attainment, teasing or similar behaviours' (Anderson & Huesman, 2003). Aggression can be an outcome of provocation, especially when the need to reciprocate is felt after an individual is provoked by another person. Though it is not always that reciprocation is an outcome of provocation, as it will depend on whether the provocation was intentional or not. When the provocation is unintentional (and there are mitigating circumstances), it will not lead to reciprocation. However, when the provocation is perceived as intentional, the likelihood of reciprocation is high.

In a research carried out by Barlett et al. (2016), two studies were conducted to investigate the role of mitigating information with reference to the link between provocation and aggression. The results indicated that weak provocations are less likely to lead to aggressive reciprocation, when compared to strong provocations. Mitigating information that is weak is less likely to decrease aggression when compared to strong mitigating information. When the provocations were weak, the varying strength of mitigating information was found to be relevant. When provocation was strong, mitigating information that was strong was found to result in decrease in aggression as opposed to mitigating information that was weak.

Cultural Influences

This is yet another situation-centred determinant of aggression and can also be categorised under situational determinants of aggression. The influence of culture is more when compared to determinants such as aversive events. Culture also has a significant influence on thinking, beliefs, attitudes and overall behaviour of people. Thus, it also plays an important role in determining aggressive behaviour. Cultural differences may exist in the display of aggressive behaviour and certain cultures may allow aggressive behaviour, whereas others may not. Here, the term culture-of-honour can also describe, that has been defined by Barrett (2017, p. 328) 'as a society in which people, especially males, are highly protective of their reputation and very sensitive and reactive to personal insults, humiliation and other threats to their honour'. The insults and humiliations, thus, can lead to display of aggressive behaviour. 'Honour killing' is one example of culture-of-honour.

In a study carried out by Cohen, Nisbett, Bowdle and Schwarz (1996) on southern white males, who were students of University of Michigan (who grew up in north or south). They were studied with regard to cognitive, emotional, behavioural manifestations and physiological reactions based on the norms that are characteristic of 'culture-of-honour'. Three experiments were carried out in this regard, in which the confederates insulted the participants after they bumped into a participant and called the participant an 'asshole'. The results indicated that students who grew up in the north were not affected by the insult. But the students who grew up in the south, displayed increased likelihood of thinking that this was a threat to their masculine reputation. The participants were also more upset, which was indicated by their increased cortisol levels, and their testosterone levels also increased indicating that they were physiologically ready for aggression. They were also cognitively ready for aggression and the likelihood of them displaying aggressive and dominant behaviour was high. Thus, the findings were consistent with what was discussed under 'culture-of-honour', that when insults lead to decrease in the reputation of a man, he will make attempts to restore his status with behaviour that is aggressive or violent.

India is not new to this kind of aggression and there are numerous incidences of honour killings. A study carried out by Deol (2014) on honour killings in India with a focus on the state of Punjab, indicated that honour killings stemmed from intolerance on the part of the families with reference to premarital relationships as well as matrimonial choices made by their daughters, more so with regard to intercaste marriages. And honour killings are not only prevalent in the northern states of India, as reported by an article in the *Deccan Chronicle* by V. Ashok Kumar (2016), there were 81 honour killings within a period of three years in Tamil Nadu.

Media Influence

Media can also be said to be a determinant of aggression. Exposure to violence through media, music and even video games can lead to increase in aggressive behaviour. The concern about media's influence on aggression has also increased due to increased exposure to and use of media in recent times.

Media violence and its links to aggression have been researched using experimental studies in both the laboratory and the field that indicated a cause and effect relationship between media violence and aggression. Cross-sectional correlational studies have also been carried out that again indicate a link between the two. Furthermore, longitudinal studies have also shown that exposure to violence on television leads to aggressive and criminal behaviour later in life (Bushman & Anderson, 2002).

In this context, the media violence hypothesis can be discussed. Media violence hypothesis states that 'exposure to violence in the media can cause aggression in the real world' (Barrett, 2017, p. 317). Anderson et al. (2003) stated that media violence led to increased chances of aggression and violence. Both, short and long terms exposure to media were found to be linked with aggressive behaviour. Further, this link with aggressive behaviour was found to be applicable to not only violence in television and films, but also to video games. Exposures to video games that are violent also lead to aggression and violence (Anderson & Bushman, 2001). Huesman et al. (2003) indicated that exposure to media violence not only has short-term effect on the adults but there were long-term negative effects on children as well. If exposed to television violence early in their life, both male and female children were prone to develop aggressive and violent behaviours as they grow up.

Short-term exposure was also seen to lead to increased chances of aggression, both verbal and physical, leading to aggressive thoughts and emotions. Anderson et al. (2003, p. 81) also described why and when aggression and violence is increased as a result of exposure to media violence. They state,

> Media violence produces short-term effects by priming existing aggressive scripts and cognitions, increasing physiological arousal and triggering an automatic tendency to imitate observed behaviours. Media violence produces long-term effects via several types of learning processes leading to the acquisition of lasting (an automatically accessible) aggressive scripts, interpersonal schemas, and aggression-supporting beliefs about social behaviour, and by reducing individual's normal negative emotional responses to violence (i.e., desensitization).

Thus media can have both short-term and long-term effects on aggressive and violent behaviours.

The extent to which media violence has an influence on an individual is also determined by various aspects such as (Anderson et al., 2003):

- The extent to which the individual identifies with the character that is displaying aggressive behaviour. This mainly focuses on the character of the viewer.
- Influence of parents, thus emphasising on the role played by social environment. And, in fact, supervision by parents and control of over use of media by children can play a role in preventing aggressive behaviour as a result of influence of media.
- Content in the media, including how attractive the aggressive person is.

Under violence related to media, we can also discuss about cyber bullying.

Cyberbullying: It is important to discuss cyberbullying because today it has emerged as a serious problem that can be attributed to increased exposure and access to mobile phones and social networking. Cyberbullying is defined as 'intended and repeated harm caused by communication via use of computers, mobile phones and other electronic devices' (Whitty & Young, 2017, p. 78). Smith et al. (2008, p. 376) defined cyberbullying as 'an aggressive intentional act carried out by a group or individual, using electronic forms of contact, repeatedly and over time, against a victim who cannot easily defend him or herself'. Cyberbullying can include posting expressions of humiliating and embarrassing information about a person online. Cyberbullying can also be deemed as a serious issue because it can occur at anytime and anywhere. There is also an added aspect that has to do with anonymity of the person who indulges in bullying, though a large audience may be involved. For example, compromising photographs of a person could be emailed or could be put on Facebook without actually revealing the identity of the person who is doing it. An article by Krishna (2015) indicates that as per the Intel Security's Teen, Tweens and Technology Study 2015, 81 per cent of respondents in the age group of 8–16 were active in social networking and 22 per cent of them had experienced cyberbullying. The four main methods of cyberbullying are direct hostility, intrusiveness, public humiliation and exclusion (Bennet et al., 2011). The consequences of cyberbullying could be more severe when compared with the conventional bullying. Adolescent victims of cyber bullying display depression, anxiety and even paranoia (Schenk & Fremouw, 2012). The victims of cyberbullying are subjected to psychological harm and can experience frustration, anger and sadness. They could also develop chronic illnesses and may even attempt suicide (Whitty & Young, 2017). Cyber laws are also not effectively enforced and it may also be difficult to catch the perpetrator as he/she could be next door or miles away.

Besides cyberbullying, there could also be cyber stalking, where an individual is stalked by using Internet, email and other electronic devices of communication (Whitty & Young, 2017). Individuals may also be subjected to cyber harassment.

CONCEPT OF ANGER

Anger can be termed as one of the basic emotions. According to Panksepp (2000), there are seven basic emotional systems. These are, seeking/expectancy, rage/anger, fear/anxiety, lust/sexuality, care/nurturance, panic/separation and play/joy. In this section of the chapter, we will mainly focus on anger.

Anger is often experienced, by an individual, as a reaction to some form of danger, threat or harm. It can be described as an emotion and may range from a mild irritation to intense rage. It can be characterised as hatred or antipathy towards something or someone who, one feels, has on purpose done wrong to him/her. Anger can also be described as a feeling infuriated due to some kind of injury or frustration. It can be termed as an internal state that has emotional, physiological and cognitive dimensions. Anger helps individuals ventilate their feelings and may even encourage them to seek solution to their problems. However, excessive and frequent anger can be detrimental to the individual's health and well-being. Thus, anger beyond an optimal level needs to be dealt with effectively so as to reduce its negative effects.

Anger is associated with certain physiological changes, such as increased heart rate, blood pressure and release of stress hormones. It can lead to increased perspiration and a feeling of being out of control. Anger also leads to decrease in cognitive processing, fine motor coordination and decrease in pain-related sensitivity. However, there is an increase in muscle strength. Besides the physiological changes, the behaviour of individuals also changes when they are angry, as they may indulge in shouting at others, throwing things around or at others, being overtly critical or withdrawing from others. It can also lead to violence and abuse, if it is not appropriately controlled.

As we discussed earlier, anger is in a way necessary to vent out one's feelings; however, it can be deemed as a problem when it interferes with one's health, work related activities, day-to-day activities, law and also interferes with one's relationship with others.

Some of the signs that indicate unhealthy anger are as follows:

1. There is verbal, emotional, physical and/or psychological abuse that accompanies anger.
2. The frequency of anger increases.
3. People around are scared or worried about the individual's anger.
4. It interferes with relationship and work-related activities.
5. Anger does not subside even after the event that triggered it has passed.
6. It interferes with other situations besides the event that triggered it.
7. The individual is anxious and worried about his/her anger.
8. There is substance abuse involved.
9. There is no focus on the problem, situation or event that triggered the anger.

It is necessary to identify anger in oneself and others so that it is adequately managed.

As such there is no cause and effect relationship between anger and aggression, though both have physiological bases and aggression is invariably learned. Every individual may experience anger at some point in life, but he/she may not always display aggression.

However, there are certain common factors that may lead to both anger and aggression; they are as follows:

1. Impairment of judgement and cautiousness, which can also be as a result of substance abuse.
2. Experiencing frequent frustrations due to inability to achieve one's goals.
3. Experiencing fear, emotional trauma, pain and discomfort can also elicit anger or aggression.
4. Post-traumatic stress disorder or desensitisation to aggression due to life experiences can also lead to anger or aggression.

Anger management: Anger management involves developing an understanding about one's anger and reasons that lead to angry behaviours and actions. It also deals with learning and developing effective ways of appropriately expressing anger or even preventing it in certain situations. With anger management, an individual is able to understand the early warnings of his/her angers and the triggers, and is able to use the techniques to calm down and manage his/her anger effectively before it gets out of control and results in negative outcomes.

According to Lerner (1985), anger is in a way an indication that something is wrong and some action needs to be taken in the direction of solving the problem. Thus, it becomes necessary to first, identify the problem and the root cause of anger, and then work towards resolving the problem. Many a time, individual may have to deal with this situation by either repressing the feelings related to anger or venting it out. Unfortunately, both these techniques may not be effective and may cause further problems. Suppressing feelings may result in an unhealthy explosion of negative feelings later and may also result in displacement of anger on others. On the other hand, venting out of anger will affect the individual and his/her relationship and image in social setting. Thus, effective management of anger is very important. Four main approaches in this regard can be of great help; they are as follows:

1. Identifying the causes of anger (whether it is frustration), one's behaviour when angry and choices in the past, wants and needs and so on. This can be done by asking oneself, 'Why am I so angry? What is troubling me?'
2. Learning effective communication skills.

3. Replacing the ineffective anger management techniques (as discussed earlier) with better and more effective techniques.
4. Having a mature and solution-focused approach to any problem or interpersonal conflict.

PREVENTION AND CONTROL OF AGGRESSION

We focused on the concept of aggression and later also discussed about theories and determinants of aggression. It is also important that, as social psychologists, we discuss about the ways in which aggression can be prevented and controlled. Some of the techniques that could be used are discussed as follows.

Punishment

Punishment is one of the techniques that has been frequently used to deal with aggression and even violence. It is assumed that punishment will lead to suppression of behaviour that is aggressive. There are also laws in place for violence and crimes such as murder, rape and so on. If punishment is appropriately used it can have a deterrent effect on aggression; however, a number of conditions needs to be kept in mind while doing so:

1. The punishments should immediately follow the aggressive behaviour.
2. The magnitude of punishment should be adequate so that it is seen as aversive by the recipient.
3. The likelihood that it is a likely outcome to an aggressive behaviour should be high.

The use of punishment to prevent and control is pretty complex as there are a number of issues and problems involved. Punishment for aggression, may further perpetuate aggression. In fact, children who were frequently punished for aggressive behaviour were found to be more aggressive later in life (Sears, Maccoby, & Levin, 1957). There could also be counter aggression as a result of fear of punishment. Punishment can also invite direct or indirect aggression.

Catharsis

Certain activities can help individuals vent out their aggressive impulses and thus help reduce aggressive behaviour. The catharsis hypothesis can be discussed here which states, indulging in activities that help individuals express or vent out their anger and hostility, in a way that is safe, will lead to decreased aggressive behaviour (Baron & Byrne, 1995).

Such activities not only help decrease anger but also help the individual to diminish emotional tension. Studies have shown mixed results with regard to the effectiveness of catharsis in reducing aggressive behaviour (Baron & Byrne, 1995).

In 1959, in a study carried out by Hornberger (Bushman, 2002), the participants were angered as they received insults from the confederates. The participants were then divided into two groups. One group had to pound nails for 10 minutes so as to vent their anger and the other group did nothing. The participants were then given an opportunity to criticise the confederate who had insulted them.

The results indicated that the hostility in the participants, who pounded the nails, was higher than the participants, who did not pound the nails.

The concept of rumination can also be discussed here. Rumination can be carried out by focusing one's attention inward, on one's self, especially on one's negative mood. It would seem that while angry, punching a pillow or a punching bag, imagining it to be the person you are angry at, could help deal with your anger. However, not many studies have actually indicated that rumination leads to decreased anger. A study was carried out by Bushman (2002) to investigate which one of the two, distraction or rumination, leads to decrease in anger. In this study, that was carried out on around 600 male and female college students, the participants were first angered as they were criticised by other participants for the essays written by them. The angered participants were then randomly assigned to rumination, distraction or control group. In the rumination group, the participants had to punch a punching bag as hard and as long as they wanted to and as they did so they had to think about the person who had angered them (the person who criticised their essay). A computer (15 inch) also displayed the photograph of this person who had criticised them. In distraction group, the participants again were told to punch the punching bag as hard and as long as they wanted to, but they were asked to think of becoming physically fit as they did so. The control group just had to sit without any activity. No efforts whatsoever were made to reduce the anger of these participants. The results indicated that the participants in rumination groups felt angrier and also more aggressive when compared to the other two groups. It can thus be concluded that rumination, in fact, increased anger and aggression rather than decreasing them and doing nothing at all (control group); was seen as a better way to vent anger.

Other Techniques to Prevent and Control Aggression

Cognitive Interventions

Cognitive interventions such as apologies and reasonable explanations can also lead to reduction in anger and aggression. For example, an individual who had an important appointment with another person is late and is not able to make it at the given time would find himself/herself at the end of anger from the other person. But if this person apologises and gives reasonable explanations, then it is possible that it will lead to diminishing of anger in the other person. The nature of excuses given also plays a role and they need to appear sincere and specific (Baron & Byrne, 1995).

Exposure to Non-Aggressive Models

Exposure to non-aggressive models could lead to decreased aggression in individuals. This was also displayed in the Bobo doll experiment carried out by Bandura et al. (1961), where the participants exposed to non-aggressive models showed less aggression when compared to the control group. Thus, when an individual is exposed to a model that is non-aggressive, the aggression displayed by him/her may decrease.

Social Skills Training

Individuals who lack social skills are more likely to display aggression, and thus, such individuals can be helped if they are provided with suitable training in social skills. A study carried out by Vahedi et al.

(2007) on effectiveness of social skills intervention to reduce aggression in preschoolers indicated that the treatment group that received social skills training displayed decrease in aggression when compared to the control group.

Incompatible Responses

This states that inducing emotional states and reactions that are incompatible with aggression can lead to decrease in aggressive behaviour. These could be empathy, humour or even mild sexual arousal. It is based on basic principles that two incompatible responses or emotional states cannot be engaged in by an individual at the same time. For example, one cannot be angry and be laughing at the same time. Further, the positive feelings that are generated by empathy, humour or mild sexual arousal will lead to reduction of negative feelings that arise as a result of frustration and annoyance experienced by the individual (Baron & Byrne, 1995).

SUMMARY

To summaries, in this chapter the concept of aggression was discussed. Aggression can be described as a behaviour that is intentional in nature and is mainly aimed at inflicting pain, psychological or physical, to another person or even object. Various forms of aggression like hostile aggression, instrumental aggression, direct and indirect aggression and violence were also discussed. The chapter further focused on aggression and anti-social behaviour. The concept of collective aggression was also described. Further, theories of aggression, including, biological theories, frustration–aggression hypothesis, cognitive neoassociationism, excitation-transfer model, learning theories and general aggression model were discussed. The person centred and situation centred determinants of aggression were also highlighted in this chapter. The chapter also focused on cyberbullying, which is important to be discussed as it has now emerged as a serious problem that can be attributed to exposure and access to mobile phones and social networking. Cyberbullying is defined as intended and repeated harm caused by communication via use of computers, mobile phones and other electronic devices. The concept of anger was further discussed, with a focus on anger management. Lastly, the chapter described prevention and control of aggression, by highlighting certain techniques like punishment, catharsis and other techniques.

QUESTIONS

1. What is aggression?
2. Explain collective aggression.
3. Discuss various theories of aggression.
4. Explain the determinants of aggression.
5. Describe the concept of anger and distinguish it from aggression.
6. Discuss the ways in which aggression can be prevented or controlled.

REFERENCES

Anderson, C. A., & Bushan, B. J. (2002). The general aggression model: an integrated social-cognitive model of human aggression. *Annual Review of Psychology*, *53*, 27–51.

Barker, R. G., Dembo, T., & Lewin, K. (1941). Frustration and regression: An experiment with young children. *University of Iowa Studies in Child Welfare*, *18*(1), 314.

Berkowitz, L., & Lepage, A. (1967). Weapons as aggression-eliciting stimuli. *Journal of Personality and Social Psychology*, 7(2, Pt.1), 202–207. Retrieved from http://dx.doi.org/10.1037/h0025008

Björkqvist, K., Lagerspetz, K. M. J., & Kaukiainen, A. (1992). Do girls manipulate and boys fight? Development trends regarding direct and indirect aggression. *Aggressive Behaviour*, *18*(2), 117–127.

Caprara, G. V., Perugini, M., & Barbaranelli, C. (1994). Studies of individual differences in aggression. In M. Potegal & J. F. Knuton (Eds.), *The dynamics of aggression: Biological and social processes in dyads and groups*. New Jersey, NJ: Erlbaum.

Caprara, G., Barbaranelli, C., & Zimbardo, P. (1996). Understanding the complexity of human aggression: Affective, cognitive, and social dimensions of individual differences in propensity toward aggression. *European Journal of Personality*, *10*(2), 133–155.

Huesmann, L. R., Moise-Titus, J., Podolski, C., & Eron, L. D. (2003). Longitudinal relations between children's exposure to TV violence and their aggressive and violent behavior in young adulthood: 1977–1992. *Developmental Psychology*, *39*(2), 201–221.

International Centre for Research on Women. (2000). Domestic violence in India: A summary report of a multi-site household survey. Retrieved from https://www.icrw.org/wp-content/uploads/2016/10/Domestic-Violence-in-India-3-A-Summary-Report-of-a-Multi-Site-Household-Survey.pdf

Lerner, M. (1995). *The politics of meaning: Restoring hope and possibility in an age of cynicism*. Reading, MA: Addison-Wesley.

Mummendey, M., & Otten, S. (2001). Aggressive behaviour. In M., Hewstone, W., Stroebe & G. Stephenson (Eds.), *Introduction to Social psychology*. Blackwell Publishers.

Panksepp, J. (2000). Emotions as natural kinds within the mammalian brain. In M. Lewis & J. M. Howland-Jones (Eds.), *Handbook of emotions* (2nd ed.). New York, NY: Guilford Press.

Weiss, W. (1969). Effects of the mass media of communication. In G. Lindzey and E. Aronson (Eds.), *The handbook of social psychology*, 2nd ed. (Volume 5, pp. 77–195). Reading, MA: Addison Wesley.

Zillmann, D. (1971). Excitation transfer in communication-mediated aggressive behavior. *Journal of Experimental Social Psychology*, 7(4), 419–434. Retrieved from http://dx.doi.org/10.1016/0022-1031(71)90075-8

FURTHER READINGS

For more information on aggression (especially, general model of aggression) refer to the following:

Anderson, A. A., & Bushman, B. J. (2002). Human aggression. *Annual Review of Psychology*, *53*(1), 27–51.

McPhail, C. (1991). *The myth of the madding crowd* (1st ed.). New York, NY: A. de Gruyter.

Warburton, W. A., & Anderson, C. A. (2015). Social psychological study of aggression. In J. Wright (Ed.), *International encyclopedia of the social and behavioural sciences* (2nd ed., Vol. 1, pp. 295–299). Oxford: Elsevier.

Following is the website related to ReThink that is an anti-cyberbullying software created by Trisha Prabhu.
http://www.rethinkwords.com

CHAPTER 11

Group Dynamics

Identify groups from the following examples:

1. *Employees working at their own desks in a chamber.*
2. *Students discussing about their assignment in social psychology.*
3. *Friends busy gossiping in food court of a mall, as they enjoy their food.*
4. *Relatives deep in conversations and interactions during a wedding.*
5. *Students sitting in a classroom and studying by their own.*
6. *Workers in an industrial set-up working on their machines on the shop floor.*
7. *Members of a sports team discussing about strategy for their next game.*

From the examples given above, examples 2, 3, 4, 7 can be termed as examples of a group and 1, 5 and 6 cannot be termed as examples of a group, as they do not fit the definition of a group, that is, three or more individuals who are interacting with each other and are also interdependent. Such members also have an influence on each other.

Thus, there could also be a group of students working on their group assignments, discussing about what information should go in the assignment and what should not, sharing their opinions and ideas.

There could be a group of people who are involved in organising a training programme on behavioural skills for the managers in their organisation, carrying out debates and discussions on what topics should be covered or the possible resource persons who could be invited, to the duration and other details of the training programme. Such groups also have formal and informal leaders.

There could also be a group of clinical psychologists having a case conferencing and discussing about what intervention strategy could be used.

Thus groups could range from family, community groups to sports teams and so on. And the members of such groups are in interaction with each other, are interdependent and also have an influence on each other's behaviour.

The focus of this chapter is not only on understanding the concept of group but also on the concepts of roles and norms. The term 'group cohesiveness' will also be discussed. The chapter will also highlight the performance of individuals in groups and explain the term 'deindividuation'. Decision-making process in groups will also be described besides focusing on leadership. In the end, the chapter will also focus on conflict and conflict resolution.

Learning Objectives

After reading this chapter, you will be able to

- ❒ Discuss the nature of group
- ❒ Explain the concepts of roles and norms
- ❒ Describe group cohesiveness
- ❒ Discuss the performance of individuals in groups
- ❒ Elucidate deindividuation
- ❒ Discuss the decision-making process in groups
- ❒ Explain leadership
- ❒ Elucidate conflict and conflict resolution

NATURE OF GROUP

A group can be described as a collection of two or more people who engage in some interaction with each other, are dependent on each other and perceive themselves as being part of the group. They may also share a common goal and have a comparatively stable relationship.

Looking at some of the definitions of group, Farnham (2005, p. 478) defined a group 'as made up of persons (more than two, which is a dyad) who communicate regularly, share goals and interact with each other over time, so building up affective bonds'.

Quick, Nelson and Khandelwal (2013, p. 320) defined group as 'two or more people with common interests, objectives, and continuing interaction'.

Barrett (2017, p. 434) defined group as 'two or more individuals who perceive themselves as part of a unit and who influence each other and are interdependent'.

To understand further about groups, they have the following main components:

- A group consists of necessarily more than two individuals.
- The members also have an influence on each other and are interdependent. They also develop a kind of relationship and are involved in social interactions.
- The members share a common goal and strive together towards achieving that goal.
- The members communicate with each other and this communication is both verbal and non-verbal.
- Certain norms, customs and procedures are expected to be followed by the group members, failing which the members may even loose the membership of the group.
- They may also engage in similar activities and the group also has some control over their actions.
- The members perceive themselves as being part of the group.

Groups can vary in terms of size; a group can be small or large in size. It could be a small group of four persons or could be a group of 20 to 30 people or even more. The group processes in smaller groups is different from that in larger groups. Furthermore, it can also vary in terms of its duration, a group such as family will exist for years together, whereas a group of, say, social workers may work on a certain case together and then disperse. Groups also vary in their values and goals or objectives; for example, a group of students performing a drama for the school get together will differ from a group of managers involved in a selection process. Based on the goals and objectives, the activities of the group also vary.

TYPES OF GROUPS

There are various types of groups that are discussed as follows:

1. **Primary groups.** A primary group is comparatively smaller in size, though the members share intimate and closer relationship with each other. A perfect example is family.
2. **Secondary groups.** These groups are less personal compared with primary groups, for example, trade unions.
3. **In-group and out-group.** In-group is the group that one identifies with. The members necessarily share common objective and goal and there is also a feeling of unity amongst the members. The members who are not part of the in-group are treated as outsiders. For example, an in-group could be based on country, that is, all Indians are in-group and those who are not are outsiders. Similarly, all Tamilians could be in-group and those who are not are outsiders. Thus, the members who do not belong to the in-group are considered as out-group.
4. **Formal groups.** As the name suggests, these are formal in nature and are created for specific purpose. Examples of such groups are different divisions in an industrial set-up. Formal groups could be temporary or permanent. A finance department in an industry could be considered as a permanent group that works on continuous and consistent basis, unless discontinued or reconfigured. A temporary group, on the other hand, is mainly created for specific purposes and discontinued once the purpose is served. For example, a group that has been created for organisation of safety week in an organisation is temporary.
5. **Informal groups.** These are not official in nature and emerge as a result of social relationship between individuals. Friendship groups and interest groups are certain types of informal groups. For example, a group of friends or a group of people in a laughter club, who just meet every day in the morning and practise laughter therapy and then disperse.
6. **Membership and reference groups.** Membership groups are the groups to which the individual belongs. For example, an individual can be a member of a certain club. Reference groups, on the other hand, are groups against which the individual will compare his/her attitudes and behaviours. Reference groups may or may not be membership groups.
7. **Part-time groups.** These are the groups that may meet regularly, but the members of these groups are members of other groups on a more full-time basis. For example, in a college, teachers from different departments may meet regularly as a part of committee that takes care of the students' welfare activities. Here, the teachers play just a part-time role as a member of the committee and their main role is that of a teacher or as an employee of the college.
8. **Temporary groups.** As the name suggests, these groups are only for a limited period of time and are dissolved as the purpose of the group is served. For example, a group of researchers carrying out research will be dissolved, as the research study is complete.
9. **Co-acting groups.** In such groups, the members work independently, though they may carry out similar or even dissimilar activities. Cohesiveness as such may not be experienced in this group due to the nature of the group and the activities carried out, though some cooperation and coordination may exist at the later stages of group functioning.
10. **Counteracting groups.** In this type of group, the members engage in competing with each other and they may also have aims that contradict with each other. There could also be struggle for power amongst the members.
11. **Common-identity groups.** This denotes attachment with the group rather than the group members. Thus, there may or may not be interaction with the group members. This is the group

where the individuals are most likely to derive their social identity from. For example, belonging to a particular nation or ethnicity.

12. **Common-bond groups.** As opposed to the common-identity groups, these groups are based on the attachment that the members have amongst each other rather than to the group. For example, a group of friends.

Group also goes through stages of development from the initial stage of orientation leading to acceptance (Miner, 1992). During this process of development, a group has to deal with a number of challenges, conflicts, delusions and so on. A group that is newly formed may lack maturity than that possessed by a group that has been for a longer period of time. The term that we use here is 'group maturity' that develops over a period of time as the group adds on to its experiences. Within the group as well, as the time passes and as the group is becoming more and more mature, the members also get to know each other well and become aware of the positive and negative aspects of every member. There is also clarity in norms, roles as well as status in the group. A group with high level of maturity is also effective in decision-making. Thus decisions are taken in a rational and collaborative manner. Group maturity thus plays a significant role in goal achievement and effective functioning of the group.

REASONS WHY PEOPLE JOIN GROUPS

There are a number of reasons why people join groups (Baron & Byrne, 1995), they are discussed as follows:

1. Certain important psychological as well as social needs of a person are satisfied by a group. For example, need to belong, and also receive attention or even recognition from others.
2. There are a number of goals that cannot be achieved by an individual by himself/herself. Such goals can be achieved when the individuals work in groups. For example, when an event (such as wedding) is to be organised, participation of a number of people is required for its successful organisation.
3. Group membership may open avenues for sharing of a certain information which otherwise would have been out of reach of the individual. For example, certain relevant information related to a company will be shared with an employee only after he/she joins the company.
4. The need for security is also fulfilled by the group. Belonging to a group also makes us feel secured. For example, belonging to a family provides security, feelings of belongingness and being cared.
5. Group also provides its members with a social identity, thus contributing to the self-concept of the individuals. For example, an individual identifies himself/herself as an employee of a particular organisation. This not only provides him/her with an identity but also enhances his/her concept of self.

But most importantly, human beings form groups, because without involvement in groups human beings would not be able to survive (Barrett, 2017).

Any group also has a structure which includes the pattern of behaviour of group members, tasks and activities performed by them and so on. In this context, we need to focus on roles and norms that are discussed in the next section of this chapter.

ROLES AND NORMS

Roles and norms are often described as building blocks of a group. They are discussed as follows:

Roles

In any group, the group members are allotted and expected to play certain roles. McKenna (2012, p. 328) defined roles as 'a set of expected patterns of behaviour attributable to a person occupying a particular position'. Roles include activities that are both formal and informal in nature and are carried out by each of the group members. These roles are also specific in nature. To discuss further about formal and informal roles, formal roles are clearly specified and defined as opposed to informal roles. Roles are internalised by individuals and are linked to their self-concept and self-perceptions (Baron & Byrne, 1995).

Role can be described as having three different aspects, expected roles (the role that each member is expected to play), perceived roles (these are the roles as perceived by the members of a group) and enacted roles (these are the actual behaviours of the members). Furthermore, roles can also be categorised as:

Task-oriented roles that relate to the task at hand.

Relationship-oriented roles that are related to the interactions amongst the group members.

Self-oriented roles that are played by the group members mainly to fulfil their own needs.

Based on the aforementioned categories, four main roles played in a group are described here.

1. **Contributor:** The role of a contributor falls under task-oriented roles. As the name suggests, while playing this role, the group member are involved in contributing relevant information and data to the group. Such a member is also actively involved in the activities of the group and is seen as a person who can be depended upon in the process of achievement of the goal.
2. **Collaborator:** This role falls under both task-oriented roles and relationship-oriented roles. Here, the member not only focuses on the group goal but also coordinates and collaborates with others. Such a member is also flexible and open to innovative ideas.
3. **Communicator:** This necessarily falls under relationship-oriented roles. Being a good communicator is essential for effective functioning of any group. This role is also important in conflict management and resolution.
4. **Challenger:** Such members are often involved in challenging the functioning as well as goals and methods of the group. Such members may also challenge the leadership in the group. Challengers are often open to taking risks in the process of goal attainment.

In the context of roles, it is also necessary to understand two main issues, role ambiguity and role conflict. Role ambiguity occurs when there is a lack of clarity in the role that the group members are expected to play. This can also be a result of gap between the expected roles and perceived roles. Role ambiguity can have negative effects on the performance of the group members. On the other hand, there could also be role conflict that occurs when the members play more than one role in the group and, thus, the performance in one role may interfere with the performance in another role.

Norms

Any group will have norms and standards of behaviour that the members have to follow. Norms are the common rules and expectations that the group members are expected to follow. Norms help guide the behaviours that are expected from the group members and state how the members should behave (termed as prescriptive norms) or should not behave (termed as proscriptive norms) in a group. Norms could be written or non-verbal and can also be implicit (indirect and to be understood) or explicit (clearly laid down). As the group develops and matures, norms may also be modified. Norms are a significant aspect of any group and conformity to the norms is important for the groups to perform effectively. Members who do not follow the norms may also lose their membership.

As roles are significant in any group, so are norms. Norms to a greater extent is a reflection of the nature of the group and also display certain central values of that group. They play an important role in guiding and regulating the behaviour of the members in the group, which is important for the effective functioning of the group. As norms also deal with any deviations from the group norms, they thus ensure continuity and survival of the group.

Some of the characteristics of norms are discussed as follows:

1. Norms are acceptable to the large majority of the group members.
2. The focus of norms is on the behaviour of the group members rather than their feelings and thoughts.
3. The most important aspects of the group are covered by the norms and they play an important role in the functioning and management of the group.
4. A varying degree of tolerance is displayed with regard to non-conformity with the norms or any deviations from them. This will depend on the norm as well as the status of the member in the group. Compliance with norms may result in members being rewarded and non-compliance with the norms may result in members being punished.
5. Norms develop over a period of time and may also be modified as the group matures.
6. Most often than not norms are difficult to change.

Norms can be categorised as central norms and peripheral norms.

Central norms: Central norms can be described as norms that are absolutely necessary to maintain the identity and survival of the group. These are the basic norms and hence are also difficult to change as they are deeply rooted. Such norms are also enforced in a stricter manner as compared to peripheral norms. Example of a central norm is involvement in group activities.

Peripheral norms: When compared with central norms, these are not as important. They are also easy to change and the enforcement of these norms is not done in as stricter manner as with regard to central norms. Example of a peripheral norm is being supportive to group members.

Guirdham, in 1995, has discussed four norms that are found in a group (Fincham & Rhodes, 1999); they are discussed as follows:

1. **Fairness.** This mainly has to do with equitability on the part of the group members, mainly with regard to the group activities.
2. **Reciprocity.** There should be reciprocity in the behaviours of the group members and if a help is received by one member, it should be reciprocated.
3. **Reasonableness.** Reasonableness denotes that the members should be rational in their behaviour and there should be no exploitation.
4. **Role expectation.** This has to do with the role that every member is expected to play.

Besides roles and norms, there is yet another term, that is, status. Status denotes one's social rank or standing (Baron & Byrne, 1995) and is reflected through various aspects. In a group, each member will also have a status of his/her own. For example, a successful and famous actor in a Hindi movie is seen as having more status when compared with a junior artist having a role in that movie. A managing director of a company again will have a higher status when compared with a supervisor on the shop floor in the same company. Thus, in a group, every member will have a social rank or status.

GROUP COHESIVENESS

Group cohesiveness, in simple terms, can be described as the cement that binds the members together in a group. The concept of group cohesion will be clear with the help of the following definitions:

Cohesion is defined by Carron (1982) as a process that is dynamic in nature and is visible in how a group remains together as it attempts to achieve the goals and objectives of the group.

Group cohesion has been defined as 'the total field of forces causing members to remain in the group' (Festinger, Schachter, & Back, 1950, p. 164). These forces could be positive or negative.

Nahavandi, Denhardt, Denhardt and Aristigueta (2015) described cohesion as 'the degree to which the members of the group are attracted to the group and to one another'.

Barrett (2017, p. 437) defined group cohesiveness as 'strength of the bonds that hold group members together and keep them in the group'.

Group cohesion is linked with performance of the group and the same has been denoted by various researches. In one such study carried out by Dorfman and Stephan (1984), the main objective was to study the relationship between group cohesiveness and organisational performance. The sample constituted of undergraduate students who were majoring in business, who had to participate and work together in management game that was based on simulated business decision-making. The results indicated a positive relationship between cohesiveness and organisational performance. Another study was carried out by Patterson, Carron and Loughead (2005) on 298 athletes from various universities, with an aim to study the effect of team cohesiveness on performance. The results indicated that higher the cohesion, the better the performance.

The cohesiveness amongst the group members is affected by various factors such as interpersonal relationship and interpersonal attraction between the members, similarities between the group members, openness, trust and even past experiences of the group members. Cohesiveness also depends on whether the goals of the individuals and that of the group match or not and also the extent to which the group is able to successfully achieve its goals. A study carried out by Synder, Lassgard and Ford in 1986 indicated that members of groups that were unsuccessful tried to distance themselves from the group, when compared with members belonging to the group that was successful (Sears, Peplau, & Taylor, 1991, p. 310). Furthermore, increased group satisfaction and morale can also have a positive impact on group cohesiveness. In certain cases, the cohesiveness could also be high because the members may not be in a position to leave the group due to lack of suitable alternatives or due to the costs or disadvantages of leaving the group being higher than remaining in it. There are a number of advantages of high cohesiveness. A group with high cohesiveness has higher levels of satisfaction and increased motivation and morale (and vice versa). Cohesiveness also has a significant impact on group success.

While discussing about cohesiveness, yet another term that can be highlighted is 'entitativity'. Entitativity implies the degree to which the group is perceived as a group by outsiders. Most often than not, cohesive groups are more likely to be seen as having high entitativity. Examples of such groups are family or even sports team. Entitativity along with group cohesiveness can provide the degrees of groupiness, that is, the extent to which the group is group-like (Barrett, 2017). This is indicated in Table 11.1.

Table 11.1 *Groupiness*

		Cohesiveness	
		High	**Low**
Entitativity	**High**	High groupiness	Moderate groupiness
	Low	Moderate groupiness	Low groupiness

Source: Author.

As can be seen in the table, groupiness can be determined based on whether cohesiveness and entitativity is high or low. High cohesiveness and high entitativity leads to high groupiness, high cohesiveness and low entitativity leads to moderate groupiness as does low cohesiveness and high entitativity. Low groupiness is a result of low cohesiveness and low entitativity.

PERFORMANCE OF INDIVIDUALS IN GROUPS

Most of the work carried out by us involves groups. It is often said that two people are better than one. And the popular belief is that when we work in groups, the work gets done faster and in a better way. Working in groups has its own advantages and disadvantages.

On one hand, when working in groups brings in varied perspectives and approaches, besides diverse knowledge and skills, and helps satisfy the need to belong, on the other hand, there are a number of disadvantages as well, especially when the group members involve in interactions that are not related to the activity. Furthermore, the individuals may also feel pressurised while working in a group and conflicts between the members could also take place, which will further affect the group's activity and delay it. A number of factors play a role in this context such as group cohesiveness, group size and also the type of activity that is carried out.

The performance of the individuals in groups and alone can be determined with the help of tasks that were stated by Steiner (1972, 1976). These tasks can be categorised in the following four categories:

- **Additive tasks:** In this, the ultimate product or output results from the combination of the contributions by each and every member of the group. For example, when four persons are moving a heavy piece of furniture, the output or movement of furniture from one place to another is a result of contributions by each member of the group.
- **Compensatory tasks.** In this, the group output of a product is a result of average of the contributions by various members of the group. For example, when a panel is taking an interview, the final marks or grade assigned to a candidate are the average of the marks or grades given by each member in the panel.
- **Disjunctive tasks.** The best member of the group will determine the output or the final product of the group. For example, in a workshop on statistics, if a group of participants are given a statistical problem to be solved, then one of its members may solve this problem that is accepted by rest of the members and the answer is then reported as that of the group.

- **Conjunctive tasks.** The weakest member of the group determines the outcome or the product of the group. For example, if in a competition involving teams, each member of the team is given different activity that is to be completed by all after which they can proceed to the other activity and so on to win the competition, then the performance of the team will be determined by the weakest of its member.

With reference to the performance in the context of these tasks, groups have been seen to perform better on additive and compensatory tasks, and in fact the performance of the group is even better than that of the best of its members. With regard to disjunctive tasks, the group performance is better than the performance by the member of the group whose performance can be considered as average, as in this case the performance of the group is mainly determined by the group member who is most effective. With reference to the conjunctive tasks, individuals perform better than the group, as the performance of the group, in this case, is determined by the group member who is least effective (Baron & Byrne, 1995).

In this context, group size can also play a role. With regard to additive tasks, larger groups can enhance group performance, but there could be issues related to coordination and decreased motivation. With regard to disjunctive tasks, the group performance may improve initially but with further increase in group size, the performance may deteriorate, again attributed to the lack of coordination between the group members.

Distraction Conflict Theory

The theory states that the individuals can get distracted from the task that they are performing in the presence of others and this leads to a conflict between the need to focus on the task and minimising the distraction due to the presence of others. This again holds good mainly in the context of tasks that are new or difficult for the individual. For example, if a person is trying to repair a complex machine, then the presence of others could lead to a conflict in his/her mind, between the need to repair the machine and decrease the distraction caused by the presence of others.

Furthermore, the presence of others while performing a task leads to the overload of information received by the individuals, which requires them to try to focus his/her attention on the task rather than on other information. Though presence of others will enhance performance on activities that involve simpler tasks, with regard to performance on activities that involve complex tasks, the performance may get negatively affected due to limited capacity of the individual to process the information in the presence of numerous stimuli. Thus, the present theory can be modified in order to provide an explanation for the process of social facilitation.

Furthermore, how groups can have an impact on the performance of the individuals in the group will also be discussed. Presence of others could lead to social facilitation or social loafing.

Social Facilitation

The term 'social facilitation' was introduced by Allport (1920). Social facilitation can be described as enhancement in performance in the presence of others. Though it has also been argued that social facilitation takes place with regard to tasks that the individual is well versed with or tasks that are easy, and that it may not occur when the task is difficult or new to the individual (Barrett, 2017).

Also implying that performance on tasks that require closer attention may not get facilitated and the quality of work may suffer though the speed with which the work is carried out may be enhanced. Though social facilitation is not specific to a group, a group does provide an environment in which social facilitation can take place.

In 1897, while Triplett was studying the cycling records of Racing Board of a cycling organisation called the League of American Wheelmen, he observed that the time recorded for cyclists were slower when they raced against the clock and they were faster when they raced against each other. Thus implying that the presence of others can have an impact on one's performance. In order to study this further, Triplett conducted an experiment. In the experiment, fishing rods were given to a sample of 40 boys and girls falling in age range of 8–17 years. These boys and girls were asked to wind the fishing rods as fast as they could. The experimental group had to wind the fishing rod in presence of others, whereas the control group had to wind the fishing rod on their own. He then tested the speed at which these children wound the fishing rod. The results obtained indicate that performance improved in the presence of others as children worked harder when others were present than when alone. Thus, it can be said that the presence of others does affect one's performance.

In certain cases, individual's may not perform well in the presence of others and this can be attributed to the evaluation apprehension, that is, apprehensions or concerns about how the performance of the individuals is being judged by others.

Zajonc proposed a theory of social facilitation in which he stated that the presence of other leads to increased arousal, which in turn leads to an increase in the likelihood of dominant response (the response most likely to be made by an individual) and decreases the likelihood of non-dominant response (Barrett, 2017). If this dominant response is correct, then the performance gets enhanced and if this dominant response is incorrect, then the performance may suffer. For example, a person has to make a presentation in front of an audience; as per the theory given by Zajonc, there will be increased arousal as a result of the presence of others. If this person is well versed with the topic of presentation and has necessary expertise in the field, his/her dominant response becomes more likely and if this dominant response is correct, then the performance will be enhanced and vice versa.

It is also possible that the presence of others interferes with the performance of the individual, this is termed as social inhibition.

Social Loafing

In social loafing, one or more members of the group do not fully contribute, to the maximum of their capacity, to the group activity. Such individuals may put their best when working alone. This not only has a negative impact on the group performance but can affect the very morale and motivation of the group. For example, if four persons are involved in shifting a piece of quite a heavy furniture, one of them may not be putting in his/her best to the activity. Similarly, while working in a project team, a member may involve in social loafing when he/she does not put in his/her best to the team activity. Though such a member will do his/her best when working at an individual level. Social loafing is also more likely to take place when the individual interests come before the group interests, thus the person is not actually bothered about group performance or objective. Social loafing also takes place when the individual's contribution to the achievement of group goal or group performance is not likely to be recognised, or when there is no possible way to determine if a particular group member is not putting his/her best.

An experiment was carried out by Williams and Harkins in 1979 (Baron & Byrne, 1995, p. 497), in which a group that constituted of male students were asked to cheer and clap as loudly as they can at certain times. This was done to determine the noise that people make in social set-ups. The participants were made to cheer and clap when alone and when in groups of two, four and six. The results indicated an inverse relationship between the sound made by the cheering and clapping and the group size. That is, as the group size increased, the magnitude of the sound created by the participants decreased. Also, this was not attributed to the lack of coordination in the group, as confirmed by the researchers.

Social loafing has a large scope, and has been seen across genders, cultures, conditions as well as tasks (whether cognitive or physical).

In this context, there is also the concept of free riding that occurs 'when group members exert little or no effort because they believe that their contribution to the group task is dispensable or not important to the overall group output' (Barrett, 2017, p. 444). For example, a person with limited skills of organising an event may not put in his/her efforts as he/she feels that their efforts may not a make huge difference to the group performance or its output.

While dealing with social loafing and free riding, it needs to be ensured that the performance of the group members are focused on and identified and a good performance is recognised. The members also need to feel the connection between the efforts and the completion of task. They need to feel that their efforts will not go for waste and they are actually contributing to the completion of the task and group output. It is easier to counter social loafing and free riding in smaller groups than in larger groups. The goals that are set also need to be meaningful and complex enough so as to challenge the group members and motivate them to achieve the goals.

Social loafing has been found to be common while performing additive tasks (Baron & Byrne, 1995).

DEINDIVIDUATION

You may have come across such news on news channels or in newspaper where a group of people lynched a person; or the doctors and nurses in hospitals were attacked by a mob or people because a child died due to inattention; or death of some public personality/leader, resulting in groups of people going about the city destroying public property.

These are example of deindividuation, where individuals cease to exist and there is just a group.

Often in the process of becoming a group member, the individual may lose his/her own self or may lose his/her self-awareness as well as the sense of personal responsibility, this is termed as deindividuation (Barrett, 2017). The behaviours observed during deindividuation include behaviours that are inhibited such as aggression, laziness, emotional, destructive and even behaviour that is childlike (Baron, 1984). Furthermore, such individuals are least concerned about how their behaviour will be evaluated and its consequences. They may also display inadequate planning and problem solving besides poor memory. In fact, the individuals may not remember how they behaved. Deindividuation also involves violent behaviour. For example, the behaviour of a group of people who get violent probably because they were not allowed to get a glimpse of their favourite sportsperson or movie star could be attributed to deindividuation.

Behaviour displayed by people during concerts is also an example of deindividuation (Zimbardo, 1969). People may get so involved with the loud music and the lighting that they get distracted from their self, and dance and sing freely to the tunes of the concert. Such behaviour can also be seen in chanting and singing of certain religious groups (Diener, 1980).

Mob behaviour is another example of how the individual behaviour gets intensified when they become a part of a group. Normal, office going, family persons, law-abiding citizens could engage in crime and violent behaviour (otherwise unexpected of them) when they are a part of a mob or larger group. Deindividuation is thus a key component to mob behaviour.

There are various reasons why such a behaviour is displayed in groups; they are as follows:

- It may occur as a result of temporary dissolution of boundary that exists between the individuals and the group, and thus the individuals lose their separate identity.
- There is a sense of anonymity. That is, such individuals feel that they cannot be identified and thus they may not be held accountable for their behaviour, thus resulting in diffusion of responsibility.
- It is also as a result of modelling, where when people see others involved in such behaviour, they feel it appropriate and safe to behave in the same manner.
- There could also be physiological basis to this behaviour as there could be excitement and physiological arousal in such set-ups (Baron, 1984). Individuals in a group may also get emotionally charged up (as in case of angry group of people who attack the doctors and nurses in the hospital).

Social Identity Model of Deindividuation Effect

This is based on the social identity theory, and it was proposed by Reicher et al. (Barrett, 2017). The model states that involvement in a group can increase the sense of self. Any individual has both a personal identity that makes him/her different from the group, as well as a social identity that reflects his/her connection to the group. As per this model, the social identity becomes more prominent, resulting in individuals abiding with the group norms. Thus deindividuation effect can take place.

DECISION-MAKING PROCESS IN GROUPS

There could be a debate on whether decision-making is better at individual level or at group level. One may feel that there is a greater advantage while making decisions in a group, due to the contributions from a number of people, which can actually help in dealing with complex issues and come up with constructive solutions. Group discussion can be a helpful process and whether it is universities, industries or other set-ups, people use group discussions to take major and crucial decisions. However, the process of decision-making is not always smooth and there could be a number of issues. Besides the problems such as the process being lengthy and time consuming, there are various other issues as well that will be discussed in the present section of this chapter.

Group Polarisation

In a study carried out by Stoner in 1961 (Sears et al., 1991), the participants were asked to read a number of situations that were complex in nature and later asked to range them from very high risk to very low risk. Initially, the participants were asked to make the decision individually and were not told that later they will be discussing the same in group. When the participants later discussed in groups to come up with a unanimous decision with regard to each situation, a strong tendency towards decision that involved greater risk was displayed by the group when compared with the average of decisions taken by the individuals. The study thus indicated that the decisions made by groups could be riskier (the risky shift) than those taken by the individuals contrary to the popular belief. The findings also indicate that decisions taken by a group are often extreme in nature. The term used to describe these extreme decisions taken by a group is 'group polarisation'. Why group polarisation may occur can be attributed to gaining of new information when interacting in a group and this will also depend on persuasiveness of the arguments put up by other group members. It is also possible that individuals, at least initially, have strong outlook about their own point of view and the information discussed during the discussion further confirms their view and this can also lead to an opinion that is extreme in nature.

Yet another reason for group polarisation is comparison of one's own opinion with that of others. There could be opinions that are similar to theirs and some opinions that are not. In this context, extreme opinions could result from the desire of the individuals to be seen in a positive light by others and therefore there could be shift in their opinion.

Furthermore, when in groups, the individuals may also feel more confident and liberal to take decisions that are riskier or extreme as compared to when alone. Group members could also go with the opinions of other members in order to maintain the group memberships, thus maintaining the group cohesiveness.

Groupthink

Most often the view is that higher the cohesiveness in the group, the better will be the group performance. However, a number of factors play a role here and a more than required focus on cohesiveness can have an impact on the group decision-making. This is where the term 'groupthink' can be discussed. The term groupthink was introduced by Irving Janis (1972, 1982). Groupthink can be defined as 'a mode of thinking by group members in which concern with maintaining group consensus overrides the motivation to evaluate all potential courses of action as accurately and realistically as possible' (Baron & Byrne, 1995, p. 508). Thus, focus is on maintaining the cohesiveness with the group members rather than on the actual decision-making.

Groupthink leads to numerous problems that negatively affect the group performance. Groupthink leads the members to think that their group can never make wrong decisions or mistakes and thus is invulnerable. Furthermore, the members may also engage in ignoring certain information that may be against the present group view, though it may be crucial for decision-making in that particular situation. This is called collective rationalisation, where all the members, together, rationalise the viewpoint of the group and any information (even from an external source) that goes against the group's approach, is ignored. The members may also feel superior to others and may consider others who do not share the view of their group as not up to the mark or wrong.

Groupthink also generates pressure on every member of the group, where they have no other choice but to go with the viewpoint or decision of the group, as otherwise they may be criticised. This can be described as self-censorship where the members refrain from commenting against the group decision and if the members even speak out, the rest of the group may actually refrain or reprimand them from doing so. There are a number of ways to counter groupthink; they are discussed in details here.

- Scepticism and open enquiry needs to be promoted amongst the group members (Baron & Byrne, 1995). The members should be encouraged to challenge and counter challenge the views put forth in the group. The group leader can play an important role in encouraging the group members to look at various alternative options and then discuss them thoroughly.

- Certain subgroups can be created who would first discuss the situation and come up with certain possible solutions, which are then discussed further in the larger group.
- Even after the group reaches a consensus or makes the final decision, a second chance can be provided to the members to challenge or question the decision that has been made.
- The leader plays a crucial role in dealing with groupthink. He/she needs to be impartial in his/her approach towards the viewpoints given by the group members.
- Members could also be assigned to evaluate and challenge the decisions taken.

Besides group polarisation and groupthink, there are other factors that could interfere with the group decision-making. These are discussed as follows:

1. The members in the group need to accept the common goal of the group. The coordination and interaction between the group members will be more effective if the common goals are accepted. Otherwise, it is also possible that certain members might not share a crucial information with other group members, which could hamper the decision-making process and its output.
2. When tasks are divided amongst the group members, it could interfere with the decision-making process. Though tasks in the group could be divided if necessary and required, due care needs to be taken with regard to coordination amongst the group members, and scope should be created for all members to participate and provide their opinions.
3. Communication pattern and status of the group members needs to be kept in mind as they can interfere with the group decision-making. Effective communication patterns that reduce the barriers and ensure free-flowing communication need to be used.
4. Larger the group, more the information. But the large size of the group could also lead to lack of coordination between the group members and problems related to interaction and communication may also increase. In larger groups, it is also possible that only few dominant members may dominate the decision-making process.
5. The composition of group whether heterogeneous or homogenous can also have an impact on group decision-making. Though heterogeneous groups are preferred and as such heterogeneity will in a way contribute to effective decision-making with regard to complex tasks, the differences amongst the group members could also lead to differences in opinion and conflict.
6. Leadership is also crucial in this context. The leader can have an impact on the members as well as the decision-making process. He/she thus has to ensure the smooth functioning of the group and deal with the factors that could interfere with the decision-making process.

LEADERSHIP

Who or what comes to your mind when we say 'leader? You would probably think of certain personalities, might be politicians or CEOs of companies. Though leaders could be at different levels. There are leaders in schools, leaders in the resident welfare associations, leaders in politics and business and so on. But leaders do share certain characteristics and one of the prominent characteristics is that they are influential and have major influence on their followers.

Leadership can be described as a process that involves one person (the leader) influencing other persons or members of the group (the followers) in order to achieve the purpose or objectives of the group.

In a group, there could be formal leaders or informal leaders. Formal leaders are either appointed or elected as leaders to the position. For example, manager of a human resource department is a formal leader.

But there could also be informal leaders in the group, who have equal or even more influence on the behaviours of the group members. If you observe a group of children busy playing, or engaged in some activity, you will probably notice that one of them will direct or tell other children what to do, though he/she has not been as such appointed or elected/selected to be a leader; through interactions, somehow this person prominently appears as the leader of this group. In industrial and organisational set-ups, focusing on informal leaderships is significant so as to understand the influence that they have on the employees. It is also possible that a leader emerges from the group over a period of time. In a group, a person who is more active and interacts more may emerge as a leader (Sears et al., 1991).

Who Becomes the Leader?

Two main aspects that need to be discussed in the context of who becomes a leader are characteristics of the person and characteristics of the situation (situational determinants). They are discussed in detail in this section.

Characteristics of the Person

A person can become a leader because of certain unique personality traits. This was mainly proposed by the 'great person' theory of leadership (Sears et al., 1991). Certain factors can be identified as follows:

- The leaders display the abilities/expertise, strength, skill and confidence that are required to achieve the group goal. For example, the player who displays these qualities is often chosen as the captain of his/her team.
- They also have enhanced interpersonal skills. As stated by Mullen, Salas and Driskell (1989), the person who were more talkative were chosen as leader by the group.
- They are ambitious and display high motivation, including achievement motivation. Leaders see a future for the group and most often have a clear idea (at least are perceived this way by the group) about where they see the group in the future and what group goals they want to achieve. The term 'leadership motivation', proposed by Kirkpatrick and Locke, can also be discussed here (Baron & Byrne, 1995). Leadership motivation denotes the desire of the leader to influence others or to lead them. Leadership motivation can be categorised as personalised power motivation (focus on status and wants to dominate the members) and socialised power motivation (leaders who seek cooperation from the members and work in coalition with them and seek power to channelise it to achieve the group goal).
- Intelligence is also associated with leadership. This characteristic is also important, as they may have to take active part in problem-solving and decision-making process.
- Personality factors also play an important role. A meta-analysis carried out by Judge, Bono, Illies and Gerhardt in 2002, indicated that leadership was positively correlated with extraversion, openness to experience and conscientiousness (Crisp & Turner, 2010).
- Even physical characteristics play a role, where physical attractiveness and height (taller) also play a part (Crisp & Turner, 2010).

Besides the aforementioned traits, some of the characteristics displayed by successful leaders are honesty, reliability and integrity, confidence in one's self, expertise and creativity, ability to adapt to the members as well as changing situations and high energy and achievement motivation (Kirkpatrick & Locke, 1991).

Characteristics of the Situation

Certain situational factors such as the size and structure of the group, besides the communication network can also play an important role in determining who becomes the leader. Furthermore, different situations call for different qualities in a leader. For example, the leadership qualities required in military are different from the leadership qualities required to lead a group of students or a group of university teachers. It needs to be mentioned here that both the characteristics of the person and characteristics of the situation are relevant determinants of who becomes a leader, and therefore there is a need for an approach that combines both these determinants in order to indicate who becomes a leader.

Theories of Leadership

Leadership theories are discussed as follows:

1. **Great person theory.** Initial research carried out on leadership stressed on personality as an important determinant of leadership. Thus, according to this theory the leaders are born leaders, and they possess certain personality characteristics that lead them to becoming leaders. The present theory thus focuses on certain inherent and dispositional factors that characterise the prominent leaders, though the theory was not able to identify any general leadership characteristics (Arvey & Chaturvedi, 2011). The theory also states that there are certain traits that are commonly found in leaders. Some of the traits identified as correlating with leadership are high extraversion and low neuroticism, conscientiousness, openness to experience, though they were not considered as essential for good leadership. Research has indicated that good leaders tend to be intelligent, self-confident and honest and they also display competence and assertiveness (Hogan and Kaiser, 2005). The great person theory not only misses out an important determinant of leadership, that is, situation, but the perspective of this theory is considered as reflecting fundamental attribution error (Barrett, 2017).
2. **Contingency model.** This model states that leadership is mainly determined by the behaviour of the leader, as well as the situational factors. As opposed to the great person theory, this model gives relevance to the situational factors along with the dispositional factors. Based on the distinction between task-oriented and relations-oriented leadership styles stated by Bales, Fiedler concluded that effectiveness of these styles depends on the leader's ability to control the situation or the group (Barrett, 2017). Task-oriented leaders are more effective with both, groups that are difficult or have low situational control and groups that are easy or have high situational control. This is so because in the first case, where there is low situational control, the group needs to focus on the task and in the second case, since the members are already motivated, and therefore, focus on interpersonal relationship may not be required (Barrett, 2017). The relationship oriented leaders, on the other hand, are effective with moderate situational control, as effective interpersonal relationship with the members is required in order to motivate the members to achieve the goals.

   Thus as stated by Fiedler in 1978, the factors that determine situational control are relationship between the leader and the group members, structure of the task and power exerted by the leader (Barrett, 2017). A positive relationship between the leader and the members lead to high situational control. The leader here is also more powerful and the tasks are also well structured. Thus lower situational control results from a negative relationship between the leader and the members and the leader does not enjoy much power and the tasks are also unstructured (Barrett, 2017). The model though has been criticised for its reliability and validity.

3. **Social identity theory.** This theory states that as the leader and the members belong to the same group, they also share social identity, thus leaders are supported by the group members because they reflect the social identity of the group. The leader thus needs to epitomise the values and outlook of the group. This membership identification also plays a role in determining how effective the leader is and whether he/she is seen as belonging to in-group or out-group (Barrett, 2017). Furthermore, when group identity is considered as important by the group, social identity that is shared is also seen as important.
4. **Transactional and transformational leadership.** Transactional leadership highlights the interaction between the leader and his/her followers. On one hand, who becomes the leader is determined by the perception and outlook of the followers, while on the other, leaders need to attend to these perceptions and views of the followers and also need to modify their leadership behaviour. Social exchange theory may play a role in this context and leaders who are perceived as lacking integrity, unrewarding or disliked may not be able to retain their position as leaders, especially in small groups, though in larger groups, leaders may be selected based on the extent to which the leader seems to have similar values and goals (Sears et al., 1991).

On the other hand, transformational leadership provides the members with a vision that captivates and inspires them in such a way that their personal goals are set aside and they work towards a goal that is comprehensive and, at the same time, reflects higher and nobler purpose (Barrett, 2017). Such leaders are also termed as charismatic leaders and can be termed as masters of impression management (Baron & Byrne, 1995). Transformational leaders do not provide monetary rewards but engage the group members with the help of inspirational motivation. They are concerned about the needs, requirements and abilities of the members as well as encourage them to think in a different manner (out of the box) and come up with new and unique ideas and solutions.

Transformational leaders besides providing group with a vision, also indicate a way in which this vision can be achieved by the group. Such leaders also engage in framing, that is, the purpose or the goal is defined in such a way that the actions and performances of the members, in the direction of achievement of that goal, is perceived as being more meaningful. Such leaders appear to be self-confident and engage in risk-taking and use typical methods and activities to achieve the goals.

Leadership Styles

Autocratic, Democratic and Laissez Faire Leadership

A study on leadership styles was carried out by Lewin, Lippitt and While in 1939. The participants of this study were 10-year-old males, who were divided in to clubs. Each club was then exposed to the three different leadership styles, authoritarian, democratic and laissez faire. The role of the leader was played by adults who were trained by the researchers to display the three leadership styles (Raven & Rubin, 1983). Each of these leadership styles and the behaviour of the leader, are discussed as follows:

- **Authoritarian leaders.** These leaders made their own decisions without seeking any opinion from the group members. They also acted detached, did not share any information with the members and did not encourage any active participation from them. Furthermore, if praise and criticism was used by them, no apparent reason for the same was given by them (Raven & Rubin, 1983).

- **Democratic leaders.** These leaders took all the decisions through consultations and active participation of the members. They engaged in meaningful communication with the group members and encouraged the members to set long-term goals. Praise and criticisms were also used by them in a concrete manner. Such group leaders were also friendlier and helpful towards the group members.
- **Laissez faire leaders.** These leaders played a very passive role. They made no suggestions to the group activities and also did not involve in any evaluation of the behaviour or performance of the group members. Though they acted in a friendly manner with the group members, they provided direction only when asked for by the group members.

Each club was thus assigned to one of the leadership styles, though, every seven weeks, the confederates were swapped so that they led in all the three leadership styles. This was also done in order to ensure that there was no confounding effect of the individual characteristics of the confederates on the leadership style. The results of the study indicated that the groups performed better under leaders who were democratic. The groups displayed high quality work, though were not as productive as the group with authoritarian leaders. The groups with authoritarian leaders also displayed over-dependence on the leaders and stopped functioning when the leaders were not present as opposed to groups with democratic leaders who continued to function and be productive even when the leaders were not present. The group with laissez faire leader did not involve in any productive activity, though they were quite friendly with the leader.

Task-Focused Versus Socio-Emotional Leadership

As the name suggests, the task-focused leader (also discussed under contingency model) focuses on the task or the goal of the group. With their excessive focus on the task, they may not have as much focus on the relationship with the group. Such leaders do not share a close interpersonal relationship with the group members, though they are perceived as being productive, methodical and knowledgeable (Crisp & Turner, 2010).

Socio-economical leaders, on the other hand, focus on dynamics of the group and ensure that the group members get along well with each other. They display empathy and are friendly with the group members.

When the three leaderships styles of autocratic, democratic and laissez faire are compared, the autocratic leaders are more task focused and less socio-economical. The laissez faire leaders are more socio-economical and less task-focused. And the democratic leaders display the qualities of both, task focused as well as socio-economical leadership.

There are also group-centred and directive leadership styles, where the group-centred leadership is similar to socio-economical leadership style and directive leadership style is similar to task-focused style.

Leadership style can also be categorised as transactional and transformational leadership that was discussed earlier.

CONFLICT AND CONFLICT RESOLUTION

Conflict can be described as 'incompatibility between parties about the desirability of some state of affairs, actual or potential' (Raven & Rubin, 1983).

The definition necessarily denotes that there are two or more than two parties that are experiencing the incompatibility and this incompatibility is with reference to certain aspect that can be actual or potential in nature. Conflicts could occur between couples, between groups or even between nations.

Myers, Sahajpal and Behera, (2012, p. 361) defined conflict as 'a perceived incompatibility of actions or goals'. This incompatibility could occur because both the parties have certain demands that are not being fulfilled by same resources at the same time. Conflict, thus, can also be defined as 'a social situation in which a minimum of two actors (parties) strive to acquire at the same moment in time an available set of scarce resources' (Wallensteen, 2015, p. 17).

Besides competing for scarce resources, conflict in groups can also be as a result of group cohesiveness. The experiment by Sherrif in 1996 (discussed in detail under chapter on social influence) displayed how intergroup conflict can be created when groups develop distinct identities as well as high group cohesiveness. And this can lead to the feeling that one's own group is better and superior to other groups and lies at the centre of everything. This tendency can be termed as ethnocentrism, which encourages the development of social identity which, in turn, could lead to negative biases directed towards others.

Conflict can be categorised as competitive conflict and hostile conflict. Competitive conflict is denoted in terms of the presence of goals that are incompatible. For example, two teams in an organisational set-up may display competitive conflict as they want to get the opportunity to work on launch of a new product or two sports teams, could compete with each other for winning the trophy. There could also be conflict with regard to the means that need to be adopted for achieving a goal that has been mutually accepted. For example, the organising committee members may show disagreement with regard to the planning process involved in organising an event in their organisation. Two researchers could display a disagreement with regard to which research method should be involved in carrying out research.

Hostile conflict, on the other hand, can be described as occurring when one party expresses its dislike for another party. This can also be related to hostile aggression described in the previous chapter on aggression. It is also possible for competitive conflict to develop into hostile conflict and hostile conflict in turn may lead to competitive conflict.

Both competitive conflict and hostile conflict could be so interwoven that determining which occurred first could be a complex activity.

Social Dilemma

Social dilemma can be described as 'a conflict in which the most beneficial action for an individual will, if chosen by most people, have harmful effects on everyone' (Aronson, Wilson, & Akert, 2014).

Aronson et al. (2014) in their book on social psychology relate an example of Stephen King and his publishing venture. Stephen King wrote just two instalments of his novel that was titled 'The Plant' and posted it online. The readers had to pay $1 for each instalment of the novel. The deal he offered in this context was that if the fee were paid by at least 75 per cent of the readers, he would keep writing the other instalments of this novel and post them online, but if less than 75 per cent of the readers paid the fee, he would discontinue writing the next instalments. Thus, it would be possible for some people to read the novel free of cost provided that others paid (at least 75 per cent in this case). Thus, Stephen King introduced a social dilemma in which if a large number of persons chose to skip paying $1, due to their self-interest, then everyone would be deprived of the next instalments of the novel.

And though initially more than 75 per cent of the readers did pay, gradually the number decreased below 75 per cent and Stephen King stopped posting the new instalments of the novel.

Experiments have been carried out on social dilemma with the use of a game called 'a prisoner's dilemma'. In this game, there are two players and each one has to choose one of the options, either option X or Y. Both the players are however not aware about what option the other player has chosen. The number of points that could be won by the players depends on the choice of option by both the players. The details in this regard are given in Table 11.2.

For example, if two players (A and B) were playing this game, if both the players (A and B) chose the option X, both the players could get 50 points each. But if player A chooses the option Y and player B chose the option X, player A will win 100 points and the player B will lose 100 points and vice versa.

It has been observed that in such games, it is most likely that the players will go with choosing option Y as if they choose option X and the other player chooses option Y, then they would lose 100 points. As a result of lack of trust on the other player and also due to increasing competition between the two, both the payers end up choosing option Y, thus both losing 10 points each.

This game can be used to explain conflicts between individuals, groups and even nations.

Though it is also possible that as the players engage in playing such a game, they may eventually go for cooperative strategy and choose option X, thus making sure that both the players win. Interaction between the players may also lead them to adopt a more cooperative strategy. Cooperation between such players can also be encouraged with the help of 'tit-for-tat strategy', in which cooperation is initially displayed by one of the parties, but later responses will depend on the stage or responses provided by the opposing party. For example, player A will initially display a cooperative stance, but in the subsequent trials if player B displayed competitive stance, then player A will also change his/her stance that of competition. And if player B displayed cooperative stance, then the player A will maintain the competitive stance.

Conflict Resolution

There are various ways in which conflict can be resolved. One way in which this is commonly done is with the use of threats, though there is not much evidence that threats can be used as an effective conflict resolution technique. Deutsch and Krauss (1960, p. 182) defined threat as 'the expression of an intention to do something detrimental to the interests of another'.

Table 11.2 ***Example Related to Prisoner's Game***

		PLAYER A	
		Option X	**Option Y**
PLAYER B	**Option X**	Both players win 50 points	Player A wins 100 points Player B loses 100 points
	Option Y	Player A loses 100 points Player B wins 100 points	Both players lose 10 points

Source: Author.

A study was carried out by Deutsch and Krauss in (1960) in which the participants (there were a total of 16 pairs of participants) had to imagine that they were in charge of a company and were carrying goods by road to a destination. The companies were named as Acme and Bolt. The participants had to carry the goods to the destinations as quickly as possible and were also paid 60 cents per trip, though 1 cent was subtracted for every second taken by them to complete the trip. The starting point and the destination point were different for the two players in a pair and the quickest way to reach their respective destination was a one-lane road that only a single truck could cross at a time. Thus, a conflict situation was introduced in this study, that if either of the player took alternative route, then they would lose 10 cents in each trial. The monetary winning and losing of the amount was imaginary and the participants were aware about the same. There were three conditions to this experiment, the first had no threat, the second had unilateral threat, that is, only one player could threaten the other, and the third had bilateral threat, that is, both the players could threaten each other. The results indicated that in the third condition with bilateral threat, the players displayed more difficulty in terms of reaching an agreement and the amount lost by them was also more at both individual and collective level.

Thus, it can be said that threat might not be a very effective technique in conflict resolution.

Communication and interaction is another way in which conflicts can be resolved; however, in another version of study carried out by Deutsch and Krauss (1962), results indicated that communication failed to develop trust between the players. And contrary to what was expected (that communication will lead to cooperation), there was no increase in cooperation in the no-threat or the bilateral-threat conditions, though some reduction in loss of amount was observed in the unilateral-threat condition.

Furthermore, in yet another version of the study carried out by Krauss and Deutsch (1966), when both the parties in the study were provided with instructions related to how they can communicate and how they could work on a solution that would benefit both the parties, there was an increase in verbal communication, the trust developed between the parties and, as a result, there was also an increase in the amount gained by both the parties. Thus, it can be said that communication that fosters trust can play a significant role in conflict resolution.

Negotiation can also play a significant role in conflict resolution. Negotiation can be defined as 'a form of communication between opposing sides in a conflict in which offers and counteroffers are made and a solution occurs only when both parties agree' (Aronson et al., 2014, p. 308). Negotiations can also be at various levels, from one's that occur during our day-to-day lives, where negotiation and bargaining is done with a shopkeeper, to negotiations that a prospective employee may carry out with employers, regarding salary and other privileges. Negotiations can also be at international level between organisations and even between nations. While carrying out negotiations, integrative solution can be kept in mind by the negotiators. Integrative solution can be termed as a solution in which the parties achieve a kind of compromise with reference to their issue based on their distinctive interest. Thus, each party concedes with regard to the issues that are not significant to them, but are significant for the other party. Although for negotiation to be effective, there has to be effective communication as well and studies indicate that face-to-face communications facilitate negotiation when compared with negotiations using technology (Stuhlmacher & Citera, 2005).

SUMMARY

To summarise, groups are part of everyone's life and it is important for social psychologists to understand group dynamics and group processes. A group can be described as a collection of two or more people who engage in some interaction with each other, are dependent on each other and perceive themselves as being part of the group. They may also share a common goal and have a comparatively stable relationship. This chapter focused on various types of groups and also highlighted roles, norms and status that are relevant while understanding the functioning of a group. Group cohesiveness that can be described as the cement that binds the members together in a group was also discussed. Furthermore, the chapter described the performance of the individuals in a groups with an emphasis on social facilitation and social loafing. The process of deindividuation, during which the individual loses his/her self-awareness and becomes one with the group, was also discussed. Yet another significant sub-topic, that is, decision-making in groups was also discussed at length with explanations on group polarisation and groupthink. Leadership was also discussed, which included descriptions of characteristics of the person and situational characteristics that determine who becomes a leader. Theories of leadership and leadership styles were also discussed. The chapter in the end discussed about conflict and conflict resolution.

QUESTIONS

1. Discuss the nature of group.
2. Explain various types of groups with examples.
3. Describe roles and norms as building blocks of the group.
4. Explain group cohesiveness.
5. Compare between social facilitation and social loafing.
6. Explain decision-making in groups.
7. Define leadership and discuss various theories of leadership.
8. Describe various leadership styles.

REFERENCES

Baron, R. S. (1984). Group Dynamics. In A. S. Kahn (Ed.), *Social psychology*. Iowa: Wm, C. Brown Publishers, College Division.

Hogan, R., & Kaiser, R. (2005). What we know about leadership. *Review of General Psychology, 9*(2), 169–180.

McKenna, E. F. (2012). *Business psychology and organisational behaviour: A student's handbook*. New York, NY: Psychology Press.

Quick, J. C., Nelson, D. L., & Khandelwal, P. (2011). *Organisational behaviour: A South-Asian perspective*. Delhi: Cengage Learning.

FURTHER READINGS

For more information on group dynamics, the following can be referred to:

Baron, R. S., & Kerr, N. L. (2003). *Group process, group decision, group action* (2nd ed.). New York, NY: McGraw-Hill.

Forsyth, D. R. (2013). *Group dynamics* (6th ed.). Belmont, CA: Thomson/Wadsworth.

Stangor, C. (2015). *Social groups in action and interaction* (2nd ed.). New York, NY: Routledge.

CHAPTER 12

Culture

A few years ago, there was an article in a leading national daily dated 10 January 1992. The article was written by Hugh and Collen Gantzer. In this article titled 'Princess in the Wilderness', they spoke about a story of a custom probably prevalent amongst Thaaru women from Terai region. When the story begins, a Sisodia King makes his daughters leave the kingdom as he gets ready to fight and may lose his life in the battlefield. He is not willing to see his daughters die in 'jauhar' (where the princesses would rather burn themselves than be humiliated by the enemy). So the King entrusts the responsibility of the princesses to the bravest of his old retainers and a group of Bhill warriors. The princesses were to be taken to a Himalayan Kingdom that the King had close ties with. However, the old retainers succumb to the difficult and strenuous journey and as the last Rajput retainer dies, the princesses and the Bhills are left with no person to show them the way or tell them about what can be done next. The princesses then take a decision that they will marry the Bhills but on one condition that their female descendants will always be superior to their males. Thus, the Thaaru women cook and carry out all the other household chores, but when it comes to serving food to their men, they place the plate with food on it and kick it towards their men.

The article does make us think of the varying cultures that exist in this world. The aforementioned story and many such stories form the ways of life of numerous people on this earth.

As social psychologist, it is important to study culture because it has a significant influence on one's social behaviour and given the variation in social behaviour that we come across in the world, understanding human behaviour in the context of culture is crucial.

In this chapter, we will discuss the concept of culture and also focus on the psychological perspectives with regard to influence of culture on behaviours. The concept of socialisation will also be explained. The chapter will also discuss the psychological perspectives of the influence of culture on behaviours and will culminate with discussion on cross-cultural research.

Learning Objectives

After reading this chapter, you will be able to

- Discuss the term 'culture'
- Describe culture and individual
- Explain the term 'socialisation'
- Describe the psychological perspectives on influence of culture on behaviours
- Discuss cross-cultural research

CONCEPT OF CULTURE

Culture in simple terms can be described as a way of life.

There are various ways in which the term culture has been described and explained. These are as follows.

The term 'culture' was first used by Taylor in 1871 who defined it as, 'that complex whole which includes knowledge, belief, art, morals, laws, customs and any other capabilities and habits acquired by man as a member of society' (cited in Berry et al., 2002).

Hofstede (2011) defined culture as, 'the collective programming of the mind that distinguishes the members of one group or category of people from others'. Though, initially culture was studied to a great extent by anthropologists, today it is a subject of study for psychologists, sociologists, evolutionary biologists and various other scientists.

The approach of psychology to culture is comparatively different from that of other subjects or disciplines. In psychology, culture can be described as ideas, meanings, traditions, behaviours, attitudes and way of life of large group of individuals that are difficult to change over time and are passed on from one generation to other. Thus, these ideas, meanings and even information are transmitted from one person to another. The mechanism of transmission is socially transmitted through the processes of enculturation and socialisation. Enculturation and socialisation are the main contributors to similarities within cultures and differences with other cultural groups (the concept of socialisation, as well as enculturation along with another term acculturation will be discussed later in this chapter).

Culture can also be termed as developing from past behaviour and it can be explained as initiator of future behaviour. Human beings contribute to culture and are also influenced by them.

Many a time, the term culture is equated with a nation or an ethnic group. Going by this, a country such as India can be said to have just one culture, which we know is not true. Thus, culture cannot be confined to national boundaries or even to a particular state (such as Gujarat, Maharashtra, Tamil Nadu), as can be said in the context of India, where culture varies amongst people even in a single state. Linton (1936) described culture as the total social heredity of mankind and Herskovits defined it as the manmade part of the human environment (Berry et al., 2002). Culture includes various aspects including religion, caste, society, property and so on.

Krorber and Kluckhohn (1952) suggested that

> Culture consists of patterns, explicit and implicit, of and for behaviour, acquired and transmitted by symbols, constituting the distinctive achievements of human groups, including their embodiments in artefacts, the essential core of culture consists of traditional (that is, historically derived and selected) ideas and especially their attached values; cultural systems may on the one hand be considered as products of action, on the other hand as conditioning elements of further action. (Cited in Berry et al., 2002)

To develop a better understanding of the term 'culture', a distinction also needs to be drawn out between explicit and implicit culture.

> The explicit culture consists of directly observable regularities in the verbal and non-verbal behaviour of the members of a society and the implicit culture consists of the beliefs, values, norms and premises, which the anthropologist infers or invents to explain observed regularities in behaviour and to explain the patterning of seemingly unrelated bits of behaviour. (Krech et al., 1983, p. 344)

Culture is influenced by the ecological variables to a great extent. For example, people in the Konkan belt (western India) eat fish and rice, as these two commodities are easily available there. People in

Punjab eat rotis made mainly from wheat as wheat is grown in that region. Clothing can be influenced by the ecological variables such as climate and temperature. Culture can also be influenced by significant events such as being ruled by another country, migration, contact with other cultural group/s, by developments in technology etc. Culture contributes to individual differences in a significant manner and as individual differences can be considered as essence of psychology, it is of utmost importance that we focus on this term. No two cultures are same, something or the other difference will exist between them. Every culture will have its own pattern and content that contributes to the differences between the cultures.

Here the term 'microculture' can also be discussed, that is, local culture. Microculture refers to certain patterns that are distinct and related to behaviour and ideas that are learned and shared. These are mainly found in local regions amongst specific groups. These could be based on ethnicity, gender, age and so on.

CULTURE AND INDIVIDUAL

There is a significant and complex relationship between an individual and his/her culture. Individual can be termed as a part and parcel of the culture and has strong conformity towards his/her cultural group. An individual's social interaction is determined by culture to a great extent. An individual is in a way also responsible for passing on the culture to the next generation.

Further, he/she may also contribute to cultural changes and modifications. Thus, it can be said that the relationship between an individual and his/her culture is not passive and is mutually interdependent. For example, on the one hand, culture determines the way we greet, eat, interact and behave. On the other hand, you must have come across numerous changes taking place in culture that can be attributed to individuals, that can range from simple changes in the food preference from probably 'parathas' to 'pizza', to more significant and complex changes of eradicating an evil system such as the 'sati'.

There also exists a relationship between culture and personality and this field was explored to a great extent by anthropologists. Culture can be said to have a significant influence on the personality of an individual. According to Whiting, personality is an outcome of childrearing practices that in turn are influenced by culture (Adamopoulos & Lonner, 2001). Thus, it can be reemphasised that the individual and culture have a vicious relationship, where they influence each other.

Studies have also been carried out to understand cultural variations in personality attributes. One such study was carried out by Hofstede (1989) that mainly focussed on values at in workplace. The researcher collected data from the IBM employees from around 50 nations and it was based on four dimensions related to cultural variations in values, namely, power distance, uncertainty avoidance, individualism and masculinity. Another dimension, truth vs virtue was added later on. Based on the data, Hofstede also drew conclusions about managerial practices. Though the work carried out by Hofstede found criticism, predictions made by Hofstede with regard to cultural differences were in general confirmed (Sondergaard, 1994).

Individuals who belong to different cultures vary with regard to various psychological processes and one of the examples here is the sense of humour. Something that is funny in one culture may not be funny in another. In similar manner, cultural variations also exist with regard to basic psychological process such as perception, motivation and so on (Heine, 2012).

Studies have indicated that self-perception, perception of others and also interpersonal relationships are influenced by culture (Markus & Kitayama, 1991; Triandis, 1989). Two studies were carried out by Cai et al. (2007) and the findings of these studies indicated that when compared with American participants, Chinese participants' appraisal about themselves was less positive on cognitive measure of self-evaluation, but no cultural variation was found with regard to the affective measure of self-regard. The results of the second study showed that there was no difference between the Chinese and the Americans with reference to self-regard, but the inclination to evaluate themselves in an excessive positive way was found to be less in the Chinese.

Culture also plays a role in the perception of non-verbal communications as was displayed by some of the studies that were discussed in Chapter 5 on social perception. Thus, there could be situations where there are cultural misunderstandings. For example, thumbs up that indicates agreement or approval and can be considered as a positive gesture in certain cultures, could be seen as a negative gesture in certain other cultures (Knapp & Hall, 2009).

Language and Culture

Human being is a social animal and is involved in communicating with each other to a great extent. Language plays an important role in facilitating this communication. Language can be defined as any set or system of vocal or written symbols, used in a more or less uniform way by the members of a community (Berry et al., 2002).

The relationship between language and culture is mutual in the same way as that between an individual and culture. Language of a particular group of people may be determined by culture; at the same time language may also lead to certain modifications and changes in culture. Language can be termed as a mirror of an individual's culture or as their crystallised thoughts and it reflects their dominant concerns and interests (Berry et al., 2002). In India for example, it is possible for us to determine the culture or region of a person from the way he/she speaks. Marathi language will vary greatly across Maharashtra. It is spoken in different ways in Mumbai, Nagpur and Malvan. So, if a person from Malvan belt speaks in Marathi, we can determine that he/she is from Malvan in Maharashtra. The same is applicable to Hindi, as spoken in different parts of North India.

Further, it is also necessary for us to understand how language influences the way individuals think and deal with objects and situations in their context. Von Humboldt stated that the structure of the language of a society, namely, the vocabulary and grammar of the language, influences an individual's concept about the world (Berry et al., 2002).

There is also a definite connection between thinking and language and thus language can have an influence on the thinking patterns of members of a particular culture (Berry et al., 1992, as cited in Spering, 2001, p. 27), though it can also be said that people who speak different languages also think differently. The term that can be stated here is linguistic relativity, that mainly focusses on the interrelationship between thinking and language characteristics. Vico, Condillac, Maupertius, Monboddo and Reid were some 18th century philosophers who worked on language and thoughts. The term linguistic relativity, is also referred to as Whorf's hypothesis (Whorf was a linguist) and sometimes referred to as Sapir-Whorf hypothesis (Sapir was a cultural anthropologist). They stressed that language is not just for communication of ideas, but is also responsible for the construction of the ideas that are communicated. Whorf in 1956 also stressed that individuals belonging to different cultures perceive and organise reality in different manners and he mainly attributed this to the language structure (Krech et al., 1983). His views were however criticised to a great extent.

Linguistic structure can also be related to behaviour. Bernstein (1959) distinguished between public language, which is spoken by uneducated people, and formal language, which is spoken by educated middle and upper middle class people (Krech et al., 1983). Bernstein also described characteristics of public language, which are discussed as follows:

1. The sentences are short, grammatically simple and many a time unfinished.
2. Certain small numbers of conjunctions, that are simple and repetitive, are used.
3. Use of adjectives and adverbs are limited and rigid.
4. The use of personal pronouns such as 'we', 'you', 'us' is frequent compared to impersonal pronouns such as 'one', 'it'.
5. Statements formulated as implicit questions are frequently used.
6. Reasons and conclusions are confounded frequently in order to construct categorical statements.
7. Traditional and idiomatic phrases are frequently used.
8. Public languages are implicit in nature.

According to Hoijer (1953), an individual's sensory perception and thought may not be limited by the linguistic patterns, though the perceptions are directed in certain channels that are habitual in nature (Krech et al., 1983).

Thus, language is an important aspect of any culture and any culture can be studied from the point of view of its language. Language is also significant in understanding overall psychology of human beings.

Intercultural Contact and Impact on the Individual

As the title suggests, the term 'intercultural contact' implies contact between two or more cultures. Intercultural contact has increased to a great extent due to the process of globalisation and has also enhanced communication technology. Today, it is easily possible to get in touch and interact with a social psychologist, say in the USA. Skype, Facebook and other social networking sites have made it extremely convenient to communicate with people from other cultures and nations. Further, the transportation by means of cheaper flights and greater connectivity has also made it simpler to travel from one part of the world to the other. This and, of course, policy decisions by governments of various countries have led to the promotion of immigration, tourism, collaborations and cooperation between nations, thus leading to more open national boundaries.

Intercultural contacts can be categorised into two (Ward, Bochner, & Furnham, 2001, as cited by Spering, 2001, p. 30):

1. The first category includes people who already live in culturally diverse nations. India, for example, is a nation with diverse culture. This is also termed as within society cross-cultural interactions.
2. The second category is between society sojourner contacts and that includes people who come in contact with another culture as they travel to another region with some purpose. The purpose can be, further studies (international students), employment and business. These people can also be termed as sojourners. There can also be other groups of people that include tourists, immigrants and also refugees, who come in contact with other cultures. As these sojourner come in contact with another culture, they have to make numerous emotional and social adjustments and they may also experience stress.

Both the aforementioned categories, within society cross-cultural interactions and between society sojourner contacts, will vary on the basis of various aspects such as the place where interaction is taking place (is it at home, away from home), the duration and frequency of interaction (short or long, rarely or frequently), the purpose of interaction or contact (education, employment etc.), the extent of involvement etc. Thus, the outcomes of this interaction can be categorised into four main categories, genocide, assimilation, segregation and integration (Bochner, 1982, as cited in Spering, 2001, p. 32). However, at the individual level, the changes would be a little different from that at the cultural level. There are various psychological adjustments that an individual might have to go through when he/she comes in contact with a new culture, before he/she adapts to it.

'According to social identification theories, identity entails a set of dynamic, complex process by which individuals define, redefine and construct their own and others' ethnicity' (Ward et al., 2001, as cited in Spering, 2001, p. 34). Identity can have both cognitive and affective components. Tajfel derived a theory of social identity that was mainly based on threats to identity as perceived by various groups, when they come in contact with other cultural groups. Also in this regard a minority group may display a greater need for identification with one's group. This identification with one's group and distinction from other groups, in a way, is necessary in order to help individuals develop positive social identity. Further, how far an individual identifies with one's culture of origin will determine his/her psychological adjustment and the extent to which he/she identifies with the culture of the other group will determine his/her socio-cultural adjustment (Spering, 2001).

The term 'intercultural contact' can be compared with the term 'acculturation'. Intercultural contact mainly deals with how members of two or more cultural systems relate to each other. Acculturation, on the other hand, describes to what extent an individual changes or modifies his/her practices and behaviours in order to adjust to the new culture. Acculturation can also be described as changes that occur as a result of the initial contact between people of different cultures. In the process of acculturation, it is also possible that the individual may have to suffer acculturative stress. 'Culture shock' is yet another term we need to explain in this context. It denotes an active process through which an individual deals with the change, as a result of contact with another culture. Cultural shock has three main components: affective, behavioural and cognitive (Ward, Bochner, & Furnham, 2001, as cited by Spering, 2001, p. 35). The affective component deals with the anxieties, confusions and stress that may be experienced by an individual during his/her initial contact with the culture. The behavioural component has to do with mainly the norms with reference to interactions. It mainly deals with the rules and norms of behaviour in a particular society. The cognitive component refers to the meanings, perceptions and beliefs shared within a particular culture.

Thus, the relationship between culture and individuals can be viewed through multiple dimensions and there are also numerous studies that have been carried out in this context.

SOCIALISATION

A concept that would be relevant to discuss in the context of culture is socialisation.

Socialisation denotes a process through which, the rules with regard to behaviour as well as beliefs and attitudes, that prepare an individual to function effectively as a member of the society, are acquired. It is a deliberate process through which an individual learns various practices and behaviours. Thus, the shaping of the individuals takes place in which certain behaviours, attitudes and beliefs are encouraged where as other behaviours, attitudes and beliefs that are not in accordance with the societal norms are discouraged. It is important to discuss socialisation in the context of culture because socialisation is determined by culture to a great extent.

Socialisation is also especially critical as it facilitates the passing on of culture to the next generation. The process of socialisation has been studied by many, including Freud, who stated that cultural values and norms are learned by individuals that lead to the development of 'superego'. Piaget attributed development of human beings to both physiological maturation and experiences that are social. Self-concept too develops as a result of reactions from others as denoted by Cooley in his term 'looking glass self'. Though the process of socialisation mainly starts with family, peers and school, even mass media can play a significant role in this process and can shape and reshape an individual's behaviour.

There are two main perspectives to socialisation. One of the perspectives views socialisation as an undirectional process, where the source of socialisation lies outside the individual and his/her behaviour is changed and regulated from outside. This holds true to an extent, as when a child is born, he/she is dependent on others for information about the cultural values.

The other perspective of socialisation perceives the child as possessing certain instincts and desires. Further, the child will be inclined to satisfy or vent his/her instincts and desires with not much concern (at least initially) for the desires and feelings of others around him/her. The children are not at the receiving end of the socialisation process, but they bring their own instincts and desires to it. The first perspective denotes that human beings are easily shaped and moulded, whereas, the second perspective denotes that human beings are not easily malleable and shaping or restraining them is difficult.

There is also a third perspective, that is, mutuality model, which highlights the reciprocal effect that the caregiver and child have on each other's behaviour (Schaffer, 1996).

It is important to study socialisation in social psychology because it contributes greatly to the development of patterns and skills that determine interactions of an individual during his/her lifetime.

Socialisation, thus, can be described as a process that is bidirectional, which encompasses not only the influence of culture on the individual but also active participation of the individual in redefining the goals and generation of strategies to achieve the goals.

Various studies have been carried out on socialisation and its impact on individual behaviour.

Whiting and Whiting (1975) carried out a study across six cultures, (Kenya, Philippines, Japan, India, Mexico and the USA) that investigated the childrearing practices and childhood social behaviour. The study was carried out on 134 children (boys and girls) belonging to the age group 3–11, whose behaviours were observed and recorded. The results indicated differences in children's pro-social behaviour. The children from the society that was most traditional displayed most pro-social behaviour and the children from the society that was most complex modern were most egoistic. A positive relationship was found between the cultural simplicity and personalities that are nurturant versus egoistic. The results also indicated the influence of modernisation on pro-social behaviour, which was attributed to the variations in childrearing practices and the dimensions of culture, namely, individualism and collectivism.

Socialisation also determines gender appropriate behaviour in individuals. A study on cross-cultural analysis of sex difference in behaviour of children aged 3–11 years, carried out by Whiting and Edwards (1973) indicated existence of sex differences that were universal in the behaviours of the samples included in the research. These were seen to be determined by socialisation process that encompassed task assignment as well as related interactions with infants, adults and peers. The results also indicated consistency in the characteristic behaviours of males and females that seems to be shaped as a result of socialisation.

Though a number of studies in socialisation focus on children, socialisation is not limited to childhood. And an individual is exposed to socialisation throughout various stages of life from adolescence to adulthood and other developmental stages. He/she faces new challenges and expectations of each developmental stage.

Parenting is a process that is both biological and social in nature and is a significant aspect when socialisation is discussed. Parenting is also directed towards raising a healthy and successful child who will contribute to his/her own self, as well as, the society and this is necessarily done through the process of socialisation, though socialisation may differ based on the parental goals. One way in which such variations can be studied is by carrying out research on the extent of acceptance of social values by the adolescents.

In a study carried out by Crystal and Stevenson (1995), adolescents from America, Japan and China and their mothers were asked a question, 'What is a bad kid?' Adolescents in America denoted substance abuse and lack of self-control as characteristics of a bad kid, whereas Chinese adolescents denoted engaging in acts that were seen as detrimental to society as characteristics of a bad kid. With regard to Japan, behaviours that interfere with interpersonal harmony were seen as characteristics of a bad kid by the adolescents. The results indicated a significant difference between the adolescents and their mothers in terms of the frequency with which they reported the types of behaviour attributed to a 'bad kid'.

The process of socialisation thus plays a significant role in determining an individual's behaviour and has an influence on his/her attitude, interpersonal relationships and overall behaviour and actions in a social set-up.

Enculturation and Acculturation

In the context of socialisation, it is also important to touch upon the terms 'enculturation' and 'acculturation'.

Enculturation is a term that has been defined by Herskovits (1948) as a process directed towards socialisation as well as maintenance of norms that are related to one's indigenous culture that encompasses the salient ideas, concepts and values of that culture. It can be described as a process that involves transmission of values, practices, language and so on to an individual, from parents, adults and peers belonging to his/her culture.

Acculturation, on the other hand, occurs when one gets in contact with another culture and adopts the beliefs and behaviours pertaining to that culture. Redfield, Linton, and Herskovits (1936) stated, 'Acculturation comprehends those phenomena which result when groups of individuals sharing different one's cultures come into continuous first-hand contact, with subsequent changes in the original culture patterns of either or both groups'. Acculturation at an individual level is termed as psychological acculturation, that denotes the impact that acculturation has on an individual (Graves, 1967). For example, an Indian immigrating to the United States would undergo a process of acculturation as he/she comes in contact with the culture there and adopts certain beliefs and behaviours of that culture.

Berry et al. (1989) explained the relationship between enculturation and acculturation in terms of integration, assimilation, separation and marginalisation. Integration (also termed as biculturalism) takes place when preference is displayed by an individual for cultural norms of both the dominant group and the indigenous group. Assimilation results when the cultural norms of the dominant group are preferred and the cultural norms of the indigenous group are rejected. Separation takes place when preference is displayed for cultural norms of the indigenous group and the cultural norms of the dominant group are rejected. Lastly, marginalisation is an outcome of lack of preference for cultural norms of both the dominant and the indigenous groups. To sum up, integration denotes high acculturation as well as high enculturation. Assimilation denotes high acculturation and low enculturation. Separation denotes low acculturation and high enculturation and marginalisation denotes low acculturation and low enculturation.

Various studies have been carried out on enculturation and acculturation that mainly focus on immigrants.

Chiu et al. (1992) carried out studies on the influence of immigration on parental behaviour and adolescent distress in Chinese families residing in two Western nations. Thus, the first generation Americans, Chinese adolescents (parents born in China but immigrated to America before the adolescent was born) and second generation American, Chinese adolescents (grandparents who were born in China but immigrated to America and parents were born in America) were compared to other Chinese adolescents from Hong Kong, and adolescents who were European American. In a second study, the first- and second-generation Chinese Australians, Anglo Australians and Chinese adolescents from Hong Kong were compared. The results indicated no difference in the adolescent problems displayed by the first- and second-generation Chinese, American adolescents and non-immigrant adolescents. No significant difference was found between the immigrant and non-immigrant adolescents with regard to relationship between behaviour of parents and distress experienced by them.

Acculturation and enculturation can also have an impact on overall psychological well-being of the individual. A study was carried out by Kim and Omizo (2010) on behavioural enculturation and acculturation, psychological functioning and help seeking attitudes among Asian American Adolescents. The sample constituted of 112 Asian-American students from high school in Hawaii. The results did not indicate relationship between high behavioural enculturation and acculturation, and psychological functioning. A post hoc assessment indicated that enculturation displayed positive relationship with general self-efficacy, cognitive flexibility and collective self-esteem dimensions of membership, private and importance to identity. Acculturation was found to display a negative relationship with importance to identity.

A study by Park (2016) on acculturation and enculturation, perception of depressive symptoms and help seeking behaviour amongst Korean Americans indicated positive relationship between acculturation and willingness to seek help for depressive symptoms, whereas a negative relationship was found between enculturation and willingness to seek help for depressive symptoms. Acculturation was significantly associated with greater likelihood of perceiving that affective depressive symptoms were problematic.

PSYCHOLOGICAL PERSPECTIVES ON INFLUENCE OF CULTURE ON BEHAVIOUR

The influence of culture on behaviour can be studied through four prominent psychological perspectives. They are cross-cultural psychology, cultural psychology, psychological anthropology and indigenous psychology (Berry, Poortinga, & Pande, 1997).

Cross-cultural Psychology

According to Berry et al. (2002),

> Cross-cultural psychology is the study of similarities and differences in individual psychological functioning in various cultural and ethno-cultural groups; of ongoing changes in variables reflecting such functioning; and of the relationships of psychological variables with sociocultural, ecological and biological variables.

Eckensberger (1972, p. 100) defined cross-cultural psychology as 'systematic comparison of psychological variables under different cultural conditions'. Cross-cultural psychology can thus be described as a study of human behaviour across cultures.

The main goals of cross-cultural psychology can be described as follows:

- It seeks to understand the diversity amongst the individuals and also identify factors that contribute to this diversity.
- It strives to research the universality of principles and theories of psychology.
- It seeks to explain how culture is one of the major influences on human behaviour and thus contributes to individual differences.
- It tries to explicitly and implicitly compare individuals' behaviour in various cultural settings using equivalent methods of assessment.

Cultural Psychology

Cultural psychology can be described as the branch of psychology which studies the effect of culture on human behaviours and thinking. It further tries to study the relationship that exists between human behaviour and culture. Cultural psychologists are interested in studying practices and behaviour in a particular culture and how these can be related to other practices and behaviours within the same culture. Cultural psychology mainly focuses on within culture analysis rather than comparisons between cultures, to seek similarities and differences, as carried out in cross-cultural psychology. The goals of cultural psychology are:

- understand the core of the culture;
- re-examine various methods in order to study the psychological processes in different cultures.

Psychological Anthropology

Psychological anthropology can be termed as an interdisciplinary subject between two main subject areas of psychology and anthropology. Anthropologists contribute greatly to the field of psychological anthropology. Bock (1988) said, 'all anthropology is psychological and all psychology is cultural' and he also focused on four approaches to psychological anthropology: they are psychoanalytic anthropology, culture and personality, social structure and personality and cognitive anthropology (as cited in Berry et al., 1997, p. 58). It mainly includes the study of relationship between culture and psychological processes.

Indigenous Psychology

Indigenous psychology emerged as a result of dissatisfaction due to the monopoly of Western theories in psychology and also due to the inability of the Western psychologists to truly understand the deeper aspects of other cultures. Thus, a particular cultural practice can be studied in the Indian context by means of indigenous psychology.

Kim and Berry (1993) defined indigenous psychologies as 'the scientific study of human behaviour that is native, that is not transported from other regions and that is designed for its people' (Berry et al., 1997, p. 60). The main goal of indigenous psychology is to have universal psychology, and in order to work in this direction, an in-depth understanding of each culture is required, which can be done with the help of indigenous psychology. Indigenous psychology also helps to understand certain psychological concepts that are locally used in a particular culture or region which may not have an equivalent meaning in English or in any other European language. Further, there are certain practices, rituals and cultural aspects that may not conform to the conventional research methods and in order to study them an indigenous research approach may be required. There are also a number of practices and rituals that cannot be approached from a Western theoretical point of view. Thus, an indigenous approach is required to understand and research such practices and rituals. Further, in order to have a comprehensive understanding of human nature, theories that emerge from indigenous psychologies need to be developed (Kao, 1997; Pandey, 1996).

CROSS-CULTURAL RESEARCH

It is necessary that cross-cultural studies on human behaviour be conducted and promoted in order to develop better understanding about the aspects of culture that have an influence on human behaviour and also to identify any universality in human behaviours. This can be a complex activity and a number of issues can crop up while carrying out cross-cultural research.

Culture can be studied with the help of emic and etic approaches. The terms 'emic' and 'etic' were introduced by Kenneth Pike, an American linguistic anthropologist in 1954 and were derived from 'phonemic' and 'phonetic'. These two terms can be used to study the cultural system. Emic approach focusses on the members of a particular culture who would be in better position to provide valid information and be a suitable judge of the culture. For example, a person belonging to a particular cultural group will understand a ritual and provide better information about it than any outsider. This approach studies the behaviour from within the cultural system and thus only one system at a time is studied. This was the perspective used mainly by cultural anthropologists who wanted to understand culture from the point of view of the 'native' (Morris et al., 1999). Method that is used here is mainly observation and involves ethnographic fieldwork. Interview method could also be used for data collection besides observation. The approach involves observation during one sitting or a few sittings, but the observation is extensive and for longer periods of time. Content analysis may also be carried out with regard to the texts based on cultural practices or rituals.

The etic approach, on the other hand, looks at the culture from the point of view of an observer who carries out observation in a scientific manner. This approach studies culture from outside the system and thus it is possible to study more than one culture at a time and compare them. This approach is based on the principles of behaviourist psychology (Morris et al., 1999). The focus of this approach is mainly on the features that are external and measurable and that can be studied in two different cultural settings. There are more than one settings involved and the observation is comparatively narrow and brief. The data is collected using multi setting surveys, cross sectional comparisons and even experiments may be carried out by having culture as a quasi-experimental manipulation.

Various qualitative approaches (that were discussed in Chapter 2) can be used to study culture. Qualitative methods involve descriptions that are detailed and in depth and this can be of great use when much information about the phenomenon is not available. For example, while studying a certain cultural practice that has not been researched much, qualitative approach can be used to gather in-depth information about that practice. One of the issues that one may face in employing qualitative methods is subjectivity, though this can be dealt with in a number of ways by using certain technical strategies such as reflexivity exercises (biases of the teams who will analyse the data are recorded before the analyses is carried out) (Karasz & Singelis, 2009). Mixed methods that include both quantitative and qualitative approaches can also be effectively used to carry out research related to culture.

Issues and Challenges While Carrying Out Cross-Cultural Research

While carrying out cross-cultural research, there are various issues as well as challenges. Some of the issues are discussed in this section of the chapter.

There are numerous issues and challenges that a researcher could face while carrying out research on individuals from other cultures (when compared with research that is carried out in one's own culture). As culture has an influence on various aspects of human psychology, most often the researchers end up employing the methods that are mostly used by a certain subfield of psychology. For example, if the researcher wanted to study effect of culture on health, the methods most often used in health psychology will be employed. Every method that is used will have its own strengths and weaknesses and thus when they are used to study people from other cultures, ambiguities could be created besides the existing ambiguities of that method (Heine, 2012).

Selecting a Culture to Carry Out Research

One of the issues while carrying out cross-cultural research is selecting a culture that one wants to study. It is suggested that a culture should not be selected randomly. Though such an approach (random selection of culture) may reveal certain cultural differences, there could be problems at the level of interpretation of results due to lack of theoretical background (that would have guided the selection of the culture).

Yet another issue that needs to be brought to light is that, despite a lot of cross-cultural research being carried out in the context of social psychology, most of the research is based on Western, Educated, Industrialised, Rich and Democratic (WEIRD) societies (Henrich, Heine, & Norenzayan, 2010). These researches are based on only a small fraction of the world populations and thus the findings of the studies carried out on this section, as such cannot be generalised. When a survey of research papers published in the history of the *Journal of Personality and Social Psychology* was carried out, 99 per cent of the paper originated from Western countries and 92 per cent emerged from United States and Canada (Quinones-Vidal et al., 2004).

One way in which the cultures can be selected is based on the theoretical variable(s) that one wants to study. For example, cultures with long-term orientation and short-term orientation can be compared to study the difference in decision-making process.

Researchers may also be interested in studying psychological universality, in which case two cultures differ to a great extent in terms of relevant theoretical variables, such as language, traditions, practices and so on are studied. Despite selecting such opposite cultures, if similarities are found in that particular psychological variable, it can be termed as having high degree of universality. Universalities with regard to childrearing practices can be studied by selecting cultures that are different from each other on various theoretical variables. Western and Eastern cultures can also be compared on similar lines.

Deriving Meaningful Interpretations from Cross-cultural Comparisons

This is the next issue that needs to be focussed on. For cross-cultural comparisons, it is important that the researcher develops an understanding about the cultures that he/she is studying. Researchers carrying out studies in their own culture may have an advantage in this regard, as they already understand the culture, and the theories and hypotheses developed by them can be guided by their observations and introspections (Heine, 2012). However, when it comes to researchers who have to study a culture that is different for their own culture, they may face certain difficulties.

Knowledge about cultures can be gathered by referring to existing texts and review besides going through ethnographies (Ethnography was discussed in Chapter 2). However, this may limit the researcher, to the perspective of the author of that text or the ethnographer. The perspective of these authors and ethnographers may also differ greatly from one another. Another way is to collaborate with a researcher from another culture, who is interested in carrying out a study on the same variables. Thus, if one wants to study relationship across different cultures, a researcher from a certain culture can be approached. Yet another way is to gather first-hand information and knowledge about the culture. Though this approach is effective, it is costly as well as time-consuming.

Another issue that needs to be focussed on while deriving meaningful interpretations from cross-cultural comparisons has to do with whether cultures that are contrasted should be similar or different. If the cultures are very different, there could be issues in using the same methods. It may not always be possible to have methodological equivalence, that is, 'methods perceived in identical ways across different cultures' (Heine, 2012, p. 117). And when different methods are used there could be other issues that result from loss of experimental control. Same methods can be used when the cultures are similar. This is one reason why a number of studies have been carried out on cultures that are similar or based on the participants' familiarity with research settings. For example, most of the educated and employed adults across different cultures would be aware about online surveys and would be able to answer them. But, then again, one would be restricting oneself to a very specific group (i.e., individuals who belong to educated or employed but do not have access to a computer). Thus, there could be problems with regard to the generalisation of the results. A study was carried out by Carroll and Patterson (2014) to investigate whether cross-cultural differences exist with regard to servant leadership (Patterson's model) phenomenon. Data was collected from 234 participants from the United States and 232 participants from India, who were employees of the IT industry. The study indicated no difference with regard to the perceptions of servant leadership between the two groups. In this study, the sample from India was selected based on whether they could read and write English fluently as it would be difficult to translate the tool used for data stats collection into the numerous languages spoken in India.

Yet another problem while deciding to select distinct cultures or similar cultures is that of the power of the study. The power of the study can be described as potential of the study to detect effect or cross-cultural difference in this context (Heine, 2012). For example, if cultures are similar there would not be variation in the independent variable (i.e., culture) and the likelihood of detecting its effect on dependent variable would be less as opposed to when the cultures are different.

Cross-cultural Research Using Surveys

There could also be other issues in the context of cross-cultural research that are related to the items in the questionnaire. Cross-cultural research may require the questionnaire to be translated in a different languages. Also, if the questionnaire is retained in a more common language such as English, the researcher cannot be sure about the English skills possessed by the respondents in a certain culture (non-English speaking). Further, persons in these non-English speaking cultures, who are well versed in English, may be more similar to their counterparts in English speaking cultures. There are also a number of issues with regard to translation, which may not be accurate, though back translation method could be used in this context, where the questionnaire is first translated from one language (example, English) to another (example, Hindi) by a translator and then retranslated into the earlier language (Hindi to English) by a different translator. It can be said that materials that are translated well are more likely to display cultural differences that are valid and reliable (Heine, 2012).

After the questionnaire has been administered and answered by the individuals from various cultures, there could also be issues with regard to response bias. Cultural variations have been observed with regard to moderacy bias and extremity bias. In moderacy bias the items that are closer to the midpoint on a scale are selected (thus in a scale of always, frequently, sometimes, rarely, never, the chances of selecting 'sometimes' are high) and with regard to extremity bias, the items that are close to the end points of the scale are selected (thus in a scale of always, frequently, sometimes, rarely, never, the chances of selecting 'always' or 'never' are high). To avoid this instead of a scale, responses in terms of 'Yes' or 'No' could be sought. But if a researcher wants to carry out assessment across a wide range of items, data can be standardised before the comparisons between the cultures are made. In this, the participants' scores are first averaged and then each item is assessed with regard to its deviation from the average score of the participants. Though there are limitations to this as well that need to be taken into consideration. There is also acquiescence bias in which the participants tend to agree with most of the statements. Cultural variations have also been displayed with regard to this bias, though this can be dealt with by having certain statements that have reverse-scored. Further, reference group effect may also play a role in cross-cultural research, where cultures may be assessed with a single standard and individuals belonging to different cultures may compare themselves with different standards as they evaluate themselves. Problems could also arise due to deprivation effect that occurs due to gap between what individuals have in reality and what they would like to have. Thus, there could be number of biases when questionnaires are used. Though there are culture fair tests, there are numerous challenges to developing such tests and they might not be absolutely accurate.

While carrying out cross-cultural assessment, there are two main equivalence that need to be considered, linguistic equivalence and psychometric equivalence. The linguistic equivalence further includes semantic equivalence, conceptual equivalence and normative equivalence. Semantic equivalence is related to the words and phrases that have identical or same meaning across cultural groups. The conceptual equivalence is related to the operationalisation of construct across cultural groups. The normative equivalence is related to the norms of a specific cultural group in which the construct is being studied. Psychometric equivalence on the other hand, can be described as 'similarities between the psychometric properties of the cultural versions of any research instrument' (İskifoğlu, 2014, p. 4655). Thus, there are a number of issues and challenges that need to be taken into consideration while carrying out cross-cultural research.

SUMMARY

To summarise, the chapter mainly focussed on the term 'culture'. While discussing the concept of culture, various definitions of culture were highlighted and the relationship between culture and individual was also described with a focus on language, culture and intercultural contact. The four psychological perspectives on influence of culture on behaviour, namely, cross-cultural psychology, cultural psychology, psychological anthropology and indigenous psychology were also highlighted. The cross-cultural research was then discussed extensively with a focus on approaches that can be used to carry out research. Issues and challenges that a researcher may face while carrying out cross-cultural research were also discussed.

QUESTIONS

1. Describe the term 'culture' and explain any one psychological perspective on the influence of culture on behaviour.
2. Explain the relationship between language and culture.
3. Differentiate between cross-cultural psychology and cultural psychology.
4. Elucidate the term 'intercultural contact' with suitable examples.
5. Discuss the issues faced by a researcher while carrying out cross-cultural research.

REFERENCES

Bernstein, B. (1959). Public language: Some sociological implications of linguistic form. *British Journal of Sociology, 10*, pp. 311–326.

Bock, P. K. (1988). *Rethinking psychological anthropology: Continuity and change in the study of human action*. Prospect Height, IL: Waveland Press.

Durkin, K. (2001). Developmental social psychology. In M. Hewstone & W. Stroebe (Eds.), *Introduction to social psychology*. Oxford: Blackwell Publishing.

Hoijer, H. (1953). The relation of language to culture. In A. L. Kroeber (Ed.), *Anthropology today*. Chicago, IL: University of Chicago Press.

Kroeber, A. L., & Kluckhohn, C. (1952). *Culture: A critical review of concepts and definitions*. Cambridge, MA: Peabody Museum, 181.

Linton, R. (1936). *The study of man*. New York, NY: Appleton- Century.

Whiting, B., & Edwards, C. P. (1973). A cross-cultural analysis of sex differences in the behaviour of children aged three through 11. *Journal of Social Psychology, 91*(2), pp. 171–188. Retrieved from http://digitalcommons.unl.edu/cgi/viewcontent.cgi?article=1607&context=psychfacpub

FURTHER READINGS

For further information on cross-cultural psychology, you may refer to the following:

Berry, J. W., Poortinga, Y. H., Breugelmans, S. M., Chasiotis, A., & Sam, D. L. (2002). *Cross-cultural psychology*. New York, NY: Cambridge University Press.

Brislin, R. (2000). *Understanding culture's influence on behavior* (2nd ed.). Belmont, CA: Wadsworth Publishing.

Hall, G. C. N. (2009). *Multicultural psychology* (2nd). Englewood Cliffs, NJ: Prentice Hall.

SECTION IV

Applied Social Psychology

CHAPTER 13

Introduction to Applied Social Psychology

In this section, the focus will be on the application part of social psychology. The field of applied social psychology will be discussed in the first chapter of this section and then application of social psychology to various areas will be in the next chapter.

In the very first section, of this book (in Chapter 1), the term 'social psychology' was discussed, besides its theories and historical developments. In this chapter, the focus will be on applied social psychology. Applied social psychology, as such, is not very different from its parent field of social psychology. Although what exactly is covered in this area will be clearer with the help of the examples mentioned here.

A psychology researcher was interested in doing research on the factors leading to suicidal ideation amongst adolescents in a city. While carrying out the research, the researcher found out that there was a considerable number of adolescents in a particular school who displayed high suicidal ideation; therefore, the researcher devised psychotherapeutic intervention to help these adolescents.

Another researcher was carrying out a study on health-related knowledge, attitude and practices of fisherfolks. The researcher was successfully able to identify certain dimensions of health that needed attention as the participants have scored low on these dimensions, thus indicating the presence of misconceptions, unhealthy practices and negative attitude. Therefore, the researcher developed a strategy to educate the fisherfolk on the dimensions of health, where they scored low.

In the above two examples, we can see that the focus of the research was not merely on the findings but also on bringing about a change. This brings us to applied social psychology, which mainly focuses on the application part of social psychology.

Thus, this chapter will discuss about the nature and scope of applied social psychology. The historical developments in applied social psychology will also be discussed. The chapter will also discuss about the role played by an applied social psychologist. Terms such as social issues and problems and social change will also be explained. The chapter in the end will cover two significant topics, namely, intervention and evaluations.

Learning Objectives

After reading this chapter, you will be able to

- Discuss the concept of applied social psychology
- Describe historical developments in applied social psychology

- ❒ Describe social psychology theories
- ❒ Explain the role of applied social psychologist
- ❒ Discuss social issues and problems and social change
- ❒ Discuss intervention and evaluation

THE CONCEPT OF APPLIED SOCIAL PSYCHOLOGY

Applied social psychology can be described as a branch of social psychology that mainly uses the theories, methods and principles of social psychology in order to understand certain social issues/problems/phenomena and then come up with suitable intervention strategies in order to deal with these issues/problems/phenomena. Developing intervention strategies is an important aspect of applied social psychology (it will be discussed later in the chapter).

The basis of applied psychology is that there are always some social components to problems related to human beings, and the most severe human problems are social in nature, for example, violence, conflict, poverty and so on. Applied social psychology in this case can be of much help in dealing effectively with such problems.

Applied social psychology can be defined as:

> The branch of social psychology that draws on social psychological theories, principles, methods, research evidence to contribute (a) to understanding social and practical problems and (b) the development of intervention strategies for improving the functioning of individuals, groups, organisations, communities, and societies with respect to social and practical problems (Schneider, Gruman & Coutts, 2012b, p. 8).

Oskamp and Schultz (1998) defined applied social psychology as 'the systematic application of social psychological constructs, principles, theories, intervention techniques, research methods and research findings to understand or ameliorate social problems'.

Applied social psychology can be categorised as theory driven or problem driven (Kok et al., 1996). The theory-driven applied social psychology focuses on how a particular theory can be tested and applied in a realistic or practical situation. This is also done in order to determine the validity of the theory. Problem-driven applied social psychology, on the other hand, focuses on developing programme activities that could help deal with certain social and practical problems.

Applied Social Psychology as Science

Applied social psychology, being a branch of social psychology, is necessarily a science and, thus, involves scientific understanding and application of core values while dealing with social issues and problems. Although there are a number of similarities between the basic social psychology and applied social psychology, there are two main differences that have been reflected in Table 13.1.

In the first chapter (while discussing about social psychology as science), four main aspects of understanding, or goals of science, namely, description, prediction, determining causality and explanation were discussed. Besides these four goals, there is also a fifth goal that is followed in applied social psychology, that is, 'control' (Christensen, 2004; Goodwin, 2003). Control involves manipulation of the

Table 13.1 *Main Differences Between Basic Social Psychology and Applied Social Psychology*

Basic Social Psychology	Applied Social Psychology
Focus is on developing theories and then testing them.	The main focus is on application, thus the objective is understanding and resolving social and practical problems.
Deductive approach is followed: How a theory will help understand a behaviour.	Inductive approach is followed: Keeping in mind a particular social problem, how a theory could be applied to a particular behaviour that is causing the problem.

Source: Author.

conditions so as to bring about changes in a particular phenomenon (Schneider et al., 2012). For example, once the researcher determines that music therapy can be effectively used with individuals diagnosed with depression, an intervention based on music therapy can be developed and implemented for such individuals. Applied social psychologists will, thus, carry out research with the main objective of bringing about a positive change. Although it also needs to be mentioned that an intervention-based study may or may not be able to achieve the goal of control as, in certain cases, the intervention may fail to bring about the expected change.

The research in applied social psychology may be conducted in order to understand a particular issue/problem/phenomena in a better manner, although their final goal may be to bring about a positive change or optimise functioning of the individuals in a society. However, sometimes they may also rely on existing researches and findings in order to develop suitable intervention strategies.

One of the most distinctive features of applied social psychology is that the research mainly starts with social issue/problem and is not based on empirical curiosity. For example, social problems related to child labour, increased in cases of HIV/AIDS and so on can be studied. Further, most of the researches in applied social psychology are interdisciplinary in nature. For example, when conducting a research on effect of social stigma on individuals with HIV/AIDS, just one viewpoint, say, of psychology, is not sufficient, and an interdisciplinary approach (including sociological, biological, economical) needs to be used. Applied social psychology research is necessarily carried out in the field set-up and they are often intervention based. While conducting any research, the researcher is guided by certain core values (like objectivity). But in this context, the role of personal values also needs to be highlighted. Personal values play a significant role in the decisions that are taken by a scientist or a researcher. For example, if a social psychologist is concerned about increased drug abuse amongst adolescents, he/she would take up a topic that would study the factors that promote drug abuse amongst the adolescents. Further, he/she may also develop an intervention based on the results obtained that can then be implemented to curb this menace. Personal values of the researcher (an applied social psychologist in this case) become even more important as he/she is involved in implementation of control (i.e., developing strategies in order to bring about a change). By developing an intervention, the applied social psychologist determines that a problem exists. However, this determination of what constitutes a problem may not be objective. Further, the decision of an applied social psychologist with reference to whether the intervention should actually be carried out or not will again depend on his/her personal values.

Research in applied psychology has also been greatly criticised mainly because of the lack of control groups, inability to carry out experimental manipulation and for its reliance on self-report and correlation. It is also questioned whether the findings of a particular study can be applied to a larger population.

Pure researches are carried out under controlled situations and, thus, have high internal validity, but it may not be possible to apply the findings to the real life situation. In addition, although the applied social psychology research may have high external validity, there is no adequate control that can affect its internal validity. Further, various communities and social groups differ in their nature and, thus, intervention that can be successful with one group may or may not be successful with another.

Humanism as a Foundation to Applied Social Psychology

Humanism also serves as a strong foundation for applied social psychology. In psychology, humanism is mainly expressed in terms of humanistic psychology that not only believes in uniqueness of the individuals but also in their potential to develop to their fullest. This has also led to the term 'humanistic social psychology' which mainly deals with how understanding of interpersonal relationships is used to achieve a state where the potentialities of the individuals are realised and achieved (Fisher, 1982). Humanism is also humanitarian and democratic in nature, which implies that individuals need to be treated equally with respect and compassion, dignity as well as equality, besides`encouraging their involvement in decision-making process with regard to issues/problems that affect them (Fisher, 1982).

It is necessary that applied social psychology is scientific as well as humanistic in its approach. On one hand, social issues/problems and situations need to be studied in a systematic and scientific manner and, on the other hand, it should not be forgotten that ultimately we are dealing with human beings who need to be respected and also need to know about and be involved in the activities and processes that are carried out with regard to issues concerning them.

HISTORICAL DEVELOPMENTS IN APPLIED SOCIAL PSYCHOLOGY

The empirical basis of applied social psychology can be tracked down to the contributions of Kurt Lewin in 1936. Numerous studies were carried out by Lewin and his colleagues on the issues such as social problems, leadership styles and so on. However, in most of the studies, the main focus was not only developing empirical understanding of these topics but also to generate solutions to these problems/ issues. He mainly emphasised on the link between the psychological theories and application leading to an amalgamation of theoretical principles, research and practice (Schneider et al., 2012).

In fact, it can be said that the work of Kurt Lewin from 1840 to 1947 contributed greatly to the emergence of applied social psychology. Lewin also emphasised on the use of action research (discussed in detail in Chapter 2). Lewin was of the view that social psychology researches can stem from the social issues and problems and that research should be carried out with the main focus on finding solutions to social issues and problems. Various organisations such as Society for the Psychological Study of Social Issues, Research Centre for Group Dynamics and National Training Laboratories, besides others, were also established by Lewin.

The Second World War and the issues and problems that were outcome of it created a situation that called for answers or solutions to numerous problems and issues. At that time, there were a number of issues related to obedience, violence, negative attitude and other social problems that called for answers from the field of social psychology.

With numerous empirical researches that were being carried out in social psychology by the likes of Lewin, Sherif and others, by 1950, applied social psychology was ready to establish itself as a significant area of study. However, this could not happen at that time due to the view that 'applied' meant low quality. This, in a way, jeopardised the smooth development of the field of applied social psychology. Further, there were also issues related to the shift in the focus of social psychology from application to an emphasis on theories and experiments related to social processes. Thus, mainly during 1940s and 1950s, the focus of social psychology shifted, thus, marring the development of applied social psychology. There was also a shift from action research to more 'pure research'.

However, in 1960s, the field of applied social psychology again started gaining momentum, mainly due to certain events that were political and social in nature, including the assassination of J. F. Kennedy, the Vietnam War, civil rights movement and so on (Schneider et al., 2012). Again, the society and the psychology community looked up to social psychology for answers and solutions to these issues. The critical outlook of social psychologists towards overemphasis on laboratory-based studies and not on field-based studies further fuelled the rise of applied social psychology.

The articles in *American Psychologist* in 1969 that mainly focused on the interaction between science and social issues/problems created avenues for applied social psychology. This field emerged as one of the prominent fields of study by 1970s. The *Journal of Applied Social Psychology* and another journal titled *Basic and Applied Social Psychology* were started in 1970–1971 and in 1980s respectively. The year 1982 saw the release of a textbook related to applied social psychology named *Social Psychology: An Applied approach by Fisher* (Schneider et al., 2012).

Thus, over the years, applied psychology has developed rapidly and emerged as a significant field of study.

SOCIAL PSYCHOLOGY THEORIES

Theory can be defined as 'a set of interrelated hypotheses or propositions concerning a phenomenon or set of phenomena' (Shaw & Costanzo, 1982, p. 4). It plays a major role in applied social psychology, as most often the interventions in applied social psychology are based on theories. Thus, before we discuss the main component of applied social psychology, that is, intervention, first, we need to update ourselves with theories in the context of social psychology. Theories in social psychology have certain characteristics. As stated by Chung-Yan and Towson (2012), these characteristics are scope, range, testability and parsimony.

- **Scope:** Scope of a theory has been described by Chung-Yan and Towson (2012, p. 27) as 'the number of different human behaviours explained by the theory'. The theories in social psychology in a way have limited scope as all human behaviour is not explained.
- **Range:** Range mainly refers to whether a theory explains behaviour of all human beings or a certain group of persons. Owing to individual difference and also varied cultural background and demographic characteristics that contribute to individual differences, the theories in social psychology cannot explain behaviour of all human beings. There are limited universal theories and behaviours that may differ from group to group.
- **Testability:** The third characteristic is testability. Any theory should be testable, that is, it should be possible to prove or disprove it. Most of the entities in social psychology are intangible and cannot be observed directly, but they are measured through their manifestations with the help of standardised psychological tools.
- **Parsimony:** It indicates that a theory should utilise as less propositions as possible while trying to explain a phenomenon (Chung-Yan & Towson, 2012). Following parsimony may not always be possible in social psychology because of the nature of theories that are mainly midlevel or minitheories and not broad enough in scope.

In order to understand the theories in the context of social psychology, it is also important to understand the scientific process. As Chung-Yan and Towson (2012) state, there are four main steps in scientific process, namely, observation, followed by theory development, specific hypotheses and hypothesis testing. Observation includes observation of the day-to-day events, research findings as well as the results of an intervention. The next step is that of theory development. A theory can be constructed based on observation. This process of deriving certain principles from observation of certain situations and events can be termed as induction. The third step in the scientific process is that of specific hypotheses, which involves deduction, where certain hypotheses are formulated from the principles or theories. The last step in the process is hypothesis testing, where with the help of research methods, research is carried out in order to test the hypothesis(es). Hypothesis testing could also involve design and implementation of intervention (especially in applied social psychology). Further, in applied social psychology, the scientific process does not end with hypothesis testing, but the results obtained from the research are further used to either modify the theories, make further observations or apply the findings to a situation/issue or problem, in pursuit of the fifth goal of science, that is control.

Functions of Social Psychology Theory

The three main functions of theory in applied social psychology are organisation, direction and guide interventions mainly in order to develop interventions. These are discussed as follows:

1. **Organisation.** Organisation can be described as 'a systematic arrangement of observations that demonstrate their relationship to one another' (Chung-Yan & Towson, 2012, p. 26). This is related to the first step of the scientific process, that is, observation. Theory in this context is necessary in order to make connections between the observations. The observations need to be systematically organised into the theoretical framework.
2. **Direction.** This function of theory is related to hypothesis(es) testing. This will help decide the focus of the research. When the research findings are obtained, these findings can direct further research or lead to modifications in the present theory or development of new theories.
3. **Guide intervention.** This is the third function of theory that can be described as an effort to bring about a change. This can be done with the help of various programmes, training programmes, counselling and so on, that can be developed based on various theories.

ROLE OF APPLIED SOCIAL PSYCHOLOGIST

As we now have a clear idea about what is applied social psychology, we also need to focus on the role of an applied social psychologist. Schneider et al., (2012) highlighted certain major roles played by applied social psychologists, which have been discussed as follows:

1. **Researcher.** The first and foremost role played by an applied social psychologist is that of a researcher. At the start of the chapter, while explaining the concept of applied social psychology, we discussed about the nature of research in applied social psychology at length. As discussed, a researcher here mainly focuses on the social problems/issues and strives to develop an intervention strategy that can help in dealing with that problem/issue.

In this context, one can also specifically talk about the role of applied social psychologist as an action researcher, which is more focused towards finding a solution to a particular social problem/issue.

2. **Programme designer.** The applied social psychologist also play the role of a programme designer; as based on the findings of the research carried by him/her or on the results of another empirical study, the psychologist develops a programme. This role requires the psychologist to focus on all the three aspects, that is, theoretical principles, research and practice.
3. **Evaluation researcher.** Any programme or intervention strategy that has been developed needs to be evaluated. Thus, the psychologist here also plays a role of an evaluation researcher. The intervention process and its outcome need to be evaluated in order to make necessary modifications in them so as to ensure better and enhanced results or outcome.
4. **Consultant.** Yet another role played by the psychologist here is that of a consultant. Applied social psychologists may work as consultants with communities, groups, organisations or individuals and, based on their competence and expertise, they may help the concerned organisation and so on deal with certain problems faced by them. For example, in an organisational set-up, when there is an increased problem of conflict, then the applied social psychologist, as a consultant, can provide a suitable intervention strategy.
5. **Advocate.** Here, the psychologist works in the area of politics in order to bring about or promote social change. For example, based on empirical findings, the psychologists may advocate a particular policy that needs to be implemented to effectively deal with malnourishment amongst children.

SOCIAL ISSUES AND PROBLEMS

'All human problems have social components, and the most serious problems are primarily social' (Fisher, 1982, p. 21). This quote sums up the significance of focusing on social problems and application of theories and principles of social psychology to these social problems. There are numerous social problems and issues that need the attention of the applied social psychology researchers. Some of the social problems will be discussed in this section, although first we will try to understand the concept of social problem.

As stated by Guerrero (2016, p. 7), 'A social problem is a social condition or pattern of behaviour that has negative consequences for individuals, our social world, or our physical world'. For example, child labour, substance abuse and so on that have a negative impact on an individual's life as well as his/her family and society at large.

Reinhardt (1952, p. 14) defined social problem as 'a situation confronting a group or a section of society which inflicts injurious consequences that can be handled only collectively'.

Social problems has both objective and subjective reality. It is not necessary for every individual to personally experience a social condition in order to consider that condition as a social problem. The existence of social problem can be confirmed with the help of data collection. This can be referred to as objective reality that denotes 'actual existence of a particular condition' (Leon-Guerrero, 2016, p. 7). Thus, a social problem related to increase in depression can be reflected based on the number of such cases provided by organisations such as the World Health Organisation (WHO). Subjective reality, on the other hand, denotes 'attachment of meaning to our reality' (Leon-Guerrero, 2016, p. 8). The idea of subjective reality is based on the social construction of reality that terms the world around us as a social creation. Thus, as per subjective reality, the conditions become social problems when human beings decide to categorise them as problems and needing intervention.

Social problems can also be described as deviations from normality and leading to undesirable consequences. They are also necessarily social in their origination and can have an impact on all the sections of the society.

Social problems could be of various types, they could be economic such as poverty and unemployment or cultural such as dowry system. It could also be biological or psychological such as HIV/AIDS or increase in relationship problems or addiction/substance abuse.

There are four main approaches, identified by Etzioni (1976), which could be used to study social problems.

1. **The consensus and structural–functional approach:** This approach focuses on how the needs of the people are met by the social structure of a society. Society is viewed as a system that has various parts that are interconnected and work in tandem so that a balance is maintained. Institutions, organisations and even governments function together to meet the needs of the people in the society. Thus, society, in this approach, is seen as an integrated system that needs to function towards meeting the needs of the people, and the individuals as well as groups need to come together to make this happen. However, it is also possible that not all segments of people get opportunities equally and not all the fundamental needs of the people are met. As we know, a lot of people do not have food to eat or even shelter to stay. Thus, as this deviation of the society from its own norms is recognised, a social issue is generated. The approach also assumes that social system will function adequately with expectation that some disparity in the extent to which the needs of the people are met, will exist. In addition, although social problems may create a threat to the society, they may also be functional for the society in some way. The model as such does not provide any measures to deal with social problems. However, as social problems, according this theory, are perceived as an outcome of breakdown in socialisation (that can be attributed to difficulties related to individuals, family and subculture), resocialisation and control are suggested as corrective measure for deviants so that they conform to the social norms. For example, juvenile delinquents are sent to corrective homes. The approach also suggests that a society goes through a process of continuous adjustment so that, most of the time, the needs of the majority of the people are met. Although the model agrees with slow change or a social reform that is gradual, a change that is rapid is not considered as it can be threatening to the social order.
2. **The conflict or alienation approach:** This approach emphasises on the existence of tension and contradictions between different classes of people in the society, the people who have the power and the people who do not have power (the haves and the have-nots). These contradictions and tensions are seen as fundamental and integral. Inequalities related to race, class, gender and so on are seen as prevalent in a society by this approach. The theory does not take consensus into consideration. In order to deal with such social problems, major social changes are required. The solution proposed by this theory involves major societal transformations so that the sharing of power and inequality between the groups is diminished or removed.
3. **Symbolic interactionism:** The focus of this approach is on difficulties that may arise in the communication between individuals and social approval. Social problems are seen as an outcome of these interactions. The theory also states that people, who are involved in behaviours that are deviant from the norms, learn these behaviours from others. Further, an individual's perception about social problems is also learned from others. These people, who deviate from the norms or

the rules, are stigmatised, labelled and could be controlled by appropriate institution. For example, persons who commit crime are labelled as criminals and put behind bars. The approach also states that social problems cannot be solved completely because of difficulties in interpersonal communication, lack of clarity in meanings and social norms will always exist.

4. **The neo-conservative approach:** This approach states that some of the persons are more fortunate (elite) and others are less fortunate due to the scarcity in resources. The approach also states that the masses are not subjected to any alienation or exploitation, but, the legitimate power is provided by them to the variety of elites in reciprocation for effective leadership in various spheres of life like, economics, politics, cultural and intellectual affairs (Fisher, 1982). There is a kind of social contract between the two sides and when this contact is failed by either of the party then social problem may arise. Thus, social problem could be as a result of issues related to authority or display of deviant behaviour and social change is not seen as necessary.

Some Prominent Social Problems

Some of the prominent social problems discussed in this section are poverty and unemployment, violence against women, domestic violence and health-related issues.

Poverty and Unemployment

These two social problems, to a greater extent, are related to each other and, therefore, will be discussed together. Henry Bernstein in 1992 stated certain dimensions of poverty, that are discussed as follows:

- Lack of means to maintain day-to-day livelihood
- Resources such as money, land and so on are inaccessible
- There are feelings related to frustrations and lack of security
- Owing to the lack of resources, social relations cannot be formed or developed

The causes of poverty can be categorised into individual causes, culture of poverty and social structure.

- **Individual:** The individual cause of poverty attributes the poverty to the failures and successes on the part of the individual. An individual may not be able to earn enough and thus may end up being poor. And this could be as a result of lack of efforts, laziness, inefficiency and so on or the part of the individual.
- **Culture of poverty:** The culture of poverty implies poverty as a way of life that has been passed down over generation. It further states that this culture of poverty leads to the maintenance of certain behaviours, lifestyles, values, norms and beliefs that serve as barrier to eradication of poverty and contributes to its perpetuation in a society.
- **Social structure:** Lastly, social structure mainly focuses on the social conditions such as lack of education, economy, unemployment and so on as reasons for poverty.

Further, mainly in the Indian context, rapidly increasing population, low agricultural productivity, resources being underutilised, lower economic developments, unemployment, rise in prices of goods and commodities and various social and political factors can be identified as resulting in or perpetuating poverty (Ahuja, 2014).

Poverty has a manifold impact on certain vulnerable groups such as elderly, women and people with disability. Caste can also be considered in this context, as Kozel and Parker (2001) found that a typical poor family was often found to be belonging to Schedule Tribe or Scheduled Caste.

Poverty can have grave consequences on the individuals and the society, as it leads to hunger and food insecurities—insufficient food to satisfy the hunger of all the family members, thus resulting in inability to live active and healthy life—and lack of shelter. But most importantly, it affects the health and well-being of the individuals. An imbalance, as well as inequalities, is also created in the society that ultimately has an impact on all sections of the society.

Unemployment can be described as the lack of remunerative work despite having the willingness as well as potentialities to work (Ahuja, 2014). Unemployment, thus, has three main elements: the individual's capability to work, willingness to work and the involvement in making efforts to find work.

Unemployment can be of various types, that are discussed as followings.

- **Seasonal unemployment:** Under this condition, the individuals are unemployed for a certain period of time in a year. For example, a person may be employed during a tourist season, and as this season ends, the person will be unemployed. Similarly, in agricultural sector as well, the person may remain unemployed for certain period of time.
- **Agricultural unemployment:** There are a number of factors that may lead to agricultural unemployment, including, smaller landholdings, that results in certain family members of working age group being not employed to cultivate the land and seasonal nature of work.
- **Cyclic unemployment:** This occurs due to fluctuations in business or trade, based on which the employees or workers are hired or fired.
- **Industrial unemployment:** With main focus on industries, this occurs because of the reasons such as increase in migration to urban areas, losses faced by industries, diminished growth of industries and so on.
- **Technological unemployment:** It is a result of technological upgradations due to which less human resource is required.
- **Educational unemployment:** It occurs when there is no fit between the educational system and the requirement of the society and the country.

The types of unemployment reflect the causes of unemployment as well. Though to the highlight, some of the causes, unemployment can be attributed to a number factors such as lack of capital and investment, technological development leading to use of machines and requirement of fewer human resource and even to the disparity between supply and demand (Ahuja, 2014). However, there are also various social factors such as increasing population and unwillingness to take up certain jobs that are perceived as degrading or below status. It can also be attributed to migration resulting in surplus availability of human resource, for example, in urban areas. Further, it can also be attributed to the misfit between the educational system and the realities of life that we discussed earlier.

It cannot be denied that India has both these social problems persisting in its society. In this direction, major interventions (in terms of policies and programmes) need to be developed to deal with these two stringent social problems.

Unemployment can have an impact on the individual as well as on the society. Individuals may develop stress, anxiety and be prone to other psychological problems, they may also be criticised by the family and significant others in their life, adding to their problems. The family of the particular individual may also suffer equally and be further deprived from fulfilment of basic needs, especially if the family is dependent on this individual. Conflicts could also increase in such families leading to disintegration of relationships and feeling of loneliness. Such individuals may also get involved into anti-social activities. Thus, unemployment can lead to disintegration of not only individuals but also their families and society as a whole.

Violence Against Women

Violence against women can range from sexual harassment, domestic violence, abuse, rape, human trafficking, female foeticide and infanticide, and female genital mutilation. As per the estimations of World Health Organization (2016), almost one in every three women all over the world are subjected to being beaten, raped or abused in their lifetime. In India as well, violence against women is increasing; in fact, there was an alarming rise in crimes against women between 2001 to 2011 (59 per cent) and the crime rated at the top was rape (John, Ahmad, & Schneider, 2013), although this can, in a way, be attributed to increase in reporting of the crime. Also, a survey carried out by National Family Health Survey (2005–2006) indicated that domestic abuse was justified by half of all the women who were surveyed.

Something that is justifiable is not seen as wrong and, therefore, is not reported. This can in a way be attributed to the patriarchal society that, in fact, may blame (indirectly) the women when their safety is violated. Patriarchal system can be explained as a social system in which men are seen as having more authority than women. In a patriarchal set-up, men are seen as having more value than females and, therefore, male child is given more preference over a female child. This inequality that is ingrained in the society does not only deprive the women's right to education, right to make a choice and so on, but also right to be born or to live. Further, women are also expected to produce a male child, which in turn may lead them to have multiple abortions when it is detected in prenatal diagnosis that the foetus is a female. This happens despite the Pre-natal Diagnostic Techniques Act, 1994 being in place. Rape is yet another violence against women that most often goes unreported mainly because the victim, and in many cases the family of the victim, experiences the fear of stigmatisation. Another fear factor involved here is the entire process of getting justice and constantly being under the radar of the media, thus being open in public may also refrain the victim and the family members from seeking justice. The onus of shame in the case of rape or sexual assault is also put on the victim rather than the perpetrator, which may further lead to subjugation and harassment of the victim.

Thus, with regard to this social problem, that is, violence against women, first of all the attitude and prejudice of the society in general needs to be targeted and suitable interventions and awareness programme also need to be created where equality between genders is promoted and measures are taken in the direction of stricter punishments for the perpetrators besides making society safe for women.

Domestic Violence

Domestic violence is a serious social issue, although is often perceived as more of an internal family affair. In a study of 90 societies, wife beating was present in 74 per cent of the societies (Levinson, 1989). In India, domestic violence, due to its increase prevalence and magnitude, is seen as a public health issue (Babu & Kar, 2009) but has also been referred to as 'crime of silence' (Pillai, 2001) because of low rates of such cases being reported or coming into open.

In order to provide protection to women from domestic violence, the Protection of Women from Domestic Violence Act, 2005, was enacted by the Parliament of India. The Section 3 of this Act provides the definition of domestic violence as (quoted from the Act):

> Any act, omission or commission or conduct of the respondent shall constitute domestic violence in case it (a) Harms or injures or endangers the health, safety, life, limb or well-being, whether mental or physical, of the aggrieved person or tends to do so and includes causing physical abuse, sexual abuse, verbal and emotional abuse and economic abuse; or (b) Harasses, harms, injures or endangers the aggrieved person with a view to coerce her or any other person related to her to meet any unlawful demand for any dowry or other property or valuable security; or (c) Has the effect of threatening the aggrieved person or any person related to her by any conduct mentioned in clause (a) or clause (b); or (d) Otherwise injures or causes harm, whether physical or mental, to the aggrieved person.

Further, in Explanation I of this section, physical, sexual, verbal and emotional abuse besides economic abuse have also been discussed.

It is to be mentioned here that although it may seem that domestic violence is mainly related to wife battering or violence by a male on the female in the family. It is not so, as is also clear from the definition given above. There could be domestic violence against the elderly, children or even men in the family. Women in India are exposed to domestic violence because of high poverty and illiteracy besides the lack of awareness and knowledge (Haq, 2013). Dowry-related violence and harassment is yet another violence that women are subjected to in this context. Dowry system still perpetuates in India despite the Dowry Prohibition Act (Ghadially, 2007).

Domestic violence can have grave effects on the victims and they could develop both physical and psychological problems. Some of the physical problems faced by the victims of domestic violence range from injuries such as cuts and bruises, loss of vision or hearing to developing hypertension, migraine and permanent disfigurement (Abbott & Williamson, 1999; Coker et al., 2009; McCaw et al., 2007). With regard to mental health, the victims could suffer from anxiety, post-traumatic stress disorder, sleep-related issues, derailment of social functioning and may also be prone to attempting and committing suicide (Abbot & Williamson, 1999; Gerlock, 1999; Howard, Trevillion & Agnew-Davies, 2010; McCaw et al., 2007). Domestic violence also has a long-term impact on the victims, including children who are subjected to or exposed to it.

It is obvious that domestic violence can have a negative impact on the victim and various laws, counselling facilities and help are available for these victims. However, what is important is to perceive domestic violence as a social issue and accordingly develop intervention strategies to deal with them. Interventions are not only required to help the victims but also to create a general awareness about the negative effects of domestic violence and need for the members of society to step up and stop such a violence when they witness it. It is also required to create and spread awareness about the facilities and help already available.

Health-related Issues

A healthy individual is not only be able to be functional and achieve his/her potentialities to the fullest but will also be in a position to support his/her family and contribute to the society. Nevertheless, ensuring health for all is not easy, and there could be a number of obstacles, starting from health-related hazards and diseases to the attitude of the people towards prevention strategies and treatment. There are a number of health-related issues that have a negative impact on the well-being of the individuals and interfere with the development of the society. These problems could be related to communicable and non-communicable diseases, such as increasing cases of HIV/AIDS, malnourishment, obesity, diabetes, malaria, tuberculosis, cancer, as well as issues related to mental illness such as increase in depression and suicide rates, besides stress and substance abuse, to name a few. Most of the problems, such as respiratory problems, are also related to various environmental factors such as pollution, which is also a major problem in itself. Inadequate garbage disposal and treatments could also add to the problem as the water gets affected, leading to waterborne diseases. When we discuss about health-related issues, it also covers issues related to hygiene and availability of adequate facilities in this regard. Thus, there are many factors significant in the context of health that can have impact on the functioning of the individual, which in turn will have repercussions for the society. The issues also become more serious due to the lack of adequate infrastructure and facilities for large number of people. Further, there is also stigmatisation attached with certain health-related issues such as HIV/AIDS and mental illnesses that can hamper the recovery process of the persons suffering from these.

It is, thus, important that besides being a medical, health is also seen as a social factor. While focusing on health as a social factor, the focus should also be on epidemiology of the illness. Epidemiology can be described as a study of patterns reflected in the frequency as well as distribution of sickness, injury and even death, and the social factors that determine the pattern (Guerrero, 2016). Epidemiology constitutes three main measures related to health status that are fertility (childbearing level), mortality (deaths in the population) and morbidity (illnesses/diseases). Epidemiology will help not only in obtaining the statistical information related to various health-related issues but also in development of health-related interventions.

While focusing on health-related issues, the factors that contribute to health inequalities such as gender and education also need to be considered. The accessibility of medical care should also be highlighted besides sanitation and hygiene, and the attitudes displayed by people.

World Health Organization (1986) stated that health can be seen as a resource that needs to be cultivated and preserved over period of time, and that can be done through the conduct of the individuals in everyday life. Thus, individuals should not only be encouraged to adopt a healthy lifestyle and focus on health on a day-to-day basis.

One reason why social psychologists study social behaviour is in order to understand and develop solutions for social problems.

SOCIAL CHANGE

Social change can be related to a change in society in order to ensure better education, employment for youth, better health care facilities, prevention of violence against women, dealing with corruption and ensuring overall development of the society. As is said, 'Change is constant' and this is one ultimate truth. The weather changes, so do people and society. Thus, there are political, economic, environmental, and climatic changes taking place all the time.

Although change is constant, bringing about social change is not an easy task. A social evil such as 'Sati' was eradicated over a period of time as a result of dedicated contributions of many and at the same time due to strict legal consequences. Thus, dealing with social problems and bringing about a social change requires interventions at many levels and by different means.

Changes, modifications and variation in political, economic and social systems can be termed as social change. Social change involves a need to change social norms. It is a process through which transformation takes place in a society.

Fisher (1982, p. 448) defined social change as 'modification or alteration in the social structure of a society- that is, in the basic arrangements of living as expressed in the society's shared values, norms, roles and so on'.

Macionis (1997) described four main characteristics of social change. The first is that social change will take place everywhere, but the rate with which these changes take place is slow. The second characteristic states that social change, most of the time, is unplanned; however, in certain cases, it can also be planned or intentional. For example, shift in the nature of families in India, from joint to nuclear, was not intentional. On the other hand, introduction of a new technology is planned. The third characteristic of social change is that it can be controversial. When widow remarriage was promoted by the likes of Raja Ram Mohan Roy, it was not easily accepted and met with cynicism and opposition. Lastly, certain changes are more relevant than others. For example, right to information (RTI) has definitely been more significant to the overall development of society compared to say a 'roti making machine'.

Social change can also be categorised in different types or categories:

1. **Process:** A change that is definite and continuous can be termed as process.
2. **Evolution:** It can be described as a process with a sense of direction. Further, it can also be explained in terms of biological development in an organism. In a social set-up, evolution denotes gradual changes in culture, social norms, technology and so on.
3. **Progress:** Progress is a change that has direction as well but it is goal oriented.
4. **Revolution:** This can be described as a change that is at much broader level. Revolution leads to change in major aspects of a society. It can be change in political or social structures.

Further, social change can also be complete or partial.

Social change was also categorised by Katz (Fisher, 1982) into the following types:

1. **Individual change:** As the name suggests this change is regarding the change in personal attributes of an individual and is independent of the social set-up in which the individual exists. This could be a change because of counselling or psychotherapeutic intervention. This may not serve as a source of wider social change at societal level. This can be brought about, for example, by making appeals or creating awareness amongst people to change their lifestyle.
2. **Incremental social change:** In this type of social change, there is alteration of the social structure but the basic arrangements, whether political, social or economic, are not dismantled. The existing system may be modified or there may be shift in a complete new direction. To bring about this kind of change, new laws may be introduced or existing laws may be modified.
3. **Radical social change:** In this type of social change, there is modification of social structure as well as reorganisation of political and economic systems. Thus, certain social structures may be dismantled in the process and new forms may take place of the old ones.
4. **Cultural change:** This denotes alterations in the attitude, values and actions of the whole society. This may not require any modifications in the social structure. Although cultural change may occur along with radical social change or incremental social change.

Various factors are responsible for social change. For instance, ecological factors can influence social change. Natural disasters can lead to migration, which in turn could bring about social change. Factors such as values, beliefs and principles can also lead to social change, besides economic and political factors. Social change is also influenced by scientific and technological developments.

The overall process of social change can also lead to eruptions of social problems. For those who have watched (if not watched, it is worth watching) the movie, *God Must be Crazy*, it shows how conflicts arise amongst a peacefully living small tribal community when they find an empty cold drink bottle. The bottle falls from an airplane flying above and is seen by the tribals as sent by Gods. Individuals in the community find creative ways of using the bottle for crushing, smoothening things, playing and so on, and each of them want to possess it for themselves. This gives rise to conflicts and fights among the members of the community. One of them ultimately decides to take the long journey to return the bottle back to the Gods. This shows how social change leads to social problems. Further, the relationship between social change and social problem is reciprocal, as social problems also call for social change.

In Indian context, the issues with regard to social problems have been in focus since early 19th century. The influence of British—their political and economic ideals as well as the Christian ideals—were one of the main factors that called for this change (Kuppuswamy, 1973).

Over the years, there have been major changes in the family structure in India. There has been a shift from joint family system to nuclear families. To some extent, caste system has also been under the radar of social change. This can be attributed to education and development in communications, policies and interventions. Social stratification has also changed. In India, the development in technology and transportation has led to increased mobility and migration within as well as outside India. There has also been mobility across professions. Changes have also taken place in the institution of marriage.

Social change in India can also be aptly described with the help of Sanskritisation, Westernisation and Modernisation as discussed here.

- **Sanskritisation:** The term sanskritisation was first used by M. N. Srinivas and was described as a deliberate adoption of practices that are social and religious. For example, shifting from being a non-vegetarian to vegetarian, chanting mantras and other such practices, mainly followed by Brahmins, that may lead to the upgradation of social status mainly in terms of caste. M. N. Srinivas (1952) described sanskritisation as a process that includes cultural mobility within the context of traditional social structure of India. It is 'the process by which a low caste or tribal or other group changes its customs, rituals, ideology and way of life in the direction of a high and frequently "twice born" caste' (Srinivas, 1966). Although the mobility in this context is an outcome of positional change and not structural change, the contemporary social change in India cannot be understood using this term.
- **Westernisation:** This is another concept that needs to be focused on while discussing social change in Indian context. Westernisation necessarily means that the Western ideas, customs and practices are adopted. Americanisation can be termed as a form of Westernisation. During British rule, Westernisation had a significant influence on Indians. As Indians were exposed to English literature, history and political institutions, some realisation occurred amongst Indians with regard to the redundancy of certain practices and customs followed by them (Kuppuswamy, 1973). Westernisation had a significant influence on the dressing style and eating habits as well as on certain values such as secularism, humanitarianism and so on. Westernisation, thus, paved the way for significant social change in India, but the influence was also restricted to the affluent class in India and the masses overall were out of its purview (Eisenstadt, 1966).
- **Modernisation:** Modernisation denotes major social changes that are quantitative and qualitative in nature. It can be described as a mass process that leads to change in attitude, values, motivations and behaviours of people. This change is also fundamental, deep-rooted and widespread. Further, such a change also brings about better living conditions for the people.

Besides encompassing changes that are social, economic and political, modernisation also brings about changes within the individual, that is, his/her attitudes, values and so on. Such internal changes are especially relevant because as stated by Inkeles and Smith (1974), 'Nation building and institution building are only empty exercises unless the attitudes and capacities of the people keep pace with other forms of development'. For example, a hospital is being built after huge investment and with the best technology in an area, but if the locals there believe that in sickness they need to consult the 'baba' who sits at the outskirts of their village, then the whole investment and the world-class technology would be waste. Thus, technological developments, and attitudes and beliefs of people go hand in hand, and both need to be taken care of to ensure modernisation. However, attitudes that are extreme and certain traditions could interfere with the modernisation process.

- **Modernity:** Modernity in simple terms can be defined as contemporary or current. Ray (1968) described modernity as 'a particular outlook or perspective of mind and a system of particular ideas and values that have gradually evolved in the course of social development'. In social science, the term 'modernity' is often used to describe qualities that are within an individual, such as values, attitudes, beliefs, besides internal locus of control, rationality of an individual, openness to novel experiences, gender equality and work ethics. Even respect towards variations in opinions are included in the concept of modernity (Inkeles & Smith, 1974; Loomis & Loomis, 1969; Mishra, 1962; Myrdal, 1968; Singh, 1984; Weber, 1958a, b).

Modernity can be analysed from two dimensions, societal dimensions and individualistic dimension. Societal dimension relates to changes that occur at societal level, for example, eradication of 'Sati' system. With regard to individualistic dimension, the focus is on the individual and his/her attitudes, valued, beliefs and behaviour, that are also necessary for mobility of an individual towards modernity.

Modernity can also be termed as a concept that is multidimensional because it involves development of various behavioural systems with unique aspects such as empathy, mobility, increased participation, achievement orientation, rational thinking and so on (Dubey, 1967).

Factors that contribute to modernity are education, media, communication, urbanisation and industrialisation. Education, especially, is an important determinant of modernity. A survey that was carried out by Inkles and Smith (1974) in six developing countries, including India, indicated a significant relationship between modernity and education.

Planned Change

Going back to the concept of change, it can be unplanned or planned. An unplanned change can be termed as operating under law of non-intervention (Fisher, 1982). Unplanned change denotes such changes that take place gradually and occur naturally. Planned changes can be defined as conscious or deliberate attempts to promote certain changes in the society (Kuppuswamy, 1973). The policies and schemes, the work carried out by non-governmental organisations and governmental organisations, awareness and intervention strategies are all planned attempts to promote change. According to Kuppuswamy (1973), in planned social change, certain specific social norms are to be set up and further how these social norms can be implemented in the society, also need to be described. These two are most crucial to facilitate any social change. Further, the goals of social change are also to be clearly stated. In India, for example, planned social change is crucial in upliftment of the downtrodden, elimination of discrimination and equal opportunity of education and employment to all. Further, India is diverse in terms of its culture, language, religion, values, beliefs and so on. Thus, in order to bring about social change, an understanding about the diverse norms prevalent in the society is required. And once this is done, the social norms that will replace the prevalent norms can be developed.

Attitude of the people is also to be taken into consideration in this regard. Participation of people in the society is of extreme relevance throughout the process of social change, especially at the level of diagnosis of the problem. Further, overall participation of people in bringing about change is also important. Discrimination and violence can also be drastically reduced if the people in the community are involved. Another relevant aspect in this regard is understanding the opposing viewpoints and empathising with people who are against social change. People who are against a construction of a highway through their locality may be doing so because a lot of families, and probably cultivation, is getting affected and the losses as a result of this development are greater compared to benefits, at least for the people in this area. This is one reason why people also protest against building of dams in their areas, as though various problems related to water and electricity may be sorted, large number of people may get be displaced. Thus, it is also important to understand the viewpoint of the people who are against the social change.

The following strategies could be employed in order to bring about a social change:

1. **The empirical rational strategy.** This strategy perceives people in society as rational beings who would change their actions for their own benefit when information regarding how change will affect them positively is provided. Thus, according to this strategy, it would be sufficient for the people to be provided with information about how wearing a helmet while riding a two-wheeler is essential to avoid head injury if any accident happens. Thus, the change agent has to work on information and knowledge that is convincing enough to bring about change. We come across awareness programme daily on radio, televisions and through other mediums but as we know, such programmes do not necessarily bring about change, as, though individuals can be considered rational beings, they are also irrational. Thus, an individual and cultural change can be brought about with the help of this strategy, but beyond that it will not play a very important role.
2. **The normative re-educative strategy:** This strategy has two main assumptions. One is that individuals are rational being and social norms have a significant influence on the actions and behaviours of the individual. Thus, change in behaviours is possible only when there is an orientation in the direction of new norms. Also, to bring about this change in orientation, attitudes, values as well as social relationships need to be change besides providing information and knowledge that promotes change. This strategy perceives individual as being in constant touch with their social situation, which plays a role in determining their behaviour. Thus, there has to be changes in the expectations and sanctions related to the norms to usher the change. The change agent thus has to work in collaboration with the target. Diagnosis is also to be carried out, where the focus is on the problem as well as need for change, besides the attitude, values and norms of the target. Action research is an example of this strategy.
3. **The power-coercive strategy.** This strategy is based on assumption that actions and behaviours of individuals can be changed only when they are forced to do so. The individuals with more power will thus control the individuals who possess less power. There is a flow of political, economic as well as moral power in one direction with a goal to bring about change. The change is especially well accepted and felt less, especially when it comes from a legitimate power. The change agents here have to use unique and innovative ways in which they could use power to bring about change.

Comparing the three strategies, in, empirical–rational strategy, knowledge is used as power and freedom to choose is uphold, and with regard to normative re-educative strategy, the influence that is reciprocal in nature is used as power and emphasis is on participative democracy. In the power-coercive strategy, power is used to force change. Thus, based on the situational needs and nature of the social problem, suitable strategy can be utilised by the change agent.

Resistance to Change

Change is often met with a great deal of resistance from individuals in society. For example, there were people who opposed education for women or widow remarriage, equality to all and so on. In fact, the proponents of social change always meet with opposition and have to struggle their way through the rigidity of the society and its individuals. Change creates challenges and, thus, meets with resistance.

Such a resistance can be as a result of personality factors or due to social factors (Kuppuswamy, 1973). Thus, there are two dimensions to resistance to social change: one that is related to an individual and the other related to society.

Personality or Individual Factors

One of the main factor here is socialisation. Socialisation (as discussed earlier) is a process through which the individuals learn about social norms. It is a way in which parents and significant others shape and influence the behaviours of individuals. Social change will always challenge socialisation. The values and beliefs incorporated in us are challenged and, thus, we resist the change. For example, certain girls/women are socialised not to speak about menstruation and related issues. As a result, these girls/women will refrain from discussing about such issues even if they are causing severe health problems.

Every social change be subjected to resistance, mainly due to socialisation. A child from a certain caste may not be allowed to eat or even sit together with other students because of the learned beliefs that are a result of socialisation. There is also the concept of re-socialisation that can be helpful in this regard where relearning of beliefs and attitudes takes place.

Further, social change also challenges the attitudes and behaviours that individuals are habitual with. It is a habitual attitude, in which, girls are made to drop out from school and learn household work so that they can be prepared for marriage. When such a habitual attitude is challenged and when parents and families are encouraged to educate their daughters, empower them and make them independent, there is resistance. This was very interestingly depicted in a Hindi movie, *Swadesh*, where the lead character, Mohan, tries his best to convince parents/families to send their daughters to school. In fact, he is criticised in the movie for being with a person from certain caste and even eating food cooked by him. Such a resistance is a result of habitual attitude, which again operates as a result of socialisation process that these individuals have gone through.

Individuals may also feel insecure about a social change. Any change will bring with it some amount of uncertainty and, thus, people will resist it. Let us take an example from an industrial set-up. A merger or an acquisition is often seen with suspicion by the employees, who will also feel insecure. This in turn will lead to resistance to such a change. In a social set-up, changes in technology, for example, use of computers or even raising a communication tower, can meet with resistance. Construction of roads, especially highways, can also meet with resistance. Social change challenges our comfort and tries to bring us beyond our comfort zone and pushes us into something that is unfamiliar. Thus, social change is looked upon with apprehension, at least initially, though as individuals become more aware of its benefits, they may gradually accept it.

It is, thus, important that these factors are taken into consideration while initiating a change or facilitating a social change.

Social Factors

Social factors can also interfere with social change and thus need to be focused. One of the prominent social factors that can interfere with social change is social norms. Social norms are rules that are prevalent in any society, and the individuals in the society are expected to follow them. For example, a social norm may permit a couple to cohabit only after being married. Thus, a live-in couple may not be easily accepted by the society as they are in way breaking the norm. Further, individuals in society readily follow these norms, as they want to conform to others and feel accepted by others in the society. Conformity and social norms are necessary to maintain harmony in the society and help individuals live together with one another and function effectively. As traffic rules are significant for the smooth flow of the traffic, social norms are significant for smooth functioning of individuals.

Another factor that leads to resistance in society is a result of attempts to protect the interests and privileges of few who are insecure that social change will result in them losing their status, privileges and benefits. Certain policies may be met with resistance because they are going to deprive a few privileged individuals in the society. Such individuals see the social change as a threat.

Social change challenges some core values of a society and, thus, they meet with resistance. Some technological developments are accepted because they do not affect the core values, whereas others are not because they interfere with the core values.

INTERVENTION

As stated by Schneider et al. (2012, p. 11), 'at the very heart of applied social psychology is a regard for addressing social problems'. Keeping this in mind, the next section of this chapter discusses about intervention and how they can be designed and implemented to deal with various issues and problems.

As discussed earlier, intervention is central to applied social psychology. Various researches in this regard have been carried out that are based on intervention. Music therapy, for example, can be used as an intervention with children to promote cognitive development. Sherif and his colleagues carried out an intervention-based study in 1966 (also refer to the experiment carried out by Sherif discussed in Chapter 2). In this study, an intervention strategy was developed to enhance the relationship amongst conflicting groups of boys. The intervention was developed by Sherif, based on the existing studies and review of literature. The main assumption behind the intervention was that the relationship amongst the conflicting groups could be improved if they cooperate with each other to achieve a superordinate goal. Superordinate goals can be described as goals that are significant and appealing to both the groups and can be achieved only when both the groups cooperate with each other. When a group of conflicting boys were presented with such superordinate goals, over the period of time, there was reduction in the conflict and the relationship between the boys improved. Thus, the intervention based on superordinate goals led to reduction in conflict and betterment of relationship.

Lodzinsky, Motomura and Schneider (2012, p. 62) defined intervention as 'a strategy (or procedure) that is intended to influence the behaviour of people for the purpose of improving their functioning with respect to some social or practical problem'. Interventions could be directed towards bringing behaviour change, attitude change or increase awareness amongst the people. National AIDS Control Organization, for example, funds projects that are aimed at creating awareness about HIV/AIDS and promoting healthy behaviour amongst migrants and high-risk groups. Similarly, a project named 'Project Sunrise' was launched (in 2016) by the Union Minister of Health and Family Welfare, J. P. Nadda. The project is of 5-year duration and is mainly directed towards the prevention of AIDS, especially among people injecting drugs in the North-eastern states.

Interventions can also be carried out at different levels, including individuals, group, organisation and community. Based on the nature of the problem/issue and the group towards which the intervention is targeted, the level can be selected.

Types of Intervention

There are various types of intervention; these are discussed in detail here.

1. **Personal interventions:** These are the interventions that are used in one's day-to-day lives. Here, the knowledge of social psychology is used in order to enhance certain circumstances or situations. Sales persons at the counter, for example, use of effective verbal and non-verbal communications to increase the sales.
2. **Programmatic interventions:** Programmes can be defined as 'an organised collection of activities designed to reach certain objectives' (Royse et al., 2006). Such programmes are used as intervention to deal with certain social or practical problems and issues. For example, an intervention can be used with students to enhance their learning skills or with employees to reduce burnout experienced by them or in a residential society to promote garbage management or rainwater harvesting.
3. **Trial interventions:** This can be categorised as the third type of intervention and, as the name suggests, these are on trial basis. Trial interventions are also known as programme efficacy studies and are aimed at finding out whether an intervention leads to the intended positive outcomes or not. For example, when an intervention is developed to promote garbage management amongst residents of a particular residential society, then it will be initially on the trial basis to find out its efficacy and, if required, based on the results of the trial, modifications and changes can be made in the intervention. Trial intervention can be of two types. The first type is when an intervention strategy has been developed by a researcher mainly to test the efficacy of the intervention programme. For example, an intervention is developed by a researcher to promote health-related awareness amongst migrants and then a research study is carried out to test the efficacy of this intervention. The second type of trial intervention is when an intervention is introduced by an organisation on pilot basis to study its efficacy and, if found effective, it can be introduced on a more permanent basis. For example, an organisation can introduce regular Yoga for its employees to deal with stress and other related problems and issues. This can initially be done on pilot basis and, if this pilot programme is successful, then it can be implemented for all the employees.

Intervention Mapping

Intervention mapping can be described as a process that involves planning based on systematic utilisation of evidence for the purpose of scientific research and theories. It mainly involves mapping the steps right from identification of the problem to implementation and evaluation of an intervention. The process of planning is of extreme importance as the success of the whole intervention is dependent on it.

This process of planning is repetitive in nature rather than linear, where each step is related to the previous step and if there is an error at any step, the development and implementation of the intervention will suffer and desirable outcomes will not be attained (Bartholomew et al., 2011). Intervention mapping also helps deal with the type III error. According to Green (2000), type III is 'failing to find intervention effectiveness because the program is poorly designed or implemented' (cited in Bartholomew et. al., 2011, p. 8).

There are four perspectives to intervention planning that are described as follows:

1. The participation perspective, that is, mainly related to the population that the intervention is intended for. It is also very healthy to seek active participation of the participants in the process of intervention design and development. This will help empower the participants and develop positive attitude towards intervention amongst the participants.
2. The second perspective has to do with the eclectic utilisation of the theories. This means that the social and practical problems should be approached with the help of multiple theories.
3. The systems perspective that denotes that interventions are mainly perceived as events that are taking place in a system, thus, there could be numerous factors that have an influence, both positive and negative, on the intervention and its outcome.
4. The last perspective is ecological perspective. This perspective gives relevance to the social as well as physical environmental conditions that could have an influence on human behaviour. These conditions are to be identified as they can have a far stronger impact on the human behaviour.

The broad steps involved in intervention mapping are discussed under the next section on design and implementation of intervention.

Design and Implementation of Intervention

As we know about what intervention is and what its types are, we now move on to how the interventions are designed and implemented.

We will discuss in detail the four main steps in the design and implementation of intervention (Oskamp & Schultz, 1998).

1. **Problem identification:** For an intervention to be designed and implemented, one must first be aware about what the problem is. Once the problem is identified, a suitable intervention can be designed. The problem also needs to be assessed in terms of its severity. One way in which more information about the problem can be gathered is by interacting with the individuals who are affected by that problem, called stakeholders. For example, with the increased level of pollution in Delhi, the people of Delhi are the stakeholders and more information about this problem, such as its impact on health and so on, can be derived from the people of Delhi. The administrators and individuals who will be involved in implementing the programme, sponsors and others who would be closely related with the delivery programme can also be termed as stakeholders. Thus, from the Chief Minister of Delhi to various departments and their employees that would be involved in the process of implementation of the programme to reduce pollution can be considered as stakeholders. This implies that there are a number of stakeholders, and an agreement between them is necessary regarding how the programme is being implemented. For example, for odd–even scheme for vehicles in Delhi, all the stakeholders,

citizens of Delhi, the government as well as the traffic police need to agree and work towards the implementation of the programme.

In order to gain more information about the problem, so as to develop a suitable intervention programme, needs assessment can also be carried out. In needs assessment, as the name suggests, the need for the programme is measured. Thus, before an intervention strategy is developed for adolescents to increase their awareness about health-related issues, first we need to assess their awareness and find out whether an intervention is required. The area in which the intervention is required is then to be identified, whether physical health, mental health or reproductive health and so on. Needs assessment can be informal or formal. In a classroom set-up, a teacher might feel a need for intervention to enhance the mathematical skills of the students. In this case, the teacher may not actually involve in a systematic study or data collection. This informal needs assessment is based on the observation and experience of the teacher in that classroom. A formal needs assessment, on the other hand, involves systematic and scientific research in which data is collected and analysed in order to assess the need. In an organisational set-up, the industrial psychologist may administer a standardised tool on stress to gather more information about stress experienced the employees and then an intervention strategy can be developed based on the results of the test. In formal assessment, various quantitative and qualitative methods of data collection can be used.

2. **Coming up with a solution:** Based on the process of identifying the problem and need assessment, a solution can be generated. But, while doing so, the factors that cause the problem, both the precipitating factors and the perpetuating factors, need to be identified. Precipitating factors are the factors that give rise to the problem and the perpetuating factors are the ones that contribute to the sustenance of the problem and interfere with the process of dealing or solving the problem. Both these factors are to be considered when coming up with a solution. If only precipitating factors are kept in mind then the solution derived will not be effective, and the perpetuating factors will not allow the problem to subside. On the other hand, if the focus is only on the perpetuating factors then one might have not attacked the problem on its roots. For example, in an industrial set-up, the root cause of low job satisfaction could be unattractive pay package (precipitating factor), but there could also be certain perpetuating factors such as lack of adequate communication between managers and employees, lack of availability of safety devices and so on. So, if this problem of low job satisfaction needs to be dealt with, then both the precipitating and perpetuating factors need to be considered.

   Once this is done, before developing an intervention strategy afresh, one needs to look for existing intervention strategies or solutions that could be used. For example, if in another industry, an intervention strategy for similar problem and causes was used successfully to deal with low job satisfaction, then the same can also be implemented in this industry. However, if there is no such intervention, or the existing intervention does not seem to be suitable (for varied reason) in the present context, then a new solution can be derived.

   The solution is then presented in the form of intervention hypotheses that are tentative statements about the intervention. For example, health-related educational intervention will lead to increased health-related awareness amongst the migrants or the short training programme based on mathematical skills will lead to enhancement of mathematical skills of the students or practicing the relaxation technique will lead to reduction in stress of the employees.

3. **Goal setting and designing the intervention:** Once we have identified the problem and derived the solution, the goals of the intervention are to be chalked out and the intervention needs to be

designed. Based on the goals (long term) and objectives (short term) of the intervention, the specific activities related to the programme need to be developed. Objectives will necessarily be based on the broader goals. For example, if the broader goal of an intervention is to help the employees deal with their stress, then one of the objectives will be helping them identify the sources of stress in their lives. Once the goals and objectives are in place, then the programme activities are developed. Each programme activity that is developed, needs to be in sync with an objective and that objective also needs to be identified. For example, carrying out an assessment (with the help of interview or standardised test) will help employees understand the sources of stress in their lives. Therefore, this activity could help achieve the objective of making the employee aware about the sources of their stress.

In this context, we also need to discuss about programme logic model that has been described by Wholey (1983) as 'an explanation or a blueprint of how the program activities lead to the attainment of the programme objectives and, in turn, how the objectives logically and operationally contribute to the eventual achievement of the programme goals' (cited in Lodzinsky et al., 2012). For example, there needs to be some theoretical logic or rationale that states that practicing relaxation techniques could lead to decrease in stress experienced by the employees. The programme logic model is mainly based on a theoretical rationale and is empirical in nature and, thus, the likelihood of its success is high. Some of the examples of programme activities leading to achievement of objectives and then goals are given in Table 13.2.

Thus the programme activities lead to achievement of the objectives and the achievement of objectives will lead to attainment of the goals.

4. **Implementation:** The last step has to do with implementation of intervention. In the previous step, the intervention was designed and goals were also set, thus, the programme is now ready to be implemented to the concerned individuals, community, organisation and so on. There are a number of aspects involved in this that are related to the staff required, what should be the educational qualification of this staff, whether the staff will require any training, space, budget and so on, that mainly depends on the size, structure and other details of the intervention. An intervention for a smaller group may not require many people or that many facilities, but an intervention that is, say, at a national level, will require a number of facilities and people with varied educational qualifications, competence and expertise. Further, the intervention needs to be implemented in such a way that its efficacy can be measured and evaluated.

Table 13.2 ***Table Showing the Examples***

Programme Activities	Objectives	Goals
Training programme on how to use safety devices	Increased use of safety devices	Decrease in industrial accidents
Programme on study habits of students	Improve study habits	Better performance in examination
Pre-marital counselling for couples	Better understanding of each other and clarity in each other's expectations	Increased marital satisfaction

EVALUATION

As the process from identifying the problem to the actual implementation of the intervention is important, so is the evaluation of intervention from time to time. Evaluation can be termed as the fifth step in the process of developing an intervention, and due to its significance, it has been discussed in a separate section.

Any type of intervention needs to be evaluated as most often interventions are based on theories that need to be tested based on the intervention hypothesis. Whether an intervention is adequate or not, or any modifications or changes are to be made, can be assessed only when the intervention is evaluated. This also adds a scientific value to the intervention as when it is tested with the help of suitable research designs and found to be adequate and effective, it can be further applied, and based on the feedback of the evaluation, theories can also be developed.

Yet another reason why the evaluation of interventions are to be carried has to do with ethics. Persons involved in the implementation of a programme should be ethical. The programmes are often targeted towards the betterment of an individual or a society as a whole or towards dealing with certain social problems. These programmes can greatly affect the lives of the persons they are intended for. For example, while implementing a programme for awareness related to HIV/AIDS, the persons implementing it need to be sensitive enough and they need to adhere to the ethical issues of beneficence and non-maleficence. In case, during HIV testing, which could be a part of the programme, if an individual has been diagnosed as positive, then the matter needs to be handled with care and in a confidential manner. Further, if the programme does not lead to any benefits to the participants, the same is redundant and needs to modified or changed or even discontinued (this is an ethical responsibility on the part of the person who implements the programme). And the programmes that have been found to be effective can also be further enhanced for more benefit.

Any intervention also involves financial investment, and any investment is always accompanied by accountability. If a programme, for example, is implemented at a very large level and a large amount has been invested in it, it is expected that the programme will be evaluated in order to know its effectiveness. Financial resources can often be scarce while dealing with the number of social and practical problems, and a particular programme is often sponsored based on its significance, need and higher possibility of positive outcome. In case, after evaluation, if it is found that a particular programme is not effective as was expected, then changes or modifications can be carried out in it or it can be discontinued so that the financial resources can be utilised somewhere else in a more optimal way. It is also possible that, though a programme has been found to be effective after evaluation, it is too costly to be continued. In such a case as well, a suitable decision needs to be taken such as whether the programme should be continued or not. Thus, all programmes carried out at a large level are to be conducted in a systematic manner by following the process right from problem identification. Yet another aspect on the basis of which a programme is evaluated is the financial accountability. Thus, any programme not only during its design and implementation but also during its evaluation needs to be assessed based on its cost and benefit ratio. If the benefit of the programme is high but the cost is low, this would be an ideal situation and the programme can be implemented or continued. If both the benefit and cost are low, such programmes could be modified or discontinued during the design and implementation stage or during the evaluation stage when the feedback of such a ratio is obtained. If the cost is high but benefit is low, again the programme can be modified or discontinued, and if the benefit is high but cost is also high, based on the nature of the problem, urgency and the overall situation, decisions can be taken about ways to bring about the balance in the ratio. In certain cases, it is possible that certain programmes with high benefit but high cost are continued due to urgency and the need of the hour.

There are four main reasons why programs or interventions could be inadequate or ineffective. These are discussed here in detail.

1. **The inadequacy of the theory or the rationale on which the programme is based:** As discussed earlier, most often the programme is developed based on a theory. If this theory is not adequate then the programme will not be effective. For example, if a theory that technique A helps reduce stress is not sound or is not based on empirical research, then the programme developed based on this rationale that technique A will lead to reduction in stress will be ineffective.
2. **Inadequate implementation:** The second aspect that may lead to the failure of the programme or intervention is that it has not been adequately implemented. In this case, it is possible that the intervention is based on an adequate theory or rationale but because of number of issues related to its implementation, the programme failed to make a positive impact. For example, while implementing a programme to enhance communication skills amongst the employees in an organisation, if the trainer did not have adequate expertise on the topic, and it is possible that the outcome of enhanced communication skills will not be achieved. In this case, the theory behind the programme; that training programme based on communication skill will help improve communication skill of the employees holds true, but its actual implementation has gone wrong.
3. **Reaction of the people/individuals for whom the programme is intended:** It is also possible that if the people for whom the programme has been designed feel threatened with it or have a negative attitude towards the programme, then the programme will be rendered ineffective. Thus, it is also important to prepare the people or clarify any misconceptions in their mind about the programme before or during the implementation of the programme.
4. **Issues and problems due to cultural incompatibility:** It is also possible that a programme that is based on a strong theory or rational and is suitably implemented, fails due to its incompatibility with the culture of the people it is intended for. Thus, during the design and implementation, the cultural background of the persons for whom it is implemented needs to be taken into consideration. For example, while creating awareness about reproductive health among women, pamphlets that are distributed should be in the local language rather than just English or Hindi, as it is possible that in certain regions in India English or Hindi may not be widely spoken. There could also be certain cultural beliefs that could interfere with the implementation of the programme, that need to be identified and dealt with sensitively.

Types of Evaluation

The types of evaluation that can be carried out are discussed here in detail.

1. **Process evaluation:** Process evaluation is also referred to as formative evaluation. This kind of evaluation mainly evaluates whether the programme has reached its target persons or not and also, whether the programme activities have been implemented as was decided and planned. This evaluation thus is a comparison between what was planned and what was implemented. Thus, for example, if weekly counselling sessions for a prescribed period of time or till the symptoms alleviate were organised for adolescents having symptoms of depression then the process evaluation will involve focusing on whether the programme is actually carried out for

adolescents showing symptoms for depression and if weekly counselling as prescribed has been carried out or not.

2. **Outcome evaluation:** As the name suggests, this evaluation focuses on the outcome or results of the programme. This is also called as summative evaluation. This evaluation will check if the stated objectives and also the goals of the programmes are met or not. For example, in Table 13.1, we discussed about certain examples of programmes with their objectives and goals. An outcome evaluation will focus on whether a programme on study habits of students leads to improved study habits and better performance in examination.

SUMMARY

In this chapter, we discussed about applied social psychology that can be described as a branch of social psychology that mainly uses the theories, methods and principles of social psychology in order to understand certain social issues/problems/phenomena and then come up with suitable intervention strategies in order to deal with these issues/problem/phenomena. The concept of applied psychology was discussed in detail, and its historical development was also discussed citing the contributions of Kurt Lewin to the development of this field as well as the developments that took place during the Second World War. The chapter also discussed about social psychology theory and its functions. The role of an applied social psychologist was then discussed in detail. Some of the roles played by an applied social psychologist are that of a researcher, programme designer, evaluation researcher, consultant and advocate. Social issues and problems were also discussed.

The term social change that has to do with transformation or change in the structure of a social system was also discussed. Further, the categories of social change such as process, evolution, progress and revolution were also discussed. Factors such as cultural, political and economic ones that influence social change were also described in the chapter. Further, this chapter focused on planned social change, resistance to social change and promoting social change. In the last subsections of the chapter, intervention and evaluation were discussed in detail, which included the description of the types of interventions and steps involved in the design and implementation of intervention. Evaluation was also discussed with the focus on its significance. Various types of evaluation were also described.

QUESTIONS

1. Define and describe applied social psychology.
2. Discuss the historical development of applied social psychology.
3. Discuss social psychology theories.
4. Explain the role played by an applied social psychologist.
5. Describe the steps involved in design and implementation of intervention.
6. Discuss the types of intervention and evaluation.
7. Describe the main reasons why programmes or interventions could be inadequate or ineffective.

REFERENCES

Chung-Yan, G. A., & Towson, S. M. T. (2012). Social psychological theory. In F. W. Schneider, J. A. Gruman, & L. M. Coutts (Eds.), *Applied psychology: Understanding and addressing social and practical problems*. New Delhi: SAGE Publications.

Eiaenstadt, S. N. (1966). *Modernization: Protest and change*. Englewood Cliffs, NJ: Prentice Hall.

Etzioni, A. (1976). *Social problems*. Englewood Cliffs, NJ: Prentice Hall.

Ghadially, R. (2007). *Urban women in India: A reader*. New Delhi: SAGE Publications.

Lodzinski, A., Motomura, M. S., & Schneider, F. W. (2012). Intervention and evaluation. In F. W. Schneider, J. A. Gruman, & L. M. Coutts (Eds.), *Applied psychology: Understanding and addressing social and practical problems*. New Delhi: SAGE Publications.

Reinhardt, J. (1952). *Social problems and social policy*. New York, NY: American Book Co.

World Health Organization. (2017). Violence against women. Retrieved from http://www.who.int/mediacentre/factsheets/fs239/en/ on 30 December 2016.

FURTHER READINGS

For more information on applied social psychology, following books can be referred to:

Buunk, B. P., & Van Vugt, M. (2013). *Applying social psychology: from problems to solutions* (2nd ed.). Thousand Oaks, CA: SAGE Publications.

Steg, L., Keizer, K., Buunk, A. P., & Rothengatter, T. (Eds.) (2017). *Applied social psychology: Understanding and managing social problems* (2nd ed.). New York, NY: Cambridge University Press.

For more information on social problems, refer to the following:

Guerrero, A. L. (2016). *Social problems: Community, policy and social action*. New Delhi: SAGE Publications.

CHAPTER 14 Application of Social Psychology

In the previous chapter, we discussed about an important field under social psychology with its focus on application, that is, applied social psychology. In this chapter, we will discuss about the areas where social psychology and its theories, principles, models and so on can be applied. Social psychology has a high application value, and it can be applied to various fields. In this chapter, we will mainly discuss about the application of social psychology to different disciplines/areas.

Jasmine is a psychology teacher in a college and recently she carried out a study on substance abuse amongst the students in her college. Although, as per her findings, there were not many who were involved in substance abuse, to her dismay, a large number of students seemed to be prone to get involved in substance abuse. Based on her findings, she identified some of the factors such as peer pressure and curiosity and willingness to try something new among others as responsible for the initiation of adolescents towards use of drugs and alcohol. She designed an intervention strategy that included workshops for adolescents as well as their parents. When post intervention, she again collected data with regard to how prone the students were to substance abuse, the number of such students had drastically gone down. The students who were already involved in substance abuse received treatment and adequate support to recover, and they showed major improvements.

Jaya volunteers with a non-governmental organisation that works in the field of HIV/AIDS. When a short study based on knowledge, attitude and practice related to HIV/AIDS was carried out by Jaya among women belonging to an area in a metropolitan city, she found that the women lacked awareness and displayed misconceptions. She, therefore, decided to create an awareness programme related to HIV/AIDS for women.

Rihan works as a human resource manager in an organisation. Very soon, his organisation is going to undergo a technological upgradation. Though as such none of the employees will lose their jobs, there is a general atmosphere of insecurity in the organisation. Employees also need to be trained to use the new technology, but most of them are not open enough and have negative attitude towards this technological advancement. Rihan is now in a fix about how to deal with insecurities and negative attitude of the employees and, at the same time, how to ensure the smooth implementation of this technological change in his organisation.

Anil is 28-year old and has a very demanding, high stress job. He has always been a high achiever, sets very high standards for himself and can be very self-critical if he fails to meet them. This was a legacy that he got from his parents who themselves were high achievers and had great expectations from Anil. Lately, Anil has been struggling with feelings of worthlessness and shame due to his inability to perform the way he always has in the past. He felt that, with this lack of performance, he was letting his parents down who had great expectations from him. He is also constantly worried that people at his workplace were going to think that he is totally worthless and incapable of even doing simple things. Due to this, he has been constantly worried and, although he has not considered suicide ever, he has found himself increasingly dissatisfied with his life and was having frequent thoughts of wishing he were dead. All this is also taking a toll on his performance at work and he is even worried that he may lose his job, which again further upsets and makes him irritable.

The principles and theories of social psychology can be applied to various fields. The first two examples from above relate to the application of social psychology to health psychology, where, with the help of social psychology research methods and intervention, Jasmine could deal with the problem of substance abuse in her college and Jaya could develop an awareness programme on HIV/AIDS for women.

In the third example, Rihan used some of the theories of social psychology to understand the employees and accordingly came up with the ways of dealing with their insecurities and negative attitudes, so that this major technological change in his organisation can take place smoothly.

The last example hints on the application of social psychology to clinical and counselling psychology. Anil is suffering from psychological problems and his situation could be understood with the help of certain social psychology theories.

In this chapter, we will discuss about the application of social psychology to fields such as health psychology, organisational psychology, sports, clinical and counselling psychology, and other areas.

Learning Objectives

After reading this chapter, you will be able to

- **Describe the application of social psychology to areas such as health psychology, organisational psychology, sports, and clinical and counselling psychology**
- **Briefly discuss the application of social psychology to other areas such as education, environmental psychology, law and consumer psychology**

APPLICATION OF SOCIAL PSYCHOLOGY TO HEALTH PSYCHOLOGY

Health psychology is a branch of applied psychology that applies the principles, theories and knowledge about psychology to the field of health, both personal and community. Modernity and development of individuals and society are not possible without focus on health; thus, it is very crucial that we focus on health. Social psychology can be used in health psychology not only to understand health-related behaviours but also to develop a suitable intervention strategy in order to modify such behaviours.

We all know that smoking is injurious to health and cautions and ill effects of smoking are displayed not only on the cigarette packets but also on television channels. People know it very well that smoking is indeed injurious to health, but they still continue to smoke. One reason for this can be the fact that they get addicted to it. However, there are a large number of people who despite all the awareness about its ill effects, start smoking. Health behaviours are thus related to the health of individuals, and healthy practices are positively correlated with good health and longevity (Stroebe, 2000).

The ideas related to the application of social psychology to the field of health psychology have been discussed in the following sections.

Relationship Between Health Attitudes and Health Behaviour

We discussed in detail about attitude, and this finds its application in this section of the book. Healthy behaviours are key to health, well-being and overall development of an individual. The attitudes that people have towards health and health-related practices can have an influence on their health-related behaviour. The relationship between health attitudes and health behaviour can be described with the help of the following beliefs (Sears et al., 1991):

- **General health values.** These pertain to the display of interests and concerns with regard to health. For example, an individual may or may not be concerned about recurrent cough that he/she is getting.
- **Threat to health.** Degree of severity of the threat of a disease or disorder to health. For example, what is the extent of threat posed by the cough and its severity? If it is just usual coughing or is more severe, related to more severe disease.
- **Vulnerability of the person.** How vulnerable is a person to the disease or disorder? For example, what is the perception of an individual with regard to how vulnerable he/she feels of developing tuberculosis or lung cancer?
- **Self-efficacy with regard to dealing with the threat.** To what extent is an individual confident that he/she will be able to deal with the threat posed by the disease or disorder? For example, to what extent does an individual feel that he/she will be able to make certain lifestyle and behavioural changes.
- **Response efficacy.** If an individual takes certain measures, will they result in the desired outcome or not? For example, what an individual feels if he/she changes his/her lifestyle and behaviour that result in the prevention from or management of the disease, in this case tuberculosis or lung cancer.

Thus, based on the aforementioned health beliefs, the health behaviour of an individual can be determined.

A number of models are available that help us understand and change health-related behaviours; these are discussed further in detail here.

Health Belief Model

This model states that the health-related behaviour of individuals depends on their presumption of the threat that is posed by the illness as well as the advantages and disadvantages of taking suitable action. The following will thus determine the action taken by an individual:

1. *Perceived susceptibility or vulnerability*. The perception of the individual about his/her susceptibility to the illness in the absence of any precaution or protective measures on the part of the individual.
2. *Perceived severity*. This mainly has to do with the severity of the illness and also the consequences of this illness (as perceived by the individual), that is, to what extent it will affect the individual—physically and socially.
3. *Perceived benefits*. This is related to the benefits (as perceived by the individual), of following, certain health-related behaviours as recommended by a medical practitioner or lifestyle coach. Whether they will reduce the perceived susceptibility/vulnerability or perceived severity or not.

4. *Perceived barriers*. This is related to the barriers or negative features (as perceived by the individual) of the health-related behaviour that were suggested by the medical practitioner or lifestyle coach.

The example of health belief model is given in Figure 14.1.

As can be seen from Figure 14.1, and based on what was discussed earlier about health belief model, if the perceived susceptibility as well as the perceived severity is high, then the threat perceived by the individual is also high (and vice versa). Further, focusing on the perceived benefits and barriers, if the benefits are high and barriers are few or negligible then the individual will believe that the health-related behaviour will be effective and thus there will be a positive change in behaviour. However, if benefits are perceived as low and there are a number of barriers, then the belief will be that the health behaviour is not as such effective and thus there will be no change in the behaviour.

The health belief model has also been criticised, mainly because of its focus only on beliefs, which is in a way narrow as individuals may display some health behaviours not because of beliefs but because of other reasons. For example, an individual may join a gymnasium just to be with his/her friends. Further, two important aspects, namely, self-efficacy (means the confidence that the individual has in one' own ability to carry out the required behaviour, for example, whether I will be able to exercise regularly and maintain healthy diet or not) and behavioural intentions have not been discussed by the model. Various beliefs with regard to health will influence the behavioural intentions and these intentions will then have an influence on the health-related behaviour, and this has not been explained in the health belief model.

Figure 14.1 ***Example of Health Belief Model***

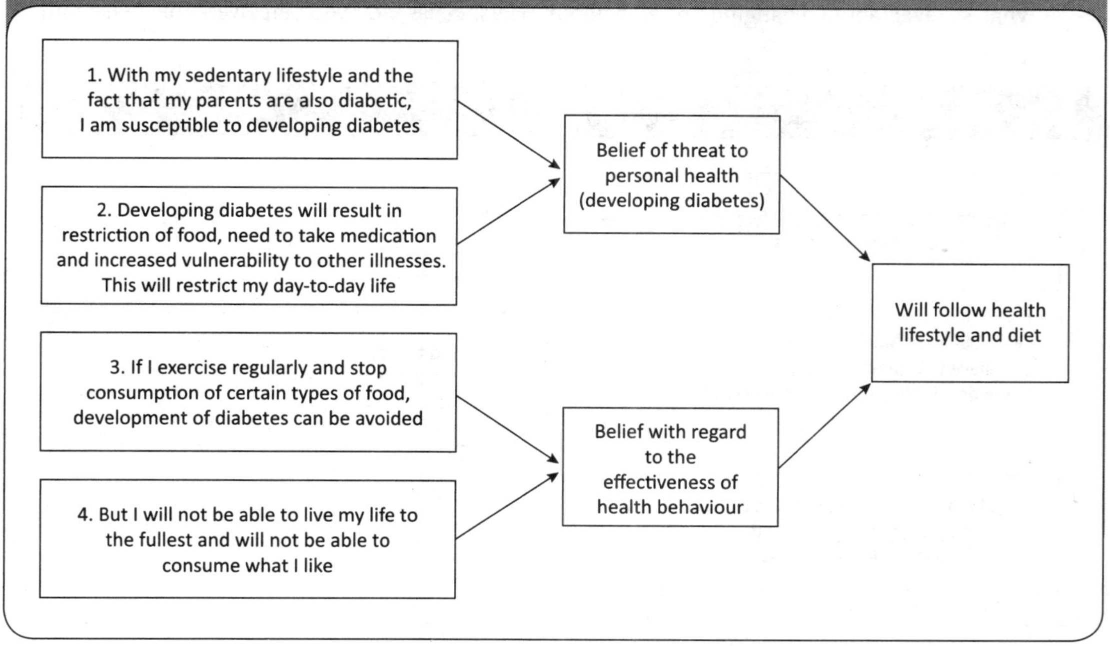

Source: Author.

Theory of Planned Behaviour

The theory of planned behaviour was proposed by Icek Ajzen and can be termed as an extension of theory of reasoned action. The theory includes perceived behaviour control as a predictor along with attitudes and subjective norms. The focus of this theory is on behavioural intensions, and the theory states that in order to bring about change in behaviour of an individual, behavioural intentions need to be focused on. Behavioural intensions in this case can be termed as a result of: (a) attitude towards the behaviour (that includes beliefs regarding the consequences and evaluation of the consequences); (b) subjective norms about the behaviour (i.e., beliefs related to other's expectations and how motivated the individual is to follow the norms); (c) the perception about the control that he/she has on the behaviour. The example of theory of planned behaviour is given in Figure 14.2.

Thus, from the example given in Figure 14.2, the attitude with regard to the consequences of yoga (that it will benefit and result in management of stress) along with the subjective norms (that my parents also believe in yoga) and the perceived control of behaviour (that I can practice yoga) leads to the intentions that 'I intend to learn and practice yoga', which in turn leads to the required behaviour.

Stages of Change Model

As the name suggests there are a number of stages through which the changes in behaviour takes place. This model was developed by Prochaska and Diclemente (1983). The stages in this model are described below.

1. **Stage 1, Precontemplation:** This is the very first stage where the individual has no intentions what so ever about changing the behaviour. He/she has not yet perceived the behaviour as

Figure 14.2 ***Example of Theory of Planned Behaviour***

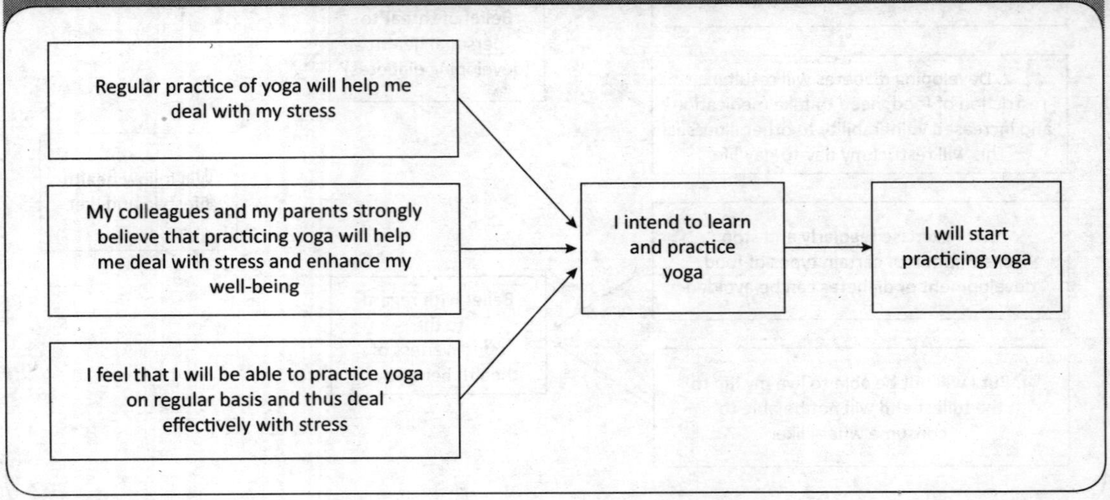

Source: Author.

causing a problem. For example, the individual has not realised that regular and frequent consumption of junk food and soft drinks could have negative consequences on his/her health.

2. **Stage 2, Contemplation:** This is the second stage where the individual realises that he/she needs to change a certain behaviour and is contemplating on changing the said behaviour. For example, the individual realises that regular and frequent consumption of junk food and soft drinks can have negative health impacts and thus, he/she is contemplating that the consumption should be either stopped or drastically reduced.
3. **Stage 3, Preparation:** Based on his/her contemplation in the second stage, the individual will make preparations to bring about the behavioural changes. He/she might also take some action in the direction of achieving the health-related behaviour. For example, they may inform friends about their decision and that they should not tempt him/her with the junk food or soft drinks henceforward or they may consult a Yoga guru to enquire about yoga classes that he/she could join to reduce stress and maintain healthy life. Individuals who experienced an unsuccessful change and are making another attempt at changing certain behaviour can also be included under this stage. For example, an individual who had failed attempts at maintaining a healthy diet (avoiding junk food) will try again.
4. **Stage 4, Action:** Here, the individual will actually change the behaviour. He/she will take necessary actions in the direction of behavioural change. For example, they will stop buying junk food and soft drinks or whenever hungry will go for alternative healthy options.
5. **Stage 5, Maintenance:** Once the health behaviour is adopted, it is really important to maintain the same and that can be difficult as well. Here, the individual with work towards maintaining the health-related behaviour. For example, the individual will maintain the behaviour of not consuming junk food or soft drinks. Individuals can be considered as entering this stage as they complete six months of successful behavioural change during the previous stage (action).

Thus, social psychology can be significantly applied to develop interventions based on these models in order to bring about change in health-related behaviours. There are other theoretical models, such as respondent and operant model, theory of reasoned action, communication–behaviour change model and trans-theoretical model that can be discussed to understand the health-related behaviour and to develop interventions.

Perspective of Social Psychology on Chronic Illnesses

Chronic illnesses obviously have a major negative impact on the individuals: their health, their activities and even their close family and friends. Most often than not, individuals suffering from any of the chronic illnesses will have a theory with regard to how they developed this illness, which could be some injury, stress, bacteria or even God's will.

They may also blame themselves or others for their illness (Sears et al., 1991). Whether the individuals blame themselves or others, this can have an impact on their coping with the illness. Research indicates that individuals who blame themselves for their illness cope poorly with their illness due to their focus on what happened or their behaviour in past rather than on the present situation and illness (Krantz & Deckel, 1983). On the other hand, research also suggests that self-blaming can actually help in coping as the individuals feel in control of the illness (Bulman & Wortman, 1977). However, it has been found that individuals who blame others are not able to adjust with the illness (Bulman & Wortman, 1977; Krantz & Deckel, 1983).

The impact of chronic illness affects all facets of an individual's life including their day-to-day activities, family life, work and leisure activities and so on. There could also be side effects of the medication and frequent trips to the doctor and financial implications. The person may go through the coping process and may or may not accept the situation that he/she is going through. This will definitely affect the social interactions of the individual that will lead to feelings of loneliness in the individual. They may also feel responsible and guilty for what their family members are going through. Further, the family members (who could also be caregivers) of the individual will have their own process of coping with the individual's illness. They may not be able to cope well or may not display the required support towards the individual who is suffering. In case the family members are not supportive, the individual is left without any help or support and may suffer further, especially psychologically. Certain chronic illnesses such as HIV/AIDS also have stigma attached to them and individuals suffering from such illnesses may be stigmatised and may not receive the required treatment and help/support. Individuals suffering from chronic illnesses and their family members may require suitable counselling or psychotherapy. Interventions can also be designed for such individuals and their family members. Also, what these individuals require is empathy and not sympathy. Organisations that run homes for chronically ill persons, such as people who have developed AIDS or a person in the last stage of cancer are also examples of pro-social behaviour in our society.

Further, while applying social psychology to the field of health psychology, there is focus on lifestyle and stress. Lifestyle to a greater extent is determined by health-related attitudes and beliefs. Also, social psychologists are interested in stress that may lead to various physiological and psychological illnesses and disorders and may interfere with social relationships.

Social psychology can also be applied to the prevention of illness and promotion of healthy behaviour besides on the relationship between the patient and practitioner whether psychologist, psychiatrist or a medical doctor. It can play a major role in dealing with certain misconceptions and negative attitudes that people may have about health-related behaviours and practices.

Thus, it is necessary to deal with the negative attitudes, beliefs and misconceptions of individuals. Based on the modernity discussed in Chapter 13, there is a term called health modernity. A. K. Singh (1983) defined health modernity as:

> Scientifically correct information, attitudes and behaviour in relation to physical and mental health, diet and nutrition, family planning and child-care including breast feeding, personal hygiene and environmental sanitation and such other issues which are essential pre-requisites for healthy living and, therefore, for human and social development.

He developed the Health Modernity Scale. In order to develop a suitable intervention to deal with health-related issues, it is important to develop a tool that can be used to measure the actual knowledge and attitudes of the people. Health Modernity Scale is one such tool that can be used to identify the areas of misconceptions and ignorance. It has 10 dimensions that are related to various aspects of health (physical health, mental health, nutrition and diet, family planning, childcare, breast feeding, mental retardation, attitude towards females, cancer and AIDS). Once the areas of misconception and ignorance are identified, a suitable intervention strategy can be developed.

Social psychology can also contribute to evaluation and improvement of health care system and health-related programme in a particular society. As was discussed in the previous chapter, the health care systems and health-related programmes prevalent in a particular society, state or a nation can be subjected to evaluation.

APPLICATION OF SOCIAL PSYCHOLOGY TO INDUSTRIAL AND ORGANISATIONAL PSYCHOLOGY

Industrial and organisational psychology is a branch of psychology that mainly includes systematic and scientific study of human behaviour at workplace. It is the application of theories and principles of psychology to an organisational set-up. Industrial psychology focuses on the individuals at workplace (the employees), whereas organisational psychology focuses on the structure and processes in organisations, including the interactions amongst the employees. An organisation can be termed as a social unit that consists of individuals who work towards achieving a common goal. Thus, the principles of social psychology can be aptly applied to the field of organisational psychology, whether it is the attitude of the employees, the factors in society that influence (social influences) the employee behaviour, aggression, culture and so on. Social psychology can also be applied to understand the discrimination or violence that exists in an organisation and its effects on the employees as well as the organisation as a whole. Various aspects of an employee's social dimension can be studied and suitable strategies/training programmes/counselling can be organised in an organisational context.

There are two important aspects that determine the productivity and performance of an employee, that is, for an employee to work effectively, he/she needs to be motivated and be satisfied with his/her job as well. Motivation can be categorised into intrinsic motivation and extrinsic motivation. Intrinsic motivation is one where the individual internally feels that he needs to work in a particular direction and extrinsic motivation is when an individual is driven to perform due to an external source. Example of intrinsic motivation is when an individual feels that he/she needs to work hard to achieve the target given to him/her, and example of an extrinsic motivation is when an individual receives encouragement to perform from his/her manager.

With regard to motivation, there are a number of theories that are available that explain how an individual is motivated. From Maslow's hierarchy of needs, need for achievement proposed by McClelland and two-factor model by Herzberg to equity theory and so on can be used to understand what drives or motivates an employee at workplace. While applying social psychology to an organisational set-up, it is necessary to understand the theories of motivation so as to develop ways in which the employees can be motivated to perform to their best and to ensure that they are satisfied with what they are doing. Based on these theories, various interventions and programmes can be devised.

Social Perception in an Organisational Set-up

In an organisational set-up, individuals are necessarily interdependent and have to work in tandem with each other, despite their differences. In this context, how employees perceive each other is also significant, and thus social perception, discussed in Chapter 5 can be highlighted here. Fiske (1993) defined social perception as 'the process of selecting and interpreting information about how we view others and ourselves'. Others are most often perceived in a subjective manner and in this there could be a number of perceptual biases. Perceptual biases can be described as errors that interfere with the process of perception. Two significant perceptual biases that can be discussed in this regard are as follows:

1. **Selective perception.** We are normally exposed to a large amount of information and it is not possible to absorb all this information. Thus, only certain information that mainly catches our attention is taken by us. In a crowd of people, therefore, we may easily notice a clown due to its distinctive costume and behaviour. Selective perception is extremely important in an organisational

set-up as from selection to performance appraisal, perceptual biases could occur that can be traced to selective perception. In this context, the schemas and heuristics that were discussed in the chapter on social cognition (Chapter 4) are also relevant.

2. **Halo effect.** In this, generalisations are made about an individual based on a single piece of information. For example, an employee who is punctual will be seen by the superior as being honest and particular about work. This may not be a reality though and thus perceptual bias can take place. Halo effect can also be as a result of 'similar to me effect', where a manager will have a favourable perception about an employee because he/she perceives the employee as being similar to him/her.

Yet another aspect under social perception that needs to be discussed is that of attribution. Most often, we also want to know why certain individuals behave or perform the way they behave. The process in which causes are assigned to such behaviours can be described as attribution process (discussed in Chapter 5 on social perception). In this context, a covariance model was suggested by Kelly in 1973 (cited in Coutts & Gruman, 2012). In this model, an individual's behaviour is attributed to either something that is internal (under control of the individual) or something external (due to factors not under control of the individual). Further, while making these attributions and deciding whether they are due to internal or external factors, three different types of information are considered.

1. **Distinctiveness.** Whether the behaviour is distinctive or not? Is it common across various situations or not? If it is common, then distinctiveness is low and if it is not common, distinctiveness is high.
2. **Consensus.** Do others behave in this manner as well or not? If yes, then consensus is high and if no, then consensus is low.
3. **Consistency.** This has to do with behaviour over the period of time. Whether the person behaves the same way in such situations in other times as well or not. If yes, then the consistency is high and if no, then the consistency is low.

Based on the above mentioned, if an individual displays high distinctiveness and consensus but low consistency, we could attribute his/her behaviour to external causes. In case if the individual displays low distinctiveness and consensus but high consistency, then his/her behaviour will be attributed to internal causes. For example, an employee who always displays leadership qualities (low distinctiveness) while working in teams, such skills have not been displayed by other team members (low consensus) and this behaviour has been displayed by the employee across period of time (high consistency), then we will attribute this quality/behaviour of the employee to the internal factors.

There could also be a number of attributional biases. To highlight, fundamental attribution error, in this context, is a behaviour that is seen as a result of internal factors, and various situational factors that might have led to such behaviours are ignored. Most often, people do not involve in an in-depth analysis of an individual's behaviour that is based on distinctiveness, consensus and consistency. Thus the influence of internal factors are emphasised as opposed to the external factors while attributing a behaviour. For example, inability to achieve targets by a salesperson will be attributed to his/her internal factors as opposed to situational factors.

There is yet another bias, that is, actor–observer bias, where though the behaviour of others is attributed to their internal factors, same behaviour on our part is attributed to external factors. For example, when a subordinate is not able to achieve his/her sales targets, the manager will attribute the inability of this salesperson to achieve the targets to his/her lack of effort. However, when this manager is not able to achieve his/her own targets, then he/she will attribute inability to do so to a slow market.

Conflict at Workplace

Conflicts could often occur when individuals are working together. Such conflicts not only affect the productivity of the individuals but also hamper the overall production and profitability of an organisation. Conflicts could be at workers level or even at higher levels of management. Either ways, it is necessary to understand them to deal with them effectively.

There are a number of causes of conflict at workplace; these are discussed here.

- **Organisational causes:** These are related to the structures and processes in an organisation. These include competition with regard to resources, power disparities, lack of clarity in roles, responsibilities and even jurisdiction, work interdependence and reward systems that are increasingly competitive in nature (Baron & Byrne, 1995).
- **Interpersonal factors:** There are also certain interpersonal factors or causes related to lack of adequate communications, attributions that are faulty, stereotypes and negative attitudes, feelings of resentment and inequality and having grievances (Baron & Byrne, 1995). What we studied in Chapter 6 on interpersonal relationship finds its application here.

As is obvious, conflicts can have a grave impact on the functioning of any organisation. And though differences in opinions are necessary to promote creativity and effective problem-solving in an organisation, conflicts need to be avoided. Therefore, necessary steps need to be taken to promote constructive arguments and criticisms, but at the same time, measures need to be taken to avoid conflicts or to resolve them effectively at the earliest.

Some of the ways in which conflicts can be resolved are as follows:

1. **Bargaining.** There is an exchange of offers, counter offers or kind of concessions between opposing parties. This can be done directly or through the representatives of the parties. The success of bargaining depends on both the techniques used to convince as well as the perceptions of the persons (of opposing parties) involved in the bargaining. The better the compatibility between these persons, the better the bargaining process. Bargaining also has various approaches or perspectives, one is the distributive perspective that results in a win–lose situation where one party gains whereas the other loses and the other is an integrative perspective where both the parties win or gain in some way.
2. **Superordinate goals.** Having goals that are common or of interest to both the parties can also be useful in resolving conflicts. The differences between the parties will resolve as they work together towards achieving a common goal. Such situations could be created within an organisation where the conflicting individuals or groups come together to achieve a certain common goal.
3. **Incompatibility response strategy.** This strategy could mainly be used to deal with any aggression that accompanies the conflict. In this the individuals displaying aggression are exposed to situations or conditions that elicit emotional responses that are not compatible with anger, for example, empathy, feelings related to amusement and so on (Baron & Byrne, 1995). A study in this regard was carried out by Baron et al. in 1990 (as stated in Baron & Byrne, 1995, p. 623). In the study, the individuals (participants) who were angered by the confederate previously were exposed to either no further manipulation (control group) or numerous treatments to elicit positive response from the participants. There were three conditions in the study. In one condition, the participants received a gift; in second, the confederate flattered them;

and in the third condition, the accomplice made self-critical remarks. The participants were asked to rate their preference for each of the five ways (avoidance, compromise, collaboration, competition and accommodation) of future conflict resolution with the confederate. The results indicated that the male participants who were exposed to the three conditions indicated stronger preference for conflict resolution through collaboration as compared to the participants in the control group. However, the same was not true with regard to female participants who went with conciliatory conflict resolution in all conditions.

Although only two main aspects were discussed in this section, it can be said that most of the chapters on social psychology covered in this book find its application to an organisational set-up. This is reflected in Table 14.1.

APPLICATION OF SOCIAL PSYCHOLOGY TO SPORTS

Sports brings to our mind teams and leadership, and social psychology has scope for application to both these areas. Also what was studied in Chapter 11 on group dynamics finds its application here. Most of you must have watched movies like *Chak De! India* and *Lagaan* that are based on teams. In both these movies, we can see how team works, what are the team dynamics and cohesion and also the role of a leader. Teams and leadership are not only significant in sports but are also significant in an organisational set-up and in any other set-up where people come together to achieve a common goal.

The focus of this section will be mainly on the application of social psychology to teams, leadership and communication.

Table 14.1 ***Application of Social Psychology Topics to an Organisational Set-up***

Social Psychology Topic	Application to an Organisational Set-up
Social cognition and social perception	Can be used to understand the thinking pattern of the employees as well as to see how they perceive each other. Could have its application from selection to performance appraisal.
Interpersonal relationship	How employees relate to each other in an organisational set-up. This is also important, as in an organisational set-up, employees may also develop friendship.
Attitudes	It is very important to focus on employee attitude towards the organisation, its structure and process and towards the people working in it. Attitude towards technology and use of safety devices and so on can also be important.
Social influence	Since employees work in groups, definitely their behaviours are influence by each other.
Group dynamics	Group dynamics can help understand the behaviour of the employees in groups and teams.

Source: Author.

Application to Teams

Team can be described as a group of people with a common goal, though it is more matured and also has a higher degree of interdependence, especially when compared to a group. Team can be described as a small group of people having skills that are complementary in nature and this group of people have common goals, purpose and strategy, for which they can be held accountable as a team (Moorhead & Griffin, 2010). Though there are different types of teams, we are mainly going to focus on teams in sports.

When we talk about teams in sports, there will be individuals who come from different backgrounds, having different skills (though complimentary), having different personalities and so on and these individuals are then expected to work together as a team and achieve the goal allotted to them and most often it is about winning a trophy or prize. These teams are also different in a way because there is an audience that is watching the game, who are emotionally charged and attached with the teams. There could be teams that represent a state or a country or a region and definitely the pressure to perform experienced by any team (especially a sports team) is huge due to various reason. Thus, when discussing about teams in the context of sports, we need to focus on interpersonal relationship, communications, conflicts, coping of each individual member with the pressures and frustrations if the goal is not achieved, social loafing and of course the role of the leader.

The application of social psychology to sports has been adequately described by Sullivan, Feltz and Dithurbide (2012). Their model includes input, output and throughput. In input, aspects such as the competencies and ability of the team members, besides their personality traits and even the coaching style, can be included. In output, we have the performance of the team and also the satisfaction or dissatisfaction and other such variables derived by the team members from their performance. However, between the input and output there is throughput, and these are some of the factors related to social psychology such as team cohesiveness and so on. These factors are not at individual level but at team level and can have an impact on the performance of the team. If one develops an understanding about these throughput factors, then the performance of the team can be improved.

One of the most significant concepts we can talk about here is team cohesion. Cohesion can be described as 'the degree to which the members of the group are attracted to the group and to one another' (Nahavandi et al., 2015).

A study carried out by Carron et al. (2002) indicated strong relationship between team cohesion and success. There are four main features of team cohesion as described by Carron et al. (1997). They are multidimensional, dynamic, affective and instrumental.

- Multidimensional means that the cohesion is a complex factor and is as a result of various factors, not single factor.
- Dynamic denotes that cohesion can change or fluctuate over a period of time despite being comparatively stable.
- Affectivity, as the name suggests, is related to the team members' or the sportspersons' emotional state.
- Instrumental mainly deals with the goals and objectives of the team towards which the team works unitedly.

The affective and instrumental characteristics of cohesion further suggest two main categories: social cohesion and task cohesion. Social cohesion deals with how united the team is as a social group, though they may not be united or organised with regard to achieving the goals of the team. A team with more focus on how the team members relate with each other than the team performance can be termed as having high social cohesion. On the other hand, a team that focuses more on the performance of the task or team goals, rather than the interpersonal relationship can be termed as having higher task cohesion. However, mostly any team needs some amount of both social and task cohesion.

Cohesion in teams can be as a result of both individual factors as well as social factors. Some of the examples of individual factors are individual personality, their socio demographic profile and so on. On the other hand, social factors include style of leadership, roles allotted to the team members and so on (Sullivan et al., 2012). Based on such a cohesion, there are also consequences that again can be categorised into individual and team consequences.

In this context, the size of the team also needs to be taken into consideration. The bigger the size of the team, the more difficult it would be to coordinate and communicate within the team. A fair knowledge of cohesion and the factors that influence it could help a social psychologist built teams that have high cohesiveness. While putting a team together the members should be selected in a way that there is high possibility of them going along well with each other so that they can function in tandem and mutually perform to achieve the goal. High cohesiveness will have positive impact on the team performance and will also lead to decreased conflict.

Yet another aspect in the teams that a social psychologist might to work on is the self-efficacy and collective efficacy. Self-efficacy can be described as 'a belief that one can perform adequately in a particular situation' (Gerrig & Zimbardo, 2006, p. 480). On the other hand, the collective efficacy has been defined by Bandura in 1997 (Sullivan et al., 2012, p. 122) as 'a group's shared belief in its ability to organise and execute the course of action required to obtain a certain outcome'. Both these terms are relevant in this context. When we talk about the collective efficacy of a team (team efficacy), there are a number of factors that we need to consider that mainly pertain to the individual team members. For example, self-efficacy of each team member will significantly contribute to the collective efficacy of the team and if the self-efficacy of each team member is high then the team efficacy will also be high. Thus, the self-efficacy of the members and the team efficacy are correlated (Feltz & Lirgg, 1998; Magyar, Feltz & Simpson, 2004). Also, collective efficacy can have a strong influence on performance and a team that is high on collective efficacy will definitely perform better than a team with lower levels of collective efficacy (MacLean & Sullivan, 2003). Further, the team cohesion also plays an important role in determining the team efficacy and studies show that they are positively correlated with each other (Paskevich et al., 1999; Spink, 1990). Study by Heuzé, Raimbault and Fontayne (2006) also indicated that relationship exists between collective efficacy and cohesion.

One of the most important tasks in team is goal setting. And in this context, the focus is on team goal setting rather than individual goal setting. However, the individual goal setting should align with that of the team for successful attainment of the team goal. In 1989, Burton (cited Sullivan et al., 2012, p. 128) stated different types of goal orientations; they are discussed as follows:

- **Outcome goals.** The focus here is on the outcome, that is, whether the team won or lost. The contribution of the team members or how they played is not considered. It does not matter whether they gave their best or did not play that well. What is important is the outcome of the game.
- **Performance goals.** In this case, the performance is more important than the outcome. The focus is on the team players' own performance and achievement of success is also based on comparison with self.
- **Process goals.** These goals focus on skills that are performed during the game.

Goal setting has a positive impact on the team performance. As stated by Locke and Latham (1985), goal setting can lead to increase in efforts put in towards the required behaviour and also results in persistence of that behaviour (cited in Sullivan et al., 2012, p. 128). Goals also help direct the performers' attention towards certain significant elements of performance and encourage the development of new learning strategies.

Application to Leadership

Leadership in sports can be viewed in two ways. First, there is the captain of the team who acts as the leader. Second, there is also the coach who also in a way plays the role of a leader guiding the team towards achieving its goals. Either ways, the theories of social psychology play an important role in this context to understand what leadership style is best suitable and what the role of a leader, whether the captain or the coach should be. We also need to remember here that it is possible that there are certain informal leaders in the team as well. And for the team to perform effectively all these leaders need to be on the same page and to work in coordination with each other. It is also possible that at one point of time one of these leaders is playing a more prominent role than others.

Leadership can be defined as 'the process through which one member of a group (its leader) influences other group members toward the attainment of specific group goal' (Yukl, 1989). We discussed at length about leadership in Chapter 11 on group dynamics. Nevertheless, it is important to note that leadership styles can be autocratic, democratic or laissez faire. In autocratic leadership, all the control is vested with the leader and all the decisions are taken by him/her without entertaining any opinions from the group or team members. In democratic leadership, the leader encourages exchange of ideas amongst the team members and promotes their participation. Members thus get to play a significant role in decision-making. In laissez faire leadership, the leader is not as such involved and is almost absent. The members have to make their own decisions, solve problems on their own and achieve the goals. Though each of these styles have their own advantages and disadvantages, which leadership style is best suited for a particular team or group will depend on the nature of that team or group. Studies indicate that autocratic leadership leads to lower task cohesion, whereas, democratic leadership leads to higher task cohesion (Sullivan et al., 2012).

A lot of studies are available as such on leadership, but our main focus will be on studies specifically carried out in the area of sports. A multidimensional model of leadership was proposed by Chelladurai (1978, 1990, 1993). The model proposed that the effectiveness of leadership is dynamic in nature and depends on sequence of interactions between the leader and the members as well as the situational constraints. The model further suggests that a balance between (a) the actual behaviour sought by the leader (example, giving positive feedback), (b) preferred leadership behaviour sought by the members (example, a leader who is supportive) and (c) the behaviour required, based on the situation at hand, will lead to the outcome such as high satisfaction and better performance. Further, factors such as the characteristics of the leader and the members will also play a role in this context and will influence the actual behaviour of the leader as well as the preferred leadership behaviour of the members.

There are a number of aspects that need to be considered when we talk about leadership in sports. And as is said by Weinberg and Gould (2003, p. 213), 'Determining what makes effective sports leadership is clearly not a simple process'. Stogdill (1974) stated that certain traits such as ability to adapt, self-confidence, persistence, intelligence and creativity could play a role in determining success. Effective communication and reinforcement, besides clear instruction, are also significant

(Crust & Lawrence, 2006). Thus, various theories of leadership can serve as a basis to enhance the leadership in sports teams. In teams, leaders play a significant role in clarifying the role that each member has to play. Role can be described as a set of behaviours that a person is expected to display when in social situations. So a goalkeeper in a football team is expected to stop a goal from the opposite team. Besides role clarity, the team members need to display both role acceptance and role performance. As defined by Sullivan, Feltz and Dithurbide (2012, p. 119), role acceptance can be described as 'the degree to which the person expected to fill a role agrees to comply with the requirements of the role' and role performance can be described as 'how well the individual actually completes the responsibilities of the role'.

Application to Communication

Smooth and free communication is also significant in any team as well as between the team members and the leader(s). In the context of team, effective team communication has been defined by Sullivan and Gee (2007) as 'interactions between teammates that result in enhanced team attributes and/or functioning'. In a study carried out by them satisfaction experienced by the athletes was positively correlated with effective communication.

Hanin in 1992 (Sullivan et al., 2012) stated four styles of communication, as discussed here.

- **Orientation messages:** Messages with regard to strategies related to planning. Team members always discuss strategies and techniques they would be using before the game. Planning is also essential component of teamwork.
- **Stimulation messages:** Messages that are used to reinforce and motivate the members. Leaders in teams often use such messages to encourage team members from performing to their best. These are mainly used during the performance.
- **Evaluation messages:** These are related to the evaluation or assessment of the members' performance with reference to their effort, ability and overall performance. These are used after the performance when the team members are given feedback with regard to their performance.
- **Task irrelevant messages:** Any communication that does not fall under the above mentioned three categories is termed as task irrelevant messages.

Besides verbal communication, there are also non-verbal communications. Crocker (1990) studied the facial and verbal expression congruencies and their effects on how the verbal and emotional feedback of a coach was perceived. The facial expressions were either congruent or incongruent and were accompanied with verbal feedback. The study was carried out on 71 students (32 females and 39 males), who were randomly assigned to four conditions. A 2 × 2 completely randomised factorial design was used. The participants were made to watch a videotape of facial–verbal pairings and then they had to evaluate the percentage of negative and positive statements and the expression of emotions by the coach. The results indicated that the expected frequency with regard to a positive feedback was distorted due to the incongruent facial expressions (in negative direction) and that the presence of a negative stimuli, whether facial or verbal, led to the perception of negative emotions or effect. Based on the results, a conclusion was drawn that lack of consistency in facial–verbal expressions has a strong impact on how the verbal feedback and emotional state is perceived.

Communication, thus, whether verbal or non-verbal, plays an important role in success of the team. Studies that were mainly carried out on golf and tennis teams (Lausic et al., 2009;

Widmeyer & Williams, 1991) indicated that the teams that loose has comparatively less interactions during and between the games than the teams that won.

Besides the above, social psychology can also be applied to sports psychology by developing interventions that could help enhance the performance of the sports persons, enhancing their communication and other skills, motivating them, training the players in leadership skills and team work and also enhance their psychological well-being.

APPLICATION OF SOCIAL PSYCHOLOGY TO CLINICAL AND COUNSELLING PSYCHOLOGY

To some extent, the readers might feel that the application of social psychology to fields such as health and organisations is quite obvious, but what about fields such as clinical and counselling psychology, that mainly deal with individuals having major or minor psychological problems or disorders. Well, social psychology has an application here as well! A term we can use here is 'social clinical interface', which is used mainly to bridge the gap that exists between basic social psychological research and clinical practices (Tashiro & Motensen, 2006).

Though bridging of this gap initially met with dead end, as it was thought that there is no connection whatsoever between social psychology and the area of mental health. Goldstein, Heller and Sechrest (1966) stated that no such thing as social psychology of psychotherapy' existed and Strong (1987) also indicated that not a single innovation in psychotherapy was as a result of contribution from social psychology.

According to Hart, Ledgerwood and Ianni (2012, p. 87), social clinical interface comprises of attempts towards comprehension, diagnoses and modification of some of the psychological problems and issues including jealousy, anger, shame, guilt, embarrassment, regret and remorse. Social psychology theories related to self, attribution theories, expectancy theories and so on can be adequately applied to understand and resolve most of these issues.

In this chapter, the application of social psychology to these two very important fields will be discussed in terms of three categories.

Social Psychology and Origin of Psychological Problems and Disorders

Human being is a social animal. This has been told to us time and again in various classes of psychology that we attended at various levels. And the roots of a lot of psychological issues/problems and disorders can be found in our social interaction or anxieties related to these interaction. Thus, it is possible that our social interactions or lack of it can lead to development of certain psychological problems and disorders. When psychological disorders and problems are discussed, heredity and environment (especially the social environment) are seen as two significant contributors to their development and their perpetuation. In this case, social can form a huge aspect of the environment.

Behaviour theories with their emphasis on the role of external stimuli in determining behaviour also gives perspective to the origins of psychological disorders and relevance of the social aspect in the development of these disorders.

Thus with regard to a psychological problem such as social anxiety, the social psychologist could identify the cognitive as well as social aspects that could lead to the development of social anxiety in a person.

Thus, a person may develop social anxiety as a result of certain past experiences and interactions with people. The social psychologists could also refer to the self-presentation theories, or theories related to self while dealing with this.

Seligman proposed the model of depression based on learned helplessness. The basis of this model was an experiment that he had carried out with dogs in 1975. In this experiment, painful electric shocks were administered to the dogs and there was no possible way that these dogs could escape the shocks. Later on, the same dogs were placed in a similar situation, though now it was possible for them to escape the electric shocks. The results of this experiment indicated that despite the opportunity available to escape the shocks, the dogs did not escape or even try to escape. They had given up and continued passively to suffer the electric shocks. Such a behaviour on the part of the dogs was attributed by Seligman to their previous experience where there was no way to escape the shocks and thus the dogs had learnt to be psychologically helpless. This model can be extended to human beings as well, and work on this was carried out by Abramson, Seligman and Teasdale (1978) (cited in Hart et al., 2012). They developed a cognitive social model of human depression and it was called as attributional reformulation of learned helplessness theory of depression (Abramson et al., 1978). The model stated that people having depression tend to make attributions that are pessimistic in nature and, in fact, they may also have pessimistic thoughts about their future. Yet another theory, the hopelessness theory of depression that was developed by Abramson, Metalsky and Alloy in 1989 (cited in Hart et al., 2012) state that depression can occur due to two main factors: first, when the person is vulnerable (a person who interprets the negative events in life negatively) and, second, when there is a negative environment.

Peer influence for example has a significant role to play in initiation of an individual to use and abuse substance. Peer pressure along with need to confirm and low self-esteem play a significant role here. Theories such as social learning theory can also be used to understand why people indulge or develop substance abuse.

Stress is yet another psychological problem that can be discussed here. Stress can be caused due to our day-to-day interactions with people (esp. significant people in our lives) around us. Stress, if ignored and not treated, can further lead to development of various other psychological problems and depression. How a person copes with stress will also depend on the social support that he/she has. Some of the experimental studies (Lepore, 1998; O'Donovan & Hughes, 2008) indicated that the cardiovascular reactivity to a stress situation decreased when the participants had the company of a friend or a stranger who was supportive.

Thus, various psychological problems and disorders can be explained with the help of various theories of social psychology.

Diagnosis

Correct diagnosis of a psychological problem or disorder is very important, as the whole treatment plan will depend on it. Based on the diagnosis using case history, Mental Status Examination, psychological tests, projective techniques and so on, the clinical psychologist has to make a decision with regard to the diagnosis. This is called as clinical decision-making, which involves not only diagnosing the problem or disorder that the person is suffering from but also determining the plan of treatment or intervention. While making clinical decisions, there could be four categories of decisions, namely, true positive, false positive, false negative and true negative.

In true positive, the person is correctly diagnosed and receives treatment as per the diagnosis. In false positive, the person receives incorrect intervention or treatment for a disorder or problem that he/she is actually not suffering from. This could create problems for the person as he/she receives unnecessary treatment for a problem or disorder that he/she actually does not have. Further, he/she fails to get treatment for a problem or condition that he/she may have. In false negative, the person does not receive treatment or intervention for the disorder or problem he/she has, as the clinical psychologist incorrectly diagnosed him/her as not having the disorder. This could be disastrous as the person's situation will not improve and it could deteriorate. This could raise ethical issues as well. Lastly, in true negative, the person is appropriately not treated for the problem or disorder he/she does not have. An example in this regard has been given in Table 14.2.

It is relevant to focus on clinical decision-making in this context (where the application of social psychology to clinical/counselling psychology is discussed) because a number of biases could creep in to decision-making that could be explained with the help of theories of social psychology. Labelling effect is one such bias that could take place. Corrigan (2007) described labelling error as 'a tendency to perceive clients in ways that are erroneous owing to the reactive effects of an existing psychiatric label'. For example, based on the case history of the person, that indicates that the person suffered from Obsessive Compulsive Disorder (OCD), the clinical psychologist may inadvertently diagnose the person as suffering from OCD due to the labelling effect. Labelling could be harmful in many ways especially in the context of psychological disorders and problems as there is stigma attached and the person may actually never be able to get the label off. This could again have negative impact on the life of the person being labelled with the psychological disorder and his/her family. The person thus may not be able to lead his/her life to the fullest and will experience decreased life satisfaction. He/she may not receive any social support, which will further aggravate the problem. It is also possible that a person is wrongly labelled and is actually not suffering from any problem or disorder.

The clinical decision-making can also be influenced by certain stereotypes that the clinical psychologists might have about certain group of people. It might be culturally or socially seen that a particular community of people is aggressive, and in case if a person from that community comes to the clinical psychologist, his/her background may influence the clinical psychologist in wrongly diagnosing the person as having behaviour problems related to aggression.

Table 14.2 ***Example of Clinical Decision-Making***

Conclusion by the Clinical Psychologist	**Persons Conditions**	
	Person has Post-Traumatic Stress Disorder (PTSD)	Persons does not have PTSD
	True Positive	**False Positive**
Person diagnosed with PTSD	Person receives appropriate treatment for PTSD. Indicating correct diagnosis and correct treatment.	Person receives treatment for PTSD despite not actually having it. Indicating wrong diagnosis.
	False Negative	**True Negative**
Person is not diagnosed with PTSD	Person has PTSD but is not diagnosed with it hence does not receive the necessary treatment. Again indicating wrong diagnosis. Thus, person does not receive any treatment.	Person is correctly diagnosed as not having PTSD and hence does not receive the treatment. Indicating correct decision as logically no treatment is given.

Source: Author.

There could also be an anchoring effect and a confirmation bias. In the anchoring effect, the initial impression of the clinical psychologist or counsellor influences the later diagnosis and decisions taken by them. And in the confirmation bias, the clinical psychologist or the counsellor will seek information that confirms their initial impression of the problem/disorder, and the information that does not confirm their initial impression is ignored.

These biases and errors in clinical decision-making can be reduced by making the clinical psychologists and the counsellors aware about the biases and errors and training them in a suitable manner to reduce the bias and be more and more objective in their diagnosis and treatment.

Treatment of Psychological Disorder

Social psychology finds application to the treatment of psychological disorders as well as where the treatment and intervention can be decided based on the inputs from social psychology. Techniques based on theories of social psychology could be used in order to help people deal with their problems and disorders. Most often, techniques to enhance social skills and relationships can also be used, especially, in the case of social anxiety and substance abuse. Most importantly, during the treatment period, adequate support of family members and friends needs to be generated. Self-presentation theory, for example, can be used while treating an individual with social anxiety. This can be done through the use of rational emotive therapy (or rational emotive behaviour therapy) that meets the outlook of self-presentation theory—if the need for social approval is reduced, then the self-presentational motivations also decrease, thus helping the person cope with social anxiety (Hart et al., 2012). Most often than not, people having psychological problems and disorders may have low self-efficacy, which can also be improved. The clinical psychologist or counsellor could work on the social environment of the person to make it more conducive for coping as well as to generate more social support. Moreover, the involvement of family members, friends and significant others can be encouraged. The theories and principles of social psychology can be used in group counselling too, besides improving the therapeutic or counselling relationship. The details covered in the chapter on group dynamics can be used in order to successfully carry out group counselling.

Besides the above, the theories of social psychology can be adequately used in the prevention of mental illness or psychological problems and disorders. They can be used to create awareness about these issues. Intervention strategies based on what was discussed in the previous chapter can be developed and implemented in a systematic manner in order to deal with these problems. A number of problems today are rooted in social networking (though they have their own advantages), which has resulted in the decreased personalised interaction. This should be studied and researched by social psychologists.

APPLICATION OF SOCIAL PSYCHOLOGY TO OTHER AREAS

Besides the areas discussed above, there are a number of other areas where social psychology can be applied.

Application to Education

Educational set-ups such as schools and colleges contribute in a major way to our overall development. It is likely that most of the individuals spend a considerable amount of time in an educational set-up such as a school, college, a university or an institution. Our behaviour gets greatly influenced by our teachers and peers. Educational set-ups in fact play an important role in the formation of our values, beliefs and attitudes. Further, the social interaction in an educational set-up is also relevant. Thus, social psychology does come into the picture. The interest and application of social psychology to education started in the late 1940s and it further accelerated in the 1970s (Fisher, 1982). Social psychologists showed great interest in studying educational institutions in order to bring about improvement in them. The application of social psychology to education mainly focuses on the behaviour in an educational set-up, that can be termed as a system in itself. Social psychology can also be applied in an educational set-up in order to deal with specific problems and issues and to improve educational output. Distance education is one such educational system that emerged as a response to socio-economic needs.

The main aim of any educational system is to provide instructions for development of skills, strive to build a cultivated society, to promote learning and convey the secular point of view of individuals. Any educational system whether conventional (i.e., face to face) or distance mode have to work towards achieving this aim. However, there are additional socio-economic needs mainly in developing countries, such as India, that need to be achieved and it may not be possible to do so with conventional mode of education. These needs are as follows:

- Need for educational system with flexible arrangements so that individuals can earn and educate themselves at the same time
- Need for specialised programmes and courses for employed individuals
- Need for certification without necessity of following the formalities of conventional education system

Further, there are other challenges such as:

- Providing education to large numbers of students who have diverse educational needs and
- Need for innovation in educational system.

In this context, the Open Distance Learning plays an important role in fulfilling the needs by providing courses in flexible form and providing courses for employed individuals that help them function in the society in a better way. However, it is important to take adequate care to provide suitable personal contact, adequate library facilities, effective delivery system and feedback system for successful implementation of a particular programme through distance mode. Distance education can be described as non-conformist and non-traditional mode of education and has emerged as a result of socio-historical needs and technological developments.

The main concepts of distance education are as follows:

1. Learner autonomy or independence
2. Indirect education where there is flexibility
3. Education in an actual or real set-up

The reach of distance education to remote areas of the country, the flexibility provided by the system and its ability to meet the socio-economic needs of individuals, are main features of distance education.

In distance education, the emphasis is on learning and the learner rather than teaching. Also, there is less stress on the academic year, that is, a learner can complete a particular programme in more than one year as per his/her learning pace and convenience. It involves effective use of communication and information technology in order to disseminate information and promote learning. This education system, thus, promotes autonomy amongst its learners. The theories of social psychology can be applied to enhance and strengthen the distance education system because a number of individuals who were not able to pursue their education though conventional mode have an opportunity here to learn and develop. Besides, the research methods in social psychology can also be used to study this system, especially the attitude that people may have about it.

Application to Law

There is no denying that crime rate is fast growing in our society. Newspapers and news channels are continuously reporting about rapes, murders and other crimes being committed. This in turn has an effect on behaviour of people as they fear for their safety and there is a feeling of insecurity. When a rape takes place in Delhi or Mumbai or any other place, questions such as why it is happening in our society and what measures need to be taken, are long-term questions, but families and women do make modifications to their schedules and take extra precautions in order to ensure their safety and that of their families. Crime can easily be termed as a social issue, especially since it is linked to poverty, discrimination, overall socio-economic status, disadvantaged groups and so on.

Though the overall relationship between psychology and law is comparatively not much researched, certain studies have been carried out on topics such as perception of eyewitnesses and his/her testimony (Fisher, 1982). Tapp (1973) identified three main areas of interaction between psychology and law, they are the process of legal socialisation in a particular community or society, the judicial processes in court of law and the criminal justice process (cited in Fisher, 1982).

Social psychology can be applied in a legal set-up to study the behaviours of the judge, lawyers, defendants, eyewitness and accused as well. It can also focus on aspects such as arrest, interrogation and prosecution (Fisher, 1982). They can greatly contribute to changes and modifications of legal and judicial procedures. Social psychology can thus contribute to improvement of the overall legal system. Further, social psychology can also be applied to build and evaluate programmes and interventions for preventing crime and ways of rehabilitating offenders.

Application to Environmental Psychology

Environmental psychology can be described as a study of relationship between behaviour and the environment (natural or created by human beings).Various environmental issues that we come across such as garbage management, pollution, crowding or even sense of alienation (even though surrounded by numerous people) can be termed as social issues. All these have an influence on health and mental health of individuals. If in India we have a marvel such as Taj Mahal, we also have a highly polluted Yamuna river flowing just next to it. Kurt Levin has suggested B = *f* (P, E), that is, behaviour is a function of both the person or an individual and environment. However, initially Lewin meant psychological environment by 'E'; as he moved towards social psychology, he broadened the concept to an environment as perceived by the individual or his/her subjective perception of the environment (Fisher, 1982). Roger Barker was one of the followers of Lewin, who focused on physical environment. He and his colleagues gave descriptions about behaviours and activities of individuals in different setting. However, his contributions did not catch the attention of social psychology, they were well received by environmental psychology. Robert Sommer (1969) carried out studies on how social interaction is influenced by the physical set-up including furniture arrangement. Edward Hall (1966) carried out research on personal space and how distance between two individuals can determine the extent of relationship between them (Fisher, 1982).

Irwin Altman and Harold Proshansky were two social psychologists who contributed greatly to the field of environmental psychology (Fisher, 1982).

Social psychology can be applied to the field on environmental psychology in the following ways:

1. Our environmental perceptions can have an influence our attitude and this can be of great interest to social psychologists as they can not only understand how attitude develops but also work towards how to modify and change individuals' attitude.
2. The theories and principles of social psychology can be used to deal with certain environmental issues such as pollution (both air and noise), garbage and overall deterioration of environment.
3. Social psychologists can study the interactions amongst individuals based on the personal space.

Application to Consumer Psychology

Consumer psychology can be defined as a branch of psychology that studies the behaviour of individuals in terms of reasons and influences on the bases of which they buy or do not buy products. Consumer psychology as a field initially started with mainly studies on advertising and sales of products. Various companies would carry out consumer surveys in order to collect information about popularity and seek feedback of the consumers in order to make their products better (Fisher, 1982). Consumer behaviour can in a way be termed as social behaviour and thus numerous developments in the fields of consumer psychology can be attributed to the theories and models of social psychology (Fisher, 1982). Various aspects such as attitude, expectations, behaviours, decision-making, influences, communication and so on need to be examined to understand the consumer behaviours of individuals (Fisher, 1982). Further, in this context we also need to focus on the economical aspect of the consumers that can determine their behaviour. Maslow's hierarchy of needs can also be applied in this context. This can be used by the marketing and sales personnel to sell their products, thus implying that their product caters to more than one need. Further, there are also various environmental factors that can have an influence on consumer behaviour, including the lighting, music and space. Thus, social psychology and its theories and principles can be effectively applied to consumer psychology.

SUMMARY

As discussed in this chapter, social psychology has vast application. In health psychology, social psychology can be applied to developing intervention programmes to create awareness about health-related issues to promote healthy behaviour. Social psychology also finds its application to industrial and organisational psychology. Organisation is like a miniature society, where there are individuals from diverse backgrounds working together to achieve common goals. Social psychology can be applied here to motivate the employees; understand the individual employee in the context of the organisation and also to resolve conflicts. In sports, it can mainly be applied to building better teams and understand leadership in the context of sports. In clinical and counselling psychology, it can be applied to understand the origins of the psychological disorders/problems, diagnosis as well as intervention. Besides these main areas, social psychology can also be applied to fields such as education, environmental psychology, law and consumer behaviour.

QUESTIONS

1. Discuss the application of social psychology to health psychology.
2. Explain the health belief model and theory of planned action with suitable examples.
3. Describe how social psychology can be applied to conflict resolution in an organisational set-up.
4. Explain the application of social psychology to teams and leadership in sports.
5. Discuss how social psychology can be applied to understand the origins of psychological problems and disorders.
6. Explain clinical decision-making with suitable examples.
7. Describe the application of social psychology to education and law.

REFERENCES

Hall, E. (1966). *The hidden dimension*. New York, NY: Doubleday.

Hart, K. E., Ledgerwood, D. M., & Ianni, P.A. (2012). Applying social psychology to clinical and counselling psychology. In F. W. Schneider, J. A. Gruman & L. M. Coutts (Eds.), *Applied psychology: Understanding and addressing social and practical problems*. New Delhi: SAGE Publications.

Prochaska, J., & DiClemente, C. (1983). Stages and processes of self-change of smoking: Toward an integrative model of change. *Journal of Consulting and Clinical Psychology*, *51*(3), 390–395. Retrieved from http://dx.doi.org/10.1037//0022-006x.51.3.390

Sommer, R. (1969). *Personal space: The behavioural basis of design*. Englewood Cliffs, NJ: Prentice Hall.

Stroebe, W. (2000). *Social psychology and health* (2nd ed.). Buckingham: Open University Press.

FURTHER READINGS

For more information on social psychology and health/health psychology, following book can be referred:

Sarafino, E. P. (2002). *Health psychology: Biopsychosocial interactions* (4th edition). New York, NY: John Wiley and Sons.

For more information on application of social psychology to clinical psychology, following books can be referred:

Weary, G., & Mirels, H. (1982). *Integrations of clinical and social psychology* (1st edition). New York, NY: Oxford University Press.

For more information on application of social psychology to sports and sports psychology, following books can be referred:

Hagger, M., & Chatzisarantis, N. (2005). *The social psychology of exercise and sport*. Maidenhead: Open University Press.

Hemmings, B., & Holder, T. (2009). *Applied sport psychology: A case based approach*. New York, NY: Wiley-Blackwell.

Horn, T. S. (2008). *Advances in sport psychology* (3rd edition). Champaign, IL: Human Kinetics.

Jowett, S., & Lavallee, D. (2007). *Social psychology in sport*. Champaign, IL: Human Kinetics.

Knowles, A. M., Shanmugam, V., & Lorimer, R. (2015). A review of 'social psychology in sport exercise: Linking theory to practice'. *Journal of Sport Psychology in Action*, *6*(2), 121–122.

Appendix

? MULTIPLE CHOICE QUESTIONS

1. _______________ defined social psychology as a discipline in which people attempt to understand, explain and predict how the thoughts, feelings and actions of individuals are influenced by the perceived, imagined or implied thoughts, feelings and action of others.

   a. Sigmund Freud b. Wolfgang Kafka
   c. Alfred Binet d. Gordon Allport

2. The four main goals of science are _______________.

   a. Description, prediction, determining causality and explanation
   b. Description, prediction, determining independent variable and explanation
   c. Description, prediction, feedback and independent variable
   d. Description, prediction, determining independent variable and explanation

3. _______________ theory was proposed by Albert Bandura.

   a. Social identity theory b. Social learning theory
   c. Social impact theory d. Social exchange theory

4. _______________ defined as interdisciplinary field devoted to the study of neural, hormonal, cellular and genetic mechanisms and to study the associations between social and biological levels if organisation.

   a. Social neuroscience b. Social biology
   c. Social psychology d. Social science

5. The year ______________ marked the publication of a text, with word Social Psychology in it, by William McDougall.

   a. 1906 b. 1907
   c. 1908 d. 1910

6. A variable that can be manipulated by the researcher or experimenter is ______________.

   a. Dependent variable b. Independent variable
   c. Extraneous variable d. Control variable

7. External validity can be categorised into two types, ______________ and ______________.

   a. Construct validity and contact validity
   b. Ecological validity and construct validity
   c. Ecological validity and population validity
   d. Construct validity and population validity

8. ______________ involves collection of data from a representative sample of a population or whole population (in case of census) regarding some behaviour or to obtain their opinion.

   a. Action research b. Correlational research
   c. Ethnography d. Survey research

9. ______________ was introduced by Glaser and Strauss in 1967.

   a. Ethnography b. Action research
   c. Grounded theory d. Correlational research

10. ______________ is defined as the total organised body of information that any given person has about himself/herself.

    a. Self-efficacy b. Self-concept
    c. Self-esteem d. Self-confidence

11. Self-perception theory was proposed by ______________.

    a. Bem b. Festinger
    c. Baron d. Binet

12. ______________ is the study of mental processes involved in perceiving, attending to, remembering, thinking about and making sense of the people in our social world.

    a. Social identity b. Social neuroscience
    c. Social cognition d. Social facilitation

13. Meer ownership effect is ______________.

    a. A tendency where the objects and things owned by us are viewed more favourably than those that we do not own
    b. A tendency to think about alternate events or outcomes
    c. A tendency to pay more attention to information that is negative
    d. A tendency where people we know are viewed in a negative manner

14. ______________ can be described as the mental shortcuts where certain instances are categorised based on how similar they are to a typical member of a particular category.

    a. Representativeness heuristic b. Availability heuristic
    c. Simulation heuristic d. Anchoring heuristic

15. ______________ is one of the dimension of causality.

    a. Controllability b. Correspondent
    c. Covariance d. Characteristics

16. In ______________, our success is attributed to internal factors and failures are attributed to external factors.

    a. Self-situational attribution b. Self-serving attribution
    c. Self-optional attribution d. Self-operating attribution

17. According to ______________ theory, individuals assess their attitudes, abilities and emotions by comparing themselves with similar others, and that they do so especially when they are uncertain about themselves.

    a. Social comparison theory b. Social identity theory
    c. Social cooperation theory d. Social impact theory

18. Loneliness can also be described in terms of four groups of feelings.

    a. Desperation, depression, control and self-deprecation
    b. Desperation, depression, impatient boredom and self-deprecation
    c. Desperation, control, impatient boredom and self-deprecation
    d. Desperation, depression, impatient boredom and control

19. Reinforcement-affect model was proposed by ______________.

    a. Bernice Lott and Albert Lott
    b. Donn Byrne and Gerald Clore
    c. Bernice Byrne and Albert Clore
    d. Donn Lott and Gerald Clore

20. ______________ is indicated by traits and characteristics possessed by the individual that he/she finds difficult to express or share while interacting with others.

a. Actual self	b. False self
c. True self	d. Artificial self

21. ______________ are the attitudes that individuals may not be conscious or aware about.

a. Dual attitudes	b. Explicit attitudes
c. Implicit attitudes	d. Applied attitudes

22. Attitude has three main components: ______________.

a. Perceptive, sensitive and reactive
b. Perceptive, behavioural and reactive
c. Cognitive, sensitive and reactive
d. Cognitive, behavioural and affective

23. Values can be categorised as ______________ and ______________.

a. Ordinal and interval	b. Terminal and interval
c. Ordinal and instrumental	d. Terminal and instrumental

24. Balance theory was proposed by ______________.

a. Heider	b. Peplau
c. Binet	d. Bem

25. The term 'stereotype' was first proposed by Walter Lippmann, in the year ______________.

a. 1921	b. 1922
c. 1923	d. 1924

26. ______________ includes viewing in-group and out-group members primarily as members of larger, mutually inclusive group, thereby diminishing the importance of intergroup differences.

a. Re-summarisation	b. Reunion
c. Re-categorisation	d. Reunification

27. ______________ can be described as pressures to go along with the crowd, to behave in the same manner as other persons in one's group or society.

a. Conformity	b. Compliance
c. Obedience	d. Reality

28. ______________ involves giving unfavourable information about oneself to convey modesty.

a. Flattery	b. Self-enhancement
c. Self-depreciation	d. Self-disclosure

29. In ______________, the person will first gain compliance for smaller requests and then puts forth his/her larger request.

    a. Ingratiation
    b. Foot-in-the-door technique
    c. Door in the face technique
    d. That's not all technique

30. The term 'norm' has been derived from Latin term, ______________.

    a. Norman
    b. Normen
    c. Norma
    d. Normes

31. ______________ can be defined as an act performed voluntarily to help someone else when there is no expectation of receiving a reward in any form.

    a. Aggression
    b. Compliance
    c. Conformity
    d. Altruism

32. The theory of reciprocal altruism that was developed by ______________.

    a. Carl Rogers
    b. Alfred Binet
    c. Robert Trivers
    d. Hamilton Baron

33. ______________ is described as a behaviour that is directed to harm another individual but the behaviour is an instrument to achieve a non-aggressive goal.

    a. Hostile aggression
    b. Instrumental aggression
    c. Violent aggression
    d. collective aggression

34. ______________ is defined as intended and repeated harm caused by communication via use of computers, mobile phones and other electronic devices.

    a. Cybersulking
    b. Cyberbullying
    c. Cyberstalking
    d. Cybertalking

35. ______________ is a set of expected patterns of behaviour attributable to a person occupying a particular position.

    a. Norms
    b. Rules
    c. Roles
    d. Status

36. Guirdham in 1995 has discussed four norms, ______________, that are found in a group.

    a. Fairness, reciprocity, reasonableness and role expectation
    b. Fairness, reciprocity, reasonableness and role feedback
    c. Peripheral, reciprocity, reasonableness and role feedback
    d. Peripheral, reciprocity, reasonableness and role expectation

37. In _____________, the ultimate product or output results from the combination of the contributions by each and every member of the group.

a. Additive tasks
b. Compensatory tasks
c. Disjunctive tasks
d. Conjunctive tasks

38. The term social facilitation was introduced by _____________.

a. Binet
b. Freud
c. Allport
d. Wundt

39. In _____________, one or more members of the group do not fully contribute, to maximum of their capacity, to the group activity.

a. Social bluffing
b. Social facilitation
c. Social working
d. Social loafing

40. _____________ is the study of similarities and differences in individual psychological functioning in various cultural and ethno-cultural groups; of ongoing changes in variables reflecting such functioning; and of the relationships of psychological variables with sociocultural, ecological and biological variables.

a. Social psychology
b. Sociology
c. Anthropology
d. Cross cultural psychology

41. In _____________, the items that is closer to the midpoint on a scale is selected.

a. Moderacy bias
b. Extremity bias
c. Sample bias
d. Population bias

42. _____________ can be defined as the systematic application of social psychological constructs, principles, theories, intervention techniques, research methods and research findings to understand or ameliorate social problems.

a. Cross-cultural psychology
b. Social psychology
c. Anthropology
d. Applied Social Psychology

43. The empirical basis of applied social psychology can be tracked down to the contributions of _____________.

a. Sigmund Freud
b. Kurt Lewin
c. Robert Trivers
d. Hamilton Baron

44. _____________ is/are a set of interrelated hypotheses or propositions concerning a phenomenon or set of phenomena.

a. Roles
b. Norms
c. Theory
d. Enquiry

45. The three main functions of theory in applied social psychology are ______________.

a. Organisation, management and guide interventions
b. Organisation, direction and guide interventions
c. Development, management and feedback
d. Development, organisation and feedback

46. ______________ can be described as a situation confronting a group or a section of society that inflicts injurious consequences that can be handled only collectively.

a. Social loafing
b. Social motivation
c. Social function
d. Social problem

47. The term sanskritisation was first used by ______________.

a. M. N. Srinivas
b. M. N. Shivnarayan
c. D. N. Srinivas
d. D. N. Sharma

48. ______________ model states that the health-related behaviour of individuals depends on their presumption of the threat that is posed by the illness as well as the advantages and disadvantages of taking suitable action.

a. Theory of planned behaviour
b. Health related model
c. Theory of planned attitude
d. Health belief model

49. ______________ are related to evaluation or assessment of the members' performance related to their effort, ability and overall performance.

a. Orientation message
b. Stimulation message
c. Evaluation message
d. Task irrelevant messages

50. ______________ can be described as a tendency to perceive clients in ways that are erroneous owing to the reactive effects of an existing psychiatric label.

a. Loafing
b. Bullying
c. Dominating
d. Labelling

Bibliography

Abbott, P., & Williamson, E. (1999). Women, health and domestic violence. *Journal of Gender Studies, 8*(1), 83–102.

Abramson, L. Y., Seligman, M. E. P., & Teasdale, J. D. (1978). Learned helplessness in humans: Critique and reformulation. *Journal of Abnormal Psychology, 87*, 49–74.

Adams, J., & Jones, W. (1997). The conceptualization of marital commitment: An integrative analysis. *Journal of Personality and Social Psychology, 75*(5), 1177–1196.

Adamopoulos, J., & Lonner, J. (2001). Culture and psychology at a crossroad: Historical perspective and theoretical analysis. In D. Matsumoto (Ed.), *The handbook of culture and psychology*. London: Oxford University Press.

Ahuja, R. (2014). *Social problems in India*. New Delhi: Rawat Publications.

Ajzen, I., & Fishbein, M. (1977). Attitude–behaviour relations: A theoretical analysis and review of empirical research. *Psychological Bulletin, 84*(5), 888–918.

Allman, J. M., & Hasenstaub, A. (1999). Brains, maturation times, and parenting. *Neurobiology of Ageing, 20*(4), 447–454.

Allport, F. H. (1920). The influence of the group upon association and thought. *Journal of Experimental Psychology, 3*, 159–182.

Anderson, C. A., & Anderson, D. C. (1984). Ambient temperature and violent crime: Tests of the linear and curvilinear hypothesis. *Journal of Personality and Social Psychology, 46*(1), 91–97.

Anderson, C. A., & Bushman, B. J. (2001). Effects of violent video games on aggressive behavior, aggressive cognition, aggressive affect, physiological arousal, and prosocial behavior: A meta-analytic review of the scientific literature. *Psychological Science, 12*(5), 353–359.

———. (2002). The general aggression model: An integrated social-cognitive model of human aggression. *Annual Review of Psychology, 53*, 27–51.

Anderson, C. A., & Huesman, L. R. (2003). Human aggression: A social–cognitive view. In M. A. Hogg & J. Cooper (Eds.), *The Sage handbook of social psychology*. London: SAGE Publications.

Anderson, C. A., Berkowitz, L., Donnerstein, E., Huesmann, R., Johnson, J. D., Linz, D., Malamuth, N. M., & Wartella, E. (2003). The influence of media violence on youth. *Psychological Science in the Public Interest, 4*(3), 81–110.

Aronoff, J., Woike, B. A., & Hyman, L. M. (1992). Which are the stimuli in facial displays of anger and happiness? Configurational bases of emotion recognition. *Journal of Personality and Social Psychology, 62*(6), 1050–1066.

Aronson, E., Wilson, T. D., & Akert, R. M. (2014). *Social psychology*. India: Pearson.

Arvey, R. D., & Chaturvedi, S. (2011). Examining the genetic basis of leadership. In S. E. Murphy & R. J. Richard (Eds.), *Early development and leadership: Building the next generation of leaders* (series in applied psychology). New York, NY: Routledge.

Asch, S. E. (1951). Effects of group pressure upon the modification and distortion of judgments. In H. Guetzkow (Ed.). *Groups, leadership, and men: Research in Human Relations* (177–190). Oxford: Carnegie Press.

———. Opinions and social pressure. *Scientific American, 193*(5), 33–35.

Ashford, J. B., & LeCroy, C. W. (2010). *Human behavior in the social environment: A multidimensional perspective* (4th ed.). Belmont, CA: Wadsworth, Cengage Learning.

Avermaet, E. V. (2004). Social influences in small groups. In M. Hewstone & W. Stroebe (Eds.), *Introduction to social psychology*. UK: Blackwell Publishing.

Babu, B. V., & Kar, S. K. (2009). Domestic violence against women in eastern India: A population-based study on prevalence and related issues. *BMC Public Health*, *9*(1), 129.

Babu, H. (n.d.) *Short essay on the recent social changes in India*. Retrieved from http://www.preservearticles.com/2012011620990/short-essay-on-the-recent-social-changes-in-india.html

Bachman, R., & Peralta, R. (2002). The relationship between drinking and violence in an adolescent population: Does gender matter? *Deviant Behaviour, 23*(1), 1–19.

Bailey, J. M., Kim, P. Y., Hills, A., Linsenmeier, J. A. W. (1997). Butch, femme, or straight acting? Partner preferences of gay men and lesbians. *Journal of Personality and Social Psychology, 73*(5), 960–973.

Baldwin, K. (2012). Canada best G20 country to be a woman, India worst. *Thomson Reuters* (online), 13 June, India.

Balsam, K. F., & Szymanski, D. M. (2005). Relationship quality and domestic violence in women's same-sex relationships: The role of minority stress. *Psychology of Women Quarterly*, *23*(3), 258–269.

Bandura, A., (2000). Social cognitive theory: An agentic perspective. *Annual Review of Psychology, 52*(1), 1–26.

Bandura, A., Ross, D., & Ross. S. A. (1961). Transmission of aggression through imitation of aggressive models. *Journal of Abnormal and Social Psychology, 63*(3), 575–582.

Bargh, J. A., McKenna, K. Y. A., & Fitzsimons, G. M. (2002). Can you see the real me? Activation and expression of the "true self" on the Internet. *Journal of Social Issues, 58*(1), 33–48.

Bargh. J. A. (1983). Automatic and conscious processing of social information. In R. S. Wyer & T. K. Srull (Eds.), *The handbook of social cognition*. Hillsdale, NJ: Erlbaum.

Barker, R., Dembo, T., & Lewin, K. (1942). Frustration and regression: An experiment with young children. *American Journal of Sociology, 47*(5), 783–784.

Barlett. C., Witkower, Z., Mancini, C., & Saleem, M. (2016). Breaking the link between provocation and aggression: The role of mitigating information. *Aggressive Behaviour, 42*(6), 555–562.

Baron, A., & Byrne, D. (1995). *Social psychology: Understanding human interactions*. New Delhi: Prentice Hall.

Baron, R. A. (1977). *Human aggression*. New York, NY: Plenum Press.

Baron, R. A., & Byrne D. (2006). *Social psychology* (10th Ed.). New Delhi: Prentice Hall of India.

Baron, R. A., Byrne, D. E., & Nyla, R. B. (2006). *Social psychology*. Boston: Pearson/Allyn and Bacon.

Baron. R. S. (1984). Group dynamics. In A. S. Kahn (Ed.), *Social psychology*. Iowa: Wm, C. Brown Publishers, College Division.

Barrett, D. W. (2017). *Social psychology: Concepts and emerging trends*. New Delhi: SAGE Publications.

Bartholomew, L. K., Parcel, G. S., Kok, G., Gottlieb, N. H., & Fernández, M. E. (2011). *Planning health promotion programs: An intervention mapping approach* (3rd ed.). San Francisco: Jossey-Bass.

Baumeister, R. F. (1995). Self and identity: Am introduction. In A. Tesser (Ed.), *Advanced social psychology*. New York, NY: McGraw-Hill.

———. (1997). Identity, self-concept, and self-esteem: The self lost and found. In R. Hogan, J. Johnson & S. Briggs (Eds.), *Handbook of personality psychology*. New York, NY: Academic Press.

Baumeister, R. F., & Bushman, B. J. (2008). *Social psychology and human nature*. Belmont, New Delhi: Cengage Learning.

Bawa, J. S. (3 September 2015). 63% want to marry virgins, but majority approve of premarital sex. *The Hindustan Times* (online). Retrieved from http://www.hindustantimes.com/india/63-want-to-marry-virgins-but-majority-approve-of-premarital-sex/story-A79JdagFgmswYwwFIxyEkO.html

Bell, P. A., Fisher, J. D., Baum, A., & Greene, T. E. (1990). *Environmental psychology*. New York, NY: Holt, Rinehart, and Winston.

Bem, D. J. (1996). Exotic becomes erotic: A developmental theory of sexual orientation. *Psychological Review, 103*(2), 320–335.

Bennet, D. C., Guran, E. L., Ramos, M. C., & Margolin, G. (2011). College students electronic victimization in friendships and dating relationships: Anticipated distress and associations with risky behaviors. *Violence and Victims, 26(4)*, 410–429.

Berkowitz, L. (1964). Aggressive cues in aggressive behaviour and hostility catharsis. *Psychological Review, 71*(2), 104–122.

———. (1969). The frustration–aggression hypothesis revisited. In L. Berkowitz (Eds.), *Roots of aggression*. New York, NY: Atherton Press.

———. (1974). Some determinants of impulsive aggression: The role of mediated associations with reinforcements of aggressions. *Psychological Review, 81*(2), 165–176.

———. (1986). *A survey of social psychology*. New York, NY: CBS Publishing.

Berkowitz, L., & Donnerstein, E. (1982). External validity is more than skin deep: Some answers to criticisms of laboratory experiments. *American Psychologist, 37*(3), 245–257.

Berman, S., & Farge, P. (1993). *Promising practices in teaching social responsibility*. Albany: State University of New York Press.

Berry, J. W., Kim, U., Power, S., Young, M., & Bajaki, M. (1989). Acculturation attitudes in plural societies. *Applied Psychology: An International Review, 38*(2), 185–206.

Berry, J. W., Poortinga, Y. H., & Pande, J. (1997). *Handbook of cross-cultural psychology* (Vol. 1: Theory and Methods, 2nd ed.). London: Allyn and Bacon.

Berry, J. W., Poortinga, Y. H., Breugelmans, S. M., Chasiotis, A., & Sam, D. L. (2002). *Cross- cultural psychology*. New York, NY: Cambridge University Press.

Best, J. W., & Kahn, J. V. (1999). *Research in education*. New Delhi: Prentice Hall.

Bettencourt, B. A., & Miller, N. (1996). Gender differences in aggression as a function of provocation: A meta-analysis. *Psychological Bulletin, 119*(3), 422–447.

Bierhoff, H. W. (2001). Prosocial behaviour. In M. Hewstone, W. Stroebe, & G. Stephenson (Eds.), *Introduction to social psychology*. UK: Blackwell Publishers.

Björkqvist, K. Lagerspetz, K. M. J., & Kaukiainen, A. (1992). Do girls manipulate and boys fight? Development trends regarding direct and indirect aggression. *Aggressive Behaviour, 18*(2), 117–127.

Blaine, B. E. (2013). *Understanding the psychology of diversity* (2nd ed.). New Delhi: SAGE Publications.

Bolton, G. M. (1974). The lost letter technique as a measure of community attitudes toward a major social issue. *The Sociological Quarterly, 15*(4), 567–570.

Bowker, N., & Tuffin, K. (2003). Dicing with deception: People with disabilities' strategies for managing safety and identity online. *Journal of Computer-Mediated Communication, 8*(2). Retrieved from http://onlinelibrary.wiley.com/doi/10.1111/j.1083-6101.2003.tb00209.x/full

Brehm, S. S., Kassin, S. M., & Fein, S. (1999). *Social psychology*. Boston: Houghton Mifflin.

Brym, R. J., & Lenton, R. L. (2001). Love online: A report on digital dating in Canada. Retrieved from http://projects.chass.utoronto.ca/brym/loveonline.pdf

Bulman, R. J., & Wortman, C. B. (1977). Attributions of blame and coping in the "real world": Severe accident victims react to their lot. *Journal of Personality and Social Psychology, 35*(5), 351–363.

Burger, J. M. (1987). Desire for control and conformity to a perceived norm. *Journal of Personality and Social Psychology, 51*(2), 277–283.

Burns, R. B. (2000). Introduction to research methods. New Delhi: SAGE Publications.

Bushman, B. J., & Anderson, C. A. (2001). Is it time to pull the plug on the hostile versus instrumental aggression dichotomy? *Psychological Review, 108*(1), 273–279.

———. (2002). Violent video games and hostile expectations: A test of the general aggression model. *Personality and Social Psychology Bulletin, 28*(12), 1679–1686.

Bushman, B. J., & Bonacci, A. M. (2004). You've got mail: Using e-mail to examine the effect of prejudiced attitudes on discrimination against Arabs. *Journal of Experimental Social Psychology, 40*(6), 753–759.

Bushman. B. J. (2002). Does venting anger feed or extinguish the flame? Catharsis, rumination, distraction, anger and aggressive responding. *Personality and Social Psychology Bulletin, 28*(6), 724–731.

Button, T., Stallings, M., Rhee, S., Corley, R., & Hewitt, J. (2011). The etiology of stability and change in religious values and religious attendance. *Behavior Genetics, 41*(2), 201–210. Retrieved from https://www.ncbi.nlm.nih.gov/pmc/articles/PMC3045647/

Byrne, D. (1961). Interpersonal attraction and attitude similarity. *Journal of Abnormal and Social Psychology, 62*(3), 713–715.

Byrne, D., Ervin, C., & Lamberth, J. (1970). Continuity between the experimental study of attraction and real-life computer dating. *Journal of Personality and Social Psychology, 16*, 157–165.

Cai, H., Brown, J. D., Deng, C., & Oakes, M. A. (2007). Self-esteem and culture: Differences in cognitive self-evaluations or affective self-regard? *Asian Journal of Social Psychology, 10*, 162–170. Retrieved from http://faculty.washington.edu/jdb/articles/Cai%20et%20al.%20(2007)%20AJSP.pdf

Capara, G. V., Perugini, M., & Barbaranelli, C. (1994). Studies of individual differences in aggression. In M. Potegal & J. F. Knuton (Eds.), *The dynamics of aggression: Biological and social processes in dyads and groups*. New Jersey, NJ: Erlbaum.

Caprara, G., Barbaranelli, C., & Zimbardo, P. (1996). Understanding the complexity of human aggression: Affective, cognitive, and social dimensions of individual differences in propensity toward aggression. *European Journal of Personality, 10*(2), 133–155.

Carroll, B. C., & Patterson, K. (2014). Servant leadership: A cross-cultural study between Indian and the United States. *Servant Leadership: Theory & Practice, 1*(1), 16–45. Retrieved from http://www.sltpjournal.org/uploads/2/6/3/9/26394582/4_patterson_-_print_v1_i1_2.pdf

Carron, A. V. (1982). Cohesiveness in sport groups: Interpretations and considerations. *Journal of Sport Psychology, 4*(2), 123–138.

Carron, A. V., Brawley, L. R., & Widmeyer, W. N. (1997). The measurement of cohesiveness in sports groups. In J. L. Duda (Ed.), *Advances in sport and exercise psychology measurement*. Morgantown, WV: Fitness Information Technology.

Carron, A. V., Burke, S. M., & ve Shapcott, K. M. (2009). Enhancing team effectiveness. In B. W. Brewer (Ed.), *International Olympic Committee medical commission handbook of sports medicine and science, sport psychology*. Oxford: Wiley-Blackwell Publishing Ltd.

Carron, A. V., Colman, M., Wheeler, J., & Stevens, D. (2002). Cohesion and performance in sports: A meta-analysis. *Journal of Sport and Exercise Psychology, 24*, 168–188.

Chaiken, S., & Baldwin, M. (1981). Affective-cognitive consistency and the effect of salient behavioral information on the self-perception of attitudes. *Journal of Personality and Social Psychology, 41*(1), 1–12.

Chapman, L. J. (1967). Illusory correlation in observational report. *Journal of Verbal Learning and Verbal Behavior, 6*(1), 151–155.

Chapman, L. J., & Chapman, J. P. (1967). Genesis of popular but erroneous diagnostic observations. *Journal of Abnormal Psychology, 72*(3), 193–204.

Chelladurai, P. (1978). *A contingency model of leadership in athletics* (Unpublished doctoral dissertation). University of Waterloo, Canada.

———. (1990). Leadership in sports: A review. *International Journal of Sport Psychology, 21*, 328–354.

———. (1993). Leadership. In R. N. Singer, M. Murphey & L. K. Tennant (Eds.), *Handbook of research on sport psychology* (pp. 647–671). New York, NY: Macmillan.

Cherry, K. (2015). 10 quick facts about social psychology. Retrieved from http://psychology.about.com/od/socialpsychology/qt/facts-about-social-psychology.htm

Chester, A. (2004). *Presenting the self in cyberspace: Identity play in MOOS* (PhD thesis). Department of Philosophy, University of Melbourne. Retrieved from https://minerva-access.unimelb.edu.au/bitstream/handle/11343/38846/66015_00000534_01_chester.pdf?sequence=1

Chiu, M. L., Feldman, S. S., & Rosenthal, D. A. (1992). The influence of immigration on parental behavior and adolescent distress in Chinese families residing in two Western nations. *Journal of Research on Adolescence, 2*(3), 205–239.

Christensen, L. B. (2004). *Experimental methodology*. Boston: Pearson. Clark, R. D., & David, J. F. (1984). Helping behaviour. In A. S. Kahn (Ed.), *Social psychology*. Iowa: Wm, C. Brown Publishers, College Division.

Cohen, D., Nisbett, R. E., Bowdle, B. F., & Schwarz, N. (1996). Insult, aggression and the southern culture of honour: An "experimental ethnography". *Journal of Personality and Social Psychology, 70*(5), 945–960. Retrieved from https://deepblue.lib.umich.edu/bitstream/handle/2027.42/92155/InsultAggressionAndTheSouthernCulture.pdf

Coker, A. L., Hopenhayn, C., DeSimone, C. P., Bush, H. M., & Crofford, L. (2009). Violence against women raises risk of cervical cancer. *Journal of Women's Health, 18*(8), 1179–1185.

Cooley, C. H. (1902). *Human nature and the social order*. New York, NY: Charles Scribner's sons. Retrieved from https://ia902707.us.archive.org/35/items/humannaturesocia00cooluoft/humannaturesocia00cooluoft.pdf

Corey G. (2001). *Theory and practice of counselling and psychotherapy*. USA: Brooks/Cole, Thomson Learning.

Cornwell, B., & Lundgren, D. C. (2001). Love on the Internet: Involvement and misrepresentation in romantic relationships in cyberspace vs. realspace. *Computers in Human Behavior, 17*(2), 197–211.

Corrigan, P. W. (2007). How clinical diagnosis might exacerbate the stigma of mental illness. *Social Work, 52*(1), 31–39.

Courage, M. L., Edison, S. C., & Howe, M. L. (2004). Variability in the early development of visual self recognition. *Infant Behaviour and Development, 27*(4), 509–532.

Coutts, L. M., & Gruman, J. A. (2012). Applying social psychology to organisations. In F. W. Schneider, J. A. Gruman & L. M. Coutts (Eds.), *Applied psychology: Understanding and addressing social and practical problems*. New Delhi: SAGE Publications.

Crisp, R. J., & Turner, R. N. (2010). *Essential social psychology*. New Delhi: SAGE Publications.

Critto, A. (1999). *Choosing models of society and social norms: Improving choices and quality of life*. Lanham, MD: University Press of America.

Crocker, P. R. (1990). Facial and verbal congruency: Effects on perceived verbal and emotional coaching feedback. *Canadian Journal of Sport Sciences, 15*(1), 17–22.

Crust, L., & Lawrence, I. (2006). A review of leadership in sport: Implications for football management. *Athletic Insight: The Online Journal of Sports Psychology, 8*(4), 28–48.

Crystal, D. S., & Stevenson, H. W. (1995). What is a bad kid? Answers of adolescents and their mothers in three cultures. *Journal of Research on Adolescence, 5*(1), 71–91.

Dalal, A. K., & Misra, G. (2002). Social psychology in India: Evolution and emerging trends. In A. K. Dalal & G. Misra (Eds.), *New directions in Indian psychology* (Vol. 1, Social Psychology). New Delhi: SAGE Publications.

———. (Eds.). (2001). *New directions in Indian psychology* (Vol. 1, Social Psychology). New Delhi: SAGE Publications.

Dave, V. R., Makwana, N. R., Yadav, B. S., & Yadav, S. (2013). A study on high-risk premarital sexual behavior of college going male students in Jamnagar city of Gujarat, India. *International Journal of High Risk Behaviours and Addiction, 2*(3), 112–16. Retrieved from https://www.ncbi.nlm.nih.gov/pmc/articles/PMC4070158/

David, M., & Sutton, C. D. (2011). *Social research: An introduction*. New Delhi: SAGE Publications.

DeBono, K. G. (2006). Self-monitoring and consumer psychology. *Journal of Personality, 74*(3), 715–738.

Deol, S. S. (2014). Honour killings in India: A study of the Punjab State. *International Journal of Social Sciences, 3*(6), 7–16.

DeRidder, R., & Tripathi, R. C. (Eds.). (1992). *Norm violation and intergroup relations*. Oxford: Clarendon.

Deutsce, M., & Krauss, R. M. (1960). The effect of threat upon interpersonal bargaining. *Journal of Abnormal and Social Psychology, 1*(2), 181–89. Retrieved from https://www.uni-muenster.de/imperia/md/content/psyifp/aeechterhoff/wintersemester2011-12/vorlesungkommperskonflikt/deutschkrauss_threatbargain_jasp1960.pdf

Deutsch, M., & Krauss, R. M. (1962). Studies of interpersonal bargaining. *Journal of Conflict Resolution, 6*(1), 52–76.

Dhangre, D. N. (1985). *India. In UNESCO report, sociology and social anthropology in Asia and the Pacific*. New Delhi: Wiley Eastern.

Diener, E. (1980). Deindividuation, self-awareness and disinhibition. *Journal of Personality and Social Psychology, 37*(7), 1160–1171.

Dindia, K., & Allen, M. (1992). Sex differences in self disclosure: A meta-analysis. *Psychological Bulletin, 112*(1), 106–124.

Ditto, P. H., & Lopez, D. F. (1992). Motivated skepticism: Use of differential decision criteria for preferred and nonpreferred conclusions. *Journal of Personality and Social Psychology, 63*(4), 568–584.

Dollard, J., Doob, L., Miller, N., Mowrer, O. H., & Sears, R. R. (1939). *Frustration and aggression*. New Haven, CT: Yale University Press.

Donath, J. S. (1999). Identity and deception in the virtual community. In M. A. Smith & P. Kollock (Eds.), *Communities in cyberspace* (pp. 29–59). New York, NY: Routledge.

Donn, J., & Sherman, R. (2002). Attitudes and practices regarding the formation of romantic relationships on the Internet. *Cyber Psychology and Behavior, 5*(2), 107–123.

Donnerstein, E. (1984). Aggression. In A. S. Kahn (Ed.), *Social psychology*. Iowa: Wm, C. Brown Publishers, College Division.

Donnerstein, M. V. (1984). Introduction to social psychology. In A. S. Kahn (Ed.), *Social psychology*. Iowa: Wm, C. Brown Publishers, College Division.

Dorfman, P. W., & Stephan, W. G. (1984). The effects of group performance on cognitions, satisfaction, and behavior. *A Process Model Journal of Management, 10*(2), 173–192.

Dubey, S. C. (1967). Modernization and its adaptive demands on Indian society. In M. S. Gore, I. P. Desai & S. Chitnis (Eds.), *Papers in the sociology of education in India*. New Delhi: NCERT.

Duck, S. W., & Craig, G. (1975). Effects of type of information upon interpersonal attraction. *Social Behavior and Personality, 3*(2), 157–164.

Dunne, G. (1997). *Lesbian lifestyles: Women's work and the politics of sexuality*. London: Macmillan.

Eagly, A. H., & Chaiken, S. (1993). *The psychology of attitudes*. Fort Worth, TX: Harcourt Brace Jovanovich.

Eagly, A. H., & Steffen, V. J. (1986). Gender and helping behaviour: A meta-analytic review of social psychological literature. *Psychological Bulletin, 100*(3), 309–330.

Eckensberger, L. H. (1972). The necessity of a theory for applied cross-cultural research. In L. H. Cronbach & P. J. D. Drenth (Eds.), *Mental tests and cultural adaptation* (pp. 99–107). The Hague, Netherlands: Mouton.

Eiaenstadt, S. N. (1966). *Modernization: Protest and change*. Englewood cliffs, NJ: Prentice Hall Inc.

Ekman, P. (1993). Facial expression and emotion. *American Psychologist, 48*(4), 384–392. Retrieved from https://www.paulekman.com/wp-content/uploads/2013/07/Facial-Expression-And-Emotion1.pdf

Ekman, P., Friesen, W. V., & Ellsworth, P. (1972). *Emotion in the human face: Guidelines for research and an integration of findings*. New York, NY: Pergamon Press.

Eysenck, M. W. (2013). *Simply psychology*. New York, NY: Psychology Press.

Farnham, A. (2005). *The psychology of behaviour at work: The individual in the organization*. East Sussex: Psychology Press.

Farooq, U. (2011). *Social problem: Definitions, effects, characteristics, classification and causes*. Retrieved from http://www.studylecturenotes.com/social-sciences/sociology/121-social-change-and-social-problem

———. (2012). *What is social change definition and meaning*. Retrieved from http://www.studylecturenotes.com/social-sciences/sociology/282-what-is-social-change-definition-and-meaning

Feldman, R. S. (1985). *Social psychology: Theories, research and applications*. New York, NY: McGraw Hill Book Company.

Felmelee, D., Orzechowicz, D., & Fortes, C. (2010). Fairy tales: Attraction and stereotypes in same gender relationships. *Sex Roles, 62*(2/3), 226–40. Retrieved from https://www.ncbi.nlm.nih.gov/pmc/articles/PMC2844533/

Feltz, D. L., & Lirgg, C. D. (1998). Perceived teams and player efficacy in hockey. *Journal of Applied Psychology, 83*(4), 557–564.

Fernandes, J. (7 October 2014). ASRO nun shower love on HIV positive kids. *The Times of India* (online). Retrieved from http://timesofindia.indiatimes.com/city/goa/ASRO-nuns-shower-love-on-HIV-positive-kids/articleshow/44528023.cms

Festinger, L., Schachter, S., & Back, K. (1950). Social pressures in informal groups. *The American Catholic Sociological Review, 11*, 268–69. Retrieved from http://dx.doi.org/10.2307/3707362

Fincham, R., & Rhodes, P. S. (1999). *Principles of organisational behaviour*. New York, NY: Oxford University Press Inc.

Fisher, R. J. (1982). *Social psychology: An applied approach*. New York, NY: St. Martin's Press, Inc.

Fiske, S. T., & Taylor, S. E. (1991). *Social cognition*. Reading MA: Addison-Wesley.

———. (1993). Social cognition and social perception. In E. W. Porter & M. R. Rosenwig (Eds.), *Annual review of psychology*. Palo Alto, CA: Annual Reviews.

Fox, C. R. (2006). The availability heuristic in the classroom: How soliciting more criticism can boost your course ratings. *Judgment and Decision Making, 1*(1), 86–90.

Frank, M., & Gilovich, T. (1988). The dark side of self and social perception: Black uniforms and aggression in professional sports. *Journal of Personality and Social Psychology, 54*(1) 74–85.

Freedom without fear is what we need to protect, to guard and respect. (22 December 2012). *News18.com*. Retrieved from http://www.news18.com/news/india/kavita-krishnan-interview-tehelka-527992.html

Fridlund, A. J. (1992). The behavioural ecology and sociality of human face. *Reviews of Personality and Social Psychology, 13*, 90–121.

Gaertner, S. L., & Divido, J. F. (1977). The subtlety of white racism, arousal and helping behaviour. Journal *of Personality and Social Psychology, 35*(10), 691–707.

Gangestad, S., & Snyder, M. (1985). On the nature of self-monitoring: An examination of latent causal structure. In P. Shaver (Ed.), *Review of Personality and Social Psychology*. California: SAGE Publications.

Gautam, A. (5 January 2017). We need Opportunities and support, not sympathy: Transgender Community. *Times of India*. Retrieved from http://timesofindia.indiatimes.com/india/transgenders-need-opportunities-and-support-not-sympathy/articleshow/56355679.cms?utm_source=toiiphoneappandutm_medium=Emailandutm_campaign=show

Gerlock, A. A. (1999). Health impact of domestic violence. *Issues in Mental Health Nursing, 20*(4), 373–385.

Gerrig, R., & Zimbardo, P. (2006). *Psychology and life*. New Delhi: Pearson Education.

Gilbert, D. T. (1991). How mental systems believe. *American Psychologist, 46*(2), 107–19. Retrieved from https:/pdfs.semanticscholar.orgd160/00a42d6f236cbd056a166d21188abe367a68.pdf

Gilbert, D. T., Tafarodi, R. W., & Malone, P. S. (1993). You cannot believe everything you read. *Journal of personality and Social Psychology, 65*(2), 221–233. Retrieved from http://www.danielgilbert.com/Gilbert%20et%20al%20(EVERYTHING%20YOU%20READ).pdf

Goldstein, A. P., Heller, K., & Sechrest, L. B. (1966). *Psychotherapy and the psychology of behaviour change*. New York, NY: Wiley.

Goodwin, C. J. (2003). *Research in psychology: Methods and designs*. Hoboken, New Jersey, NJ: Wiley.

Graves, T. D. (1967). Psychological acculturation in a tri-ethnic community. *Southwestern Journal of Anthropology, 23*: 337–350.

Green, R. J., & Mitchell, V. (2002). Gay and lesbian couples in therapy: Homophobia, relational ambiguity, and social support. In A. S. Gurman & N. S. Jacobson (Eds.), *Clinical handbook of couple therapy*. New York, NY: Guilford Press.

Gregory, W. L., Cialdini, R. B., & Kathleen, C. M. (1982). Self-relevant scenarios as mediators of likelihood estimates and compliance: does imaging make it so? *Journal of Personality and Social Psychology, 43*(1), 89–99.

Griffitt, W. B., & Guay, P. (1969). "Object" evaluation and conditioned affect. *Journal of Experimental Research in Psychology, 4*, 1–8.

Guerrero, A. L. (2016). *Social problems: Community, policy and social action*. New Delhi: SAGE Publications.

Hall, J. A., & Veccia, E. M. (1990). More "touching" observations: New insights on men, women, and interpersonal touch. *Journal of Personality and Social Psychology, 59*(6), 1155–1162.

Hansen, R. D. (1984a). Attribution. In A. S. Kahn (Ed.), *Social psychology*. Iowa: Wm, C. Brown Publishers, College Division.

———. (1984b). Person perception. In A. S. Kahn (Ed.), *Social psychology*. Iowa: Wm, C. Brown Publishers, College Division.

Haq, R. (2013). Intersectionality of gender and other forms of identity: Dilemmas and challenges facing women in India, gender in management. *An International Journal, 28*(3), 171–184.

Harries, K. D., & Stadler, S. J. (1983). Determinants revisited: Assault and heat stress in Dallas, 1980. *Environment and Behaviour, 15*(2), 235–256.

Harrigan, J., Lucic, K., Kay, D., McLaney, A., & Rosenthal, R. (1991). Effect of expresser role and type of self-touching on observers' perceptions. *Journal of Applied Social Psychology, 21*(7), 585–609.

Hartnack, C. (2016). The interlinkages between Western and indigenous psychology in 20th- and early 21st-century India. In M. Kuhn & H. Vessuri (Eds.), *Contributions to alternative concepts of knowledge*. Stuttgart: Ibidem-Verlag.

Hedin, D. P. (1989). Power of community service. *Proceedings of the Academy of Political Science, 37*(2), 201–213.

Heine, S. J. (2012). *Cultural psychology*. New York, NY: W. W. Norton and Company.

Henrich, J., Heine, S. J., & Norenzayan, A. (2010). The weirdest people in the world? *Behavioural and Brain Sciences, 33*, 61–135. Retrieved from http://www2.psych.ubc.ca/~henrich/pdfs/Weird_People_BBS_final02.pdf

Herskovits, M. J. (1948). *Man and his works: The science of cultural anthropology*. New York, NY: Knopf.

Heuzé, J. P., Raimbault, N., & Fontayne, P. (2006). Relationships between cohesion, collective efficacy, and performance in professional basketball teams: An examination of mediating effects. *Journal of Sports Sciences, 24*(1), 59–68.

Hewstone, M., Stroebe, W., & Jonas, K. (Eds.). (2007) *Introduction to social psychology: A European perspective* (4th ed.). London: Blackwell.

Hixon, J., & Swann, W. (1993). When does introspection bear fruit? Self-reflection, self-insight, and interpersonal choices. *Journal of Personality and Social Psychology, 64*(1), 35–43.

Hodgetts, D., Drew, N., Sonn, C., Ottilie, S., Nikora, L. W., & Curtis, C. (2010). *Social psychology and everyday life*. New York, NY: Palgrave Macmillan.

Hoffman, M. L. (1975). Sex differences in moral internalization and values. *Journal of Personality and Social psychology, 32*(4), 720–729.

Hofstede, G. (2011). Dimensionalizing cultures: The Hofstede Model in context. *Online Readings in Psychology and Culture, 2*(1). Retrieved from http://dx.doi.org/10.9707/2307-0919, p.1014.

———. (1989). Culture's consequences: International differences in work-related values. New York, NY: SAGE Publications.

Holmberg, B. (1981). *Status and trends of distance education*. London: Kogan Page.

How Sindhutai converted every adversity into an achievement. (5 March 2016). Retrieved from http://www.moneylife.in/article/how-sindhutai-converted-every-adversity-into-an-achievement/45810.html

Howard, L. M., Trevillion, K., & Agnew-Davies, R. (2010). Domestic violence and mental health. *International Review of Psychiatry, 22*(5), 525–534.

Huesmann, L. R., Moise-Titus, J., Podolski, C., & Eron, L. D. (2003). Longitudinal relations between children's exposure to TV violence and their aggressive and violent behavior in young adulthood: 1977–1992. *Developmental Psychology, 39*(2), 201–221.

Indian Woman refused abortion in Ireland, dies. (15 November 2012). *The Times of India*. Retrieved from http://timesofindia.indiatimes.com/india/Indian-woman-refused-abortion-in-Ireland-dies/articleshow/17222804.cms

Inkeles, A., & Smith, D. H. (1974). *Becoming modern: Individual changes in six developing countries*. Cambridge: Harvard University Press.

International Center for Research on Women. (2000). *Domestic violence in India: A summary report of a multi-site household survey*. Washington, DC: International Center for Research on Women. Retrieved from https://www.icrw.org/wp-content/uploads/2016/10/Domestic-Violence-in-India-3-A-Summary-Report-of-a-Multi-Site-Household-Survey.pdf

İskifoğlu, G. (2014). Approaches to study culture, equivalence and bias: Triadic notions in developing research instruments for cross-cultural comparative studies. *Proceedings of INTED2014 Conference*. Retrieved from https://www.researchgate.net/publication 261702002_APPROACHES_TO_STUDY_CULTURE_EQUIVALENCY_AND_BIAS_TRIADIC_NOTIONS_IN_DEVELOPING_RESEARCH_INSTRUMENTS_FOR_CROSS-CULTURAL_COMPARATIVE_STUDIES

Janis, I. (1972). *Victims of groupthink*. Boston: Houghton Mifflin.

———. (1982). *Groupthink*. Boston: Houghton Mifflin.

John, D., Ahmad, O., and Schneider, M. (2013) India: Violence against women. Current challenges and future trends. Retrieved from http://www.freiheit.org/Aktuelle-Berichte/1804c27055i1p/index.html

Jones, J. M. (1997). *Prejudice and racism*. New York, NY: McGraw Hill.

Judge, T., Bono, J., Ilies, R., & Gerhardt, M. (2002). Personality and leadership: A qualitative and quantitative review. *Journal of Applied Psychology, 87*(4), 765–780.

Jussim, L., Cain, T., Crawford, J., Harber, K., & Cohen, F. (2009). The unbearable accuracy of stereotypes. In T. Nelson (Ed.), *Handbook of prejudice, stereotyping, and discrimination* (pp. 199–227). Hillsdale, NJ: Erlbaum.

Kahn, A. S., & Donnerstein, E. (1984). Social influence. In A. S. Kahn (Ed.), *Social psychology*. Iowa: Wm, C. Brown Publishers, College Division.

Kakar, S. (1995). *The colors of violence*. New Delhi: Oxford University Press.

Kao, H. S. R. (1997). *Asian perspectives on psychology*. New York, NY: SAGE Publications.

Karasz, A., & Singelis, T. M. (2009). Qualitative and mixed methods research in cross-cultural psychology: Introduction to the special issues. *Journal of Cross Cultural psychology, 40*(6), 990–916.

Kelley, H. H. (1950). The warm–cold variable in first impressions of persons. *Journal of Personality, 18*(4), 431–439.

Kernis, M. H., & Wheeler, L. (1981). Beautiful friends and ugly strangers: Radiation and contrast effects in perception of same sex pairs. *Personality and Social Psychology Bulletin, 7*(4), 617–620.

Kerlinger, F. N. (1995). *Foundations of behavioural research*. Bangalore: Prism Books Pvt Ltd.

Kern, H., & Yeaton, W. H. (2010). Lost and found, letters and methods: Assessing attitudes toward chiropractic and medical care. *Journal of Methods and Measurement in the Social Sciences, 1*(1), 35–44.

Kim, B. S., & Omizo, M. M. (2010). Behavioral enculturation and acculturation, psychological functioning, and help-seeking attitudes among Asian American adolescents. *Asian American Journal of Psychology, 1*(3), 175–185. Retrieved from https://www.ncbi.nlm.nih.gov/pmc/articles/PMC3092711/

Kimball, M. M. (1986). Television and sex role attitudes. In T. M. Williams (Ed.), *The impact of television: A natural experiment in three communities* (pp. 265–301). Orlando, FL: Academic Press.

Kirkpatrick, S. A., & Locke, E. A. (1991). Leadership: Do traits matter? *Academy of Management Executive, 5*(2), 48–60.

Klein, S. B., & Loftus, J. (1988). *The nature of self-referent encoding: The contributions of elaborative and organizational processes: Correction to Klein and Loftus. Journal of Personality and Social Psychology, 55*(1), 5–11.

Klein, S. B., Loftus, J., & Burton, H. A. (1989). Two self-reference effects: The importance of distinguishing between self-descriptiveness judgments and autobiographical retrieval in self-referent encoding. *Journal of Personality and Social Psychology, 56*(6), 853–865.

Knapp, M. L., & Hall, J. A. (2009). *Nonverbal communication in human interaction* (7th ed.). Boston: Wadsworth.

Kok, G., Schaalma, H., De Vries, H., Parcel, G., & Paulussen, T. (1996). Social psychology and health education. In W. Stroebe & M. Hewstone (Eds.), *European review of social psychology* (Vol. 7, pp. 241–282). Chichester: John Wiley and Sons Ltd.

Kozel, V., & Parker, B. (2001). Poverty in rural India: The contribution of qualitative research in poverty analysis. Poverty Reduction and Economic Management Unit, South Asia Region. Washington DC: World Bank.

Krantz, D. S., & Deckel, A. W. (1983). Coping with coronary heart disease and Stroke. In T. G. Burish & L. A. Bradley (Eds.), *Coping with chronic disease: Research and applications*. New York, NY: Academic Press.

Krauss, R. M., & Deutsce, M. (1966). Communication in Interpersonal Bargaining. *Journal of Personality and Social Psychology, 4*(5), 572–577.

Krech, D., & Crutchfield, R. S. (1948). *Theory and problems of social psychology*. New York, NY: McGraw-Hill.

Krech, D., Crutchfield, R. S., & Ballachey, E. L. (1962). *Individual in society: A textbook of social psychology*. London: McGraw-Hill.

Krishna, G. (2015). India: A country of cyberbillies? *Business Standard*. Retrieved from http://www.business-standard.com/article/specials/india-a-country-of-cyberbullies-115110501365_1.html

Kumar, A., & Tiwari, V. K. (2003). Knowledge, attitude and behaviour towards pre-marital sex: A study among youths from two city slums in India. *Health and Population: Perspectives and Issues, 26*(4), 126–134. Retrieved from http://medind.nic.in/hab/t03/i4/habt03i4p126.pdf

Kumar, V. A. (15 March 2016). 81 honour killings in three years in Tamil Nadu. *Deccan Chronicle*. Retrieved from http://www.deccanchronicle.com/nation/crime/150316/81-honour-killings-in-three-years-in-tamil-nadu.html

Kuppuswamy, B. (1973). *Elements of social psychology*. New Delhi: Vikas Publishing House Pvt. Ltd.

Kurdek, L. A. (1993). The allocation of household labor in gay, lesbian, and heterosexual married couples. *Journal of Social Issues, 49*(3), 127–139.

———. (2004). Are gay and lesbian cohabiting couples really different from heterosexual married couples? *Journal of Marriage and the Family, 66*(4), 880–900.

———. (2005). What do we know about gay and lesbian couples? *Current Directions in Psychological Science, 14*(5), 251–254.

Lamont, E. P. (Ed.). (2009) *Social psychology: New research*. New York, NY: Nova Science Publishers, Inc.

Larson, C. L., Aronoff, J., & Stearns, J. J. (2007). The shape of threat: Simple geometric forms evoke rapid and sustained capture of attention. *Emotion Review, 7*(3), 526–534.

Latane, B. (1981). The psychology of social impact. *American Psychologist, 36*(4), 343–356.

Lausic, D., Tennenbaum, G., Eccles, D., Jeong, A., & Johnson, T. (2009). Intra-team communication and performance in double tennis. *Research Quarterly for exercise and sports, 80*(2), 281–290.

Leone, C., and Hawkins, L. B. (2006). Self monitoring and close relationships. *Journal of Personality, 74*(3), 739–778.

Lepore, S. (1998). Problems and prospects for the social support-reactivity hypothesis. *Annals of Behaviour Medicine, 20*(4), 257–269.

Lerner, M. (1995). *The politics of meaning*. Reading, MA: Addison-Wesley.

Levenson, R. W., Ekman, P., & Friensen, W. V. (1990). Voluntary facial action generates emotion-specific autonomic nervous system activity. *Psychophysiology, 27*(4), 363–384. Retrieved from https://www.paulekman.com/wp-content/uploads/2013/07/Voluntary-Facial-Action-Generates-Emotion-Specific-Autom.pdf

Levinson, D. (1989). *Family violence in cross-cultural perspective* (Frontiers of Anthropology). New Delhi: SAGE Publications.

Lewis, M., & Brooks, J. (1978). Self knowledge in emotional development. In M. Lewis & L. Rosenblum (Eds.), *The development of affect*. New York, NY: Plenum.

Loomis, C. P., & Loomis, Z. K. (1969). *Socio-economic change and the religious factor in India: An Indian symposium of view on Max Weber*. New Delhi: Affiliated East-West Press.

Macionis, J. (1997). *Sociology* (1st ed.). Upper Saddle River, NJ: Prentice Hall.

MacLean, D., & Sullivan, P. (2003). A season long case study investigation of collective efficacy in male intercollegiate basketball. *Athletic Insight: The Online Journal of Sports Psychology, 5*(3). Retrieved from http://www.athleticinsight.com/Vol5Iss3/BasketPDF.pdf

Macrae, C. N., Hood, B. M., Milne, A. B., Rowe, A. C., & Mason, M. F. (2002). Are you looking at me? Eye gaze and person perception. *Psychological Science, 13*(5), 460–464.

Madlow, L. (1972). *Anger: How to recognize and cope with it*. New York, NY: Schribners.

Magyar, T. M., Feltz, D. L., & Simpson, I. P. (2004). Individual and crew level determinants of collective efficacy in growing. *Journal of Sport and Exercise Psychology, 26*(1), 136–154.

Markus, H. R., & Kitayama, S. (1991). Culture and the self: Implications for cognition, emotion, and motivation. *Psychological review, 98*(2), 224–253.

Marsh, H., Byrne, B., & Yeung, A. (1999). Causal ordering of academic self-concept and achievement: Reanalysis of a pioneering study and revised recommendations. *Educational Psychologist, 34*(3), 155–167.

Matsumoto, D., & Hwang, H. S. (2011). *Reading facial expressions of emotion*. Retrieved from http://www.apa.org/science/about/psa/2011/05/facial-expressions.aspx

McCanne, T. R., & Anderson, J. A. (1987). Emotional responding following experimental manipulation of facial electromyographic activity. *Journal of Personality and Social Psychology, 52*(4), 759–768.

McCaw, B., Golding, J. M., Farley, M., & Minkoff, J. R. (2007). Domestic violence and abuse, health status, and social functioning. *Women and Health, 45*(2), 1–23.

McCorduck, P. (April 1996). Sex, lies and avatars. *Wired*, 106–10, 158–164.

McDavid, J. M., & Harari, H. (1994). *Social psychology: Individuals, groups and societies*. New Delhi: CBS Publishers.

McGarty, C. (1999). *Categorisation in social psychology*. London: Cambridge University Press.

McLeod, S. (2007). Social psychology. *Simply psychology*. Retrieved from http://www.simplypsychology.org/social-psychology.html

Mezulis, A. H., Abramson, L. Y., Hyde, J. S., & Hankin, B. L. (2004). Is there a universal positivity bias in attributions? A Meta-analytic Review of Individuals, Developmental and Cultural differences in the Self- serving.

Midlarsky, E., Bryan, J., & Brickman, P. (1973). Aversive approval: Interactive effects of modeling and reinforcement on altruistic behavior. *Child Development*, *44*(2), 321–28. Retrieved from http://dx.doi.org/10.1111/j.1467-8624.1973.tb02158.x

Milgram, S. (1963). Behavioural study of obedience. *Journal of Abnormal and Social Psychology, 67*(4), 371–378.

———. (1977). *The individual in a social world*. New York, NY: McGraw-Hill.

Miller, D. T. (1977a). Altruism and threat to a belief in a just world. *Journal of Experimental Social Psychology, 13*(2), 113–124.

Miller, D. T. (1977b). Personal deserving versus justice for others: An exploration of the justice motive. *Journal of Experimental Social psychology, 13*(1), 1–13.

Miner, J. B. (1992). *Industrial and organisational psychology*. New Delhi: McGraw- Hill, Inc.

Ministry of Health and Family Welfare Government of India. (2005–2006). *National Family Health Survey (NFHS-3)*. Mumbai, India: International Institute for Population Sciences. Retrieved from http://dhsprogram.com/pubs/pdf/FRIND3/FRIND3-Vol1[Oct-17-2008].pdf

Mishra V. (1962). *Hinduism and economic growth*. Bombay: Oxford University Press.

Montepare, J., Koff, E., Zaitchik, D., & Albert, M. (1999). The use of body movements and gestures as cues to emotions in younger and older adults. *Journal of Nonverbal Behaviour, 23*(2), 133–152.

Moore, M. G. (1973). Towards a theory of independent learning and teaching. *Journal of Higher Education, 44*(9), 661–679.

Moorhead, G., & Griffin, R. W. (2010). *Organisational behaviour: Managing people and organisations*. Mason, OH: South Western Cengage Learning.

Morris, M. W., Leung, K., Ames, D., & Lickel, B. (1999). Views from inside and outside: Integrating emic and etic insights about culture and justice judgement. *Academy of Management Review, 24*(4), 781–796.

Moscovici, S., & Personnaz, B. (1980). Minority influence and conversion behaviour in perceptual task. *Journal of Experimental Social Psychology, 16*(3), 270–282.

Moscovici, S., Lage, E., & Naffrechoux, M. (1969) Influence of a consistent minority on the responses of a majority in a colour preparation task. *Sociometry, 32*, 365–379.

Moscowitz, G. B. (2005). *Social cognition: Understanding self and others*. New York, NY: Guilford Press.

Mostyn, B. (1978). *The attitude behaviour relationship* (1st ed.). Bradford: MCB Publications. Retrieved from https://dspace.lib.cranfield.ac.uk/bitstream/1826/2968/1/MCRC%2015.PDF

Mother of orphans. (n.d.). Retrieved from http://ckpally.tripod.com/mother/

Mullen, B., Salas, E., & Driskell, J. (1989). Salience, motivation, and artifact as contributions to the relation between participation rate and leadership. *Journal of Experimental Social Psychology, 25*(6), 545–559.

Mummendey, A., & Otten, S. (2004). *Aggressive behaviour*. In M. Hewstone & W. Stroebe (Eds.), *Introduction to social psychology*. UK: Blackwell Publishing.

Myers, D. G., Sahajpal, O., & Behera, P. (2012). *Social psychology*. New Delhi: Tata McGraw Hill Education Private Limited.

Myrdal, G. (1968). *The Asian drama: An inquiry into poverty of nations*. London, Allen Lane: The Penguin.

Nahavandi, A., Denhardt, R. B, Denhardt, J. V., & Aristigueta, M. P. (2015). *Organisational behaviour*. New Delhi: SAGE Publications.

National Commission for Women, India. (n.d.). *Domestic Violence Act 2005*. Retrieved from http://ncw.nic.in/acts/TheProtectionofWomenfromDomesticViolenceAct2005.pdf

Nemeth, C. J. (1986). Differential contributions of majority and minority influence. *Psychological Review, 93*(1), 23–32. Retrieved from http://scholar.berkeley.edu/sites/default/files/nemeth/files/differential_contributions_of_majority_and_minority_influence.pdf

Newcomb, T. M. (1961). *The acquaintance process*. New York, NY: Holt.

Newman, R. S. (2001). *Of umbrellas, goddesses and dreams: Essays on Goan culture and society*. Goa: Other India Press.

Nisbett, R. E., & Wilson, T. D. (1977). Telling more than we can know: Verbal Reports on Mental Process. *Psychological Review, 84*(3), 231–259.

O'Donovan, A., & Hughes, B. (2008). Access to social support in life and in the laboratory: Combined impact on cardiovascular reactivity to stress and state anxiety. *Journal of Health Psychology, 13*(8), 1147–1156.

Oaluck, E. L. (2009). What's in a norm? Sources and processes of norm change. *Journal of Personality and Social Psychology, 96*(3), 594–600.

Olson, J., Vernon, P., Harris, J., & Jang, K. (2001). The heritability of attitudes: A study of twins. *Journal of Personality and Social Psychology, 80*(6), 845–860.

Oskamp, S., & Schultz, P. W. (1998). *Applied social psychology* (2nd ed). California: SAGE Publications.

Otis, M. D., Rostosky, S. S., Riggle, E. D. B., & Hamrin, R. (2006). Stress and relationship quality in same-sex couples. *Journal of Social and Personal Relationships, 23*(1), 81–99.

Pallak, S. R. S., Pittman, T. S., & Pallak, M. S. (1984). Attitudes: Their nature, formation and change. In A. S. Kahn (Ed.), *Social psychology*. Iowa: Wm, C. Brown Publishers, College Division.

Pandey, J. (1996). *Asian contributions to cross cultural psychology*. New York, NY: SAGE Publications.

Pandey, J., & Singh, P. (2005). Social psychology in India: Social roots and development. *International Journal of Psychology, 40*(4), 239–253.

Panksepp, J. (2000). Emotions as natural kinds within the mammalian brain. In M. Lewis & J. M. Howland-Jones (Eds.), *Handbook of emotions* (2nd ed.). New York, NY: Guilford Press.

Parameswaran, E. G., & Beena, C. (2004). *An invitation to psychology*. Hyderabad: Neelkamal Publications Pvt Ltd.

Park, K. (2016). *Acculturation and enculturation, perception of depressive symptoms, and help-seeking behaviors among Korean Americans*. Retrieved from http://digitalcommons.odu.edu/cgi/viewcontent.cgi?article=1033andcontext=psychology_etds

Paskevich, D. M., Brawley, L. R., Dorsch, K. D., & Widmayer, W. N. (1999). Relationship between collective efficacy and team cohesion: Conceptual and measurement issues. *Group Dynamics: Theory, Research and Practice, 3*(3), 210–222.

Pass, J. A., Lindernberg, S. M., & Park, J. H. (2010). All you need is love: Is the sociometry especially sensitive to one's mating capacity? *European Journal of Social Psychology, 40*(2), 221–234.

Patterson, M. M., Carron, A. V., & Loughead, T. M. (2005). The influence of team norms on the cohesion–self-reported performance relationship: A multi-level analysis. *Psychology of Sport and Exercise, 6*(4), 479–493.

Payne, V. L., & Crowley, R. S. (2008). *Assessing use of cognitive heuristic representativeness in clinical reasoning*. AMIA Annual Symposium Proceedings Archive. Retrieved from https://www.ncbi.nlm.nih.gov/pmc/articles/PMC2656076/#

Peplau, L. A. (1982). Research on homosexual couples. *Journal of Homosexuality, 8*(2), 3–8. Retrieved from http://dx.doi.org/10.1300/j082v08n02_02

Peplau, L. A., & Cochran, S. D. (1990). A relationship perspective on homosexuality. In D. P. McWhirter, S. A. Sanders & J. M. Reinisch (Eds.), *Homosexuality/heterosexuality: Concepts of sexual orientation*, (pp. 321–349). New York, NY: Oxford University Press.

Peplau, L. A., & Fingerhut, A. W. (2007). *The close relationships of lesbians and gay men. Annual Review of Psychology, 58*(1), 405–424.

Peters, O. (1971). Theoretical aspects of correspondence instruction. In O. Mackenzie & E. L. Christensen, (Eds.), *The changing world of correspondence study*. Pennsylvania: Pennsylvania University Press.

Pillai, S. (2001). Domestic violence in New Zealand: An Asian immigrant perspective. *Economic and Political Weekly,* 36(11), 965–974.

Pittman, T. S., Pallak, S. R., & Pallak, M. S. (1984). Attitudes and behaviour. In A. S. Kahn (Ed.), *Social psychology*. Iowa: Wm, C. Brown Publishers, College Division.

Prasad, K. N., Kumar, P. S. V., & Poovitha, R. (2014). Premarital sex and age at first sex among collegiate men in Pondicherry. *Scholars Academic Journal of Biosciences,* 2(9): 618–22. Retrieved from http://saspublisher.com/wp-content/uploads/2014/09/SAJB-29618-622.pdf

Project Sunrise launched to control HIV in North East. (7 February 2016). Retrieved from http://meghalayatimes.info/index.php/front-page/33205-project-sunrise-launched-to-control-hiv-in-north-east

Quick, J. C., Nelson, D. L., & Khandelwal, P. (2011). *Organisational behaviour: A South Asian perspective*. Delhi: Cengage Learning.

Quinones-Vidal, E., Lopez-Garcia, J. J., Penaranda-Ortega, M., & Tortosa-Gil, F. (2004). The nature of social and personality psychology as reflected in JPSP, 1965–2000. *Journal of Personality and Social Psychology, 86*(3), 435–452.

Rao, K. R. (2002). *Consciousness studies: Cross-cultural perspectives*. Jefferson: McFarland.

———. (2011). *Cognitive anomalies, consciousness and yoga*. New Delhi: Centre for Studies in Civilisations.

Raven, B. H., & Rubin, J. Z. (1983). *Social psychology*. USA: John Wiley and Sons, Inc.

Ray, N. (1968). *Modernity and contemporary India literature*. Shimla: Indian Institute of Advanced Study.

Redfield, R., Linton, R., Herskovits, M. J. (1936). Memorandum on the study of acculturation. *American Anthropologist, 38*(1), 149-152.

Reiss, D., & Marino, L. (2001). *Mirror self-recognition in the bottlenose dolphin: A case of cognitive convergence*. Retrieved from http://www.pnas.org/content/98/10/5937.full

Reitan, H. T., & Shaw, M. E. (1964). Group membership, sex-composition of the group, and conformity behaviour. *The Journal of Social Psychology, 64*, 45–51.

Riggio, H. R., & Garcia, A. L. (2009). The power of situations: Jonestown and the fundamental attribution error. *Teaching of Psychology, 36*(2), 108–112.

Roberts, J., & Monroe, S. (1992). Vulnerable self-esteem and depressive symptoms: Prospective findings comparing three alternative conceptualizations. *Journal of Personality and Social Psychology, 62*(5), 804–812.

Rosenthal, R. (1966). *Experimenter effect in behavioural research.* New York, NY: Appleton-Century-Crofts.

Rosenwasser, S. M., Lingenfelter, M., & Harrington, A. F. (1989). Nontraditional gender role portrayals on television and children's gender role perceptions. *Journal of Applied Developmental Psychology, 10*, 97–105.

Ross, L. D., Amabile, T. M., & Steinmetz, J. L. (1977). Social roles, social control, and biases in social-perception processes. *Journal of Personality and Social Psychology, 35*(7), 485–494.

Royse, D., Thyer, B. A., Padgett, D. K., & Logan, T. K. (2006). Programme evaluation: An introduction. Belmont, CA: Thomson Brooks/Cole.

Ruane, J. M. (2016). Introducing social research methods: Essentials for getting the edge. UK: John Wiley and Sons Ltd.

Sandage, S. J., Worthington Jr, E. L., Hight, T. L., & Berry, J. W. (2000). Seeking forgiveness: Theoretical context and an initial empirical study. *Journal of Psychology and Theology, 28*, 21–35.

Sanderson, C. A., & Cantor, N. 1997. Creating satisfaction in steady dating relationships: The role of personal goals and situational affordances. *Journal of Personality and Social Psychology* 73, 1424–1433.

Schaster, S. (1951). Deviation, rejection and communication. *Journal of Abnormal and Social Psychology, 46*(2), 190–207.

Schenk, A. M., & Fremouw, W. J. (2012). Prevalence, psychological impact, and coping of cyberbully victims among college students. *Journal of School Violence, 11*(1), 21–37.

Schneider, F. W., Gruman, J., & Coutts, L. M. (2012a). *Applied social psychology understanding and addressing social and practical problems* (2nd Ed.). New Delhi: SAGE Publications.

———. (2012b). Defining the field of applied social psychology. In F. W. Schneider, J. A. Gruman & L. M. Coutts (Eds.), *Applied psychology: Understanding and addressing social and practical problems*. New Delhi: SAGE Publications.

Schwarz, N., Bless, H., Strack, F., Klumpp, G., Rittenauer-Schatka, H., & Simmons, A. (1991). Ease of retrieval as information: Another look at the availability heuristic. *Journal of Personality and Social Psychology, 61*(2), 195–202.

Sears, D. O., Peplau, A. L., & Taylor, S. E. (1991). *Social psychology*. Englewood Cliffs, NJ: Prentice Hall.

Sears, R. R., Maccoby, E., & Levin, H. (1957). *Patterns of child rearing*. Evanston, IL: Row, Peterson.

Sedikides, C. (1992). Attention effects on mood are moderated by chronic self-conception valence. *Personality and Social Psychology Bulletin, 18*(5), 580–84. Retrieved from am from http://www.southampton.ac.uk/~crsi/Attentional.pdf

Sharf, R. S. (2000). *Theories of psychotherapy and counselling* (2nd ed). Belmonte, CA/Boston: Brooks/Cole/Thomson Learning.

Sharma, R. R., Pardasani, R., & Nandram, S. (2014). The problem of rape in India: A multi-dimensional analysis. *International Journal of Managing Projects in Business, 7*(3), 362–379.

Shaw, M. E., & Costanzo, P. R. (1982). *Theories of social psychology*. New York, NY: McGraw-Hill.

Sherif, M. (1936). *The psychology of social norms*. New York, NY: Harper Collins.

Sherif, M., Harbey, O. J., White, B. J., Hood, W. R., & Sherif, C. W. (1961). *Intergroup conflict and cooperation: The Robers' cave experiment*. Norma, Oklahoma: University of Oklahoma Book Exchange.

Sigall, H. F. (1984). Interpersonal attraction. In A. S. Kahn (Ed), *Social psychology*. Iowa: Wm, C. Brown Publishers, College Division.

Simpson, J. A., & Gangestad, S. W. (1991). Individual differences in sociosexuality: Evidence for convergent and discriminant validity. *Journal of Personality and Social Psychology, 60*(6), 870–83.

———. (1992). Sociosexuality and romantic partner choice. *Journal of Personality, 60*(1), 31–51.

Singh, A. K. (1983). Health modernity education in India. *Social Change, 12*(2), 27–34.

———. (1984). Health modernity: Concept and correlates. *Social Change, 14*(3), 3–16.

Sinha, D., & Tripathi, R. C. (1990). *Individualism in a collective culture: A case of coexistence of dichotomies*. Paper presented at the International Conference on Individualism and Collectivism: Psychocultural Perspectives from East and West, Seoul.

———. (1994). Individualism in a collective culture: A case of coexistence of opposites. In U. Kim, H. C. Triandis, C. Kagitcibasi, S. Chai, & G. Yoon (Eds.), *Individualism and collectivism: Theory, method and application* (pp. 123–136). Thousand Oakes: SAGE Publications.

Sinha, J. B. P., & Pandey, A. (2007). Indians' mindsets and the conditions that evoke them. *Psychological Studies, 52*, 1–13.

Sirswal, D. R. (2011). *Philosophy of social change: Need of an Indian model*. Retrieved from http://niyamakphilosophy.blogspot.in/2011/02/philosophy-of-social-change-need-of.html

Smith, E. R., Coats, S., & Walling, D. (1999). Overlapping mental representations of self, in-group, and partner: Further response time evidence and a connectionist model. *Personality and Social Psychology Bulletin, 25*, 873–882.

Smith, P. K., Mahdavi, J., Carvalho, M., Fisher, S., Russell, S., & Tippett, N. (2008). Cyberbullying: Its nature and impact in secondary school pupils. *Journal of Child Psychology and Psychiatry, 49*(4), 376–385.

Snyder, M., & Ickes, W. (1985). Personality and social behaviour. In G. Lindsey & E. Aronson (Eds.), *The handbook of social psychology*. New York, NY: Random House.

Snyder, M., & Swann, W. B. (1978). Hypothesis testing processes in social interaction. *Journal of Personality and Social Psychology, 36*(11), 1202–12. Retrieved from http://www.communicationcache.com/uploads/1/0/8/8/10887248/hypothesis-testing_processes_in_social_interaction.pdf

Sondergaard, M. (1994). Research note: Hofstede's consequences. A study of reviews, citations and replications. *Organization Studies, 15*(3), 447–456.

Spering, M. (2001). *Current issues in cross-cultural psychology: Research topics, applications, and perspectives*. Retrieved from http://www.psychologie.uni-heidelberg.de/ae/allg_en/mitarb/ms/cross-cultural%20psy.pdf

Spink, K. S. (1990). Collective efficacy in the sport setting. *International Journal of Sport Psychology, 21*(4), 380–395.

Spunt, R. P., & Lieberman, M. D. (2013). The busy social brain: Evidence for automaticity and control in the neural systems supporting social cognition and action understanding. *Psychological Science, 24*(1), 80–86.

Srinivas, M. N. (1952). *Religion and Society among the Coorgs of South India*. Oxford: Claredon Press.

Srivastava, A. K., & Misra, G. (2007). *Rethinking intelligence: Culture and conceptualization of competence*. New Delhi: Concept.

Staat, A. W. (1983). Paradigmatic behaviourism: Unified theory for social personality psychology. In L. Berkowitz (Ed.), *Advances in experimental social psychology* (Vol. 16, pp. 126–179). New York, NY: Academic Press.

Staats, A., Staats, C., & Crawford, H. (1962). First-order conditioning of meaning and the parallel conditioning of a GSR. *The Journal of General Psychology, 67*(1), 159–167.

Steiner, I. D. (1972). Process and productivity. New York, NY: Academic Press.

———. (1976). Task Performing group. In J. W. Thibaut, J. T. Spence & R. C. Carson (Eds.), *Contemporary topics in social psychology*. New Jersey: General Learning Press.

Stogdill, R. (1974). Handbook of leadership. New York, NY: Free Press.

Storms, M. D. (1973). Videotape and the attribution process: Reversing actors' and observer's point of view. *Journal of Personality and Social Psychology, 27*(2), 165–175. Retrieved from https://www.uni-muenster.de/imperia/md/content/psyifp/aeechterhoff/sommersemester2012/sozialekognition/storms_videoperspattribution_jpsp1973.pdf

Strack, F., Martin, L. L., & Stepper, S. (1988). Inhibiting and facilitating conditions of the human smile: A nonobtrusive test of the facial feedback hypothesis. *Journal of Personality and Social psychology, 54*(5), 768–777. Retrieved from http://datacolada.org/wp-content/uploads/2014/03/Strack-et-al-1988-cartoons.pdf

Strong, S. R. (1987). Social-psychological approach to counselling and psychotherapy: 'A false hope?' *Journal of Social and Clinical Psychology, 5*(2), 185–194.

Stuhlmacher, A. F., & Citera, M. (2005). Hostile behaviour and profit in virtual negotiations: A meta-analysis. *Journal of Business and Psychology, 20*(1), 69–93.

Suddendorf, T., & Collier-Baker, E. (2009). The evolution of primate visual self-recognition: Evidence of absence in lesser apes. *Proceedings of the Royal Society B: Biological Sciences, 276*(1662), 1671–1677.

Sullivan, P. J., & Gee, C. (2007). The relationships between athletic satisfaction and intra-team communication. *Group Dynamics: Theory, Research, and Practice, 11*(2), 107–116.

Sullivan, P., Feltz, D. L., & Dithurbide. (2012). Applying social psychology to sports teams. In F. W. Schneider, J. A. Gruman & L. M. Coutts (Eds.), *Applied psychology: Understanding and addressing social and practical problems*. New Delhi: SAGE Publications.

Suls, J., & Rosnow, J. (1988). Concerns about artefacts in behavioural Research. In M. Morawski (Ed.), *The rise of experimentation in American psychology* (pp. 163–87). New Haven, CT: Yale University Press.

Tajfel, H., & Turner, J. (1986). The social identity theory of intergroup behaviour. In W. Austin & S. Worchel (Eds.), *The social psychology of intergroup relations* (pp. 33–48). Chicago, MI: Nelson-Hall Publishers.

Tashiro, T., & Mortensen, L. (2006). Translational research: How social psychology can improve psychotherapy. *American Psychologist, 61*(9), 959–1269.

Taylor, D. A. (1984). Race prejudice, discrimination and racism. In A. S. Kahn (Ed.), *Social psychology*. Iowa: Wm, C. Brown Publishers, College Division.

Tesser, A. (1993). The importance of heritability in psychological research: The case of attitudes. *Psychological review, 100*(1), 129–142.

TheFamousPeople. (n.d.) *Baba Amte Biography*. Retrieved from http://www.thefamouspeople.com/profiles/baba-amte-5328.php

Thorne, B. (1993). *Gender play: Girls and boys in school*. New Brunswick, NJ: Rutgers University Press.

Thurstone, L. L., & Chave, C. J. (1930). *A Scale of Measuring Attitude toward the Church*. Chicago, IL: University of Chicago Press.

Tidwell, N. D., Eastwick, P. W., & Finkel, E. J. (2012). *Perceived, not actual, similarity predicts initial attraction in a live romantic context: Evidence from the speed-dating paradigm*. Retrieved from http://faculty.wcas.northwestern.edu/eli-finkel/documents/InPress_TidwellEastwickFinkel_PersonalRelationships_000.pdf

Triandis, H. C. (1989). The self and social behavior in differing cultural contexts. *Psychological Review, 96*(3), 506–520.

Turkle, S. (1995a). Ghosts in the machine. *Sciences, 35*(6), 36-39.

———. (1995b). *Life on the screen: Identity in the age of Internet*. New York, NY: Simon and Schuster.

———. (1997a). Computational technologies and images of self. *Social Research, 64*(3), 1093–1111.

———. (1997b). Multiple subjectivity and virtual community at the end of the Freudian century. *Sociological Inquiry, 67*(1), 72–84.

Turner, R. N., Crisp, R. J., & Lambert, E. (2007). Imagining intergroup contact can improve intergroup attitudes. *Group Processes and Intergroup Relations, 10*, 427–441.

Tversky, A., & Kahneman, D. (1974). Judgement under uncertainty: Heuristics and bias. *Science, 185*(4157) 1124–1131. Retrieved from http://psiexp.ss.uci.edu/research/teaching/Tversky_Kahneman_1974.pdf

Ullman, C. (1987). From sincerity to authenticity: Adolescent's view of the 'true self'. *Journal of Personality, 55*(4), 583–95.

Uono, S., Hietanen, J. K. (2015). Eye contact perception in the West and East: A cross-cultural study. *PLoS ONE, 10*: e0118094. doi:10.1371/journal.pone.0118094

Vahedi, S., Fathiazar, E., Hosseini-Nasab, S. D., Moghaddam, M., & Kiani, A. (2007). The effect of social skills training on decreasing the aggression of pre-school children. *Iran Journal of Psychiatry*, 2, 108–14. Retrieved from https://www.researchgate.net/profile/Shahram_Vahedi/publication/235769303_The_Effect_of_Social_Skills_Training_on_Decreasing_the_Aggression_of_Pre-school_Children/links/5411418d0cf2f2b29a412327/The-Effect-of-Social-Skills-Training-on-Decreasing-the-Aggression-of-Pre-school-Children.pdf

Valle, A., Núñez, A. C., Cabanach, R. G., González-Pienda, J. A., Rodríguez, A., Rosário, P., Muñoz-Cadavid, M. A., & Cerezo, R. (2009). Academic goals and learning quality in higher education students. *The Spanish Journal of Psychology, 12*(1), 96–105. Retrieved from http://citeseerx.ist.psu.edu/viewdoc/download?doi=10.1.1.1030.7215andrep=rep1and type=pdf

Verweij, K. J. H., Shekhar, S. N., Zietsch, B. P., Eaves, L. J., Bailey, M., Boomsma, D. L., & Martin, N. G. (2008). Genetic and environmental influences on individual differences in attitude towards homosexuality: An Australian twin study. *Behaviour Genetics, 38*(3), 257–65. Retrieved from https://www.ncbi.nlm.nih.gov/pmc/articles/PMC2292426/

Wallensteen, P. (2015). *Understanding conflict resolution*. New Delhi: SAGE Publications.

Walster, E., Aronson, V., Abrahams, D., & Rottman, L. (1966). Importance of physical attractiveness in dating behavior. *Journal of Personality and Social Psychology, 4*(5), 508–516.

Ward, C. A., Bochner, S., & Furman, A. (2001). *The psychology of cultural shock* (2nd ed.). UK: Routledge.

Waskul, D., & Douglas, M. (1997). Cyberself: The dynamics of self in online chat. *The Information Society: An International Journal, 13*(4), 375–397.

Weber, M. (1958a). *The protestant ethic and the spirit of capitalism* (T. Parsons, Trans.). New York, NY: Charles Scribner's Sons.

———. (1958b). *The religion of India: The sociology of Hinduism and Buddhism* (I-1.H. Gerth & D. Martindale, Trans.). Glencoe: The Free Press.

Wedemeyer, C. A. (1977). Independent study. In A. S. Knowles (Ed.), *The International Encyclopedia of Higher Education* (Vol. 5, pp. 2114–2132). Boston, MA: CIHED.

Weinberg, R. S., & Gould, D. (2003). *Foundations of sport and exercise psychology* (3rd ed.). Champaign, IL: Human Kinetics.

Weiss, W. (1969). Effects of the mass media of communication. In G. Lindzey & E. Aronson (Eds.), *The handbook of social psychology*, (2nd ed., Vol. 5, pp. 77–195). Reading, MA: Addison Wesley.

Weiten, W., Hammer, E. Y., & Dunn, D. S. (2012). *Psychology and contemporary life human adjustment*. Boston: Wadsworth Cengage Learning.

Whiting, B., & Whiting, J. W. M. (1971). Task assignments and personality: A consideration of the effect of herding on boys. In William W. Lambert and Rita Weisbrod (Eds.). Comparative Perspectives on Social Psychology. Little, Brown and Co. 33–45

———. (1972). *Children of six cultures: A psycho-cultural analysis*. Cambridge, MA: Harvard University Press.

Whitty, M. T., & Young, G. (2017). *Cyberpsychology*. UK: John Wiley and Sons Ltd.

Widmeyer, W. N., & Williams, J. (1991). Predicting cohesion in coaching sport. *Small Group Research, 22*(4), 548–570.

Williams, J. & Solano, C. (1983). The social reality of feeling lonely: Friendship and reciprocation. *Personality and Social Psychology Bulletin, 9*(2), 237–342.

Wilson, T. D., & Kraft, D. (1993). Why do I love thee? Effects of repeated introspections about a dating relationship on attitudes toward the relationship. *Personality and Social Psychology Bulletin, 19*(4), 409–418.

Wishner, J. (1960). Reanalysis of 'impressions of personality'. *Psychological Review, 67*(2), 96–112.

Woike, B., Gershkovich, I., Piorkowiski, R., & Polo, M. (1999). The role of motives in the content and structure of autobiographical memory. *Journal of Personality and Social Psychology, 76*, 600–612.

World Health Organization. (2005). *WHO multi-country study on women's health and domestic violence against women: Initial results on prevalence, health outcomes and women's responses*. Geneva: World Health Organization.

———. (1986). *Ottawa charter for health promotion*. Retrieved from http://www.who.int/healthpromotion/comferences/previous/ottawa/en/

Wright, S. C., Aron, A., McLaughlin-Volpe, T., & Ropp, S. A. (1997). The extended contact effect: Knowledge of cross-group friendships and prejudice. *Journal of Personality and Social Psychology, 73*(1), 73–90.

Yukl, G. (1989). *Leadership in organisations*. New Jersey, NJ: Prentice Hall.

Zajonc, R. B., Murphy, S. T., & Inglehart, M. (1989). Emotions research: Some promising questions and some questionable promises. *Psychological Science, 3*(1), 70–74.

Zanna, M. P., & Hamilton, D. L. (1972). Attribute dimensions and patterns of trait inferences. *Psychonomic Science, 27*(6), 353–354.

Zillmann, D. (1979). *Hostility and aggression*. Hillsdale, NJ: Erlbaum.

———. (1988). Cognitive-excitation Interdependencies in aggressive behaviour. *Aggressive Behaviour, 14*(1), 51–64.

Zillmann, D., Johnson, R. C., & Day, K. D. (1974). Attribution of apparent arousal and proficiency of recovery from sympathetic activation affecting excitation transfer to aggressive behaviour. *Journal of Experimental Social psychology, 10*(6), 503–515.

Zimbardo, P. G. (1969). The human choice: Individuation reason and order versus deindividuation, impulse and chaos. In W. J. Arnold & D. Levine (Eds.), *Nebraska symposium on motivation* (Vol. 17). Lincoln: University of Nebraska Press.

Answers to Multiple Choice Questions

1. d. Gordon Allport
2. a. Description, prediction, determining causality and explanation
3. b. Social learning theory
4. a. Social neuroscience
5. c. 1908
6. b. Independent variable
7. c. Ecological validity and population validity
8. d. Survey research
9. c. Grounded theory
10. b. Self-concept
11. a. Bem
12. c. Social cognition
13. a. A tendency where the objects and things owned by us are viewed more favourably than those that we do not own
14. a. Representativeness heuristic
15. a. Controllability
16. b. Self-serving attribution
17. a. Social comparison theory
18. b. Desperation, depression, impatient boredom and self-deprecation
19. b. Donn Byrne and Gerald Clore
20. c. True self
21. c. Implicit attitude
22. d. Cognitive, behavioural and affective
23. d. Terminal and instrumental
24. a. Heider
25. b. 1922
26. c. Re-categorisation
27. a. Conformity
28. c. Self-depreciation
29. b. Foot-in-the-door technique
30. c. Norma

31. d. Altruism
32. c. Robert Trivers
33. b. Instrumental aggression
34. b. Cyberbullying
35. c. Roles
36. a. Fairness, reciprocity, reasonableness and role expectation
37. a. Additive tasks
38. c. Allport
39. d. Social loafing
40. d. Cross-cultural psychology
41. a. Moderacy bias
42. d. Applied Social Psychology
43. b. Kurt Lewin
44. c. Theory
45. b. Organisation, direction and guide interventions
46. d. Social problem
47. a. M. N. Srinivas
48. d. Health belief model
49. c. Evaluation message
50. d. Labelling

Index